AT FREEDOM'S EDGE

AT FREEDOM'S EDGE

BLACK MOBILITY AND THE SOUTHERN
WHITE QUEST FOR RACIAL CONTROL
1861–1915

William Cohen

LOUISIANA STATE UNIVERSITY PRESS   BATON ROUGE AND LONDON

Copyright © 1991 by Louisiana State University Press
Manufactured in the United States of America

Louisiana Paperback Edition, 1991
00 99 98 97 96 95 94 93 92   5 4 3 2

Designer: Amanda McDonald Key
Typeface: Bembo
Typesetter: G&S Typesetters, Inc.

Library of Congress Cataloging-in-Publication Data

Cohen, William, date.
    At freedom's edge : black mobility and the Southern white quest
for racial control, 1861–1915 / William Cohen.
      p.   cm.
    Includes bibliographical references and index.
    ISBN 0-8071-1621-1 (alk. paper). — ISBN 0-8071-1652-1 (pbk. :
alk. paper)
    1. Afro-Americans—Southern States—Migrations. 2. Afro-
Americans—Kansas—Migrations. 3. Migration, Internal—United
States—History. 4. Southern States—Population—History.
5. Afro-Americans—Southern States—Economic conditions. 6. Kansas—
Population—History. I. Title.
E185.6.C66   1991
305.8'96073075—dc20   90-44493
                                                                 CIP

Some of the material in this book has appeared in a slightly different form in "Black
Immobility and Free Labor: The Freedmen's Bureau and the Relocation of Black Labor,
1865–1868," *Civil War History,* XXX (1984), 221–34; and "Negro Involuntary Servitude in the South, 1865–1940: A Preliminary Analysis," *Journal of Southern History,*
XLII (1976), 31–60.

For
Margie,
Alan, Elizabeth, and Mia

CONTENTS

TABLES

PREFACE

This book had its origins in the late 1960s, when issues of racial justice and urban violence were very much in the headlines. In Washington, policy makers were looking for answers that might enable them to reduce the explosive potential of black ghettos across the country. In academia, scholars were seeking a better understanding of how and why the ghettos had developed as they had. Out of the convergence of these interests was born a federally funded project at the University of Chicago entitled "The Urbanization of the Negro American in the Twentieth Century."

At the outset, my part in the project was to collaborate with John Hope Franklin on a book that would deal with twentieth-century black migration and its roots. I began my work predisposed to believe that the massive migration of World War I and later was primarily a function of white oppression. Early on, however, the secondary literature of black migration persuaded me that this was not the case and that, overwhelmingly, the Great Migration was a direct response to economic forces like sharply rising job opportunities in the North. Having reached this conclusion, I was not sure that I had much of significance to add to what had already been said on the subject.

I had other grounds as well for hesitating. Although my commitment as a professional historian would not allow me to disregard the evidence that pointed toward an economic interpretation, my personal commitment to the cause of equality made it difficult to work enthusiastically on a book that might have the effect of diverting attention from prejudice and discrimination as sources of the oppression suffered by blacks.

Increasingly, I was drawn toward the years prior to 1916, when black movement out of the South had been minimal. I began to wonder why black migration to the North had not started earlier, and I concentrated my research attention on the South. Soon, I stumbled across a structure of post-Reconstruction laws that seemed to aim at limiting black movement. My first instinct was to conclude that it was this set of statutes that had prevented blacks from coming north. I now explored the possibility that laws of involuntary servitude had created a situation in which blacks could not move north because they were physically restrained from doing so. But that would not wash. Strong evidence suggested that in the years from 1865 to 1915, blacks in the South had considerable freedom of movement and that within the region they usually could move from one place to another without hindrance. The laws of involuntary servitude were very real, but so was the evidence of extensive black movement.

More and more, what had started as a book on twentieth-century black migration was becoming a book about why blacks had not gone north in significant numbers in the fifty years before 1916. As I followed this path, Professor Franklin gave me full support. At the same time, however, there was no getting away from the fact that as the inquiry moved ever farther from its original conception, it was becoming my book rather than our book. Professor Franklin generously encouraged me and went on to other things, never frowning because I took my own road with a book he had conceived quite differently.

In retrospect, it is clear that I pulled the book toward the nineteenth century in large part because of my intense discomfort with purely economic interpretations of black migration. I should have realized that the very thing that made me uneasy in dealing with twentieth-century migration would still be there when I worked on the nineteenth century. For a while, however, I had a respite from such concerns. Federal funding for our project came to an end in 1971, and I moved to another institution. I put the question of black mobility *per se* on the back burner and turned my attention to exploring the system of involuntary servitude that I found embedded in southern law. Mindful of how much black movement there was within the South, I came to view involuntary servitude as a sort of "now you see it, now you don't" system that tended to be implemented in times and places where labor shortages were especially acute.

In a 1976 article, I sought to describe the system of involuntary servitude as I then understood it. The article showed the dense fabric of labor-control laws designed to limit black movement. It showed too that those laws were actually applied, but it was vague about how often. Conceding that blacks usually moved freely within the South, the article laid out my conclusion that laws of involuntary servitude came into play largely at times when labor was in short supply. Clearly, though, these statutes did not go far toward explaining why so few blacks went north in the fifty years before World War I.

When I returned to the subject of black migration in the nineteenth century, I gave attention to back-to-Africa movements and to the well-known Exodus of 1879. Both were rooted in racial oppression, but in each case there was not much economic opportunity for poor blacks in the destination area. As a result, only a relative handful of blacks left the South for the North, and even fewer went to Africa. In the end, then, these "migrations" proved to be more important as political statements than as instances of black movement. Their history reinforced the idea that black migration was an essentially economic phenomenon.

Increasingly, it became evident that to deal adequately with black mobility before World War I, several interwoven stories had to be told. I would need to deal with the emergence of black mobility and free labor after the Civil War. I would have to show how central mobility was to the concept of freedom. At the same time, however, it would be necessary to demonstrate how black poverty placed sharp limits on the possibility of large-scale independent movement. The story of black mobility would have to be told, as well, against the background of southern white efforts to circumscribe black freedom of movement. Ultimately it became clear that the tension between black mobility, on the one hand, and white efforts to control blacks, on the other, would be the dynamic that held this book together.

Of great importance, then, are the legal measures by which southern whites attempted to exert control over the black population. At first I was concerned only with laws aimed at limiting black mobility, but as the research neared its conclusion, it became clear that statutes aimed at controlling black labor could only be fully understood when seen as part of a more comprehensive legal effort to assert white control on all fronts. Laws to limit black mobility came into being simultaneously with statutes whose purpose was to drive blacks from the political arena and with enactments aimed at separating the races in the social sphere.

The movement to enact such legislation began even before Reconstruction was over, and it was largely successful by 1890. Historians concerned with southern laws of repression have placed considerable emphasis on the black codes of 1865–1867 and on the repressive legislation of the 1890s and later. They have said less about the statutes of the 1870s and the 1880s. This book treats the laws of the 1870s and the 1880s as of central importance. Taken together, the laws of the period from the 1870s to about 1910 represented a major and continuing white effort to reassert hegemony over blacks in all areas of life.

Thus, as my work was drawing toward its end I began to see that the evidence was leading me toward conclusions quite at variance with the dominant interpretation of postbellum southern history. The prevailing interpretation emphasizes class factors and treats the effort to segregate, disfranchise, and control blacks as part of a larger class conflict between planters and other moneyed interests, on the one hand, and poor farmers, both black and white, on the other. It views racial conflict as largely the product of planters' efforts to use the race issue to undermine the struggles of the poor for economic justice, and it tends to find in the rise of Populism the catalyst that led to the erection of the South's rigid racial system.

When I began studying black mobility, I accepted this interpretation, but I became increasingly troubled by evidence that the legal structure of black oppression dated at least as much from the period before 1890 as from the years after that date. Considerable continuity existed between the events of the 1890s and those of the preceding decades. In the 1870s and the 1880s, before Populism posed a problem for the planter class, there were systematic efforts to reestablish white control over blacks on every front, from school segregation to labor regulation. Throughout the postbellum era there was class struggle aplenty in the South, but by and large the struggle was conducted separately by whites and blacks. On the matter of racial equality, whites, rich and poor, usually possessed a common cultural outlook.

By 1890, southern whites had already established the broad out-lines of a legal structure aimed at asserting white racial control in every area of life. By then, most southern states had disfranchisement laws of one sort or another aimed at keeping blacks out of office and away from the ballot box. Almost everywhere, miscegenation acts and school-segregation measures pointed toward a castelike social struc-ture based on a belief in black inferiority. In most southern states a variety of labor-control laws sought to prevent black workers from moving without the consent of their employers.

In the years from 1890 onward, southern whites would elaborate the new system with additional legislation, but the groundwork had already been completely laid. Even when the entire panoply of repres-sive law was in place, however, blacks retained some freedom. Dis-franchisement and segregation were almost universal, but involuntary servitude was not. Southern blacks could still move about with con-siderable freedom, and when they learned of jobs in the North, they experienced relatively little difficulty in leaving the South.

Paradoxically, it was differences between whites that made this freedom possible. If southern whites were united in their convictions about black inferiority, they divided on policies concerning mobility. Planters seeking to hold on to the workers they already had might favor draconian measures to keep blacks from leaving, but those des-perate for new labor pulled in the opposite direction. Nor was it just a matter of competing interests among planters. Whites who de-pended for their livelihood on black labor favored legislation to pre-vent black migration. Whites who did not employ black workers were more likely to favor plans that promised to reduce the black population.

In addition, there existed a small cadre of southern federal judicial officials whose jobs required them to protect the rights of all persons, including blacks. Many of these officials did not carry out their federal responsibilities to blacks with any great vigor. Some, however, took their duties seriously indeed, and they erected a series of legal barriers against peonage and involuntary servitude that played a key role in protecting black freedom of movement. Thus, within a limited range, national values were imposed on the South by men whose service as federal officials gave them a dual identity.

Whites played an important role in the story of black mobility, but it was the blacks themselves who played the largest part, by resisting efforts to immobilize them. Deprived of many of the most basic rights of citizenship, they clung tenaciously to that most important of rights, the right to move. They were often cheated and exploited, and poverty placed sharp limits on their ability to make long-distance moves without assistance. Still, they took what autonomy they could by moving whenever they found a chance to better their condition. They moved from one local employer to another in a continuing quest for better wages and fair treatment. They moved back and forth between the agricultural and semi-industrial sectors of the economy. And when the chance came their way, they made long-distance moves in pursuit of a better life. White employers complained interminably about black unreliability and did what they could to immobilize their labor, but in the long run they were powerless to prevent the blacks from leaving. To that extent, and to that extent only, the free labor system imposed by the North after the Civil War was a success.

If the process by which this book has come into being has been a long one, the list of persons who have given me their advice or assistance is even longer. Indeed, about the only good thing I can think to say about taking twenty years to write a book is that it gives you ample time to learn from others.

My debt to John Hope Franklin goes back even farther than twenty years. It was he who inspired me to become a historian, and it was he who nurtured my initial interests in black and southern history. He has been a role model for me, a mentor, a colleague, and a friend. His generosity in inviting me to collaborate on a book about black migration is directly responsible for launching me on the path to this book.

My initial research was conducted in 1968–1971, when I was a research associate at the Center for Urban Studies of the University of Chicago. It was an exciting place, where graduate students, faculty, and research associates from various disciplines came together in sporadic combat over how to interpret the world. It was there that Zahava Blum, Peter Goheen, and John Gardner dragged me, kicking and screaming, to examine a way of thinking in which unique historical events count for less than quantifiable patterns of human behavior.

While at the Center for Urban Studies, I was privileged to have the talented research assistance of Barbara Yondorf, Shirley Ray, and John

Robb. Mr. Robb was at the time a graduate student in history, and when, some years later, he decided to leave the field of history, he kindly gave me the notes he had been gathering for a dissertation on labor agents. I am much in his debt for this.

I am grateful too for the assistance of the library and archival staffs at the Library of Congress, the National Archives, the University of Chicago, Duke University, the Georgia Department of Archives and History, Louisiana State University, Michigan State University, the Mississippi Department of Archives and History, the University of Texas, Tuskegee Institute, and Western Michigan University. I owe special thanks to Dick Burtt, Elaine Cline, Kelly Jacobsma, and Carol Juth-Gavasso, of the Hope College Library, for their unfailing assistance in locating and obtaining distant materials.

I have been assisted toward the completion of this book by an NEH Category B Research Fellowship and by a series of summer grants from Hope College. In regard of the latter, I am deeply grateful to Provost Jacob Nyenhuis for his consistent support and for his faith that my project would come to fruition. I owe much also to Carole Boeve for an almost flawless typing job, for her work in moving the text onto a word processor, and for the way she saved me from the commission of innumerable careless errors.

Among those who have read and commented upon my manuscript in one or another of its incarnations are Edward Ayers, Barry Castro, LaWanda Cox, Stanley Engerman, Eric Foner, John Hope Franklin, Michael Lewis, George Rappaport, Loren Schweninger, and my wife, Margaret Cohen. My colleagues in the Hope College history department have been enormously supportive in a wide variety of ways, and three of them—Marc Baer, Earl Curry, and Larry Penrose—have read the manuscript as well. I am deeply indebted both for the praise that kept me going and for the criticism that made this a better work than it would otherwise have been. No one has read this work with more care than my editor, Barry Blose, of the Louisiana State University Press, whose sharp eye and hard questions have done much to improve the book. For the faults that remain, the responsibility lies with me alone. I am under a special obligation to LaWanda Cox, whose encouragement and criticism have meant a great deal to me.

Finally, a word of thanks to my family, without whom this book certainly would have been finished much sooner but without whom my world would be a desolate place. My wife, Margie, has had to share me with this project ever since we met. We both look forward to finding out what life is like without its lurking in the background of our lives. As for the children, they helped in their special ways. Alan assisted me with the index and in getting the bibliography into proper form. Elizabeth helped fix the spacing at the end of sentences, and Mia, who has just reached eight, turned handsprings.

ABBREVIATIONS

ACS	American Colonization Society
Ascom	Assistant Commissioner
BRFAL	Bureau of Refugees, Freedmen, and Abandoned Lands (Freedmen's Bureau)
DJ	Department of Justice
EB	Endorsement Book
HD	House Document
HXD	House Executive Document
LC	Library of Congress
LR	Letters Received
LS	Letters Sent
NA	National Archives
Regletrec	Register of Letters Received
Source-Chron	Source-Chronological Files
SXD	Senate Executive Document
WD	War Department

PART ONE

BLACK MOBILITY
IN THE RECONSTRUCTION ERA

1

THE BIRTH OF A FREE LABOR SYSTEM

The history of black mobility from the Civil War to World War I occupies a time when southern blacks lived at freedom's edge, suspended between the world of slavery that had once been theirs and a world of freedom that still belonged mostly to whites. The extent of black freedom varied with time and place, but always the right to move without hindrance was one of its most important measures.

Central to slavery had been the ability of the masters to control black movement; central to freedom was the right of former bondsmen to pick up and move when they wished. Long after emancipation, southern whites continued to believe that they had every right to limit black freedom in virtually any way they chose, and the fifty years after the Civil War were marked by a continuing struggle over how much freedom of movement blacks should have.

The story of black mobility is, then, a study in continuity and change. Emancipation transformed southern society, destroying bondage and paternalism and, in theory at least, leaving blacks and whites free to work out new ways of existing together. But it had little effect, if any, on deep-seated white attitudes about blacks. Southern whites continued to see blacks as constituting an inferior order with no rights a white person was bound to respect. After the Civil War, these interwoven forces of continuity and change shaped the worlds of blacks and whites alike.

The forces of change were especially conspicuous just after the Civil War, when the North tried to impose its vision of freedom on the South. In that effort the Freedmen's Bureau was central. It presided ᴜver the transition from a slave labor economy, where decisions about black movement rested with masters and slave traders, to a free labor economy, where blacks could make their own choices but where poverty and a lack of opportunity raised major barriers to movement.

Still, resistance to the pressures for equality was everywhere. Even as free labor institutions were taking hold, they were reshaped by a culture of racism that presumed black inferiority. The same kind of resistance could be found throughout the southern society, and it was inevitable that, as the North lost its will to maintain the occupation of the South, Reconstruction would be overthrown. When that happened, a wave of fear swept the black community, leading a few blacks to make plans for an exodus to Africa and others to look toward Kansas. There was, however, little demand for unskilled black migrants in Kansas, and less still in Africa. As migrations, these events were failures, but they are significant because of what they contributed to the cultural and intellectual stream that became black nationalism.

One of the most significant constants of the postwar era was the effort of southern planters to find ways of legally restricting black movement. Almost from the moment slavery ended, whites who employed black labor sought to re-create a main element in the old system by preventing blacks from moving about freely. In 1865 and 1866, they worked for the adoption of black codes to tie the freedmen to the farms, and until the eve of World War I, they continued to search for legal formulas that could keep blacks from deserting their employers. But though the laws of labor control undoubtedly helped create an ethos unfriendly to migration, planters were rarely able to use their legal instruments effectively enough to interdict seriously black movement from one state to another. Throughout the period up to World War I, blacks in most parts of the South appear to have moved with relatively little interference when jobs were available.

White southerners were, nevertheless, largely successful in using legislation to drive blacks from the political arena and in erecting a massive wall of segregation statutes between the races. Why was it that they were so much more effective in limiting the political and social freedoms of blacks than in controlling black movement? At the heart of the matter is white solidarity. Clearly solidarity existed when it came to segregation and, to a somewhat lesser extent, political exclusion. Believing in black inferiority, whites of all classes united in support of those goals. On the question of limiting black movement, however, whites divided among themselves.

There was first of all the difference that arose out of the competition for labor. Planters in areas undergoing substantial out-migration were in favor of stringent measures to limit black movement, but those in regions with labor shortages often paid recruiters to bring in blacks from far away. In that, they acted without the slightest concern that they might be "stealing" another person's labor. But beyond such competition stood sharp differences between whites whose livelihoods and well-being depended on the use of black workers and those whose did not. White supremacists who needed black labor liked to suppose that black inferiority justified special measures to prevent Negroes from moving on their own. White supremacists who got along without black labor would have been happy to see an all-white South. Accordingly, their enthusiasm for immobilizing blacks was less than the planters'. In an era when repression was the order of the day, this division of opinion in the white community gave blacks a small margin of freedom.[1]

Tradition thinks of the world of slavery as a static place, with blacks typically remaining on one plantation all their life. The reality was quite different. Migration with masters, the interstate slave trade, and slave hiring were major facts of life for antebellum blacks which involved involuntary uprootings and cruel separations from family and friends.[2]

The slave trade provided a brutally efficient mechanism for keeping

1. Often overlapping with traditional class differences, the division described here also cuts sharply across class lines. On one side were those whose living depended on black labor, whether wealthy planters or ordinary farmers with one or two hired hands. Employers from the industrial and semi-industrial sectors, like sawmill and turpentine operators, also fitted in this category. On the other side were factory workers, urban folk, newspaper editors, and other independent professionals, as well as the poorest whites and white people of all sorts from counties with very few blacks.

2. Herbert Gutman and Richard Sutch, "The Slave Family," in *Reckoning with Slavery: A Critical Study in the Quantitative History of American Negro Slavery,* ed. Paul A. David *et al.* (New York, 1975), 99–110.

labor demand in balance with supply. The trade worked simply and naturally enough along free-market lines. Virginia had a surfeit of slaves, and therefore slave prices in that state were low. Mississippi planters were acutely short of labor, so slave prices there were high. Between the two extremes, the Negro traders made a market in human beings, providing the South with the labor elasticity needed for survival in the modern world. There is considerable debate over the precise size of the domestic slave trade, but simply from the number of people involved in the buying and selling, it seems clear that it was extensive indeed.[3]

The slave trade served to make gross adjustments in the geographic distribution of the work force, but the fine tuning came from a hiring system that provided forced labor for rent. In rhythm with southern agriculture, hiring was arranged largely through annual contracts that ran from January through December. That pattern was especially strong in the cotton South. When a Georgia slaveholder tried to get back a slave she had rented out for a year, the state supreme court held that it was the "universal practice in a cotton county to hire negroes for the year, if hired at the beginning of the year."[4] The labor system

3. In 1842, a New Orleans directory listed 185 persons as having the occupation of "trader," and in 1848 a Louisville directory cataloged 44 traders in that city. In the 1850s, no fewer than a hundred trading firms were active in South Carolina. Such figures say nothing of the myriad auctioneers, commission merchants, brokers, real-estate agents, and others who bought and sold human beings as an adjunct to their main business. See Frederic Bancroft, *Slave Trading in the Old South* (1931; rpr. New York, 1959), 128–29, 314–15; and Michael Tadman, "Slave Trading in the Ante-Bellum South: An Estimate of the Extent of the Inter-Regional Slave Trade," *Journal of American Studies*, XIII (1979), 218n. For the dispute over the extent of the slave trade, see also Robert William Fogel and Stanley L. Engerman, *Time on the Cross* (2 vols.; Boston, 1974), I, 48–55, II, 48–54; William Calderhead, "How Extensive Was the Border State Slave Trade? A New Look," *Civil War History*, XVIII (1972), 42–55; Michael Tadman, *Speculators and Slaves: Masters, Traders, and Slaves in the Old South* (Madison, Wis., 1989); Donald M. Sweig, "Reassessing the Human Dimensions of the Interstate Slave Trade," *Prologue*, XII (1980), 5–21; and Gutman and Sutch, "The Slave Family," 99–112.

4. *Hobbs* v. *Davis*, 30 Ga. 423 (1860). On the slave hiring system, see Clement Eaton, "Slave-Hiring in the Upper South: A Step Toward Freedom," *Mississippi Valley Historical Review*, XLVI (1960), 663–78; Kenneth Stampp, *The Peculiar Institution: Slavery in the Antebellum South* (New York, 1956), 67–73; Robert S. Starobin, *Industrial Slavery in the Old South* (New York, 1970), 128–37; Ulrich B. Phillips, *American Negro Slavery* (1918; rpr. Baton Rouge, 1969), 405–14; and Fogel and Engerman, *Time on the Cross*, I, 52–53, 55–57.

that emerged after emancipation would borrow more than a little from the prewar hiring system.

Still, from a legal perspective, slave hiring agreements were more like rental leases than labor contracts and, therefore, would have made a poor starting point for the establishment of a new free labor system.[5] But the hiring system existed side by side with a system by which antebellum free Negroes made labor contracts with their white employers, and the two systems had enough similarities that the one sometimes seems to shade into the other. An antebellum white proudly claimed that "free colored workers hire themselves annually upon the same terms and conditions as slaves and are subject to the same discipline." But as similar as the two sets of arrangements might seem, there was a crucial distinction: the contracts of free Negroes were labor agreements not leases.[6] When freedom came, southern whites would reach back to both the slave hiring system and the regulations governing antebellum free Negroes for models.

The labor system that replaced slavery had its immediate origins in the Civil War and was very much a product of black movement and the fear of black movement. Everywhere the northern soldiers went, their presence undermined slavery and disrupted agriculture. This posed major problems for the advancing Union army, since military necessity required that the blacks in conquered areas be kept at work but political and moral considerations made it impossible to hold them as slaves. As a result, Union commanders groped toward intermediate arrangements.

The question of what to do about the blacks arose first in April, 1861, at Fortress Monroe, Virginia, when General Ben Butler refused to return three fugitive slaves to their owners, declaring that they were contraband of war and arguing that local slaves were being used to construct Confederate fortifications. The contrabands were simulta-

---

5. When a slave died while hired out, the hirer had no liability unless the contract had been violated. Thus, masters suing for damages in such situations sought to show that their property had been abused in violation of the terms of the contract. See, e.g., *Bedford and McCall* v. *Flowers,* 30 Tenn. 242 (1850); and *Wallace* v. *Seales,* 36 Miss. 53 (1858).

6. Quoted by Ira Berlin in *Slaves Without Masters: The Free Negro in the Antebellum South* (New York, 1974), 228. See also pp. 92–94, 165, 166*n*, 208–209, 327–31 in the same book, and John Hope Franklin, *The Free Negro in North Carolina, 1790–1860* (Chapel Hill, N.C., 1943), 63–64, 72.

neously property to be denied the enemy and, as Butler would recall a year later, men to be treated as "human being[s] wrecked upon a civilized coast."[7]

In November, 1861, the Yankees captured the Sea Islands, off the South Carolina coast, from which the entire white population had fled, leaving behind ten thousand contrabands and sixty thousand acres of arable land. With the masters absent, this seemed an ideal place to stage a "rehearsal for Reconstruction" that tried various approaches to free labor. The Port Royal Experiment did indeed show that the blacks could work without coercion, but there was too much conflict among the various northern elements at Port Royal for it to prove much more than that. Besides, the absence of southern whites that made experimentation so easy also created artificial conditions quite unlike those that came to exist in the rest of the South.[8]

In the end it was Louisiana that set the pattern for the South's new labor system. On April 25, 1862, New Orleans fell before a northern naval onslaught, and Butler, then commander of the Department of the Gulf, was put in charge of the city and its hinterland. Almost immediately he faced a major exodus from the plantations to New Orleans, and his efforts to halt that movement profoundly affected the shape of the new labor system.[9] Despite Butler's best efforts, the exodus from the farms had created a labor shortage by the fall of 1862 that threatened the gathering of the crops. Consulting with at least

7. Louis S. Gerteis, *From Contraband to Freedman: Federal Policy Toward Southern Blacks, 1861–1865* (Westport, Conn., 1973), 12–13; Benjamin Butler to Edward M. Stanton, May 25, 1862, in *The War of the Rebellion: A Compilation of the Official Records of the Union and Confederate Armies* (130 vols.; Washington, D.C., 1880–98), Series I, Vol. XV, p. 439 (hereafter cited as *OR;* unless otherwise indicated all citations are to Series I); Hans L. Trefousse, *Ben Butler: The South Called Him Beast!* (New York, 1957), 77–79.

8. Willie Lee Rose, *Rehearsal for Reconstruction: The Port Royal Experiment* (Indianapolis, 1964); Gerteis, *Contraband to Freedman,* 48, 49–62, 301–15, 351–58; James M. McPherson, *The Struggle for Equality: Abolitionists and the Negro in the Civil War and Reconstruction* (Princeton, 1964), 158–67. See also William S. McFeely, *Yankee Stepfather: General O. O. Howard and the Freedmen* (New Haven, 1968), 130–48.

9. Trefousse, *Ben Butler,* 104–106, 130; Butler to Stanton, May 25, 1862, in *OR,* XV, 441, 440. On conditions in Louisiana at this time, see William F. Messner, "Black Violence and White Response: Louisiana, 1862," *Journal of Southern History,* XLI (1975), 24–25, 31–34.

one local planter, Butler devised a contractual arrangement meant to assure labor stability. What is striking about the "labor contract" is that it was between the government and the planters. Unlike the annual labor contracts that would emerge later, it was an agreement that blacks were not parties to.[10]

Under the "arrangement" worked out, the government promised to "employ all the persons heretofore held to labor by loyal planters in St. Bernard and Plaquemines parishes." The blacks were to be worked as before, "under the charge of the loyal planters and overseers of said parishes." Planters were barred from whipping their slaves, and discipline was given over to the army. Provost marshals were authorized to punish "insubordination or refusal to perform suitable work."[11]

In mid-December, 1862, Butler was succeeded by General Nathaniel P. Banks, but labor policy in Louisiana continued along the same lines as before. For about the next year, General Banks continued to use a contract system according to which agreements were between the planters and the military and the mere presence of blacks on a plantation was deemed evidence of their having "acquiesced" to the terms of the contract.[12] By late 1863, however, it was clear that if any

10. "Memorandum of an arrangement entered into between the planters, loyal citizens of the United States, in the parishes of St. Bernard and Plaquemines, in the State of Louisiana, and the civil and military authorities of the United States in said State" [October, 1862], in *OR*, XV, 594–95; C. Peter Ripley, *Slaves and Freedmen in Civil War Louisiana* (Baton Rouge, 1976), 37–38, 44–45. The degree to which Butler consulted local planters is unknown, but he surely had help from his trusted confidant Christian Roselius, who was the Unionist owner of a large plantation in Carrollton. See Ripley, *Slaves and Freedmen*, 33–34; Benjamin Butler to President Lincoln, July 30, 1862, in *OR*, XV, 533; and Christian Roselius to Benjamin Butler, August 20, 1862, in *Private and Official Correspondence of Gen. Benjamin F. Butler During the Period of the Civil War*, ed. Jessie A. Marshall (5 vols.; Norwood, Mass., 1917), II, 207 (hereafter cited as *Butler Correspondence*).

11. Memorandum of an arrangement [October, 1862], in *OR*, XV, 594–95.

12. Fred H. Harrington, *Fighting Politician: Major General N. P. Banks* (Philadelphia, 1948), 90–93, 104–106; Trefousse, *Ben Butler*, 122–33; General Order No. 12, January 29, 1863, in *OR*, XV, 667; Ripley, *Slaves and Freedmen*, 48; Contract Form Issued by the U.S. Sequestration Commission, February 5, 1863, and Signed on February 20, 1863 (Edward J. Gay Family Papers, Troy H. Middleton Library, Louisiana State University); Gerteis, *Contraband to Freedman*, 75.

farming was to get done, the whites would have to deal directly with the blacks. In October, 1863, the wife of a plantation manager in Iberville Parish said she feared that contracting under Banks's plan might lead to the impressment of her blacks, and she suggested that "it would be better to let the authorities entirely alone, and make the best arrangements possible with the negroes themselves."[13]

In February, 1864, Banks revised his labor program and, for the first time, recognized black laborers as parties to the contract. He said, "Laborers will be permitted to choose their employers, but when the engagement is made, they will be held to their engagements for the year, under the protection of the government."[14] It was a grudging concession, but it was of enormous importance. The labor contract was to be an agreement between laborers and planters rather than between planters and the government. By mid-1865, when the Freedmen's Bureau took over the work of supervising the contractual process, that principle was universally accepted.

Central to the evolving system was the army's role in coercing laborers into returning to the plantations. In January, 1863, Banks proclaimed that those who left their employers would be "compelled to support themselves and families by labor upon the public works." A year later he was still making the threat.[15] Banks built coercion into the fabric of his free labor system. He invested provost marshals with broad powers to supervise labor relations and to deal with vagrants. As under slavery, blacks needed written proof that they were authorized to be off the plantation. A newly created Bureau of Negro Labor was given overall charge of the black labor force and of the disposition of vagrants.[16]

With good reason, the free blacks of New Orleans and many New

13. Mrs. L. M. Clark to Edward J. Gay, October 22, 1863, in Gay Family Papers.
14. General Order No. 23, February 3, 1864, in OR, Vol. XXXIV, Part 1, p. 229.
15. General Order No. 12, January 29, 1863, in OR, XV, 667; General Order No. 23, February 3, 1864, in OR, Vol. XXXIV, Part 1, p. 229.
16. General Order No. 64, August 29, 1863, in OR, Vol. XXVI, Part 1, p. 704; Barnes Fletcher Lathrop, "The Pugh Plantations, 1860–1865: A Study of Life in Lower Louisiana" (Ph.D. dissertation, University of Texas, 1945), 258–59; Bell Irvin Wiley, Southern Negroes, 1861–1865 (1938; rpr. Baton Rouge, 1974), 256; Gerteis, Contraband to Freedman, 81, 92–94, 101, 104; Ripley, Slaves and Freedmen, 61–63, 91–92.

England abolitionists charged that General Banks was not creating a free labor system at all.[17] And yet it is a mistake to see Banks's system as an extension of slavery, for it required that wages be paid, it denied masters the right to whip their workers, and it ended the purchase and sale of human beings. Perhaps the way to characterize it is to say, with Edward Messner, that it was a "compulsory free labor system."[18]

As the contract system was evolving in Louisiana, it was spreading to other parts of the South. In the Mississippi Valley, John Eaton and General Lorenzo Thomas introduced it to large areas of Tennessee and the Lower South. In South Carolina, General Rufus Saxton attempted to arrange for the blacks to buy confiscated lands, but when that plan failed, he turned instead to a contract system like the one in Louisiana.[19] When the war was ending, Congress flirted briefly with the idea of black landownership. In March, 1865, it created the Bureau of Refugees, Freedmen, and Abandoned Lands to preside over the transition from slavery to freedom, and in the law establishing it, mandated that every male freedman "shall be assigned not more than forty acres of [abandoned or confiscated] land." For a period of three years, the freedman could rent the land with an option to buy. If he purchased it, he would be given "such title thereto as the United States can convey."[20] Ambiguous as the language about land titles might be, Congress had given blacks reason to believe that, in one way or another, the government would give them land. Unfortunately, the end of the war quickly dulled the northern taste for land confiscation, and by the close of 1865 it was clear that such proposals had become politically unrealistic.[21]

With large-scale land distribution out of the question, there was

17. Ripley, *Slaves and Freedmen*, 74–75, 87; McPherson, *The Struggle for Equality*, 290–93.

18. Messner, "Black Violence," 34.

19. John Eaton, *Grant, Lincoln, and the Freedmen: Reminiscences of the Civil War* (1907; rpr. New York, 1969), 110–11, 146, 155–56; Joel Williamson, *After Slavery: The Negro in South Carolina During Reconstruction, 1861–1877* (Chapel Hill, N.C., 1965), 68.

20. *Statutes at Large of the United States . . . from December, 1863, to December, 1865* (38 vols.; Boston, 1866), XIII, 508.

21. McFeely, *Yankee Stepfather*, 133. On northern attitudes about land for the freedmen, see Eric Foner, *Politics and Ideology in the Age of the Civil War* (New York, 1980), 128–49.

little alternative to the "compulsory free labor" program pioneered by Butler and Banks. Pressed by the need to get southern agriculture back on its feet and to make the freedmen self-supporting laborers, the Freedmen's Bureau set out to get the blacks back into the fields as quickly as possible. Reflecting this mood, Thomas W. Conway, the assistant commissioner for Louisiana, instructed a subordinate: "Give patches to families. . . . Hire them out! Cut wood! Do anything to avoid a state of idleness."[22] Across the South in late 1865 and early 1866 the Freedmen's Bureau began to take drastic steps to put the new labor system into operation. Everywhere rations for the destitute were reduced, and in one state after another bureau officials threatened to jail as vagrants any freedmen refusing to work. In Georgia, the bureau chief simply directed his subordinates to make contracts for blacks who refused to make them themselves.[23]

Watching such activities, white southerners could not help wondering whether the differences between northern and southern attitudes were not more apparent than real. The Louisville *Democrat* mocked:

> We shall have to read a lecture to some of those agents of the Freedmen's Bureau, Gen. Howard amongst the rest. They tell the negro he must go to work immediately. He must make contracts and stick to them, do a good day's work. One fellow went so far as to say, if they did not he would make them. It is not in order to talk that way to freedmen. . . . Let's have no more of this baby talk to men; it is impertinent and unbecoming in men pretending to be loyal. It is just the way slaveholders used to talk to contrabands.[24]

Knowing of the intense northern desire to get the freedmen back to work, white southerners felt on firm ground when they began assembling a permanent structure of laws to control black labor. The whites

22. John A. Carpenter, *Sword and Olive Branch: Oliver Otis Howard* (Pittsburgh, 1964), 94; Thomas Conway to L. S. Gardner, Assistant Superintendent (Selma, Alabama), June 20, 1865, in Assistant Commissioner, Louisiana, Letters Sent, Vol. XV, Records of U.S. Bureau of Refugees, Freedmen, and Abandoned Lands, National Archives, Record Group 105 (hereafter such records will be cited using the form Ascom, Louisiana, LS, XV, BRFAL, NA; a list of abbreviations appears at the front of the book); Circular 11, July 12, 1865 (WD, Circulars Issued, CXXXIX, BRFAL, NA).

23. George R. Bentley, *A History of the Freedmen's Bureau* (Philadelphia, 1955), 84.

24. Quoted in Jackson (Miss.) *Daily Clarion*, December 6, 1865.

framed black codes defining the status of the former slaves and using the labor contract as the keystone of a new system of labor control (see Chapter 2). Northern authorities quickly struck down the most discriminatory aspects of the new laws, and by 1867 many of the labor-control provisions of the codes were dead.

Southerners were surprised at the sharpness of the northern reaction. After all, on the surface, these laws simply sought to achieve what the northerners themselves seemed to be attempting: the return of the blacks to work. And there were indeed crucial areas of similarity between the positions of the northerners and white southerners. Both wanted the freedmen to make contracts, both wanted the blacks to observe the agreements once they had been made, and both were willing to use compulsion to attain their goals. Still, the gulf between the two was enormous. The planters saw compulsion as an absolute prerequisite for black labor, whereas bureau officials saw it as a way-stop on the road to a genuine free labor system in which wages and conditions would be determined by the economic marketplace.[25]

In stark terms, Wager Swayne, the assistant commissioner for Alabama, explained his view of what made men work: "The true incentives to labor are hunger and cold; the true security of labor in the free states is when the laborer finds himself ill-treated, or his wages insufficient or unsafe, he can quit without having to account to anybody." From that perspective the compulsory measures that the government took were excusable only until the natural workings of the labor market obviated the need for artificial intervention.[26]

The planters had a dramatically different perspective, which is captured by the remarks of a southern planter who told a northern reporter, "All we want, is that our Yankee rulers should give us the same privileges with regard to the control of labor which they themselves have." When the northerner explained that in his section, workers did not have to sign annual contracts and there were no criminal penalties for leaving one's job, the planter could hardly be-

25. Foner, *Politics and Ideology*, 103–104.

26. *Reports of the Assistant Commissioners of the Freedmen's Bureau Made Since December 1, 1865*, 39th Cong., 1st Sess., Senate Executive Document No. 27, pp. 63–64 (hereafter cited as SXD 27); Foner, *Politics and Ideology*, 102–103. Swayne was more proplanter than most of the assistant commissioners, but still his views typify northern free labor thought.

lieve it: "How can you get work out of a man unless you compel him in some way?"[27]

Despite the chasm between planters and bureau officials, they were agreed in late 1865 on the urgent need for some sort of intervention. It appeared then as though the whole black population was on the move. Emancipation triggered an enormous amount of black migration as the freedmen set about testing their new status, reuniting their families, and finding new situations.[28] To northerners and southerners alike, the tide of migration appeared responsible for a labor shortage of massive proportions.

It is now clear that the labor shortage that emerged in 1865 was not simply a transient consequence of the first adjustments to freedom. When emancipation came, blacks all over the South decided that if freedom meant anything, it meant the right to reject slavery's hours and slavery's pace. With freedom, blacks chose to reduce their working hours to something more akin to what other free people were used to, and the participation of women and children in the work force declined significantly as blacks sought to take for themselves the same standards of domestic life as were held by whites.[29] The cumulative impact of these individual decisions permanently altered the productivity of the southern economy. Taking account of productivity differences between men, women, and children, Roger Ransom and Richard Sutch have concluded that, on a per capita basis, after the Civil War the black population of the "Cotton South" worked between 28 percent and 37 percent fewer hours than before the war. Had other things been equal, that would have meant that the blacks produced 28 to 37 percent less.[30] But other things were not equal, and it stands to reason that in the absence of the whip there occurred

27. Quoted by Foner in *Politics and Ideology,* 104.

28. Leon Litwack, *Been in the Storm So Long: The Aftermath of Slavery* (New York, 1981), 292–335.

29. Roger L. Ransom and Richard Sutch, *One Kind of Freedom: The Economic Consequences of Emancipation* (New York, 1977), 6–7, 44–47, 55, 232–36; Herbert G. Gutman, *The Black Family in Slavery and Freedom, 1750–1925* (New York, 1976), 167–68.

30. Ransom and Sutch, *One Kind of Freedom,* 6. Though some econometricians have suggested that the decline in the black labor supply may not have been as large as Ransom and Sutch suggest, almost all seem to agree that a significant drop took place in black labor-force participation. See Claudia Goldin, "'N' Kinds of Freedom: An Intro-

a decline in the intensity of labor. That makes the decline in per capita production even larger than the estimates of Ransom and Sutch suggest.

The impact of the labor shortage was exacerbated by a black agenda that dovetailed with neither the needs of the planters nor the expectations of the northern occupiers. Seeking independence from white control, they resisted the work forms of slavery, refusing to labor in gangs or to take direction from overseers or even drivers. Through the prism of racial prejudice, such behavior entered the minds of whites as idleness and indolence and served as confirmation that blacks needed white supervision. Moreover, the labor scarcity worked to magnify the importance of every instance of supposed idleness. Typical of the many who complained of black labor was a Mississippi white who said, "The negro . . . is an eyesore to the planter [who] has to mourn over the dreadful failure in his crops, and bear the indolence and stupidity of a set of 'freed' negroes."[31] His anger and frustration were widely shared by southern whites. Everywhere, it seemed, the bottom rail was on top. In 1867, V. T. Rogers had to earn his living recruiting black labor for others, and he could barely stand it. He told his employer: "This is a horrible business[.] I certain[ly] have never done anything more humiliating than mixing with those miserable drunken wretches and talking on terms of familiarity in order to obtain their services[.] [T]hey feel themselves better than a white man when they have a few dollars in their pockets." The same sense that the world was out of joint was expressed more prosaically

---

duction to the Issues," *Explorations in Economic History,* XVI (1979), 10; and Gavin Wright, "Freedom and the Southern Economy," *Explorations in Economic History,* XVI (1979), 94–95.

31. *Southern Cultivator,* November, 1866, p. 260; Foner, *Politics and Ideology,* 106–107. See also Litwack, *Been in the Storm,* 396. The planters were fond of attributing the failure of their crops to problems with black labor. In fact, many of their troubles came from nature. The years from 1864 to 1867 were marked by too much rain in the spring and too little in the fall, as well as by flooding and an invasion of army worms. See Lawrence N. Powell, *New Masters: Northern Planters During the Civil War and Reconstruction* (New Haven, 1980), 145–46. As James Roark has noted, the planters often ignored the role of the weather and placed all the blame for the crop failure on their former bondsmen (*Masters Without Slaves: Southern Planters in the Civil War and Reconstruction* [New York, 1977], 160–61.

by a Georgian who in 1874 complained that the blacks "have now reached a point where they are able to dictate their own terms and have things their own way."[32]

The comments of whites show what a difficult time they were having in getting beyond the mentality of slavery, but they also reflect the leverage that blacks had gained as a result of the labor shortage. In August, 1865, blacks working on the Virginia Central Railroad near Noels Turnout stopped work because they were not paid. In January, 1868, the local agent of the Freedman's Bureau at Opelousas, Louisiana, reported that black laborers were resisting planters' efforts to fix the price of labor, by refusing to make contracts. In 1871, the blacks in Marion County, Alabama, organized a labor union and threatened to emigrate if they did not get better contracts than they had the year before.[33]

Edward J. Gay, a prominent New Orleans commission merchant and sugar planter, found himself confronted with black labor militancy at almost every turn. In 1868, one of his managers closed a bargain with a neighboring planter for his cane, explaining at the same time that the laborers had made themselves parties to the transaction. The manager wrote Gay, "In order to get the hands to move the cane, they forced Mr. Clark to turn the pay roll of back wages over to me and look to me for the money which I wish you would send up as soon as possible." On another occasion, one of Gay's clients pleaded that his draft to pay his laborers be honored: "Unless you do this for me Mr. Gay I must lose my crop. I have not got the money to pay my laborers, and unless they are paid promptly they will not work."[34]

The labor shortage gave black workers the leverage to demand that they be paid promptly and in full, but it should not be imagined that it guaranteed them high wages or fair treatment. Labor was never *that* scarce. Overall, there was in the years of Reconstruction a sort of

32. *Southern Cultivator,* January, 1874, pp. 7–8; V. T. Rogers to Edward J. Gay, February 5, 1867, in Gay Family Papers.

33. Col. Orlando Brown to Capt. T. F. Crandon, August 9, 1865, in Ascom, Virginia, LS, XII, O. M. Violet to Assistant Commissioner, January 15, 1868, in Ascom, Louisiana, Regletrec, X, both in BRFAL, NA; William Warren Rogers, *The One-Gallused Rebellion: Agrarianism in Alabama, 1865–1896* (Baton Rouge, 1971), 12.

34. Roman Daigre to Edward J. Gay [1868], Gilbert A. Daigre to Edward J. Gay, October 6, 1872, both in Gay Family Papers.

rough balance betwen black labor and white capital. But in particular counties and on particular plantations there was a continually shifting labor supply, and this in turn had very direct effects on labor conditions. Witness the remarks of a Louisiana plantation manager who counseled his employer, "I think it good policy to keep the Hands as well satisifed as possible until we can get the Corn planted and then give them the choice of signing a contract or leaving."[35]

The labor shortage was real enough, but so was the advantage of being white. Though the former slaveholders were, for the moment, relatively weak in the public arena and though they had to pay competitive wages, they still wielded much authority on the farm itself. Over and over again, the freedmen complained that they were cheated at settlement time or that they were driven off the farms without any pay at all. One Louisiana worker whose account showed that there was nothing due him exclaimed, "I done wuck mighty hard fo' you, chop briars and roll logs and you haint paid me nuffin at all." A former Kentucky slave said that after the war he stayed with his old master and worked on halves as a sharecropper "and that was when the real slavery start, for when we got our c[r]op made it done take every bit of it to pay our debts and we had nothing left to buy winter clothes or pay doctor bills." Similar feelings must have existed on the cotton plantation of General M. St. John R. Liddell, in Catahoula Parish, Louisiana. When Liddell settled up with his workers on January 21, 1867, six laborers received amounts from $7.01 to $52.97; twenty-eight others got notice that they were in debt for sums ranging up to $88.10.[36]

Certainly the masters had expenses, and certainly in the devastated state of southern agriculture after the war the blacks would not have received the amounts expected by some even if there had been no cheating at all. But there was cheating, and it was widespread. On December 28, 1868, one of Gay's plantation managers wrote to ask

35. John W. Austin to Edward J. Gay, March 23, 1867, in Gay Family Papers; Foner, *Politics and Ideology*, 118.

36. Litwack, *Been in the Storm*, 422; George P. Rawick, ed., *The American Slave: A Composite Autobiography* (19 vols.; Westport, Conn., 1972–78), Vol. IV, Part 1, p. 238; Account of Wages Paid, January 2, 1867 (Liddell Family Papers, Troy H. Middleton Library, Louisiana State University). See also Joe M. Richardson, *The Negro in the Reconstruction of Florida, 1865–1877* (Tallahassee, Fla., 1965), 60–61.

that money be sent so he could "square up with our laborers for the present year." He specified that he wanted more than half the money "in Small Bills of $1 or $2 & even 50c/ pieces in convenient order in order to make the Pile look big." He went on to explain: "Negroes are somewhat peculiar concerning money[.] [T]hey will voluntarily accept less in Small bills providing they are new ones & such as they fancy." Testifying in 1883, an Alabamian admitted that there was a "good deal" of cheating in his area. He asserted, however, that "the better class of planters and the majority of planters" eschewed such dealings as both unjust and bad policy.[37]

Right after the war, all too many planters sought to cheat the blacks by driving them off the farms just before settlement was due. Sometimes they ordered the freedmen off the land. Other times they harassed them relentlessly until they "broke" their contracts. That way the planter had no responsibility to pay the laborer anything. A South Carolina freedman described the process: "There's a many masters as wants to git de colored peoples away, ye see; an' dey's got de contrac's, an' dey can't do it, ye see, lawful; so dey 'buses dem, an' jerks 'em up by de two fums, an' don't give 'em de bacon, an' calls on 'em to do work in de night time an' Sun'ay, till de colored people dey gits on easy an' goes off." In both 1866 and 1867, many Alabama planters acted in that way. Peter Kolchin quotes one 1867 Black Belt resident as saying, "They will all be turned loose without homes[,] money or provisions[;] at least no meat."[38]

The labor system that replaced slavery came into being, then, under conditions of enormous strain. Southern whites with deep-seated prejudices that had been shaped in the time of slavery found themselves forced to bargain about economic matters with people they felt subhuman. Blacks who wanted land and independence from white control found themselves facing insurmountable pressures to accept a system of labor contracts that gave little promise of earning

37. Testimony of Willard Warner, November 15, 1883, U.S. Senate, Committee on Education and Labor, *Report on the Relations Between Capital and Labor* (5 vols; Washington, D.C., 1885), IV, 273; [Roman] O. Daigre to Edward J. Gay, December 28, 1868, in Gay Family Papers.

38. Peter Kolchin, *First Freedom: The Responses of Alabama's Blacks to Emancipation and Reconstruction* (Westport, Conn., 1972), 42, 41; Sidney Andrews, *The South Since the War, As Shown by Fourteen Weeks of Travels and Observation in Georgia and the Carolinas* (Boston, 1866), 204.

them their way to autonomy. Northerners who despised slavery but who had a desperate fear of encouraging black dependence found themselves coercing blacks to work even as they forced white southerners to recognize that they had no proprietary right to black labor.

The new labor system was then the resultant of what amounted to a three-way tug of war in which blacks, northern whites, and planters pulled in different directions. As the system developed, sharecropping began to emerge as the dominant means of organizing southern agricultural labor, and that was a direct consequence of a continuing stalemate between the planters and their black workers. Built atop the annual contract system that gained a foothold during the Civil War, the sharecropping system was a compromise between the desire of blacks, on the one hand, to distance themselves as far as possible from slavery and white control and the desire of the employers, on the other, to retain control over the production process.[39]

Just after the war the freedmen were generally hired as wage laborers. But there was at the time an acute shortage of cash, which led to the rise of an arrangement whereby the workers agreed to accept as wages a portion of the crop to be distributed at the end of the season. Those who made agreements to take their wages in crops remained wage laborers in the fullest sense of the term. Their employers kept control over all aspects of the production process, and they had no legal right to the crop itself. By and large, the planters tried to maintain the work routines of slavery using drivers, overseers, and the gang system.[40]

Seeking a chance to be free from white control, the blacks resisted.

39. For recent accounts of the emergence of sharecropping, see Ransom and Sutch, *One Kind of Freedom*, 56–61; Gavin Wright, *Old South, New South: Revolutions in the Southern Economy Since the Civil War* (New York, 1986), 84–87; Harold D. Woodman, "Post–Civil War Southern Agriculture and the Law," *Agricultural History*, LIII (1979), 319–37, esp. 322–25; Jonathan M. Wiener, *Social Origins of the New South: Alabama, 1860–1885* (Baton Rouge, 1978), 66–73; Litwack, *Been in the Storm*, 446–48; Joseph D. Reid, Jr., "Sharecropping as an Understandable Market Response—the Postbellum South," *Journal of Economic History*, XXXIII (1973), 106–30; Joseph D. Reid, Jr., "White Land, Black Labor, and Agricultural Stagnation: The Causes and Effects of Sharecropping in the Postbellum South," *Explorations in Economic History*, XVI (1979), 31–55; and Ralph Shlomowitz, "The Origins of Southern Sharecropping," *Agricultural History*, LIII (1979), 557–75.

40. Woodman, "Post–Civil War Southern Agriculture," 322; Litwack, *Been in the Storm*, 446; Ransom and Sutch, *One Kind of Freedom*, 61.

They wanted their own land, or if that was not possible, they wanted to rent land they could use as they saw fit. Only a relative handful had the capital to buy land; more succeeded in renting land as share tenants. That is, they paid their annual rent with a share of the crop, but they had the legal status of renters. Describing the transition to share tenantry, a Georgia farmer said of the freedmen, "[They] will almost starve and go naked before they will work for a white man if they can get a patch of ground to live on, and get from under his control."[41]

Sharecropping, a third system, came into being as a way of organizing the labor of those who could neither buy land nor rent it but were unwilling to continue working under the old forms of plantation superintendence. Reflecting the widespread white belief that without white supervision the freedmen would not produce effectively, it left control of the productive process in the hands of the planter. At the same time, in subdividing the plantations into small plots, the planters yielded to the blacks' rejection of the gang system and to their aversion to white overseers. Individual families signed annual contracts to work these plots and received a share of the crop *as wages* at the end of the year.[42]

Superficially, tenantry and sharecropping were similar. Tenants and sharecroppers both worked individual plots of land, and both divided their crops with the landowner according to the terms of a prearranged annual contract. But there the similarities ended. Tenants owned the crops they grew, croppers did not. Tenants were free to make their own decisions about what to plant, when to plant it, and the like. Croppers had to accept employer supervision of virtually every dimension of their farming activity. Landlord lien laws weakened the position of the tenants, but, even so, crop ownership gave them a large advantage as compared with sharecroppers.[43]

The legal distinctions between tenantry and cropping could be significant, but the tendency of tenants and croppers alike to fall into debt to their landlords or to local merchants often had the practical effect

41. *Southern Cultivator,* March, 1867, p. 69; Ransom and Sutch, *One Kind of Freedom,* 87–91.

42. Ransom and Sutch, *One Kind of Freedom,* 88–91, 68–70; Huntsville (Ala.) *Advocate,* October 27, 1868.

43. Woodman, "Post–Civil War War Southern Agriculture," 325–34; Ransom and Sutch, *One Kind of Freedom,* 88–91.

of blurring the differences. Once caught in the trap of debt, the tenant too might have to accept white supervision, whether he liked it or not. In 1867, the annual report of the commissioner of the Freedmen's Bureau noted that in Mississippi the plantation laborer was often charged so heavily for negligence or incidental expenses that "at the end of the year he is poorer than at the beginning."[44]

Still, at its inception, sharecropping was far more popular among blacks than the annual-wage system. In giving the cropper an individual plot of land to work, sharecropping provided at least the illusion of independence. By late 1866, the movement toward sharecropping was fairly well under way, and even those planters who did not like the system must have found it hard to resist. In November, 1866, a report to the Freedmen's Bureau dealing with the area around Memphis said that 20,836 freedmen were working on shares, as against 8,539 for wages. At the same time, a Florida bureau official said that half the freedmen in that state were working for a share of the crop. In March, 1868, a local agent of the bureau in Louisiana asserted that the freed people in his parish "universally desire to contract for a share of the crop, and refuse to work for wages."[45] By January, 1869, the movement toward sharecropping in Louisiana was so strong that one plantation manager who was still using the wage system predicted difficulty, saying, "It is a hard matter for the negroes to stand the inducements and promises offered them by many who want to work on shares, it puts we that are hiring to a great deal of trouble and wise working to Keep our old hands." Two months later another Louisiana farmer glumly predicted, "This is about the last year they will work in gangs or large squads."[46]

It was so in much of the South, and by the early 1870s most south-

---

44. "Report of the Commissioner of the Bureau of Refugees, Freedmen, and Abandoned Lands, November 1, 1867," in *Annual Report of the Secretary of War,* 40th Cong., 2nd Sess., House Executive Document No. 1, pp. 680–81.

45. A. M. Murtagh to Capt. Lucius M. Warren, March 31, 1868, Abbeville, Louisiana, in Trimonthly Reports to the Ascom, Louisiana, BRFAL, NA; "Station Memphis" (Report prepared by Fred Palmer, chief superintendent, November 9, 1866; Ascom, Tennessee, LR, XXXI, BRFAL, NA; Palmer's report made no distinction between tenants and croppers); Maj. Gen. J. G. Foster, Ascom, Florida, October 1, 1866, in *Reports of the Assistant Commissioners of Freedmen . . . [for 1866],* 39th Cong., 2nd Sess., Senate Executive Document No. 6, p. 43 (hereafter cited as SXD 6).

46. Sam Postilthwaite to "Uncle Gillespie," March 14, 1869, in James A. Gillespie

ern land was cultivated by sharecroppers. According to Ransom and Sutch, by 1880 traditional plantations accounted for only 8.9 percent of the croplands cultivated in the area of their study. On the other hand, over half of all the farms in the Cotton South were cultivated by "tenants." Of the tenant farms, 72 percent were sharecropped.[47] Moreover, it seems a fair assumption that, even at this early stage, whites accounted for a disproportionate share of the renters and blacks for a disproportionate share of the sharecroppers.

The emergence of sharecropping marked the conclusion of the search for a labor system to replace slavery. Wrought from the conflicting needs and perceptions of freedmen, planters, and northerners, the new labor system was shaped by the postwar labor shortage. There can be little doubt that it was only because of the combination of labor scarcity and the northern presence that southern whites accommodated themselves at all to the demands of the blacks. Still, the new system had strong roots in the southern past. The annual contract system was not just an invention of the occupying northerners but had antecedents in the slave hiring system, in the prewar agreements between free Negroes and employers, and in the very rhythms of southern agriculture.

Such continuities must not obscure, however, the way the new labor system was indeed a free labor system in which blacks had the right to move about and to bargain with their employers over terms. It gave them vastly more independence than they had had under slavery. The new labor system was rife with the potential for abuse—in particular, it lent itself to cheating at settlement time and to the development of debt servitude—but it was a free labor system of sorts. Whether it could survive a withdrawal of northern support for Reconstruction was another question.

Family Papers, Troy H. Middleton Library, Louisiana State University; Roman Daigre to Edward J. Gay, January 4, 1869, in Gay Family Papers.

47. Ransom and Sutch, *One Kind of Freedom*, 87–88, 68–70 (the "Cotton South" is defined on pp. xii and xx [map]).

2

THE PLANTER QUEST

FOR CONTROL

Just how free was the system of free labor that emerged after the Civil War? And, if there was indeed a genuine free labor system in the Reconstruction era, did it remain free in the decades afterward? Were blacks generally free to go where the wages and working conditions were best, or were planters able to exert substantial control over black mobility?

Who was responsible for the attempt to turn back the clock and destroy black freedom in the years after the Civil War? Did the effort emanate largely from the planter class, as historians concerned with class analysis have argued, or did it stem from a broadly based white racism that cut across class boundaries?[1] Such questions are of crucial import, for on the answers to them hinges our conception of what happened in the post–Civil War South.

---

1. Charles Flynn has suggested that it is wrong to look at the question as a matter of whether class oppression is more important than racial oppression or vice versa. Rather, he says, "the central theme of southern history can be found in the interplay between the South's culturally defined caste and economically defined class systems" (*White Land, Black Labor: Caste and Class in Late Nineteenth-Century Georgia* [Baton Rouge, 1983], 2). The point is an excellent one. The two systems are interrelated. Still, it is legitimate to ask which of the two had the more powerful influence.

Put in the starkest and most oversimplified terms, the debate of historians over the extent of black mobility ranges from the contention that blacks experienced the South as a vast jail run by the planter class to the thesis that although racial oppression was real enough, it stopped where free-market economic principles began.

In works dealing with peonage and involuntary servitude, Pete Daniel, Daniel Novak, and I have each described southern coercive labor practices. Novak and I have concentrated on exploring the legal framework for involuntary servitude. Daniel has described southern peonage in the twentieth century. None of us has had direct evidence concerning the extent of these practices, but we all inferred from the material at our disposal that forced labor of one sort or another was relatively common. Indeed, Novak went so far as to say that for much of the region's history, involuntary servitude "held a majority of the black population of the South in thrall."[2]

As I was writing about involuntary servitude, I became troubled by the apparent contradiction between the evidence that planters were coercing black labor and the other evidence that large numbers of blacks were moving about as they chose. I resolved the paradox by arguing, in essence, that involuntary servitude was an optional system that planters could invoke or not, and that they resorted to it especially when threatened by labor shortages. At other times, I said, blacks were pretty much free to move at will.[3] Daniel, Novak, and I dealt extensively with the efforts of southern planters to limit black movement, but beyond this none of our works was concerned with class analysis as such. Clearly, planters had a special interest in black labor, but it seems equally true that racial oppression came from virtually all directions.

For Jonathan Wiener, on the other hand, class is all-important. He argues that after the Civil War the planters regained control of the South and crushed both black and white workers under their heels

2. Daniel A. Novak, *The Wheel of Servitude: Black Forced Labor After Slavery* (Lexington, Ky., 1978), 84; Pete Daniel, *The Shadow of Slavery: Peonage in the South, 1901–1969* (Urbana, Ill., 1972), 11, 21–22; William Cohen, "Negro Involuntary Servitude in the South, 1865–1940; A Preliminary Analysis," *Journal of Southern History,* XLII (1976), 31–60. See also Pete Daniel, "The Metamorphosis of Slavery, 1865–1900," *Journal of American History,* LXVI (1979), 88–99.

3. Cohen, "Negro Involuntary Servitude," 59–60.

as they traveled along a Prussian Road to modernization. Wiener strongly implies that as this process unfolded, the South became a large prison for blacks, or almost so. He says:

> Large-scale black migrations from the South took place only twice between Reconstruction and the Depression: the "Kansas Fever" exodus of 1879–80 and the migration during World War I. Aside from these two movements, the migration rate from the Southern states was significantly lower than that from other areas of the country, another measure of the success of repressive law and regional practice.[4]

Other advocates of a class analysis have questioned whether the power of the planters was as complete as Wiener suggests. Although focusing on the persistence of plantation society into the era of freedom, Jay Mandle rejects the argument that peonage practices prevented migration. He reasons that the large-scale movement from one plantation to another that took place at contract time shows that blacks did have the right to move if they wished.[5]

Taking a similar view, Harold Woodman has challenged Wiener's insistence that tenants and sharecroppers operated within a system of "bound labor." He notes that southern black laborers moved "more often and regularly than their northern counterparts." Labor could not be bound and mobile at one and the same time. Woodman says we need to see the period from 1870 to 1900 as a time when the various southern classes were being transformed as they grappled with the necessity of adapting to a capitalist framework of employer-employee relations.[6]

Much of the vigor of the recent debate comes from the contribu-

4. Jonathan M. Wiener, "Class Structure and Economic Development in the American South, 1865–1955," *American Historical Review*, LXXXIV (1979), 983. See also Wiener, *Social Origins of the New South*, 69–73. Another work that argues for the "Prussian Road" is Dwight B. Billings' *Planters and the Making of the "New South": Class, Politics, and Development in North Carolina, 1865–1900* (Chapel Hill, N.C., 1979). Billings, however, has the planters becoming industrialists, whereas Wiener sees them resisting economic modernization.

5. Jay R. Mandle, *The Roots of Black Poverty: The Southern Plantation Economy After the Civil War* (Durham, N.C., 1978), 20–21.

6. Harold Woodman, "AHR Forum: Class Structure and Economic Development in the American South, 1865–1955," *American Historical Review*, LXXXIV (1979), 997–1001.

tions of econometricians who have attempted to apply quantitative techniques to the study of postbellum southern economic history. Along the way they have challenged a host of traditional notions about the southern economy, forcing historians to deal with arguments rooted in the principles of market economics.

The first book-length study of the southern economy in the post-bellum era, Stephen J. DeCanio's *Agriculture in the Postbellum South,* is an ambitious work that tries to address directly the question of whether the southern labor market was free. Applying a sophisticated regression analysis to common census data (like the value of farm implements, the number of improved acres, and the rural population), DeCanio seeks to determine whether black sharecroppers were paid an amount equal to the marginal product of their labor. If so, he argues, it cannot be said that they were exploited. He concludes that in the years from 1880 to 1910 the South had a competitive economy in which black labor was not oppressed. Despite a formidable technical apparatus, however, the study contains a flaw that renders its results invalid. Lacking adequate information on the size of the black and white labor forces, DeCanio makes the assumption that data on the rural population are an acceptable substitute for data about the labor force.[7]

In an important study of blacks in the American economy during the period from 1865 to 1914, Robert Higgs has claimed that black economic history of the postbellum era was in essence the result of the interaction between "two systems of behavior: a competitive economic system and a coercive racial system." Higgs grants the considerable importance of the coercion blacks experienced, but he sees the coercion as emanating almost exclusively from the public sector, where government discriminated against blacks in a myriad of ways.[8] Pulling in a quite opposite direction, according to him, was the economic sphere, where competition and self-interest forced southerners

---

7. Stephen J. DeCanio, *Agriculture in the Postbellum South: The Economics of Production and Supply* (Cambridge, Mass., 1974), 10–15, 262–64, 302–303. The weakness of DeCanio's assumption becomes apparent when one asks whether the labor-force participation rates for white and black women were—or could have been—approximately equal.

8. Robert Higgs, *Competition and Coercion: Blacks in the American Economy, 1865–1914* (New York, 1977), 13, 132–33.

to choose between their desire to discriminate and their desire to acquire wealth. In the economic realm the most precious freedom that blacks had was the right to move from one place to another and from one job to another. In the free agricultural labor market, where most blacks operated, says Higgs, "discrimination in employment and wages scarcely existed."[9]

Bridging the gap between historians and econometricians is Gavin Wright, who operates with equal ease in both worlds. In a sweeping reinterpretation of southern economic history since the Civil War, he notes that one of the most crucial changes that resulted from emancipation was a revolutionary transformation in the nature of the planter class. Those who had been "laborlords" in the antebellum era were transformed into "landlords," with significantly different kinds of economic concerns from the slaveholders, whose wealth had been concentrated more in slaves than land.[10]

Like Mandle and Woodman, Wright argues that black movement was simply too extensive for there to have been any large-scale system of unfree labor. In support of his position he observes that plantation records for Alabama and Georgia "show not only that tenants frequently left but that they were often *more* likely to leave if they were heavily in debt."[11] Beyond this, however, Wright argues that although the southern labor market was free, it was also separate, distinct, and isolated from the northern market. That striking interpretation helps explain how there could be vigorous migration within the South even while there was only a trickle of movement to the North. It also helps explain continuing southern backwardness in a host of areas ranging from literacy to industrialization.[12]

It is clear that the view of the South as a vast prison for blacks distorts historical reality, but it is equally clear that things were going on in the postbellum South that led many people—contemporaries as well as modern historians—to believe that view correct. A central goal of this book is to make sense of the conflicting evidence in this matter. To do so it is necessary to examine both planters' efforts to control the black labor force and the reality of continuing black movement.

9. *Ibid.*, 119, 130, 132.
10. Gavin Wright, *Old South, New South*, 33–34, 47–50.
11. *Ibid.*, 65.
12. *Ibid.*, 64–70, 78–80.

Mobility and the effort to limit it need to be seen as well, however, within a larger context that emphasizes that racial oppression had a life of its own and was not simply an expression of class conflict.

When emancipation came, neither planters nor slaves had a choice but to interpret it through eyes and ears shaped by slavery. They had no other frame of reference for judging the new conditions they were experiencing. It is no wonder, then, that although the North had little trouble destroying the institution of slavery *per se,* the underlying premises on which it had rested proved far more resilient. Long after slavery was laid to rest, the great majority of whites continued to believe that blacks belonged to an inferior race, that whites had a right to control the members of the lower race, and that whites had the right to appropriate black labor for themselves.

Over and over again in 1865 and 1866 former slaveholders mourned the loss of control over their blacks and expressed a determination to keep them in subordination. An Alabama planter and lawyer spoke for much of the South when he said, "I look upon slavery as gone, gone, gone beyond the possibility of help," adding, "We have the power to pass stringent police laws to govern the negroes—This is a blessing—For they must be controlled in some way or white people cannot live amongst them." George Fitzhugh insisted: "A great deal of severe legislation will be required to compel negroes to labor as much as they should do, in order not to become a charge upon the whites. We must have a black code." [13]

The state legislatures agreed and, by June, 1866, eight of the former Confederate states had enacted laws of the sort Fitzhugh believed necessary. Aimed at redefining the place of blacks in southern society, the codes generally recognized the end of slavery by making it legal for the freedmen to marry, to own property, and to sue and be sued. The main functions of the new codes, however, were to replace the labor controls of slavery and to limit the mobility of the black labor force. Sidney Andrews, a northern correspondent with radical proclivities, quoted an Arkansas lawyer:

13. *DeBow's Review,* June, 1866, p. 579; J. B. Moore Diary, June 3, 1865, quoted by Kolchin in *First Freedom,* 36.

I know a good many of these men they've sent to the [Arkansas] legislature; and I know there'll be private talk this session, even if there isn't an open effort, to make the penal code take [the freedman] back into the condition of slavery. It'll be called "involuntary servitude for the punishment of crime," but it won't differ much from slavery. Why, I know men right here in this very town who believe in making the breaking of a contract a crime for which the nigger may be sold.[14]

It was not accidental that this lawyer chose contract enforcement as illustrating the new slavery. If the planters had their way, the annual contracts that northerners saw as keystones to free labor would become instead chains of servitude. Contract laws would tie the freedmen to their employers. Vagrancy laws would discipline those who refused to obey the contract laws, and sanctions against "enticement" would punish whites who threatened the system by hiring blacks already under contract to another.[15]

Mississippi enacted the first black code after the Civil War, and though soon repealed, it embodied the system of involuntary servitude southerners were trying to construct. Among the most draconian features of the Mississippi black code was its requirement that after the second Monday in January of each year all blacks show written evidence (for example, a contract) that they have homes and occupations. Other sections mandated that civil officials arrest and return any black abandoning a contract without good cause.[16]

Complementing the contract law, Mississippi's new vagrancy law provided that all blacks with "no lawful business or occupation" were subject to fines of up to fifty dollars and imprisonment for up to ten days. Those who could not pay their fines within five days were to be hired out by the sheriff "to any person who will, for the shortest period of service, pay said fine or forfeiture and all costs: Provided, a preference shall be given to the employer, if there be one, in which

14. *Report of the Joint Committee on Reconstruction*, 39th Cong., 1st Sess., 1866, I, 112, III, 175.

15. Schurz, *Report on Condition of the South*, 39th Cong., 1st Sess., Senate Executive Document No. 2, pp. 24–25; Greensboro *Alabama Beacon*, September 15, 1865; Whitelaw Reid, *After the War: A Tour of the Southern States, 1865–1866* (1866; rpr. New York, 1965), 336–37.

16. Mississippi, *Laws*, 1865, pp. 83–85.

case the employer shall be entitled to deduct and retain the amount so due or to become due." Rounding out the labor provisions of the code, an apprentice law gave preference to former masters when apprentices were bound out by the courts.[17]

The announcement of Mississippi's code provoked a storm of protest. Understandably, northern critics saw it as a vehicle for reenslavement. The radical Chicago *Tribune* threatened that Mississippi would be turned into a "frog pond" before such laws were allowed to disgrace the Union. But warnings like that were not fully heard by other southern states, and within six weeks South Carolina and Florida had enacted their own equally harsh regulations.[18]

The legislatures of Alabama and Louisiana appear to have been as oblivious to the northern furor as South Carolina and Florida. Both went ahead and passed laws making the violation of labor contracts a criminal offense. In each of these states, however, the governor intervened to prevent the law from taking effect. By the fall of 1866 it was clear that northern public opinion would not tolerate southern statutes that smacked of reenslavement. Even so, the Texas senate adopted a stringent contract statute requiring that "all common laborers" make contracts early in January each year. By the time the bill reached the governor, cooler heads had prevailed, and the provision was removed. Yet, clearly, only the fear of antagonizing northern opinion prevented the entire South from following Mississippi's lead.[19]

Reacting to northern criticisms, the southern states that were still drafting black codes began to cast the labor provisions in them in non-discriminatory language. On paper they applied equally to everyone. The states also refrained from passing contract laws that required all

17. *Ibid.*, 92, 90–91, 86–87.

18. William C. Harris, *Presidential Reconstruction in Mississippi* (Baton Rouge, 1967), 141; South Carolina, *Acts,* 1865, pp. 10–44; Florida, *Laws,* 1865–66, pp. 28–35.

19. Theodore Brantner Wilson, *The Black Codes of the South* (University, Ala., 1965), 76–77, 108–109; John Rose Ficklin, *History of Reconstruction in Louisiana, Through 1868* (Baltimore, 1910), 138–40. The Louisiana contract bill is sometimes described as having become law, but Ficklin shows that this was not the case (p. 139). A thorough check of Louisiana, *Laws,* 1865 (Extra Sess.) confirms his position. A partial text of the bill appears in *Documents of American History,* ed. Henry Steele Commager, 7th ed. (2 vols.; New York, 1963), I, 455–56.

workers to have contracts by a certain date.[20] Limited in this manner, the states still sought to control black mobility through the creation of an unobtrusive legal structure that could be selectively applied to enforce the contract system.

To give legal force to the contract system, all that was absolutely needed was a vagrancy statute and an enticement law. Vagrancy legislation allowed planters and sheriffs to coerce blacks into making and keeping their contracts. Enticement statutes protected white planters from competition with one another in the labor market. In the two years after the Civil War, every Confederate state except Tennessee passed an enticement law, and in the same period all except Tennessee and Arkansas adopted new vagrancy laws. Tennessee finally swung into line in 1875, when on successive days it enacted first an enticement law and then a vagrancy law. Arkansas did not adopt a new vagrancy statute until 1905 but, like most states, had a serviceable law on the subject from the antebellum era.[21]

More than any other legislation, the enticement acts embodied the essence of the system of involuntary servitude southerners were trying to build. These laws aimed at re-creating in modified form the proprietary relationship that had existed between master and slave. With precedents going back to fourteenth-century England, they had an

---

20. Georgia provides an excellent example of this retreat. See Alan Conway, *The Reconstruction of Georgia* (Minneapolis, 1966), 55–56.

21. For the enticement laws passed in 1865–1867, see Alabama, *Acts*, 1865–66, pp. 111–12; Arkansas, *Acts*, 1866–67, p. 300; Florida, *Acts*, 1865–66, p. 33; Georgia, *Acts*, 1865–66, pp. 153–54; Louisiana *Laws*, 1865 (Extra Sess.), 24–26; Mississippi, *Laws*, 1865, p. 85; North Carolina, *Public Laws*, 1866 (Special Sess.), 122–23, 1866–67, pp. 197–98; South Carolina, *Acts*, 1865, pp. 36–37; Texas, *General Laws*, 1866, p. 80; Virginia, *Acts*, 1865, p. 38. For the vagrancy laws of this period, see Alabama, *Acts*, 1865–66, pp. 119–21; Florida, *Acts*, 1865, pp. 28–29; Georgia, *Acts*, 1865–66, pp. 234–35; Louisiana, *Laws*, 1865 (Extra Sess.), 18, 20; Mississippi, *Laws*, 1865, pp. 90–93; North Carolina, *Public Laws*, 1865–66 (Special Sess.), 111; South Carolina, *Acts*, 1865, pp. 43–44; Texas, *General Laws*, 1866, pp. 102–104; Virginia, *Acts*, 1865–66, pp. 91–93. The later enticement and vagrancy laws of Tennessee are given in Tennessee, *Acts*, 1875, pp. 168–69, 188–89. For the history of Arkansas vagrancy legislation, see Arkansas, *Revised Statutes* (Ball and Roane), 1837, Chap. 154; Arkansas, *Digest of Statutes* (Sandel and Hill), 1894, secs. 1916–22; Arkansas, *Acts*, 1905, pp. 702–703.

extensive history in criminal and civil law. Seventeenth-century Americans often viewed the enticement of a servant as a crime against society, that is, as a violation of criminal law, but later generations took the matter less seriously and treated it as a civil wrong involving only private rights. By the mid–nineteenth century, criminal prosecutions for enticing a servant had become virtually nonexistent, and civil cases were rare.[22] Thus, it is highly significant that when the South resurrected the enticement laws after the Civil War, only Virginia chose to treat the offense as a civil matter. Georgia's statute made it criminal to entice a worker "by offering higher wages or in any other way whatever." Louisiana levied criminal penalties on those who "shall persuade or entice away, feed, harbor or secrete any person who leaves his or her employ."[23]

In Alabama and Louisiana, the text of the new vagrancy laws of late 1865 and early 1866 shows the intent of the legislators. The Alabama statute supplemented existing statutory definitions of who was a vagrant by mentioning: "a stubborn or refractory servant; a laborer or servant who loiters away his time, or refuses to comply with any contract for a term of service without just cause." Louisiana's vagrancy law held that "if the accused be a person who has abandoned his employer before his contract expired, the preference shall be given to such employer of hiring the accused."[24] For the most part, however, the new vagrancy laws give few clues to the intent of the legislators who wrote them. All the former Confederate states had vagrancy laws in the antebellum period. Alabama, Mississippi, and Louisiana replaced their prewar laws with statutes that were clearly harsher than the old ones. Elsewhere, and most plainly in Georgia and Texas, the text of the laws was unrevealing, and the penalties might actually have been lighter than before.[25]

22. Richard B. Morris, *Government and Labor in Early America* (New York, 1946), 414–34; *Century Edition of the American Digest: A Complete Digest of All Reported American Cases from the Earliest Times to 1896* (164 vols.; St. Paul, Minn., 1897–1904), XXXIV, 2055–63.

23. Louisiana, *Laws,* 1865 (Extra Sess.), 24, 26; Georgia, *Acts,* 1865–66, pp. 153–54.

24. Louisiana, *Laws,* 1865 (Extra Sess.), 18; Alabama, *Acts,* 1865–66, p. 119.

25. For the relevant post–Civil War vagrancy laws, see *n*21 above. These may be compared with antebellum vagrancy laws by consulting Alabama, *Code,* 1852, secs. 3794–98; Florida, *Digest of Laws* (Thompson), 1847, p. 500; Georgia, *Digest of Laws*

Still, there can be no doubt that all the former Confederate states had a similar conception of the purpose for which they were creating the new vagrancy laws. Since all had had adequate vagrancy laws before the war, the new statutes were not necessary except as a way of warning blacks that idleness would not be tolerated and that contracts had to be made and obeyed.

The southern convict laws enacted in 1865 and 1866 are rarely seen as part of the black codes, but that is a mistake. The main purpose of the codes was to control the freedmen, and the question of how to handle convicted black lawbreakers was very much at the center of the control issue. Of the nine states that adopted vagrancy laws in 1865–1866, all except North Carolina provided for the hiring-out of vagrants. These same states also enacted convict laws allowing for the hiring-out of other county prisoners who could not pay their fines and costs. In addition, Alabama, Georgia, South Carolina, Texas, and Virginia made it legal for county authorities to put prisoners to work on public projects such as roads and bridges.[26]

Taken as a whole, the new black codes were firmly rooted in the southern heritage. Resting on the widely held belief that blacks would not work without coercion, the codes were an amalgam of familiar ideas and institutions. A provision in the Mississippi code pertaining to the apprehension of runaway contract breakers harks back directly to provisions in the Mississippi slave code dealing with fugitives.[27] Too, there are interesting parallels between the labor provisions of the

---

(Cobb), 1851, p. 820; Louisiana, *Laws*, 1855, pp. 149–50; Mississippi, *Revised Code*, 1857, p. 629; North Carolina, *Revised Statutes*, 1854, pp. 210–11; South Carolina, *Revised Statutes*, 1872, pp. 382–83 (giving the antebellum law); Tennessee, *Code*, 1857, secs. 1710–12; Texas, *Code*, 1857, pp. 168–69; Virginia, *Code*, 1860, p. 802.

26. For laws authorizing the hiring-out of vagrants and other county convicts, see Alabama, *Acts*, 1865–66, p. 199; Florida, *Acts*, 1865–66, p. 28; Georgia, *Acts*, 1865–66, p. 234; Louisiana, *Laws*, 1865 (Extra Sess.), 18; Mississippi, *Laws*, 1865, p. 93; South Carolina, *Acts*, 1865, p. 43; Texas, *General Laws*, 1866, pp. 103–104; Virginia, *Acts*, 1865–66, p. 92. For laws authorizing the use of county prisoners on public projects, see Alabama, *Penal Code*, 1866, secs. 217–20; Florida, *Acts*, 1865–66, p. 22; Georgia, *Acts*, 1865–66, p. 27, as amended by Georgia, *Acts*, 1866, p. 26; Mississippi, *Laws*, 1865, pp. 166–67; South Carolina, *Acts*, 1865, p. 16; Texas, *General Laws*, 1866, pp. 119, 193; Virginia, *Acts*, 1865–66, pp. 216–17.

27. Compare Mississippi, *Laws*, 1865, p. 84 (Section 7) with Mississippi, *Code*, 1857, p. 238 (Article 16).

black codes and antebellum legislation that governed free Negroes. The prewar laws of North Carolina, Delaware, and Maryland dealing with free Negro vagrants bear a close resemblance to the southern vagrancy laws of 1865 and 1866. The hiring-out of county convicts also had antebellum roots. Before the war southern courts had hired out both free Negroes and poor whites who could not pay what the courts ordered. By the end of the antebellum period the practice of hiring out white paupers was declining, but no change was taking place in the rate at which the courts were hiring out free Negroes.[28]

Had the South been left free to arrange its own affairs, the new scheme of things embodied in the black codes almost certainly would have created the situation envisioned by Carl Schurz when he wrote that in consequence of these laws "the blacks at large belong to the whites at large." But because the codes were so obviously reminiscent of slavery, the South was not allowed to have its way. In December, 1865, General Wager Swayne, the assistant commissioner of the Freedmen's Bureau in Alabama, ruled that a new state contract law was discriminatory and, therefore, null and void. A short while later the governor of Alabama, mindful of the northern presence, vetoed the law.[29]

In January, 1866, acting on the advice of South Carolina moderates who feared a northern reaction, General Daniel Sickles nullified South Carolina's black code by military fiat. In January, 1867, the assistant commissioner of the bureau in Texas ruled that his local agents should disregard the new Texas contract law. It was not until 1871, however, that the Texas legislature repealed the measure.[30] Elsewhere the repeals generally came a bit faster, and by 1868, as a result of adverse northern public opinion and the events of Military Reconstruction, the most discriminatory laws in the black codes had been repealed in most southern states.[31]

28. Almont Lindsey, "Freedmen's Rights in the South, 1865 to 1866" (M.A. thesis, University of Illinois, 1930), 16; Richard B. Morris, "The Measure of Bondage in the Slave States," *Mississippi Valley Historical Review,* XLI (1954), 223–25.

29. Schurz, *Condition of the South,* 24; Huntsville (Ala.) *Advocate,* December 21, 1865.

30. Williamson, *After Slavery,* 77; General Order No. 2, January 3, 1867, from J. B. Kiddoo (Ascom, Texas, Special Orders, BRFAL, NA); Texas, *General Laws,* 1871, p. 91.

31. The pattern of repeals: The Alabama vagrancy law was repealed by Alabama,

Even with the repeals, a significant residue remained through Reconstruction and beyond. There was no attempt to remove the laws providing for the hiring-out of county prisoners convicted of minor offenses. If laws did not manifest obvious discrimination against the freedmen, they often survived. Thus, when Reconstruction came to an end, the enticement laws of Alabama, Georgia, and North Carolina remained on the books. Florida's enticement law was packaged together with a draconian contract-enforcement statute that punished both "wanton impudence" and "abandonment of the premises" as vagrancy. When enacted, this measure applied only to "persons of color." In December, 1866, it was amended "to extend to all persons without discrimination," and in this form it continued through the Reconstruction era. In Georgia, North Carolina, Texas, and Virginia, the vagrancy laws of 1866 survived. Enacted after the northern displeasure with the early black codes was clear, the wording of the laws was generally mild and nondiscriminatory.[32]

Acts, 1866–67, p. 504. The Arkansas contract and enticement act passed in 1867 was apparently repealed by its milder replacement, Arkansas, *Acts,* 1873, p. 183. Florida's stringent vagrancy law was replaced in Florida, *Laws,* 1868, p. 99. The entire Louisiana black code was repealed by the Louisiana Constitution of 1868. See Francis Thrope, ed., *The Federal and State Constitutions . . . of the . . . United States* (7 vols.; Washington, D.C., 1909), III, 1467. In early 1867, the Mississippi legislature ended the worst aspects of the black code by repealing all laws that discriminated in the punishment of blacks (Mississippi, *Laws,* 1866–67, pp. 232–33). The harshest part of the North Carolina black code was that state's apprentice law, which was repealed in North Carolina, *Public Laws,* 1866–67, pp. 10–11. Like Georgia's, North Carolina's vagrancy and enticement statutes contained no discriminatory provisions and remained intact throughout Reconstruction and beyond. The South Carolina black code nullified by General Sickles was formally repealed by South Carolina, *Acts,* September 16, December 21, 1866. Virginia's contract and enticement law was removed from the books by Virginia, *Acts,* 1870–71, p. 147.

32. On the whole, the laws authorizing the hiring-out of county convicts survived the Reconstruction era unscathed. See Alabama, *Code,* 1876, sec. 4468; Florida, *Digest of Laws* (McClellan), 1881, p. 321; Georgia, *Code,* 1882, secs. 4814–15; Texas, *Revised Statutes,* 1879, sec. 3062; Virginia, *Code,* 1873, p. 1264. The four enticement laws that were not repealed during Reconstruction continued in existence well into the twentieth century. With amendments, these laws last appeared in *Code of Alabama Recompiled,* 1958, titles 26–331 to 26–333; Florida, *Statutes,* 1941, sec. 448.02; *Code of Georgia Annotated,* 1966 Revision, secs. 66–9904, 66–9905; *General Statutes of North Carolina,* 1969 Replacement, secs. 14–347, 14–348, 14–358. Aside from the enticement laws, the only contract law that lasted through the 1870s was Florida's (Florida, *Digest of Laws*

The black codes show the kind of labor control white southerners wanted to achieve. What is less clear is the extent to which the laws actually went into operation. In South Carolina, the military order nullifying the code followed so closely upon its enactment that enforcement was hardly possible. In Mississippi, the northern reaction against the code led influential citizens in Jackson and Vicksburg to try to prevent the use of the new vagrancy law. Elsewhere, however, small-town mayors "generally insisted on carrying out the letter of the law." In most parts of the state, the law requiring that blacks doing job work have a special certificate was rigorously enforced. In Mississippi's interior counties the new apprentice law became a popular tool for impressing the labor of black teenagers, but the practice was by no means universal.[33]

Alabama too had an apprentice law, and the statute received a good deal of use, especially in the state's Black Belt counties. Little is known, however, about how fully the rest of this state's black code was carried into practice. Nor is much evidence available about the extent to which Louisiana and Florida enforced their black codes. Joe Richardson indicates that in Florida the Freedmen's Bureau acted to prevent the widespread enforcement of discriminatory legislation, but he does not speak directly of the degree to which Florida applied its contract, apprenticeship, and vagrancy laws. Richardson's study makes it appear that the vigorous efforts of the Florida Freedmen's Bureau to compel blacks to make contracts obviated the need for much civilian enforcement.[34]

[McClellan], 1881, Chaps. 29, 47). Surviving vagrancy laws included Georgia, *Code*, 1882, sec. 4560; North Carolina, *Revisal of Public Statutes* (Battle), 1872–73, p. 319; Texas, *Criminal Statutes* (Willson), 1889, secs. 634–38; Virginia, *Code*, 1887, secs. 884–85.

33. Harris, *Presidential Reconstruction*, 148–49; Vernon Lane Wharton, *The Negro in Mississippi, 1865–1890* (1947; rpr. New York, 1965), 91–92.

34. Kolchin, *First Freedom*, 63–66; Richardson, *The Negro in the Reconstruction of Florida*, 43–47, 59–65, 135–36; Florida, *Laws*, 1865–66, pp. 28, 32–33, 34, 1866–67, pp. 21–22. With the exception of the works by William Harris and Vernon Lane Wharton, the secondary literature has relatively little to say about the enforcement of the codes in the months and years before they were repealed or modified. See, e.g., Joe Gray Taylor, *Louisiana Reconstructed, 1863–1877* (Baton Rouge, 1974), 99–103, 152. John B. Myers shows that the courts and jails of Alabama were extremely crowded with blacks who were prosecuted for minor violations in the months after the passage of the

That enforcement of the black code played a role in inducing some freedmen to sign contracts in early 1866 seems certain, but the role can be overestimated. Many blacks, hoping to obtain land and distrusting their former masters, had refused to make agreements in December, 1865. By February, 1866, however, freedmen were making contracts and settling down in large numbers. That was as true in Georgia, North Carolina, Virginia, and Texas, where the codes had not yet been adopted, as it was in Mississippi, Louisiana, and Florida, where they were already on the books.[35] It is unlikely, therefore, that those statutes played a decisive role in getting most blacks back to work.

Neither the passage of the black codes nor the return of the freedmen to the fields was enough to resolve the southern labor problem. Every year the region's agricultural journals were filled with the complaints of men who had been used to having total control over their labor force but who now had to deal with a labor supply that seemed as undependable as the price of cotton. In February, 1869, a Georgia planter lamented: "Once we had reliable labor, controlled at will. Now we depend upon chance for labor at all. It is both uncertain and unreliable; and our contracts must often be made at great disadvantage." A South Carolina farmer summed up the white perception of the labor problem when he explained that in practical terms the phrase "Labor is Scarce . . . means, the nigger won't work."[36]

---

black code, but he gives no indication whether many were charged with vagrancy ("The Freedmen and the Law in Post-Bellum Alabama, 1865–1867," *Alabama Review*, XXIII [1970], 56–69).

35. Conway, *The Reconstruction of Georgia*, 119. After touring the area between the Brazos and Colorado rivers, the assistant commissioner for Texas asserted that 90 percent of the blacks were under contract and that only sixty-seven persons were on relief (*Report by the Commissioner of the Freedmen's Bureau of All Orders Issued by Him or Any Assistant Commissioner, March 19, 1866,* 39th Cong., 1st Sess., 1866, House Executive Document No. 70, p. 305 [hereafter cited as HXD 70]). For North Carolina, see Report of Col. E. Whittlesey, Assistant Commissioner, January 15, 1866, in *Report of the Joint Committee on Reconstruction,* II, 191. For Virginia, see the Trimonthly reports Lt. J. M. Kimball to Capt. Stuart Barnes (*re* Lawrenceville, Brunswick County), March 31, 1866, Capt. Samuel Carpenter to Capt. Frank Crandon (*re* Madison Court House and vicinity), February 28, 1866, both in Ascom, Virginia, Reports of Bureau Affairs, XXVII, BRFAL, NA.

36. *Southern Cultivator,* July, 1870, p. 198, February, 1869, p. 53.

In essence, white southerners were caught between a very real labor shortage and a set of unrealistic racial convictions that led them to believe that blacks ought to work as long and as hard as they did in slavery, for as little as they received in slavery. The whites, seeking to end the shortage on terms consistent with their racial outlook, created the labor provisions of the black codes in order to restore the racial power relations of the antebellum era.

Even as legislators devised the black codes, some planters despaired of ever using free black labor and looked instead to schemes for the importation of northern or foreign workers into the South. In 1867, a newspaper in Columbus, Mississippi, remarked that projects for importing white labor were "seriously occupying the minds of our people." It worried that the freedmen did not work as before. Instead, black "men are out looking for land to buy—women are quitting the fields, the children flock to the neighboring schools."[37]

In Texas, Thomas Affleck concluded, "We must & we will have other labor." Affleck's solution was to import "intelligent labor," and by this he meant white Europeans, preferably Scots. Others shared his view. The Montgomery *Advertiser* said, "The people of Alabama would do well to encourage emigration to this State, and to obtain an abundant supply of free white labor, rather than trust alone to the efficacy of freedmen contracts and vagrant work-house laws." Less than five months after the guns of war had fallen silent, the Huntsville *Advocate* was inviting "honest, intelligent, thrifty" northern farmers to come South and take up the slack created by a "deficient" and "demoralized" black labor force.[38]

Commenting, "We have already more than enough of a low-grade race here now," Affleck adamantly rejected proposals for the importation of Chinese coolies, but other planters were more receptive. A Georgia planter urged, "Bring them here in competition with the

37. Columbus (Miss.) *Index*, n.d., quoted in *DeBow's Review*, June, 1867, pp. 584–85.

38. Thomas Affleck to Henry W. Hayman, November 22, 1865, in Thomas Affleck Collection, Troy H. Middleton Library, Louisiana State University; Hunstville (Ala.) *Advocate*, August 31, 1865; Montgomery *Daily Advertiser*, August 3, 1865; Affleck to Hayman, November 22, November 15, 1865, Thomas Affleck to Charles Congrere and Sons, November 24, 1865, Thomas Affleck to M. Bass, July 31, 1866, all in Affleck Collection.

negroes, and the latter may find it to their interest to quit stealing and going to the Legislature, and go to work in the cotton fields where they belong."[39]

Reflecting such sentiments, all the southern legislatures enacted measures designed to encourage the settlement of foreign workers. In the period 1865–1876, Virginia passed twelve laws that aimed at encouraging immigration to the state. In 1866, Louisiana and South Carolina established bureaus of immigration. Alabama incorporated a German association and passed a law to protect employers and foreign immigrants from each other.[40]

At the same time a small host of "emigration agents" and immigration societies offered their service of bringing laborers to the South for a fee. Among the many local immigration societies that sprang up across the South were the Eastern North Carolina Immigration Association (1868), the Arkansas River Valley Immigration Company (1869), and the Immigration Society of Newberry, South Carolina (1869). At Okolona, Mississippi, citizens organized a society to import "hardy, sober Danes," and the agents associated with the project boasted that they would furnish five thousand Danes within twelve months.[41]

The five thousand hardy, sober Danes never arrived; neither did the tens of thousands of Scots, Germans, Swedes, Irish, and Chinese

39. *Southern Cultivator*, September, 1869, p. 281; Affleck to Hayman, November 22, 1865, in Affleck Collection. See also *Southern Cultivator*, April, 1870, pp. 108–109.

40. Bert J. Lowenberg, "Efforts of the South to Encourage Immigration," *South Atlantic Quarterly*, XXXIII (1934), 370; Taylor, *Louisiana Reconstructed*, 338; Williamson, *After Slavery*, 119; Sylvia Krebs, "Will the Freedmen Work? White Alabamians Adjust to Free Black Labor," *Alabama Historical Quarterly*, XXXVI (1974), 154. See also Rowland T. Berthoff, "Southern Attitudes Toward Immigration, 1865–1914," *Journal of Southern History*, XVII (1951), 328–60.

41. Jackson (Miss.) *Weekly Clarion*, December 16, 1869; Joseph F. Steelman, "The Immigration Movement in North Carolina, 1865–1890" (M.A. thesis, University of North Carolina, 1947), 28–29; Thomas S. Staples, *Reconstruction in Arkansas, 1862–1874* (1923; rpr. Gloucester, Mass., 1964), 341–42; Broadside, Immigration Society of Newberry, September 6, 1869 (Thaddeus S. Boinsett Collection, William R. Perkins Library, Duke University). For examples of the many advertisements placed by agents for the importation of foreign labor, see Natchez (Miss.) *Democrat*, November 20, 1865; New Orleans *Picayune*, December 25, 1865; Memphis *Daily Appeal*, December 14, 1865; and Richmond *Daily Enquirer*, March 3, 1866.

that were expected in so many parts of the South. In the years from 1860 to 1880 over five million immigrants came to American shores, but only a handful went south. Even fewer stayed for any length of time. The foreign-born population of the former Confederate states rose from 233,651 in 1860 to 279,619 in 1880, with these numbers including an increase of 71,194 in the foreign-born population of Texas. Texas aside, the South suffered a net decrease of about 11 percent in its foreign-born population during the period from 1860 to 1880.[42]

Here and there, ten, twenty, fifty, or even a hundred immigrant laborers did go South, but when they did, the results were often disastrous. In early 1866, James Trowbridge reported that of one hundred Germans who had recently gone to Louisiana to work on sugar plantations, thirty had deserted for higher wages within a day of their arrival. That same year a Georgia newspaper suggested that the German Emigration Societies established in Alabama had proved to be swindlers: "One planter who was foolish enough to try it, had a lot of crop-eared bounty jumpers sent to him who deserted after having their passage paid and receiving the first installment of their wages."[43]

In the end, foreign immigration turned out to be a chimera, because southerners could not afford to match the wages offered in the North and West, because many of the prospective immigrants had an aversion to competing with black labor, and because the planters had no real comprehension of the meaning of free labor. Those who had imagined immigration a solution were as baffled and angry at the unwillingness of foreigners to accept southern wages and living conditions as they were at the refusal of blacks to continue working and living as they had under the lash. Most planters, however, never succumbed to the illusion that immigrant labor might supplant the blacks. A Georgia planter explained his opposition to the importation

42. Figures calculated from data in U.S. Census Office, *Population of the United States in 1860* (Washington, D.C., 1864), xxix, Vol. I of *Eighth Census* (hereafter cited as *Eighth Census, Population, 1860*); U.S. Census Office, *Statistics of the Population of the United States at the Tenth Census, June 1, 1880* (Washington, D.C., 1883), xxxix, Vol. I of *Tenth Census* (hereafter cited as *Tenth Census, Population, 1880*); U.S. Bureau of the Census, *Historical Statistics of the United States, Colonial Times to 1970* (2 vols.; Washington, D.C., 1975), I, 106.

43. Milledgeville (Ga.) *Federal Union*, July 17, 1866; John T. Trowbridge, *The South: A Tour of Its Battlefields and Ruined Cities* (Hartford, Conn., 1866), 414.

of foreigners, on the grounds that they were "not like the negro who is satisfied with plenty of 'hog and hominy,' and a shelter to turn the rain." An Alabamian bluntly rebutted an argument in favor of imported labor: "The negro constitutes our labor, and it is the cheapest we can get. He bears the *same relation* to us now, *de facto* as *heretofore*. We controlled his labor in the past (at our own expense), and will control it in the future (at his). His condition before the war and since are almost identical."[44] Cheap labor and control of the work force remained central goals of the planter class. If this Alabamian was overly sanguine in his estimate of how much control the planters had in November, 1865, he was certainly correct in identifying control as what mattered most.

Even as the planters were devising black codes, they experimented with other ways of controlling their labor. Foremost among these was the planter association. In one place after another white farmers organized themselves into combinations to ensure a common position on black labor. In June, 1865, the citizens of Nelson County, Virginia, held a meeting where they compacted with one another not to pay more than five dollars a month for field hands and not to hire any freedman without first getting permission from his previous employer. Elsewhere a black seeking work often had to present a discharge certificate corroborating that he had fulfilled his previous contract. A month after the Nelson County meeting a similar gathering was held in Franklin County, Virginia, that provoked the Freedmen's Bureau to ban planters' meetings for fixing wages or setting the conditions of employment.[45]

Beyond Virginia, planter associations are known to have existed in Monroe, Conecuh, and Clarke counties in Alabama, and in Coahoma, Attala, and Hinds counties in Mississippi. In 1867 and 1868, still other such organizations came into being in Opelousas and Madison Parish, Louisiana, in Amite and Madison counties, Mississippi, and in Summerville, Alabama. The Opelousas group operated in secret and went by the name of CLUB.[46] There were doubtless numerous other

---

44. Huntsville (Ala.) *Advocate,* November 9, 1865; *Southern Cultivator,* September, 1869, p. 277, December, 1869, p. 374.

45. New York *Times,* June 27, August 1, 1865.

46. O. M. Violet to Ascom, January 15, 1868, in Ascom, Louisiana, Regletrec, X, BRFAL, NA; Testimony of George H. Thomas and Clinton B. Fisk, January 30, 1866,

such groups, and even where formal organization did not exist, planters sometimes tried to keep wages down by informal agreement. In 1873, a planter in Plaquemines Parish, Louisiana, wrote Edward J. Gay to say that Gay's manager was offering too much money for labor. He complained: "I regret to say that your Correspondent Mr. G. A. Daigre is disposing to *overbid* for hands on My place & other plantations in the Neighborhood. . . . For the benefit of the Parish[,] if not of Mr. Daigre individually[,] I trust you will enter your protest to high wages[.] We are all making a terrible *last* struggle & I see no hope for success if Daigre is to offer such prices."[47]

The evidence is clear and unmistakable. All over the South planters eagerly sought to act collectively to hold down wages and to enforce contracts. The evidence is just as clear, however, that such efforts to "combine in self defense" generally ended in failure. Most of the planter associations encountered Freedmen's Bureau opposition at their inception and their efforts at wage fixing never gained the sanction of law. Each group was, therefore, largely dependent on the voluntary cooperation of local farmers. That such unanimity was almost impossible to achieve is suggested by a steady stream of contemporary complaints. A Louisiana farmer protested the lack of planter unity that was allowing black tenants and croppers to make "so much money that all the others will be dissatisfied with their wages." Then he lamented, "What a pity it is for the planters to act so when they have it all in their own hands & could establish[,] if they wished[,] a regular system of wages by a little concert of action."[48] An article by a cotton planter claimed: "There was no concert of action on the part of the planters [to resist exorbitant black wage demands;] . . . on the contrary every man tried to out bid his neighbor, and to fill up his requisite quota of hands at the expense of everybody else."[49]

Perhaps the strongest evidence of the ineffectiveness of the planter

---

in *Report of the Joint Committee*, III, 27, 30; Krebs, "Will the Freedmen Work?" 157–58; Roark, *Masters Without Slaves*, 198–203; Ross H. Moore, "Social and Economic Conditions in Mississippi During Reconstruction" (Ph.D. dissertation, Duke University, 1938), 54–59; *DeBow's Review*, February, 1868, pp. 224, 212–13. See also Litwack, *Been in the Storm*, 415–16.

47. H. Von Ihil to Edward J. Gay, January 4, 1873, in Gay Family Papers.

48. Postilthwaite to "Uncle Gillespie," March 14, 1869, in Gillespie Family Papers.

49. *DeBow's Review*, February, 1869, pp. 152–53; *Southern Cultivator*, May, 1870,

associations is in the simple fact that they were almost always ephemeral. Few if any remained in business much beyond their founding meetings. In view of the acute labor shortage, such associations would surely have persisted had they been effective tools for limiting the competition for labor.

From the perspective of the planters the postwar effort to control the labor force was in a shambles within just a few years of Appomattox. With the exception of the convict laws, most of the black-code legislation was void, dormant, or so watered down as to be of little help in controlling black labor. The effort to control black labor through planter cooperation was just as unsuccessful. In the late 1860s, it was still too early to tell whether efforts to encourage foreign immigration would bear fruit, but certainly there were no signs of early success.

Members of the planter class seemed certain that the bottom rail was on top, but blacks would hardly have agreed. With good reason they complained of being exploited and oppressed on the farms, even as they gained the right to vote and hold office. In fact, there was during the Reconstruction era something of a stalemate between black labor and white capital.[50] The labor shortage and the northern occupation gave blacks real leverage in their struggle with the planters but were hardly enough to offset the wealth, education, and experience of white society in general and of the planter class in particular.

---

p. 141. See also Ralph Shlomowitz, "'Bound' or 'Free'? Black Labor in Cotton and Sugarcane Farming, 1865–1880," *Journal of Southern History,* L (1984), 569–72.

50. Foner, *Politics and Ideology,* 118.

3

THE FREEDMEN'S BUREAU AND THE
REALLOCATION OF BLACK LABOR

As planters and freedmen struggled over the shape of the new labor system and over the issue of control, old patterns of black movement persisted. It might have been expected that emancipation would unleash a flood of migration to the North but, despite a significant push from the Freedmen's Bureau, that did not happen. Instead, the direction of black movement quickly returned to about what it had been before the war. Attracted by promises of higher wages and better conditions in labor-starved southwestern states like Mississippi, Louisiana, Arkansas, and Texas, significant numbers of freedmen opted to abandon the older southern states.

Impoverished as the freedmen were, they could not migrate unassisted. Just as antebellum movement had taken place under the auspices of slave traders who functioned to keep the labor supply in balance with demand, postwar movement was presided over by labor agents. In the first years after the war the Freedmen's Bureau had a big part in this. Initially reluctant to do anything to increase black movement, bureau officials eventually concluded that the only way to cope with postwar unemployment was by turning the organization into a gigantic labor agency and sponsoring the relocation of those who could not find work.

In addition, planters from the Lower South and their representatives flocked to the Southeast in search of hands. It was in this context that the new southern occupation of the labor agent came into being. The agents were middlemen who made a regular business of providing workers for a charge. These labor recruiters were never alone, however, for many planters preferred not to pay their fees and instead came to the Southeast themselves or sent relatives or employees to do the job.

If southeastern blacks wanted to go to the Southwest, where the jobs were more plentiful and the pay was better, their poverty left them no choice but to accept the free transportation that the labor agents offered. But the freedmen were not pawns either. If they could not pay for long-distance moves on their own, they could search out local job opportunities to work as extra hands, or as laborers in the semi-industrial sector of the southern economy. In this they exasperated their employers with their "unreliability," but they were in fact making a rational decision about how to maximize their income. The pay for working in railroad construction or as day laborers at harvest time was far better than for working as sharecroppers with annual contracts. Moreover, since many blacks moved back and forth between their farms and other jobs, their returns from sharecropping were not lost. That sort of movement was not really new. It replicated what had been occurring before the war under the slave hiring system.

Still, all was not merely a repetition of the past. Freedom made a difference. Those who migrated might find the racial conditions at their destinations as bad as what they had left, but at least they were moving of their own accord. Even more important, postbellum migration did not bring with it the forced separation from relatives and friends that had occurred under slavery. Like people everywhere in the modern world, blacks moved from one place to another in tune with the rhythms of the labor market, going where the promise of economic betterment was greatest. The focus of this chapter and of the two chapters that follow will be upon precisely this kind of economically inspired movement. Some blacks, however, saw migration more as a political response to racial oppression than as a matter of economics, and subsequent chapters will explore migration efforts that were more political than economic.

*   *   *

In 1865 and 1866, with the Freedmen's Bureau superintending the transition to a free labor system, politically motivated migration was not an issue. Adopting the position that the blacks had to sign contracts but that a return to slavery in any form would not be tolerated, the bureau stood as the embodiment of Yankee determination to remake the southern economy in the northern image. It was one thing, however, to decree a return to work; it was quite another to be able to supply jobs where the freedmen were concentrated.

All over the South, or so it seemed, labor supply and labor demand were out of phase. While southwestern planters hungered for hands and offered premium wages, the chief of the Freedmen's Bureau in Virginia was suggesting that only a large-scale exodus of blacks could relieve the labor surplus in his state. A similar oversupply existed in the District of Columbia and in certain parts of Georgia and North Carolina. The freedmen in those places often confronted job shortages that were for them every bit as serious as labor scarcity was for southwestern planters.[1]

At first, the response of the Freedmen's Bureau to the labor imbalances was confused and uncertain. Two weeks after General Oliver Otis Howard became commissioner of the bureau in mid-May, 1865, he was told that a large number of freedmen had been removed from Weldon, North Carolina, to Virginia. Angrily, he ordered Orlando Brown, the assistant commissioner for Virginia, to provide for them at once. Simultaneously, he declared, "All such removals are prohibited. Any change of considerable numbers of the people from one district to another will only be made on agreement between the respective commissioners or as ordered by me." Less than two months later, when Brown wrote to Washington for advice about transporting freedmen from one place to another within Virginia, he was told, "Use your judgment." Cost considerations played a major role, however, and the one concrete guideline Brown received was that he should "determine if it will be cheaper to transport them to another place or provide for them where they are."[2]

Quickly, the assistant commissioners began to see that their efforts

1. Reports of Edgar M. Gregory, January 31, 1866, Orlando Brown, November 31, 1865, both in SXD 27, pp. 78, 146.

2. Assistant Adjutant General to Orlando Brown, July 25, 1865, Oliver Otis Howard to Brown, May 31, 1865, both in WD, LS, I, BRFAL, NA.

to get the blacks back to work and reduce dependence on government rations were linked to their ability to bring labor to where it was needed. Thus, when an ambiguously worded directive from Washington seemed to imply that even intrastate transportation orders had to be approved by Howard himself, the assistant commissioner for North Carolina protested that the order was creating "much mischief and Suffering." A week earlier the assistant commissioner had transported a hundred laborers to jobs in Edgecombe County. Now he asked, "Must they be kept here & fed in idleness for want of the power to give them transportation to a place where they can be earning their own living?"[3]

A similar complaint came from Wager Swayne, the bureau head in Alabama, who had been providing transportation for groups of as many as fifty refugeed freedmen from states to the west who were en route to their homes in South Carolina and other southeastern states. Reluctant to care for them in Alabama, Swayne asked permission to continue them on their way. As it turned out, neither he nor the North Carolina bureau chief had genuine cause for worry. The directive in question had been ambiguously written and applied only to the granting of transportation to blacks bound for the North.[4]

Increasingly, it became clear that transportation had to be an essential part of any plan for restarting the southern economy on the basis of free labor. If the maldistribution of labor was a major part of the problem and if this maldistribution bore on the price of labor and on the cost of government support for the indigent, why not give the freedmen the opportunity to go where they could get the most for their labor? In September, 1865, Brevet Major General John Hawkins put forward a plan to do just that.[5]

Stationed at Alexandria, Louisiana, Hawkins concluded that black freedom would never make headway among southerners "as long as circumstances compel [the blacks] to remain with their former

3. Eliphalet Whittlesey to James Fullerton, Assistant Adjutant General, August 7, 1865, in Ascom, North Carolina, LS, BRFAL, NA.

4. Wager Swayne to O. O. Howard, August 30, 1865, in Ascom, Alabama, LS, IV, Eliphalet Whittlesey to Capt. John F. Barnett, August 14, 1865, in Ascom, North Carolina, LS, both in BRFAL, NA.

5. Bvt. Maj. Gen. John Hawkins to Samuel Thomas, September 9, 1865, in Ascom, Mississippi, LR, Box 2, BRFAL, NA.

masters, or while their masters may suppose that circumstances will compel them to remain." Writing to Samuel Thomas, the assistant commissioner for Mississippi, Hawkins suggested a remedy. Some of the labor from the Alexandria area could be transferred to depopulated districts of Mississippi, where labor was scarce. His plan, he said, would raise wages in his part of Louisiana, it would provide workers where they were needed, and it would prevent the Alexandria planters from "throwing their negroes on the hands of the government for support."[6]

Hawkins sent his plan to Howard. It must have piqued the interest of the general or of someone from his office, for the Washington headquarters asked Thomas what he thought of the Hawkins plan. Thomas was unimpressed. He rejected the idea of the government's transporting freedmen from one area to another, as an impractical interference with the workings of the marketplace. His response revealed some crucial limits, however, to the laissez-faire thinking of bureau officers. Agreeing with Hawkins' emphasis on the importance of labor competition, Thomas concluded that labor "rather needs *protection* than *control*." He said it would be futile for the government to move labor from one place to another. If the demand for labor was not strong already, intervention would hardly increase the need for black workers. If, on the other hand, the demand for black labor was indeed strong, such intervention would be unnecessary.[7] Thomas conceded that the war had undermined the equilibrium between labor supply and labor demand, and he agreed that "the equilibrium thus disturbed should be restored." Instead of accepting that the government transport black laborers, however, he suggested a plan for it to "assist the evil to cure itself and yet allow 'labor to take care of itself.'" His idea was for the Freedmen's Bureau to function as a central informa-

6. *Ibid.*

7. Bvt. Maj. Gen. John Hawkins to Samuel Thomas, September 10, 1865, in Ascom, Mississippi, Regletrec, I, BRFAL, NA; Samuel Thomas to O. O. Howard, October 12, 1865, in Ascom, Mississippi, LS, 1865, BRFAL, NA. The above account of Thomas' position differs somewhat from that which I presented in "Black Immobility and Free Labor: The Freedmen's Bureau and the Relocation of Black Labor, 1865–1868," *Civil War History,* XXX (1984), 225–26. The present version incorporates the results of a thorough rechecking of the relevant records.

tion agency, assisting planters who wanted labor and freedmen who needed jobs to find each other across a broad area.[8]

It was the response of a believer in laissez-faire and free labor whose mission was to use the powers of government to restructure an entire labor system. Seeing that the marketplace was not effectively bringing planters and laborers together, Thomas could only justify government intervention by casting it as an attempt at the restoration of a lost equilibrium.

Within the bureau, ambivalence about government intervention remained a constant, but the agency was increasingly drawn toward policies that required it to play the part of both an information bureau and a source of transportation. General Howard and his assistant commissioners all shared a commitment to laissez-faire and to free labor, but in their efforts to build a free labor system in the South, they all found themselves drawn toward solutions that required more of a government presence than philosophically they would have preferred.[9]

The acceptability of the government's resettling the black laboring population came sharply into question during the deliberations over the phasing-out of Camp Nelson, Kentucky. The camp had begun as a recruiting and training center for black soldiers, but it soon became a refuge for their wives and children as well. At the end of the war it continued to be home to three thousand black refugees, who were supported by the army and the Freedmen's Bureau. Although other smaller camps were quickly phased out, Camp Nelson remained in operation, and by July, 1865, Howard was telling Clinton B. Fisk, the assistant commissioner for Kentucky and Tennessee, that it was not a good idea to allow such an enclave to exist permanently. He told Fisk to break it up gradually, making a "careful distribution" of its inhabitants.[10]

8. Thomas to Howard, October 12, 1865, in Ascom, Mississippi, LS, 1865, BRFAL, NA.

9. On Howard's position about such matters as free labor and laissez-faire, see Carpenter, *Sword and Olive Branch*, 124–26. Whether the Hawkins plan to transport blacks from Louisiana to Mississippi was carried forward is not known, but it certainly foreshadowed later attempts by the bureau to resolve the maldistribution of labor by providing transportation for unemployed black workers.

10. O. O. Howard to Clinton B. Fisk, July 15, 1865, in WD, LS, I, BRFAL, NA;

Fisk responded by commanding that all able-bodied persons in the camp go out and get work. That, plainly, was more easily said than done. Speaking in behalf of the inhabitants, the camp chaplain, John G. Fee, pointed out that it would be impossible to settle the blacks in the immediate area of the camp. The refugees were strangers to the region and were hated by the local residents. Fee, an old-line abolitionist, was deeply concerned that the freedmen find good homes, and he urged the employment of an agent to scour the state for jobs. He said that if the residents of Kentucky did not give the blacks jobs, there were "localities where lands can be purchased—cheaply—and where these people could be settled." [11]

Fisk gave the authority for the kind of job search Fee had suggested, but by November, 1865, it was clear that Kentucky simply could not supply places for all the inhabitants of Camp Nelson. As a result, someone, perhaps Fee, began to talk about transporting the freedmen to work in Ohio and Indiana. Writing for General Howard, Max Woodhull ruled out such an approach by skeptically asking if the freedmen were likely to find employment across the Ohio River. He concluded, "It is not considered advisable to clear Kentucky of Freedmen and then have to feed them in Ohio and Ind." [12]

In the meantime, Fee did what he could. He tried to persuade others to buy lands and give them to the blacks so that the refugees could establish a self-sustaining community, but nobody would participate in the plan. Strapped for funds, he borrowed five hundred dollars, and his wife sold some land she owned in a free state. The money enabled them to buy 130 acres of Kentucky land for long-term repurchase by the freedmen. Twenty-five years later, forty-two black families were living on land that Fee and his wife had helped them buy. [13]

John G. Fee to Clinton B. Fisk, July 17, 1865, in Ascom, Tennessee, LR, 1865, BRFAL, NA; John G. Fee, *Autobiography of John G. Fee, Berea, Kentucky* (Chicago, 1891), 178–79.

11. Fee to Fisk, July 17, July 18, 1865, both in Ascom, Tennessee, LR, 1865, BRFAL, NA.

12. Max Woodhull to Clinton B. Fisk, November 10, 1865, in WD, LS, I, BRFAL, NA; endorsement of Fisk in Fee to Fisk, July 18, 1865, in Ascom, Tennessee, LR, 1865, BRFAL, NA.

13. Fee, *Autobiography*, 183.

Most inhabitants of Camp Nelson were not so lucky. R. E. Farwell, the special agent charged with closing the camp, was a well-meaning man apparently sincere in the desire to provide good homes for the blacks, but he was under heavy pressure from Fisk and from Washington to close the camp as soon as possible. Thus, when a "General Banbridge" and his partners offered to take as many as five hundred laborers to their Mississippi plantation, Farwell found it difficult to say no, even though he had serious doubts about the character of at least one of the partners. On December 22, he told Fisk that Banbridge was a "clever man" but that one of his partners was a "very good specimen of the swell head Whiskey drinking southern planter." He ended by saying that he would not feel justified in getting up the party for Mississippi "were it not for the confidence I feel that you will follow and protect the people."[14]

Fisk gave little indication of similar qualms. Three days later he told Farwell that the Banbridge plan had been approved and that transportation would be granted to all the inmates of Camp Nelson who could be induced to go to Mississippi. The children in the party were to be apprenticed at Vicksburg by the assistant commissioner there. He concluded by urging, "Close the camp as rapidly as possible. Washington is impatient at its continuance into winter."[15]

Washington's concern was linked to its disinclination to support indefinitely a large population of indigent freedmen and to its growing realization that in certain parts of the South the size of the black labor force exceeded the capacity of the local economy to support it.[16] Increasingly, it seemed that any solution to the southern labor problem would have to include measures aimed at moving "surplus" blacks from one place to another.

The problem was particularly acute in Virginia, where the devastation of the war years combined with the long-term forces that had made the state an exporter of slaves in the antebellum years to create a large population of unemployed freedmen. By November, 1865,

14. R. E. Farwell to Clinton B. Fisk, December 22, December 21, 1865, both in Ascom, Tennessee, LR, 1865, BRFAL, NA.

15. Clinton B. Fisk to R. E. Farwell, December 25, 1865, in Ascom, Tennessee, LS, VII, BRFAL, NA.

16. Bentley, *Freedmen's Bureau*, 76–77.

Orlando Brown was estimating that only an emigration of fifty thousand blacks would relieve the problem, and he eagerly embraced proposals that had that end in view. On a number of occasions he had urged his superiors to consider encouraging black movement from Virginia to the public lands of Florida, and in late November, 1865, Woodhull invited him to ready his plan for consideration at headquarters.[17]

Over the next eight months, Brown's plan underwent a tortuous evolution that emasculated it and turned it into the Southern Homestead Act of 1866. That law opened federal lands in Florida, Alabama, Mississippi, Louisiana, and Arkansas to settlement in eighty-acre plots and barred former Confederates from making claims to the lands until January 1, 1867. Earlier, General Howard had tried to place confiscated and abandoned lands in the hands of the freedmen but had been decisively defeated. The new law appeared to present an alternative by which at least some blacks could have the opportunity to become self-sufficient farmers. At the same time, it had the potential to drain off the surplus laboring population of places like Virginia and Georgia.[18]

These hopes were doomed from the start. Howard and Brown both understood that homesteading required capital and that for the bill to achieve its purpose, it would be necessary to provide stock, tools, and a means of subsistence to the new settlers. Since the law provided none of those things, it was virtually guaranteed to fail. Still, Howard did his best. He urged his subordinates to make the blacks in their states aware of the opportunity the act held for them and to help secure lands for freedmen who wished to take advantage of it. For those who took up the challenge, the bureau provided free transportation and a month's subsistence. That was hardly enough support, but given the circumstances, it was all the bureau could do. In 1868,

17. "Report of Orlando Brown, November 31, 1865," SXD 27, p. 146; Bentley, *Freedmen's Bureau*, 96–97; Max Woodhull to Orlando Brown, November 21, 1865, in WD, LS, I, BRFAL, NA; O. O. Howard to Orlando Brown, December 19, 1865, in Ascom, Virginia, LR, Box 11, BRFAL, NA.

18. Bentley, *Freedmen's Bureau*, 134; Claude F. Oubre, *Forty Acres and a Mule: The Freedmen's Bureau and Black Land Ownership* (Baton Rouge, 1978), 82–87. For a different interpretation of General Howard's role, see McFeely, *Yankee Stepfather*, 157–59.

when the homesteaders were in dire straits, the agency came up with additional rations that doubtless helped many survive the year.[19]

The Southern Homestead Act was in effect for about six years, and in that time only about four thousand black families obtained land under its terms. Roughly three thousand of the families were in Florida, and of these, only about a third managed to keep their land to 1870. From the beginning, the odds were heavily against success. The available public lands were either of poor quality or far from the railroads, and the new settlers often found themselves torn between the need to improve their farms and the imperative of feeding their families. Many hired themselves out to local planters and tried to build their farms after hours, but for most this proved impossible. Having come to the new land without capital, they lacked even the most basic agricultural tools, and many worked with nothing more than an ax and a hoe.[20]

Beyond their poverty, the new settlers were often harassed by white neighbors who objected to black landownership. Philip Sheridan saw that in Louisiana such attitudes posed a "great hindrance to the successful carrying out of the Homestead Act." He went on to say that in some portions of the state "it would be unsafe for the freedmen to settle . . . except in large colonies for mutual protection, as they would either be killed or driven away." Given the hostility of whites in the areas of settlement, given the poverty of the freedmen, and given the poor quality of the lands available to them, it is no wonder that so few chose to become homesteaders. No wonder, either, that few succeeded in making good their claims to the land.[21]

Long before the Southern Homestead Act took effect, however, the bureau was exploring a very different way of resolving the problems

19. "Report of Orlando Brown, October 27, 1866," in SXD 6, p. 168; McFeely, *Yankee Stepfather*, 214–17; Richardson, *The Negro in the Reconstruction of Florida*, 77–78.

20. Richardson, *The Negro in the Reconstruction of Florida*, 77–79; Bentley, *Freedmen's Bureau*, 145–46; "Report of the Commissioner of the Bureau of Refugees, Freedmen, and Abandoned Lands, October 20, 1869," in *Annual Report of the Secretary of War [1868–1869]: Accompanying Reports*, 41st Cong., 2nd Sess., House Executive Document No. 1, Part 2, p. 505 (hereafter cited as "Report of the Commissioner, October 20, 1869").

21. "Report of Philip H. Sheridan, October 31, 1866," in SXD 6, p. 72; Richardson, *The Negro in the Reconstruction of Florida*, 73–74.

of unemployment and indigency. Here too the approach involved re-location, but it had nothing to do with land distribution. In areas of serious unemployment, the bureau would operate as a gigantic long-distance labor agency, making contracts between black workers and employers and arranging free transportation to the workers' new homes.

The seeds of the new system had been present in the first few months of the bureau's existence. Almost from the beginning, the bureau had maintained employment offices. As these offices were originally conceived, they were local undertakings whose purpose was to bring planters together with freedmen for the making of annual contracts. In June, 1865, the assistant commissioner for Virginia instructed agents to keep registers of all able-bodied unemployed freedmen in their subdistricts and to use the registers to aid those needing jobs in finding work. Still, no provisions existed for coordinating the requirements of subdistricts that needed labor with those that had workers to spare.[22]

Unemployment was particularly severe in Virginia, but Brown was exceedingly cautious about doing anything to move the freedmen from one place to another. Though it was he who had urged the necessity of an emigration of fifty thousand blacks, he repeatedly acted to carry out both the letter and the spirit of Howard's injunction of May 31, 1865, that considerable numbers of freedmen should not be moved from one district to another. In July, Brown admonished the superintendent of the Petersburg district that "no more negroes [should] be sent to another state without authority from these Head-quarters." In August, when a subordinate visited Boston, he told him to go no farther in the matter of sending freedmen north than to satisfy himself that a demand existed for their services. Beyond that, he believed that nothing could be done "until further instructions have been received from Washington." In November, Brown reported that he had called upon his superintendents to "discourage as far as possible the disposition of the freedmen to remove from one locality to another, except so far as it might be necessary for uniting members of

22. Circular letter, Orlando Brown to "Captain," June 15, 1865, in HXD 70, p. 120.

separated families, or to find profitable employment"[23] Those were powerful exceptions, but there is little to indicate that, up to that time, Brown had done anything to help blacks from one district to find employment in another.

In Georgia, the assistant commissioner, Davis Tillson, took a far more active approach. Believing that starvation would result if the labor situation was not brought under control, he ordered his subordinates to make "immediate and vigorous efforts" to find jobs for all unemployed freedmen. Toward that end, agents were to keep a record of the labor needs of all persons in their subdistricts, and private employment agencies were to be encouraged. Most important, the agents in each subdistrict were to inform Tillson's office "whenever it shall appear that there is more or less labor than can find profitable employment" so that the assistant commissioner could take steps to see "that the needed distribution be secured." As early as October, 1865, Tillson had adopted a policy of actively moving freedmen around in order to coordinate the labor supply with demand.[24]

Clearly, Tillson was more willing than Brown to intervene to resolve problems of unemployment. He was a conservative on racial matters and had come to Georgia in September, 1865, certain that the blacks would not work without compulsion. He appointed white Georgians to serve as bureau agents throughout his state. He supported Andrew Johnson's approach to Reconstruction. It is possible that for him relocation was simply the solution to a problem in economics and logistics and that he gave little thought to its human consequences. At the same time, he was well within the ambit of the northern free labor ideology. Though he favored the planters on many questions, he did not shrink from using force against them when they tried to prevent the freedmen from choosing their own employers.[25]

23. Orlando Brown to O. O. Howard, November 31, 1865, in SXD 27, p. 145; Orlando Brown to Capt. Stuart Barnes, July 20, 1865, Orlando Brown to C. B. Wilder, August 3, 1865, both in Ascom, Virginia, LS, XII, BRFAL, NA.

24. Circular No. 2, October 3, 1865, Ascom, Georgia, in HXD 70, p. 58.

25. Bentley, *Freedmen's Bureau,* 129, 238*n,* 15. See also McFeely, *Yankee Stepfather,* 202–203, 248–49, 255. Tillson was by no means an uncritical supporter of Johnson. Fearing that the president would interfere with the bureau courts in Georgia, he said that in that event, "all hope of justice to the freed people, for the present, will be lost.

Tillson's approach to the unemployment question anticipated that of the bureau, but it is not known whether his ideas directly influenced General Howard. Even before Tillson took up his post in Georgia, Howard had concluded that it was better to move workers to places where jobs were available than to support them in idleness on government rations. For that reason, he had asked the adjutant general's office to issue General Orders No. 138 providing that upon request from the commissioner or from the assistant commissioners, transportation would be furnished to "such destitute Refugees and Freedmen as are dependent upon the government for support," who were to be carried "to points where they can procure employment and subsistence and support themselves and thus relieve the government" of the need for caring for them. The orders specified that the assistant commissioners could authorize transportation only within the limits of their own states.[26]

General Orders No. 138 was a crucial step in the development of the bureau's relocation program, for it provided a basis upon which the assistant commissioners could act independently to redistribute the labor force. Still, it said nothing about how to carry out the relocation. It was not until December, 1865, that Howard began to point the way in that regard, and when he did, his plan was remarkably similar to the one Tillson had devised. Howard said that because he found the freedmen going to the cities and military posts even though there were no jobs there, he decided to have bureau agents "adopt a system like the ordinary intelligence office, and use every effort in their power to procure good places" for the freedmen.[27]

Howard's report made it sound as though the bureau had been

I shall decline to act in my present position when no longer able to protect the freed people—it would be too mortifying to be endured" (Carpenter, *Sword and Olive Branch*, 134).

26. General Orders No. 138, September 16, 1865 (WD, Adjutant General's Office, BRFAL, NA); *Report of the Commissioner of the Bureau of Refugees, Freedmen, and Abandoned Lands, December 19, 1865,* 39th Cong., 1st Sess., House Executive Document No. 11, p. 14 (hereafter cited as HXD 11).

27. HXD 11, pp. 12, 14. The orders and circulars issued by Howard prior to December, 1865, make no mention of the term "intelligence office[s]," though it was occasionally used by other bureau officials to refer to the employment work being done in Virginia, Georgia, and the District of Columbia.

carrying out relocation all along. A comparison of Tillson's aggressive measures in Georgia with Brown's much more cautious approach in Virginia brings home clearly that up to December, 1865, there was no single bureau policy on the matter. In January, 1866, moreover, seeking to make sure that the assistant commissioners understood the *new* policy, Howard had his adjutant general draw particular attention to the part of his December report that dealt with intelligence offices.[28] Tacitly admitting the newness of the policy, the adjutant wrote, "No general instructions have been issued from the bureau on this subject, as it is not the wish of the Commissioner to add unnecessarily to the number of officers on duty with the Bureau." In his letter, however, he put on record that Howard wanted the assistant commissioners to consider the "proposition of establishing through individual enterprise a system of agencies in each State, with the design of bringing labor and capital together." He concluded by observing that such a system might be self-supporting and even remunerative "if conducted in the same manner as similar institutions are carried on in our large cities at the North." The day before he sent the letter, Tillson had written a report for Howard that said, "The bureau in [Georgia] is an extensive intelligence office, finding homes for freed people and laborers for employers."[29]

The system of employment agencies that came out of Howard's plan was both more and less independent of the Freedmen's Bureau than he envisioned. By and large, the employment agencies that the bureau supervised in the South were simply extensions of the bureau itself. In July, 1867, there were thirty-four bureau employment agents in the District of Columbia, where the agency was especially anxious to solve the unemployment problem. Elsewhere the task was usually handled by regular agents of the bureau, but in either case the effort to find jobs for the unemployed was a top priority. While the bureau was getting into the placement business, there arose in the South a small number of independent labor agents who dealt with it regularly

28. Circular letter, Max Woodhull to the assistant commissioners, January 10, 1866, in WD, LS, II, BRFAL, NA.

29. Davis Tillson to O. O. Howard, January 9, 1866, in SXD 27, p. 89, circular letter, Woodhull to the assistant commissioners, January 10, 1866, in WD, LS, II, BRFAL, NA.

as they sought to procure workers for their clients. In a few instances, the bureau briefly gave its imprimatur to private agencies, but such arrangements generally turned out badly.[30]

In February, 1866, Howard removed all doubt that the bureau had become fully committed to relocation. Responding to an inquiry from Brown, he said through an assistant, "Should there be an excess of labor in one quarter of the state and a demand for it in another . . . the surplus negroes from the overstocked districts, should be removed to where they can find employment; those only, going, who can be induced voluntarily to do so."[31] The emphasis on voluntary movement was important, for it underscored the free labor goals of the bureau leadership. In the months that followed the adoption of the relocation policy, there would be instances where agents compelled movement by applying heavy pressure—including the threat of cutting off rations. On the whole, however, it appears that the great majority of those who moved under the program did so of their own will.

The relocation policy was a new departure, but it reflected the same free labor ideology that had guided the bureau from the outset. Sharing the general northern conviction that American liberty required a self-sufficient citizenry, bureau officials could hardly envision the nation with a permanent black pauper class dependent upon government for its survival. And yet the bureau not only was responsible for managing the transition from slavery to freedom but also had the responsibility of giving relief to the needy.[32] From the beginning there was this tension. Simple humanity and the devastated condition of the South required that the bureau aid the hungry and care for the weak, but fears of encouraging dependence pulled in the opposite direction, toward limiting the issuance of government rations. Within a month

30. Elaine Everly, "The Freedmen's Bureau in the National Capital" (Ph.D. dissertation, George Washington University, 1972), 164–65; letters of appointment as employment agents sent to thirty-four recipients, including O. S. B. Wall and Josephine Griffing, July 25, 1867, in Ascom, District of Columbia, LS, VIII, BRFAL, NA. On the bureau's bad experiences when it endorsed private agencies, see pp. 69–71 below.

31. WD, BRFAL, to Orlando Brown, February 10, 1866, in Ascom, Virginia, LR, Box 11, BRFAL, NA. See also circular letter, O. O. Howard to the assistant commissioners, February 23, 1866, in HXD 70, p. 199.

32. Foner, *Politics and Ideology*, 101–103; Bentley, *Freedmen's Bureau*, 76–79.

of when he took charge, Howard, speaking through an adjutant, had warned of being too generous with government aid. He had remarked that people who could walk ten or twenty miles carrying great loads of rations were in no danger of starving and that "the same exertion put forth to draw supplies from the government, applied to some useful occupation, would earn enough to support wives and children that may be really destitute."[33]

But what if "useful occupations" simply were not available where they were needed? In that case, government aid in the form of relocation assistance was a legitimate means of encouraging black self-sufficiency and of reducing the relief burden of the government. On that premise, the Freedmen's Bureau and the army gave transportation assistance to tens of thousands of blacks in the period from 1865 to 1868.[34]

In December, 1865, as Howard was reshaping his policy in Wash-

33. Quoted by Carpenter in *Sword and Olive Branch*, 104–105. See Bentley, *Freedmen's Bureau*, 76–79.

34. The annual reports of Commissioner Howard give a running total of the transportation provided to destitute refugees and freedmen. These reports show that in the period from May 30, 1865, until September 30, 1868, the bureau transported 29,402 freedmen. This figure is large, but there is good reason to believe that it substantially undercounts the number who received such assistance. As will be seen, the assistant commissioners for Mississippi and Georgia gave transportation to many thousands of unemployed blacks in late 1865 and early 1866. At about the same time, 6,352 blacks were reportedly transported out of the District of Columbia. And yet the summary figures Howard gave in 1869 acknowledge a mere 8,509 blacks to have been moved in 1865–1866. Howard's total was 1,803 below the combined numbers for the District of Columbia and Georgia alone. When it is remembered that thousands were moved in Mississippi and that significant relocations occurred in Kentucky and other states, it becomes clear that Howard's figure of 8,509 greatly understates the extent of government-sponsored movement during the period. For the offical figures, see "Report of the Commissioner of the Bureau of Refugees, Freedmen, and Abandoned Lands, November 1, 1866," in *Annual Report of the Secretary of War: Appendix*, 39th Cong., 2nd Sess., House Executive Document No. 1, p. 711 (hereafter cited as "Report of the Commissioner, November 1, 1866"); and "Report of the Commissioner, October 20, 1869," 515. Why did the discrepancy occur? How many blacks were transported by the Freedmen's Bureau? The answers are not clear. Certainly, granting free transportation was a sensitive subject, and certainly Howard would have wished to minimize the count. It seems not unreasonable to guess that the number transported by the bureau may have been double the number reported, that is, perhaps fifty or sixty thousand freedmen in the period from May 30, 1865, to September 30, 1868.

ington, Samuel Thomas took direct action to cope with the maldistribution of labor in Mississippi. A few months earlier he had voiced reservations about the relocation that General Hawkins had recommended. Now he himself began moving black labor in a big way. In Mississippi, large numbers of freedmen were clustered in the interior, poor sections of the state while planters along the river were desperate for labor, so Thomas began transporting large numbers of the unemployed to the "Mississippi Bottoms," where, he believed, they would be "well-treated, fed and paid by kind employers." Writing on January 2, 1866, he predicted that many thousands would "change their homes in this manner." On January 10, he told Washington that after consulting with the army commander in Mississippi, he had transported "large numbers" to the rich lands even though his orders regarding transportation did not meet the case.[35]

Even earlier, Tillson had embarked on a relocation plan of his own in Georgia. When he arrived, in September, 1865, planters were offering the freedmen wages of from two to seven dollars a month. Believing that low wages were connected with the maldistribution of labor, he addressed both problems at once. In November, he told his agents to disapprove contracts that did not provide "fair and reasonable compensation." He explained, "It is useless to expect reliable and profitable labor for inadequate wages, or [to expect] a successful working of the free labor system." Five weeks later, Tillson sought to establish a de facto minimum wage by formally announcing that the going rate in upper and middle Georgia was twelve to thirteen dollars a month and that along the coast and in the southwestern part of the state it was fifteen dollars.[36]

To give effect to his demand for fair compensation, Tillson encouraged emigration from the state. He had come to Georgia from duty with the Freedmen's Bureau at Memphis, and he brought with him a trusted subordinate, Major William Gray, formerly of the 1st United States Colored Artillery. Gray served as Tillson's inspector, and he was

35. Samuel Thomas to O. O. Howard, December 28, 1865, January 2, 1866, in SXD 27, pp. 30–31, 37; Samuel Thomas to O. O. Howard, January 10, 1866, in HXD 70, p. 264.

36. Circular No. 4, November 15, 1865, Circular No. 5, December 22, 1865, in HXD 70, pp. 62, 65; Davis Tillson to Bvt. Maj. Gen. Donaldson, January 16, 1866, in Ascom, Georgia, LS, II, BRFAL, NA.

the key figure in arranging an exodus of Georgia's "surplus" blacks. Shortly after the arrival of Tillson and Gray in Georgia, George R. Campbell was assigned to duty as the acting subassistant commissioner for the district of Atlanta. Like Gray, Campbell had been an officer with the 1st Colored Artillery, and like Gray, he was to be deeply involved in the work of transporting blacks out of the state.[37]

In early December, 1865, Gray asked George Curkendall, the bureau agent in Atlanta, to provide him with hands for work in Arkansas. Curkendall promised to round up a large number of workers if the bureau would send an agent to care for them. The next day, Gray sent almost identical letters to Curkendall and the bureau agent in Columbus, asking each, "Have you contracted with the 200 hands to go to Arkansas[?] The parties are here to take them away."[38]

One of the men seeking hands for Arkansas was quite probably a former Tennessee acquaintance of Gray's. He was a Colonel Thurston, who had come from Memphis to secure laborers for his Arkansas plantation. The freedmen who emigrated appear to have done so voluntarily, but at least one army officer on duty with the bureau did suggest that cutting off relief rations might impel many to go to work for Colonel Thurston. The colonel apparently got his hands, for in mid-December, 1865, Tillson's office requested transportation for two parties of two hundred each, one from Atlanta and the other from Washington County.[39]

Just after the new year opened, Tillson wrote transportation orders for seven hundred freedmen solicited by agents for plantations in Tennessee and Arkansas. On January 8, 1866, he endorsed the trans-

37. Headquarters, BRFAL, to Col. T. S. Bowers, September 9, 1865, in WD, LS, I, BRFAL, NA; Special Orders No. 130, October 23, 1865, Headquarters (Ascom, Georgia, Orders and Circulars, XXVI, BRFAL, NA).

38. William Gray to George Curkendall, William Gray to Capt. Phillip Slaughter, both December 6, 1865, in Ascom, Georgia, LS, I, BRFAL, NA; George Curkendall to William Gray, December 5, 1865, in Ascom, Georgia, Unregistered LR, 1865, BRFAL, NA (National Archives Microfilm Publications M-798, roll 24; hereafter, microfilm versions of Freedmen's Bureau records will be cited in the form microfilm M-798, roll 24).

39. W. W. Deane to George Curkendall, December 9, 1865, in Ascom, Georgia, Records of the Atlanta Office, Box 7, Ascom, Georgia, to Col. C. R. Smith, chief quartermaster, letter press copy dated between December 8 and December 18, 1865, in Ascom, Georgia, LS, I, both in BRFAL, NA.

portation request of John Woods, who was taking 150 freedmen out of Georgia. Like the other assistant commissioners, Tillson could authorize transportation only within Georgia. What he did, there-fore, was send the blacks as far as the border with Tennessee at Chattanooga.[40]

During the second week in January, Tillson's policy of sending blacks out of the state began to change. On January 9, he wrote General Howard: "The almost painful anxiety I have had as to the future of the freed people in this State is entirely relieved. . . . I can provide all the able-bodied freed people, young and old with employment . . . and a promise of kind treatment. The demand for labor and the price paid for it are increasing every day." He went on to say that although he had been sending some freedmen to the Mississippi Valley, where they were getting excellent wages, he had stopped that when the demand at home became too great.[41]

In line with what Tillson told Howard, Gray answered an inquiry from Memphis by saying that there was now a large demand in Georgia for labor priced in the range of twelve to fifteen dollars a month, that he would give all the assistance he could to "any agent you may send here," but that he could not furnish transportation "until the local demand for labor is satisfied." At about the same time, he turned down the request of a planter in Elberta, Georgia, for the approval of labor contracts that paid less than twelve dollars a month, saying that there were a "number of people . . . here from Mississippi, Missouri, & Arkansas, scouring the Country for labor and in many cases offer[ing] $20–$25/mo for first Class field hands."[42]

An exception to Tillson's general policy of favoring the interests of Georgia farmers over those of out-of-state planters and labor agents occurred in the case of A. T. Reeve. Like Gray and Campbell, Reeve had been an officer in a black unit during the war, and like Gray, he had served with the Freedmen's Bureau at Memphis. As superintendent of the Memphis subdistrict, Reeve had been deeply involved

---

40. George Curkendall to Davis Tillson, January 1, 1866, in Ascom, Georgia, Unregistered LR, 1866, BRFAL, NA (microfilm M-798, roll 25).

41. Davis Tillson to O. O. Howard, January 9, 1866, in HXD No. 70, pp. 315–16.

42. William Gray to William Haslett, Esq., January 22, 1866, William Gray to T. H. Ayres, January 8, 1866, both in Ascom, Georgia, LS, II, BRFAL, NA.

in finding jobs for freedmen. On December 23, 1865, he resigned his positions in the army and the bureau, becoming a civilian. Five weeks later he was in Georgia working as a labor agent.[43] On January 31, he wrote Tillson to say that he had accompanied Gray on a tour of Wilkes and Elbert counties and that he had found most of the freedmen there working for two to six dollars a month, with board but without any clothing or medical care provided. Reeve said that the blacks knew that most of the employers in Elbert County were determined "to avail themselves of the labor of the freedmen with no remuneration beyond their board and clothes," but that so far they had "not dared to leave the county for fear of personal violence."[44]

Reeve may well have been genuinely concerned about the situation, but he was also a businessman capable of using the events in Elbert County as a point of argument in trying to get government aid for crossing Tennessee. He had already been granted help with transportation in Georgia, but securing it in the neighboring state was more difficult. He wrote Fisk, the assistant commissioner for that area, to ask that two hundred hands from Elbert County be given transportation at the government rate from Chattanooga to Memphis "if not inconsistent" with Fisk's policies.[45]

Reeve emphasized that Tillson had given him just this sort of aid in Georgia, and he evinced concern for the Elbert County blacks. He offered assurances that they would have kind and just treatment from planters in the Mississippi Valley and that they would be paid "at the rates of from $15 to $18 per month." He dwelled on the desperate situation of the blacks he had encountered in his tour of Elbert County. He and Major Gray had found whites "who hardly realized the war was over" and who nearly mobbed the officer. Conditions were so bad, he said, that the major went to Augusta and returned

43. Special Orders No. 97 (paragraph 3), December 6, 1865 (Ascom, Tennessee, Orders and Circulars, XXIII, BRFAL, NA); Special Orders No. 107 (paragraph 2), December 23, 1865 (*ibid.*); Ascom, Tennessee, to Major A. T. Reeve, December 19, December 23, 1865, both in Ascom, Tennessee, LR, VII, BRFAL, NA.

44. A. T. Reeve to Davis Tillson, January 31, 1866, in Ascom, Georgia, Unregistered LR, File 2, BRFAL, NA (microfilm M-798, roll 28).

45. A. T. Reeve to "General [Clinton B. Fisk]," February 2, 1866, in Ascom, Tennessee, LR, XXI, BRFAL, NA (microfilm M-999, roll 11).

with a detachment of twenty-five soldiers, vowing to "'emancipate' the colored people" of Elbert County.[46]

Gray himself wrote to Fisk: "Gen'l Tillson has authorized me to give [Reeve] transportation at gov't rates to Chattanooga. Will you deem it improper for me to ask you to render him similar assistance through your state?" The answer came addressed directly to Reeve. General Fisk could not grant the transportation requested, since the rule of the Tennessee bureau that employers transport their own employees was "invariable." Fisk's refusal was softened only slightly by his declaration that if he could make exceptions, he "would be glad to do so for you."[47]

Though the labor situation in Georgia eased for a while, the fall of 1866 brought a miserable harvest, and in its train, unemployment and destitution. Again, Tillson's response was to encourage emigration to the west, "where there is an abundance of food and employment." Since he had issued transportation orders for 3,960 freedmen in the year ending November 1, 1866, and since he had allowed his officers to act as recruiting agents, it seemed certain he would do the same after the fall crisis of 1866. But he did not.[48]

In late 1866, W. H. Morgan, a Memphis attorney, wrote for aid in securing five hundred hands. Tillson responded, "I can neither assist in getting up hands, nor allow my officers to do it, without subjecting myself to charges of corruption or malfeasance in office (already have been charged with that)." He went on to explain that the only way to get hands in the state was "to employ some person not connected with the Bureau." He recommended "Captain [George R.] Campbell, formerly of the 1st USC aty[,] now at Augusta and who has engaged in furnishing hands and has been quite successful." Campbell was no

46. *Ibid.*

47. Assistant adjutant general to A. T. Reeve (c/o Major William Gray), February 11, 1866, in Ascom, Tennessee, LS, IX, BRFAL, NA; William Gray to Ascom, Tennessee, February 2, 1866, in Ascom, Tennessee, LR, XXI, BRFAL, NA (microfilm M-999, roll 11).

48. Davis Tillson to William Finch, October 10, 1866, Davis Tillson to bureau office, Washington, Georgia (name of addressee illegible), October 19, 1866, Davis Tillson to Governor Charles S. Jenkins, December 4, 1866, all in Ascom, Georgia, LS, V, BRFAL, NA; Conway *The Reconstruction of Georgia*, 79n.

longer in the service and, according to Tillson, was therefore free to make any arrangement he saw fit.[49]

All over the South the postwar imbalance between the supply of and the demand for labor created severe problems. Despite the changes that the war wrought, the underlying economic forces behind the southwestward slave traffic before the war remained strong. The slave traders were gone, but the southern economy still needed some agency to mediate the relationship between labor supply and labor demand. The situation in Georgia after the war reflected that reality, which General Tillson understood. He took actions to send unneeded laborers out of the state, and he shifted workers around within Georgia. Here he was replicating prewar patterns. In the 1850s, Georgia had been a net exporter of slaves but the southwestern portion of the state had remained labor-hungry.[50] When Tillson turned his agency into an "extensive intelligence office," he was responding to the same sort of labor demand that had driven the slave trade. The one crucial difference, however, was that the blacks were now free to drive their own bargains. To put the newly freed laborers in touch with those who needed their labor, Tillson and other bureau officials found it expedient to encourage the activities of private labor agents.

Indeed, the line between the government operations of the bureau and the private activities of the labor agents was sometimes fuzzy. Successful bureau agents like Reeve and Campbell would soon quit and go into business for themselves. Bureau officers still working for the government had no hesitation about cooperating closely with their former colleagues, and they gave them "every assistance." In addition, although Tillson had no authority to grant transportation to places like Arkansas, he was able to provide it to Georgia's western border. He used that power freely, giving transportation to Chattanooga to many parties heading west. Across the border, General Fisk disapproved; he refused to provide transportation through his district, because he believed the planters "could well afford" to pay full rates.[51]

49. Davis Tillson to W. H. Morgan, December 3, 1866, in Ascom, Georgia, LS, V, BRFAL, NA.

50. On the pattern of the slave trade in Georgia before the war, see Michael Tadman, *Speculators and Slaves,* 12.

51. Clinton B. Fisk to O. O. Howard, February 10, 1866 (Endorsement regarding

Charges of corruption in the recruiting of Georgia labor for the Mississippi Valley surfaced on several occasions in 1866. In November, 1866, the Columbus *Daily Sun* asserted that bureau officials were largely motivated by the recruiting fees that desperate planters from other states readily paid. It also alleged that black women were being taken out of the state for purposes of prostitution.[52]

Certainly Tillson assisted planters and labor agents generously by giving free passage to Chattanooga. Certainly his officers were extremely helpful to out-of-staters seeking labor, particularly to former associates like Reeve and Colonel Thurston. On a few occasions at least, transportation designated for the use of one individual was sold for use by another. Still, there is no evidence that anyone at the upper levels of the Georiga bureau was making a profit from its activities. It is impossible to rule out corruption, but the available evidence is consistent with Tillson's and Gray's genuinely believing that only a substantial emigration could avert "starvation and death" and save the government from supporting thousands of helpless dependents. Of course, it is possible that in this instance, corruption and good intentions went hand in hand.[53]

One of the most interesting parts of the story of labor recruiting in Georgia just after the war involved what might be called the Tennessee connection, which linked officers of the Georgia bureau with officers and recruiters from the Memphis area. Tillson, Gray, and Reeve all had served with the Freedmen's Bureau in the Memphis area. Tennessee bureau officers were thrust by the nature of their work into contact with hundreds of labor-starved planters from the Mississippi Valley,

letter from Sam Tate to George Thomas, January 16, 1866), in Ascom, Tennessee, Endorsement Book 20 (T-18), BRFAL, NA.

52. Conway, *The Reconstruction of Georgia, 79n;* Davis Tillson to Governor Charles S. Jenkins, December 4, 1866, in Ascom, Georgia, LS, V, BRFAL, NA.

53. Regarding transportation abuses in Georgia, see A. J. White to Ascom, Georgia, January 22, 1866, in Ascom, Georgia, Regletrec, I, Davis Tillson to D. C. Poole (Telegram), February 7, 1866, in Ascom, Georgia, LS, II, Davis Tillson to George R. Campbell, November 9, 1866, in Ascom, Georgia, LS, V, O. O. Howard to Davis Tillson, November 17, 1866, in WD, LS, II, all in BRFAL, NA. Aside from indicating charges concerning the sale of transportation orders, these letters show that Tillson responded to the charges by investigating and by taking steps that seem to have aimed at halting the practice.

and they must have learned early that the southerners were willing to pay well for hands. No wonder Reeve, and later Campbell, resigned to go into the business of recruiting.

It is also significant that Gray, Reeve, and Campbell had been officers in black regiments during the war. Lawrence Powell shows in his work on Yankee planters in the South that it was not uncommon for those who led such units to work as labor brokers and plantation supervisors in the years just after the war. Such officers were more likely to have the confidence of their men, and of other black troops as well, than were any other group of whites on the southern scene. Consequently, white planters sought them out and paid them a premium both for the hands they could bring and, afterward, for helping to retain black labor. The former Confederate general Nathan Bedford Forrest said that when he took up planting in Mississippi just after the war, seven federal officers "got me my hands and they kept my hands engaged for me"[54] It seems a good guess that the seven officers had served with black regiments.

In the postwar South, survival and success depended on the ability to get and hold black labor. One of the people who learned this early was W. H. Morgan, the Memphis attorney who had asked Tillson for five hundred hands. Morgan was a former Union officer who, upon being mustered out, remained in Memphis, where he had been stationed, and opened a law office to serve local planters he had come to know while with the army. His practice consisted, at least in part, of supplying the planters with hands, and in December, 1865, he wrote General Fisk to say: "Major Reeve [the same A. T. Reeve who would soon go to Georgia] . . . tells me it is impossible for him to supply them. Can you help me[?]"[55]

Morgan was not overly fussy about the character of his business associates, and at some time between the end of the war and November, 1866, he entered into an association with General Forrest. Before

54. U.S. Congress, *Report of the Joint Select Committee to Inquire into the Condition of Affairs in the Late Insurrectionary States . . . and Testimony Taken* (Washington, D.C., 1872), XIII, 24 (hereafter cited as Ku Klux Report); Powell, *New Masters,* 10, 50, 199*n,* 117.

55. W. H. Morgan to Clinton B. Fisk, December 18, 1865, in Ascom, Tennessee, LR, 1865, BRFAL, NA.

the war, Forrest had been a leading Memphis slave dealer; during the war, he had been associated with the infamous Fort Pillow massacre; after the war, he would play a leading role in the Ku Klux Klan. According to his own testimony he had been worth $1.5 million before the conflict but emerged from defeat penniless. It appears that one of the first postwar activities of the old slave dealer was a labor speculation in which he, with the aid of federal officers, brought two hundred Georgia hands to Mississippi for his own use and an even larger number for the use of his neighbors.[56]

By late 1866, Morgan and Forrest were working together with Sam Tate, a former Confederate colonel, to build the Memphis and Little Rock Railroad. Tate was the president of the road, Forrest was the contractor, and Morgan functioned as the line's recruiting agent. It was as recruiting agent that Morgan had written to Tillson for hands. On Forrest's behalf he had promised to pay the laborers a dollar a day.[57]

Ultimately, Forrest corresponded directly with General Howard. Although the bureau chief might have been expected to shun plans from such a notorious source, he gave them his cautious endorsement. He told Forrest, "Your propositions are practical and commend themselves to my judgment." Even so, Howard worried about the way Forrest might treat his black employees. He instructed the assistant commissioner for Arkansas to select a capable and discreet officer for duty as superintendent of the district through which the railroad would pass.[58] The commissioner could hardly afford to ignore a proj-

56. Ku Klux Report, XIII, 24; Lt. George Carliss to Lt. Stuart Eldridge, April 9, 1866, in Ascom, Mississippi, LR, 1866, BRFAL, NA. Carliss described in his report a tour of inspection of the area around Friars Point, Mississippi. He said that most of the hands in the neighborhood and all of Forrest's laborers were from Georgia. Since the seven federal officers rented lands from Forrest and his neighbors, the suggestion is that the freedmen were imported not only for Forrest's use but for his neighbors' as well. (Powell, New Masters, 50).

57. W. H. Morgan to O. O. Howard, November 26, 1866, referred to in WD, EB, LXXXIV, 118, BRFAL, NA; Davis Tillson to W. H. Morgan, December 3, 1866, in Ascom, Georgia, LS, V, O. O. Howard to E. O. C. Ord, December 29, 1866, in WD, LS, II, F. B. Sewell to Sam Tate, R. C. Braikly, et al., December 26, 1866, in WD, LS, II, all in BRFAL, NA.

58. O. O. Howard to E. O. C. Ord, December 29, 1866, O. O. Howard to Nathan Bedford Forrest, December 15, 1866, both in WD, LS, II, BRFAL, NA.

ect that promised to give work to five hundred freedmen just when the crop failures of 1866 seemed to presage a new wave of unemployment and hardship.

Though it is tempting to conclude that Forrest, the former Negro trader, had simply adapted his calling to conditions of the postwar world and become a labor agent, that would be inaccurate. He may have begun his postemancipation career partly as a labor agent, but his subsequent ventures involved recruitment not as a means of earning commissions from others but as a way of getting workers for his own projects. By 1870, he had become the president of the Selma, Marion and Memphis Railroad, and it was in that role that he appeared in Greensboro, North Carolina, to gather hands for the construction of his road. From 1874 until his death in 1877, he engaged in planting, using convicts for his labor force. In the end, this former Memphis slave trader had found a way to beat the uncertainties of dealing in a free labor market.[59]

Another military man concerned with the southern labor market was General James Longstreet. In January, 1866, he proposed to carry 100,000 unemployed blacks from Virginia, North Carolina, and Kentucky to the Gulf area, where, as he put it, plantations were lying in waste for want of labor. Responding to this proposition on Howard's behalf, Woodhull said that the commissioner could not organize an enterprise for the removal of large numbers of blacks from one section to another. He added, however, that Howard would not oppose private efforts toward that end and might even indirectly aid the project by issuing transportation for the freedmen.[60]

It was a good opportunity for an enterprising labor agent, but for reasons unknown, Longstreet dropped the plan. In October, 1866, the New Orleans firm of Van Ornum and Trigant (later, W. H. Van Ornum and Company) proposed to do just the sort of thing Longstreet had proposed. As a preliminary, it applied for and received appointment as "Special Agents of this Bureau (without pay) for the

59. Allen W. Trelease, *White Terror: The Ku Klux Klan Conspiracy and Southern Reconstruction* (New York, 1971), 211–12; Memphis *Daily Appeal,* October 30, 1877.

60. Max Woodhull to Absalom Baird, February 20, 1866, in WD, LS, II, James Longstreet to Absalom Baird, January 31, 1866, in Ascom, Virginia, LR, both in BRFAL, NA; Bentley, *Freedmen's Bureau,* 83.

purpose of obtaining employment for freedmen." Soon thereafter the firm let the public know that it had great plans indeed. Advertising as Van Ornum and Trigant Great Southern Land and Immigrant Agency, it boasted of connections in New York, Liverpool, and Le Havre and offered to furnish "white or colored" laborers for plantation and other work. The firm's purposes included, in addition, the securing of capital for the South, the sale and lease of real estate, and the settlement of immigrants.[61]

With such grand corporate objects, it is no wonder that the day after the company's appointment, the Van Ornum and Trigant agency was chafing under the petty restraints of the Freedmen's Bureau. Writing to explain that the authority conveyed by its appointment was insufficient to cover its plans, it asked that the bureau permit it to dispense rations and transportation. To bolster its cause, it enclosed a petition from the factors and commission merchants of New Orleans recommending the importation of freedmen from the East. After due consideration the bureau rejected the firm's request, on the ground that the company was a private enterprise.[62]

On January 3, 1867, Van Ornum and Trigant began soliciting business in earnest, using the classified columns of the New Orleans *Times* to notify planters and cotton factors of its selection as "Special Agents of the Freedmen's Bureau for the purpose of transferring freedmen from the more Eastern and Northern States to work on plantations in Louisiana." Further emphasizing its official connection with the bureau, the firm said: "This enterprise is under the direct supervision and control of Government, and no applications will be approved unless made by responsible parties. We shall be able to furnish labor at a very reasonable rate, as the Government defrays the cost of transportation to the place of delivery."[63]

One could hardly help thinking that Van Ornum and Company had an exclusive franchise to dispense government transportation, and that is probably just the impression the firm hoped to leave. The

61. New Orleans *Times,* November 11, 1866; Special Orders No. 131, October 29, 1866 (Ascom, Louisiana, Orders and Circulars, XXVII, BRFAL, NA).

62. Van Ornum and Trigant to Ascom, Louisiana, October 30, 1866, in Ascom, Louisiana, Regletrec, IV, BRFAL, NA. For the bureau's reaction, see Endorsements Dated November 24, 1866 (WD, EB, LXXXIV, BRFAL, NA).

63. New Orleans *Times,* January 3, 1867.

Freedmen's Bureau demurred, however, and on January 15 it placed an advertisement of its own "to correct a false impression" about the matter of obtaining government transportation for freedmen from other states. In no uncertain terms the assistant commissioner for Louisiana said that "any party" could apply to the bureau for such aid and that "no person or persons have any appointment which gives them the sole right to transact this business in this state." Eight days later, W. H. Van Ornum abruptly resigned his company's commission, and at some time during the following year the Great Southern Land and Immigrant Agency simply evaporated.[64] Its downfall was due at least in part to its expectation that the Freedmen's Bureau would dispense transportation on a no-questions-asked basis. Although the bureau was far from perfect in controlling the transportation it offered, it never gave free transportation with anything like carte blanche.

Throughout the life of the bureau, transportation policy was a thorny problem indeed. There were, in the first place, heavy pressures from Andrew Johnson and others to keep transport expenditures to a minimum. For conservatives anxious to limit the initiatives of the bureau, that was a natural focus, and Johnson did what he could to prevent the bureau from moving blacks. Besides, it certainly was true that providing free travel for the unemployed opened up broad possibilities for corruption and abuse.[65] At the same time, given the absolute poverty of the black population and the disruptive impact of the Civil War, relocation at public expense seemed the only feasible and humane answer to unemployment. As Howard repeatedly argued, it was cheaper to transport the freedmen to new jobs than to feed them in idleness. That was especially so in late 1866, when it became apparent that the year's poor harvest would seriously exacerbate unemploy-

64. *Ibid.*, January 15–17, 26, 29, February 7, 1867. The bureau warning appeared on January 15 and continued for two more days. It reappeared on January 26 and remained in the paper for a month. At some time between January 27 and January 29, Van Ornum responded by changing the text of his advertisement to make it clear that planters had to apply directly to the bureau for transportation. Though Van Ornum's original advertisement was paid in advance for the period until April 2, 1867, the version that continued in its stead appeared for the last time on February 7, 1867.

65. See the corrupt transportation practices in Charlotte, North Carolina, described in Chapter 5 below.

ment. On the other hand, the bureau also had a mission to protect the freedmen, and any large-scale relocation plan opened the possibility of blacks' being exploited by unscrupulous planters and labor agents.

Attempting to deal with all these problems at once, Howard issued Circular No. 21, which provided new transportation guidelines. The circular virtually offered free transportation to any planter who needed labor, at the same time that it established a series of criteria to protect the freedmen against abuse and the public against corruption. Transportation was to be given only to freedmen who were currently dependent on government support or who were likely to become dependent. Planters who wished to import labor had to show that they would provide the blacks with "comfortable homes and reasonable wages," that government transportation orders would not be sold or transferred, and that the assistant commissioner of the state the blacks were leaving approved of their departure.[66]

To meet these requirements, those who applied for government transportation orders had to contract in advance with the intended emigrants and the contracts had to be approved by bureau officials. In addition, the planters had to post bond to guarantee that transportation orders would be used only for their intended purpose. In Louisiana, the bond generally amounted to about one hundred dollars for each freedman transported, far more than the value of the transportation itself. The bond contained the pledge that the planter was importing the freedman for his own use in the pursuance of a legitimate business. Howard also continued to insist that his office retain responsibility for approving or disapproving all interstate transportation requests.[67]

The system was hardly foolproof. From a Washington vantage point, Howard had little alternative but to accept the assurance of an assistant commissioner who wrote, "I deem this a meritorious case." In turn, each assistant commissioner had to place a heavy reliance on his local agents and superintendents. Thus, it was possible for Captain

66. The content of Howard's circular is given in Circular No. 24, December 20, 1866 (Ascom, Texas, Special Orders, IX, BRFAL, NA); Transportation Bond Signed by William Edgar and William J. Darden, January 1867 (Ascom, Louisiana, LR, BRFAL, NA).

67. Circular No. 24, December 20, 1866 (Ascom, Texas, Special Orders, IX, BRFAL, NA).

Ernest Hunter, at Charlotte, North Carolina, to do a brisk business charging for the processing and approval of transportation requests.[68] On the other hand, despite such examples, the requirements for contracts and for transportation bonds provided a considerable check on the abuse of freedmen and on corruption.

In early 1867, J. W. Bondurant brought a hundred freedmen from Virginia to his plantation in Morehouse Parish, Louisiana. When, in a few months, Bondurant died of yellow fever, his successor discharged the Virginia blacks, conceding them only partial payment for their services. Learning of this, the Virginia bureau agent who had handled matters when Bondurant was collecting hands in the East informed the bureau in Louisiana of the situation, with the result that the agent at Morehouse Parish seized the Bondurant plantation to secure the claims of the freedmen.[69]

The bureau agent in Iberville Parish, Louisiana, showed similar initiative. In early 1867, Edward J. Gay imported well over a hundred blacks from North Carolina and Virginia. A year later some of Gay's laborers complained that "they had received no final payment for last year's labor." It is not known whether these particular freedmen were the ones he had brought from the East. What is clear is that the local agent acted decisively to protect their rights. He told Gay that he had no reason to doubt their word, since the freedmen "showed me their hand books (kept by your overseer)," and he threatened that in the absence of a settlement with the blacks, he would "take steps to secure them their pay, provided there is property enough on the plantation to Satisfy their claim."[70]

Not all bureau agents were that vigorous in protecting the contrac-

68. Ascom, Mississippi, to O. O. Howard, November 24, 1866, in Ascom, Mississippi, EB, XXIII (316), BRFAL, NA; Endorsement of Transportation Application Made in John and F. B. Willis to Ascom, Mississippi, November 24, 1866 (Ascom, Mississippi, Reletrec, IV [W-187], BRFAL, NA).

69. Capt. R. S. Lacey to Ascom, Louisiana, October 18, 1867, in Ascom, Louisiana, Regletrec, VIII, Capt. R. S. Lacey to Ascom, Virginia, October 18, 1867, in Ascom, Virginia, Regletrec, VII, both in BRFAL, NA; Endorsement Regarding Capt. R. S. Lacey to Ascom, Virginia, October 18, 1867 (Ascom, Virginia, EB, XXIX, BRFAL, NA); Ascom, Virginia, to J. W. Bondurant (Telegram), February 9, 1867, in Ascom, Virginia, LS, BRFAL, NA.

70. Charles E. Merrill, assistant subassistant commissioner, to Edward J. Gay, February 24, 1868, in Gay Family Papers.

tual rights of the freedmen, and some were completely subservient to the planters. Still, protection was common enough to ensure that the contracts signed by those wishing transportation were something considerably more than meaningless scraps of paper.[71] It seems a fair conclusion that, although the bureau was anxious to relocate unemployed freedmen and although it was even capable of using pressure tactics to achieve its aim, it was serious about seeing that the blacks it relocated went only to places where they would find "comfortable homes and reasonable wages."

Among the men who journeyed east making promises were Texas planters. Desperate for labor, they pleaded with the assistant commissioner for Texas to import workers from other states, but the only thing he could do was write letters of introduction for those who traveled east in their own search for hands. And write he did, over and over again, asking his counterparts in other states to do what they could for this labor agent or that planter. In behalf of a Milam County recruiter, he told Tillson that he was "of the firm opinion that the experiment of free labor can be better tested on the rich and fertile plantations of [Texas] than in the older and more worn-out Cotton states." More usually, he just endorsed the bearer of the letter, spoke of the scarcity of workers in Texas, and asked the recipient to give what help he could.[72]

So acute was the Texas labor shortage that in early 1866, when Howard recommended that the assistant commissioners encourage the establishment of intelligence offices in their states, the Texas bureau chief responded by saying that since the demand for labor in Texas greatly exceeded the supply, his state had no need for such offices. His successor, Joseph B. Kiddoo, echoed the theme, and in midsummer,

71. Whether local bureau agents worked to protect the contract rights and interests of the blacks is a matter of controversy. McFeely says that the agents generally sided with the planters, but his research is focused more on the office of General Howard than on what was occurring at the local level (*Yankee Stepfather*, 157–59). A more balanced view is given by Donald G. Nieman in *To Set the Law in Motion: The Freedmen's Bureau and the Legal Rights of Blacks, 1865–1868* (Millwood, N.Y., 1979), 162–70, 209–10.

72. Joseph B. Kiddoo to Davis Tillson, January 5, 1867, Joseph B. Kiddoo to Ascom, Louisiana, August 13, 1866, Joseph B. Kiddoo to Ascom, North Carolina, October 11, 1866, Joseph B. Kiddoo to Ascom, Alabama, August 28, 1866, all in Ascom, Texas, LS, IV, BRFAL, NA.

1866, he reported that planters were offering as much as a third or even a half of their crops "to anyone who will furnish hands and Secure them." He recommended that some system be created under the auspices of the bureau "that will bring freedmen from other States where there is a Surplus of labor."[73]

A month later, when Howard did not respond, Kiddoo wrote a follow-up letter stressing the proportions of the shortage and urging that the assistant commissioners in states with a surplus of labor be empowered to send their extra blacks to Texas at will. General Howard would not agree. He insisted on retaining control of the interstate transportation of freedmen and explained his reluctance to send blacks to Kiddoo's state in particular: "I am very hesitant to encourage negroes to go to Texas, as long as it is reported that they are killed and outraged, and have so little show of justice." Still, Howard's reply was not an outright prohibition of movement. The commissioner was willing to see blacks go to Texas provided they did so of their own free choice. He told Kiddoo that one company of freedmen had already started for Texas, and he said he had sent representatives of groups of freedmen from Fortress Monroe, Yorktown, and New Berne "to look at the country and see what are the prospects for the colored people."[74]

Howard was plainly seeking to spur Kiddoo to do all he could to stem the violence in Texas. At the same time, the commissioner could act only within a limited sphere. There is no evidence that he did anything to warn blacks against going to Texas or to impede their migration to that state. Indeed, in early January, 1867, he provided transportation to a Texas labor agent carrying eighty-four freedmen from Winnsboro, South Carolina, to Brenham, Texas. Later in the month, Thomas Stubblefield, another Texas labor agent, went to Washington in search of hands, and Charles H. Howard—General

73. Joseph B. Kiddoo to O. O. Howard, July 23, 1866, Edgar M. Gregory to Max Woodhull, January 29, 1866, both in Ascom, Texas, LS, IV, BRFAL, NA.

74. O. O. Howard to Joseph B. Kiddoo, September 11, 1866, in Ascom, Texas, LR, Box 2, James B. Kiddoo to O. O. Howard, August 29, 1866, in Ascom, Texas, LS, IV, both in BRFAL, NA. The assistant commissioners were perpetually asking Howard to give them authority to issue interstate transportation orders. See, e.g., Thomas J. Wood to O. O. Howard, December 7, 1866, in Ascom, Mississippi, LS, XVIII, BRFAL, NA.

Howard's brother and the assistant commissioner for the District of Columbia—instructed one of his employment agents to "devote yourself entirely to procuring this lot." On February 4, Stubblefield and two other Texans in Washington for labor received authorization to take ninety-nine blacks back to Texas. So far as can be determined, however, they succeeded in getting only fifty-eight.[75]

At war's end the black labor supply was out of phase with demand. Unemployment was rife in many parts of the Southeast at the same time that places like Arkansas and Texas could not get enough laborers. Voluntary relocation at government expense was an obvious answer to the problem, but the free labor ideology of the North posed a serious obstacle to such a solution. This ideology fostered the belief that with emancipation, normal market forces would create an appropriate equilibrium between the supply of black labor and the demand for that labor. From top to bottom, the Freedmen's Bureau was staffed by men who subscribed to that view.

The agency's primary mission, however, pulled in the opposite direction. The bureau had been created to use the power of government to establish a free labor system in the South, and an important measure of its success was its effectiveness in reducing the number of blacks who depended on government relief rations. Thus, although bureau officials often spoke the language of market economics, they had little alternative but to move toward a solution according to which the government aided the freedmen to reach places where there were jobs. To do that the bureau transformed itself into a vast "intelligence office" to which planters could look in seeking labor and to which blacks could look for work. At the same time, the bureau became a provider of transportation to those who needed to move long distances to get jobs.

Attracted by the prospect of free transportation for black workers,

75. Charles H. Howard to Mrs. L. M. Ricks, January 25, 1867, in Ascom, District of Columbia, LS, VII, George Grant to O. O. Howard, January 3, 1867, in Ascom, South Carolina, LR, Box 5, both in BRFAL, NA; Contract Signed by Thomas Stubblefield, February 4, 1867 (Ascom, Texas, LR, Box 4, BRFAL, NA); Contract Signed by Green and Cox, February 4, 1867 (Ascom, Texas, LR, Box 4, BRFAL, NA); Transportation Order Dated February 4, 1867, and Issued by Order of O. O. Howard (Ascom, Texas, LR, Box 4, BRFAL, NA).

a small band of agents and planters from labor-hungry areas descended on the offices of the bureau. There was money to be made by those who knew how to use the bureaucratic structure of the Freedmen's Bureau to find labor, make contracts, and arrange transportation. In Georgia, and probably elsewhere as well, some prominent labor agents were men who had recently worked for the bureau and who were thoroughly familiar with its procedures for arranging these matters. They had the additional advantage that the officials with whom they had to deal were often former associates.

In arranging the relocation of blacks, the Freedmen's Bureau faced a conflict of interest. It was responsible simultaneously for creating a free labor system in the South and for protecting the freedmen. In its first obligation, it had an almost obsessive preoccupation with getting the blacks back to work. Bureau officers dreaded the possibility that the government rations they distributed to the freedmen might somehow lead to dependence. In its second obligation, however, the bureau had to see that relocation did not turn into a vehicle for the reenslavement or exploitation of the blacks. Thus it was that the whole process came to be encumbered with regulations about the posting of transportation bonds by employers and the guarantee in writing of "comfortable homes and reasonable wages" for the freedmen. Always the resources of the bureau were too meager to allow it to protect completely the mass of southern freedmen against exploitation and violence. What is remarkable is that, with its personnel spread so thinly, the bureau did create a system in which labor contracts made in Virginia really could be enforced in Louisiana a year later.

4

LOOKING NORTH

Given southern oppression and violence, it might be expected that significant numbers of blacks would seek escape by moving north. In fact, few did. Although the Freedmen's Bureau tried to cure unemployment in the District of Columbia by sending black workers north, that failed to spark further movement. Indeed, in the postwar era, opportunities for blacks existed only at the margins of economic life, and as a result, black migration at this time is best characterized as minimal.

The last thing the Freedmen's Bureau wanted was to get involved with black migration to the North, but the question of what to do about black unemployment in the District of Columbia quickly became so urgent that agency officials felt they had no choice. Ever since the bureau came into being, the presence of large numbers of destitute blacks in the District and its environs had been a source of embarrassment and concern. During the war the capital had become a refuge for runaways, and afterward it became the home of significant numbers of black soldiers who were mustered out there. Before the war the federal census counted 14,316 blacks in the District. In 1866, a Freedmen's Bureau census enumerated 31,549, and in 1870 the census office set the figure at 43,404.[1] The steady growth of the black

1. U.S. Bureau of the Census, *Negro Population, 1790–1915* (Washington, D.C., 1918), 44; "Report of the Commissioner, November 1, 1866," 709–10, 730.

population may have been a sign that the number of jobs open to blacks was increasing, but black unemployment remained a problem throughout the decade.

The effort of the Freedmen's Bureau to end black indigency in the District of Columbia began in July, 1865, with the opening of an employment office devoted to establishing contracts between freedmen and Maryland farmers. Then, for a brief period, the commissioner permitted Josephine Griffing, a social worker and old-line abolitionist, to send blacks to jobs in the North using the government transportation rate.[2]

In early September, General Oliver Otis Howard, the commissioner of the Freedmen's Bureau, abruptly ended that aid, pending the issuance of new transportation regulations by the secretary of war. Once the new rules were in place, however, he hesitated for several months before renewing efforts to relocate the District's unemployed blacks. Certainly he must have been worried about how northerners would react to any plan that would send substantial numbers of blacks in their direction.[3] But with Washington crowded with unemployed blacks, it was hard to rule the idea out. In what may have been a trial balloon, the assistant commissioner for the District of Columbia noted in his year-end report that "several calls for labor" had been received from northern railroad and mining companies. Ambiguously, he continued, "For various reasons these calls have not been answered." Certainly the bureau had reason to believe that northern employers were open to the idea of using black labor. In the months from July to November, 1865, inquiries about the availability of black labor were received not only from major centers like Boston and New York but also from Pittsburgh; Grand Rapids; Auburn, New York; Portland, Maine; Manchester, New Hampshire; Paterson, New Jersey; Danby Four Corners, Vermont; Bucyrus, Ohio; and Springfield, Massachusetts.[4]

2. "Report of the Assistant Commissioner for the District of Columbia," December 15, 1865, in HXD 70, p. 120; Everly, "The Freedmen's Bureau in the National Capital," 78–79.

3. Everly, "The Freedmen's Bureau in the National Capital," 79; V. Jacque Voegeli, *Free but Not Equal: The Midwest and the Negro During the Civil War* (Chicago, 1967).

4. "Report of the Assistant Commissioner for the District of Columbia, December 15, 1865," in HXD 70, p. 381. The places listed above were among the datelines of

Black unemployment in the District of Columbia was a special worry because of its symbolism. There, at the commissioner's doorstep, were the problems of unemployment and pauperization writ large, just where the federal government could be expected to have more control than anywhere else. If the bureau could not solve the problem of unemployment in Washington, would that not prove that black unemployment was due to black indolence? Would it not prove that the white South had been right all along about the need for control?

Whether the changes in the bureau's approach to relocation were primarily in response to the situation in the District is uncertain, but General Howard must have seen a convergence between the situation in the capital and that in the South. No wonder, then, that in early 1866, as the new relocation policy was being put forward, the bureau began once again to give free transportation to unemployed District freedmen. By March, 1866, District blacks in significant numbers were being sent both north and south. In April, Charles H. Howard, the assistant commissioner for the District of Columbia, requested that freedmen's relief organizations in Philadelphia, Boston, New York, Providence, and Allegheny City, Pennsylvania, set up unemployment offices to find jobs for freedmen from Washington.[5]

Just as the new program was getting under way, Andrew Johnson brought it to a sharp halt. With crocodile concern for the freedmen, he seized on a newspaper story that charged the bureau with forcing them to go south by threatening to cut off relief rations. Voicing alarm that the blacks would be exploited by labor brokers and employers, he taxed the bureau with countenancing "another form of slavery."

---

letters of inquiry to be found in Local Superintendent, District of Columbia, LR, LXXIV, BRFAL, NA.

5. "Clark, AAAG" to James E. Rhoades, corresponding secretary, Pennsylvania Freedmen's Relief Association, March 31, 1866, AAAG to James E. Rhoades (Telegram), March 30, 1866, both in Ascom, District of Columbia, LS, VII, BRFAL, NA; Everly, "The Freedmen's Bureau in the National Capital," 95; Bentley, *Freedmen's Bureau*, 124–25. O. O. Howard said in his annual report for 1866 that between November 11, 1865, and September 30, 1866, 6,352 freedmen were transported to jobs in the North. Howard's figures for transportation granted by the bureau in early 1866: January, 51; February, 143; March, 614; April, 1602; May, 154; and June, 581 ("Report of the Commissioner, November 1, 1866," 710–11).

Johnson's charges were exaggerated, but it cannot be denied that William Spurgin, the local superintendent for the District of Columbia, had suggested in March that "all who cannot give a satisfactory account of their ability to provide for themselves be considered vagrants and forced to leave." Spurgin's proposal was never adopted as official policy, but the fact that its author ranked second only to Charles Howard in the bureau's District hierarchy suggests that considerable pressure may have been brought to bear on those who resisted leaving.[6]

Defending his agency against Johnson's charges, General Howard said the freedmen had been sent away so that they could get good jobs and become self-supporting and so that the government could be relieved of the responsibility of supporting them. He maintained that he had not discriminated against any section of the nation in sending them out and that the employers who had received hands had in every instance been highly recommended by Union men. He stressed that the employers had been required to guarantee the payment of good wages. But the commissioner did not address himself to the matter of coercion.[7]

Acting at the president's insistence, Howard ordered all transportation ended, but he left sufficient time between the order and its effective date that his subordinates could rush through a flurry of transportation requisitions. Even though transportation was cut off after April 15, official figures suggest that the bureau moved almost twice as many blacks in April as it did in the previous month.[8]

Despite the president's opposition, the bureau persisted in efforts to relocate the unemployed. Charles Howard wrote asking help of Lewis Tappan, the veteran abolitionist who had become active in freedmen's relief work. He said that even though relocation efforts had been "checked" by the lack of transportation, the bureau would be

6. The quotations are given by Everly in "The Freedmen's Bureau in the National Capital," 97; and by Bentley in *Freedmen's Bureau,* 125.

7. O. O. Howard to Edward M. Stanton, April 17, 1866 in WD, LS, II, BRFAL, NA.

8. C. H. Howard to William Spurgin, April 11, 1866, in Ascom, District of Columbia, LS, VI, C. H. Howard to Edward M. Stanton, April 17, 1866, in WD, LS, II, both in BRFAL, NA. For the effect of the president's order, see the figures given in *n*5 above.

glad to carry on the work to the extent that the means of the freedmen's aid societies would permit. That is, the bureau remained willing to provide laborers if ways could be found of getting them to their new jobs.[9]

In July, 1866, the new Freedmen's Bureau Act became law, and the agency returned in earnest to the business of transporting freedmen out of Washington. By November, bureau officials were presenting a confusing variety of overlapping statistics that all suggested the development under bureau sponsorship of a growing movement of blacks toward the North. General Howard's annual report of November 1, 1866, claimed that, between November 11, 1865, and September 30, 1866, 6,352 freedmen had been transported "to homes where they could find employment in different parts of the North." At another point, Howard said that the bureau and the National Freedmen's Relief Association of the District of Columbia—of which Josephine Griffing was general agent—had jointly furnished jobs to 5,192 freedmen during the previous year. In her report on the six months running from April 20 to October 20, 1866, Griffing recorded that her group had sent 2,224 freedmen to jobs in other states. Of these, 458 had gone to places in the South, including Missouri, and 300 had gone to the Middle West. The remaining 1,466 had traveled to places in New England and the Middle Atlantic states.[10]

Bureau officials appear to have had no difficulty learning of jobs in the North. Announcements of openings came from all over. J. Ammerman and Company, of Broad Tap, Pennsylvania, wanted two hundred laborers to work in its coal mines; Thomas Butcher, of Philadelphia, wanted farmhands and house servants; J. M. Moorehead, of Ida, Iowa, wanted a family of freedmen; Charles Round, a labor agent, said he could obtain places for fifty or more colored servants with a large number of families in Calais, Maine; Henry Gardiner, of New London, Connecticut, wanted twenty Negro men as farmhands; J. C. Leonard, of Saginaw, Michigan, needed freedmen to

9. C. H. Howard to Lewis Tappan, April 21, 1866, in Ascom, District of Columbia, LS, VII, BRFAL, NA.

10. "Report of the Commissioner, November 1, 1866," 730, 710; Josephine Griffing, Six Month Report on the Activities of the National Freedmen's Relief Association in the District of Columbia, October 20, 1866 (Ascom, District of Columbia, LR, 1867, BRFAL, NA).

work in his salt works, as well as two female house servants. G. A. Wadsworth, of East Hartford, Connecticut, wanted fifty men to chop wood for one year and, as an office summary says, a "light complexioned girl 18 years old to go to school with his daughter as a room mate."[11]

Taken by itself, Wadsworth's letter seems reasonable enough, but his later dealings with the bureau show that he was exploitative and dishonest. A month after he placed his order for laborers, the bureau still could not fill it. J. W. Vandenburgh, the new local superintendent for the District of Columbia, tried to tell him why: "Its up Hill business when the farmers and Contractors pay $1.00 per cord for chopping wood here and you offer only 75 cents." He suggested that if Wadsworth would pay the same as what laborers were making in Washington, he would "get better men and more of them"[12] Vandenburgh himself had no scruples about delivering laborers to Wadsworth, and despite the low wages being offered, he promised that "we may in a few days get a few ready to send on." The next day he sent fifty men, and a week later he sent twenty-four more. As it turned out, Wadsworth was not interested in just cheap labor. In April, 1867, Charles Howard explained to his brother that the Connecticut man had employed many freedmen "under false pretenses" and defrauded them of their pay.[13]

In the period from July, 1865, through October, 1867, when the bureau ceased giving free transportation to Washington blacks, at least nine thousand freedmen accepted relocation in the North. Still, if the population figures for the District of Columbia are anywhere near correct, it was a losing battle. Between 1866 and 1870, the black population of Washington rose by about 38 percent. It appears that even as

11. The letters from J. Ammerman and Thomas Butcher are dated August 10 and September 8, 1866, respectively, and are summarized in Ascom, District of Columbia, Regletrec, I, BRFAL, NA. Those from G. A. Wadsworth, J. M. Moorehead, Charles Round, Henry Gardiner, and J. C. Leonard bear dates of October 13, 1866, February 28, March 18, May 7, and November 26, 1867, and are summarized *ibid.*, II.

12. J. W. Vandenburgh to G. A. Wadsworth, November 19, 1866, in Local Superintendent, District of Columbia, LS, LXXVII, BRFAL, NA.

13. Ascom, District of Columbia, to O. O. Howard, April 25, 1867, in Ascom, District of Columbia, EB, XXIII (543), Vandenburgh to Wadsworth, November 19, 1866, in Local Superintendent, District of Columbia, LS, LXXVII, both in BRFAL, NA.

the bureau was making every effort to reduce the number of the city's blacks through relocation, it was helpless to prevent new blacks from coming.[14]

Worse still, from the bureau perspective, was that many blacks resisted relocation. Charles Howard explained in his report of October, 1866, that though the surest way of relieving the government of the need to support black indigents in Washington was by removing them "with their own consent" to states where there were jobs, getting that consent was by no means easy: "There seems to be a great reluctance on the part of the majority to leave even the miserable homes they have established here, and start forth to parts of the country new and strange to them."[15] Over and over, bureau officials pleaded with, cajoled, and even threatened the freedmen, in an effort to get them to take jobs elsewhere. In October, 1866, the commissioner himself sent a circular letter to the black clergy of Washington urging them to impress on their congregations the necessity of getting work for the winter. Howard warned, "If they do not [get jobs] they must expect to suffer." Charles Howard and his adjutant went out among the blacks, carrying the same message.[16]

The reluctance of the freedmen to take advantage of the government's offer of free transportation was rooted in some very real misgivings. In January, 1866, the assistant commissioner for the District of Columbia explained to General Howard that it was difficult to get the freed people to go to any southern state even with good wages as a lure. Clearly, fear of racial oppression was part of the reason they did not want to go south, but that fear does not explain why they were also loath to go north.[17]

The image of black resistance to going north comes to some extent from our tendency to see things through the eyes of officials of the Freedmen's Bureau. According to figures already given, nine thousand blacks received transportation out of Washington in the

14. Everly, "The Freedmen's Bureau in the National Capital," 98.

15. "Report of Assistant Commissioner for the District of Columbia, October 22, 1866," in "Report of the Commissioner, November 1, 1866," 730.

16. Quoted by Everly in "The Freedmen's Bureau in the National Capital," 97.

17. Ascom, District of Columbia, to O. O. Howard, January 26, 1866, in Ascom, District of Columbia, EB, XXIII (116), BRFAL, NA.

period 1865–1867, mostly to jobs in the North. The figure of nine thousand represents 28.5 percent of the 31,549 blacks who were living in the District of Columbia shortly after the war. When over one-fourth of a population leaves within a span of about three years, that is a highly significant population movement. Still, from the perspective of white Washington, it mattered less that some nine thousand blacks departed from the District than that even larger numbers had been coming in to replace those who took jobs elsewhere.

Moreover, when one looks carefully at the opportunities open to blacks who went north, it becomes clear that the freedmen had good reason for resisting the bureau. Many of the jobs in the North were for persons without families. Equally important, the wages were pitifully low. When N. B. Blackman, of Howell, Michigan, offered to employ five or six hundred men "at good fair pay" in constructing a railroad from Detroit to Lansing, Charles Howard responded personally, "Please inform me whether you can arrange to receive families as on that will greatly depend our success in inducing them to go." About a month later the bureau received a solicitation from S. A. Forbes, who was recruiting labor for the same railroad as Blackman. Forbes said he wanted four hundred laborers and that he could provide places for families in a ratio of one family for every twenty laborers. He offered eight dollars a month and board.[18]

A bureau official responded to Forbes that at the wages he was offering, it was not probable that he would get the laborers he needed in the Washington area. The official added, "The demand for labor is so great, that good hands can obtain twelve to fourteen dollars per month almost anywhere." He might also have said that in North Carolina, Arkansas, and elsewhere, *southern* railroads were generally offering common laborers a dollar a day in addition to board. The official ended, "It would be hardly possible to send so large a number of men without families[,] but if sufficient wages were offered no doubt part could be obtained." The conclusion must be, not that the

18. H. B. Blackman to Ascom, District of Columbia, February 22, 1867, S. A. Forbes to Ascom, District of Columbia, March 18, March 25, 1867, all in Ascom, District of Columbia, LR, BRFAL, NA (microfilm M-1055, rolls 7, 8); Charles H. Howard to H. B. Blackman, March 7, 1867, in Ascom, District of Columbia, LS VII, BRFAL, NA.

blacks refused to take jobs in the North, but that they manifested an enormous lack of enthusiasm for jobs that debarred families and for work that paid less than what they might obtain in the South.[19]

The demand for black workers in the North was largely a marginal one emanating from employers looking for a big bargain in the wages they had to pay. In 1860, farm laborers from the Middle Atlantic states earned $12.75 a month and board and were the lowest paid in the North. In 1870, farm workers from the East North Central area were the lowest paid in the northern states, receiving $16.94 a month in addition to board. Both these figures were considerably higher than the wages being offered the freedmen by northern employers just after the war. No attempt was made to study systematically all the wage offers received by the bureau, but, in the course of the research for this book, only two wage offers were recorded that appear even to approach the 1860 figure of $12.75 a month and board. L. W. Huff, of Lancaster County, Pennsylvania, said he wanted a small family to work on a farm and offered $150 a year rent free to the man and $5 a month to the woman for housework "if she earns it." J. H. Moore-head, of Ida, Iowa, promised $30 a month for a family of freedmen, the males (plural) for farm work, the female to work in the house.[20]

Had there been a strong demand for black laborers in the North, the freedmen could be expected to have commanded wages at least as high as those paid in most of the South. Northern employers could also be expected to have sought such workers actively and perhaps even to have sent labor agents after them. That is certainly what happened in the early twentieth century, when a heavy demand for black laborers did arise. One would expect, too, to see those who went north writing home to tell their relatives about the good opportunities available, and one would expect many of those kinfolk to join the migration stream to the North.[21]

19. AAAG [District of Columbia, BRFAL] to S. A. Forbes, April 9, 1867, in Ascom, District of Columbia, LS, VIII, BRFAL, NA.

20. L. W. Huff to Ascom, District of Columbia, April 3, 1867, J. H. Moorehead to Ascom, District of Columbia, February 28, 1867, both in Ascom, District of Columbia, Regletrec, II, BRFAL, NA; U.S. Bureau of the Census, *Historical Statistics,* I, 163.

21. Literature of the migration process that provides a basis for these expectations: Charles Tilly, "Race and Migration to the American City," in *The Metropolitan Enigma: Inquiries into the Nature and Dimensions of America's "Urban Crisis,"* ed. James Q. Wilson (Cambridge, Mass., 1968), 141–43; John S. MacDonald and Leatrice MacDonald,

Such scanty statistical evidence as there is suggests that to the extent that this kind of a process was going on in the North after the Civil War, it was proceeding at a snail's pace, especially in the Northeast. Though northern job placements by the Freedmen's Bureau tended to concentrate heavily in New England and the Middle Atlantic states, the only black movement to the North of any real significance occurred in the Middle West.[22]

Table 1 shows the size of the black population outside the South in 1850, 1860, and 1870. The numbers here suggest that black migration to the North and West in the 1860s was minimal. In this decade the black population of the North and West rose by 114,911. Adjusting that number for the impact of natural increase and of black military casualties in the Civil War leaves an estimated net gain from southern migration of about 108,832.[23] That represents a net out-migration rate of 2.4 percent of the blacks living in the South in the 1860s, a

---

"Chain Migration, Ethnic Neighborhood Formation, and Social Networks," *Milbank Memorial Fund Quarterly*, XLII (1964), 82–97; Morton Rubin, "Migration Patterns of Negroes from a Rural Northeastern Mississippi Community," *Social Forces*, XXXIX (1960), 59–66; Thompson P. K. Omari, "Urban Adjustment of Rural Southern Negro Migrants in Beloit, Wisconsin" (Ph.D. dissertation, University of Wisconsin, 1955), 49–55.

22. For a discussion of the nature of the statistical evidence of migration in the United States, see Appendix A, "About Migration Statistics."

23. The extent of the black natural increase in the North and West at this time is difficult to estimate. In the 1830s the black population of those areas rose by 21.8 percent. In the 1840s and the 1850s the comparable figures were 14.4 percent and 15.1 percent respectively, as calculated from figures in U.S. Bureau of the Census, *Negro Population*, 44–45. Although runaway slaves did go north in those years, their numbers were small and it is unlikely that many identified themselves to the census enumerators. Virtually nothing is known of free Negroes who left the South in the antebellum era, and it is assumed that their numbers were small. The estimate of the black natural increase for the 1860s is based, first, on the assumption that the rise in the black population of the North and West in the 1850s was roughly equivalent to the black natural increase in those years. It is based, also, on the assumption that the rate of natural increase for the 1860s was about the same as it was in the previous ten years. During the Civil War, 29,362 northern blacks served in the Union army. Applying a casualty rate of 38 perent to this number yields 11,158 military deaths (see *OR*, series 3, IV, 1269–1270; and Dudley Taylor Cornish, *The Sable Arm: Negro Troops in the Union Army, 1861–1865* [New York, 1966], 288). Summarizing the calculation: 114,911 minus 15 percent for natural increase is 97,674. Adjusting this figure by 11,158 military casualties yields a net gain of 108,832.

TABLE 1

Black Population of the North and West, 1850, 1860, and 1870,
with Place of Birth of Northern and Western Blacks, 1850 and 1870

REGION OF RESIDENCE	BLACK POPULATION			BORN OUTSIDE STATE OF RESIDENCE, 1850	BORN IN SOUTH, 1870[a]
	1850	1860	1870		
New England	23,021	24,711	31,705	6,892	8,298
Middle Atlantic	126,741	131,290	148,033	28,638	33,811
East North Central	45,195	63,699	130,497	23,453	68,444
West North Central[a]	372	2,037	24,512	305	17,344
Western	1,241	4,479	6,380	775	3,184
Nonsouthern total	196,570	226,216	341,127	60,063	131,081

SOURCES: U.S. Bureau of the Census, *Negro Population, 1790–1915* (Washington, D.C., 1918), 44; U.S. Census Office, *The Seventh Census of the United States, 1850* (Washington, D.C., 1853), Table XVII, p. xxxviii; U.S. Census Office, *The Statistics of the Population of the United States* (Washington, D.C., 1872), 328–35, Vol. I of *Ninth Census [1870]*.

[a]For the purposes of this table, Missouri, which had 114,931 slaves in 1860, has been defined as a southern state. In other respects, geographic sections conform to standard census definitions.

low figure when compared with twentieth-century black migration rates.[24]

The limited extent of movement from the South to the North in the 1860s confirms the impression that the northern demand for black labor was marginal at best, especially in the Northeast. Though New

24. This estimated net out-migration rate was arrived at by dividing the figure of 108,832 by the average southern black population during the decade of the 1860s. The average black population of the South was calculated as 4,538,288, with Missouri included as southern and with an adjustment for the undercount of 1870. A total black national population of 4,880,009 from the 1870 census plus a 6.6-percent upward adjustment for the undercount is 5,202,090. Subtracting 341,127 northern and western blacks, as given in Table 1, leaves a hypothetical southern black population of 4,860,963 in 1870. Ten years earlier, in 1860, the black population of Missouri and the rest of the South was 4,215,614 (U.S. Bureau of the Census, *Negro Population*, 45). Averaging the 1860 and 1870 figures yields an average southern black population of 4,538,288. On net migration rates, see Appendix A, "About Migration Statistics," and Hope T. Eldridge

England and the Middle Atlantic states received the heaviest concentration of Freedmen's Bureau placements, their arrival failed to produce the kind of chain migration that occurs when economic conditions are favorable.[25] The data in Table 1 show just how limited black movement was from the South to the Northeast. In 1870, there were only 8,298 southern blacks living in New England. That a considerable minority of these had come to the area before the Civil War is suggested by the 1850 census, which lists 6,892 New England blacks as having been born outside their state of residence. There is no way of knowing how many came from the South rather than from other northern states. Nor can it be known how many survived to 1870 or how many unenumerated runaways were living in New England before the Civil War.

Considering these variables, it seems a reasonable guess that the blacks who came to New England from the South during the decade of the Civil War cannot have numbered much in excess of 5,000 and may have been a good deal fewer than that. The same kind of reasoning applies to the Middle Atlantic states, which had 33,811 southern-born blacks in 1870 but which in 1850 had had 28,638 black residents who had been born outside their home states. It seems a reasonable conjecture that new arrivals from the South to the Middle Atlantic states did not amount to more than 20,000 in the decade of the 1860s.

Black migration to the Middle West was not very extensive either, but it was greater than movement to the Northeast. In the East North Central section there were 68,444 southern blacks in 1870. Twenty years earlier the number of out-of-state blacks living in the section had been only 23,453. If none of these out-of-state blacks died or migrated

---

and Dorothy Swaine Thomas, *Demographic Analyses and Interrelations* (Philadelphia, 1964), 68–70, 99, Vol. 3 of *Population Redistribution and Economic Growth, United States, 1870–1950*, ed. Simon Kuznets and Dorothy Swaine Thomas, 3 vols. On migration rates in the twentieth century, see Table 5 below.

25. A tabulation of 1,094 placements made by the three intelligence offices of the Freedmen's Bureau in the District of Columbia in the period from January 28 to June 28, 1867, reveals that 31.7 percent of the applicants were sent to New England. Another 39.1 percent went to the Middle Atlantic states, and 14.6 percent were sent to the Middle West. Yet another 5.1 percent went south, and 10.1 percent went to local jobs in the district (Reports of Business of Employment Offices at East Capital Barracks, at 394 North Capital Street and at Seventeenth and I streets [Local Superintendent, District of Columbia, Miscellaneous Files, 1866–68, Box 3, BRFAL, NA]).

TABLE 2

State of Birth of Southern-Born Blacks
Living in the North and West, 1870

STATE OF BIRTH	REGION OF RESIDENCE					
	NEW ENGLAND	MIDDLE ATLANTIC	EAST NORTH CENTRAL	WEST NORTH CENTRAL	WESTERN	TOTAL
Maryland, Delaware, or District of Columbia	2,334	16,454	1,874	282	618	21,562
Virginia	3,975	13,050	18,475	1,861	664	38,025
North Carolina	884	1,253	5,247	583	141	8,108
South Carolina, Georgia, or Florida	671	1,844	2,129	410	210	5,264
Alabama or Mississippi	83	234	3,463	734	180	4,694
Kentucky or Tennessee	161	594	31,159	4,271	533	36,718
Louisiana, Texas, or Arkansas	165	324	1,502	1,364	263	3,618
Missouri[a]	24	58	4,595	7,839	575	13,091
Total	8,297	33,811	68,444	17,344	3,184	131,080

SOURCE: U.S. Census Office, *The Statistics of the Population of the United States* (1872), 328–35.
[a]For the purposes of this table, Missouri, which had 114,931 slaves in 1860, has been defined as a southern state. In other respects, geographic sections conform to standard census definitions.

before 1870, the infusion would have to be no fewer than 44,991 southern-born blacks in the period 1850–1870. It seems reasonable to assume then that the number of migrants was well in excess of 50,000, and that most came after 1860.

Where did the migrants come from, and under what circumstances did they come? Table 2 shows the origins of southern blacks living in the North and West in 1870. The table confirms the truism that migrants usually move in greatest numbers to nearby areas. Those who went to the Middle Atlantic states generally came from Maryland and Virginia; those who went to Kansas, Nebraska, Minnesota, and the Dakota Territory generally came from the closest southern areas, like Missouri, Kentucky, and Tennessee. The table also appears to show Virginia as one of the largest contributors to the northward migration. That is probably so, but because Virginia blacks bulked so large in the slave trade there may have been many Virginia-born blacks who came North only after residing in other southern states.

The most striking movement that Table 2 shows is from Kentucky and Tennessee to the Midwest, with 31,159 blacks from those two states living in the East North Central section alone. Table 3 gives a more detailed perspective on the origins of this movement. It identifies Kentucky as the state that sent the largest number of migrants into the East North Central section, and Ohio and Indiana as the main destination areas for those Kentuckians.

The black exodus from Kentucky to the North had its origins in the final years of the war, when about twenty-nine thousand blacks enlisted in the army in Kentucky. At the close of the war, the officer commanding these troops began to issue free transportation to his men and their families so that they could find work. The search took many across the Ohio River, and by October, 1865, the Cincinnati *Gazette* was guessing that ten thousand blacks had come north from Kentucky. The freedmen arrived just when the Midwest was experiencing an acute farm-labor shortage. As a result, the newcomers had little difficulty in finding work.[26]

Other Kentucky freedmen came as domestics and servants. In December, 1865, a Miss Hager, who was an agent of the Christian

26. David A. Gerber, *Black Ohio and the Color Line, 1860–1915* (Urbana, Ill., 1976), 29–32.

TABLE 3

State of Birth of U.S.-Born Blacks Living
in the East North Central Section, 1870

| | STATE OF RESIDENCE | | | | | |
STATE OF BIRTH	OHIO	INDIANA	ILLINOIS	MICHI-GAN	WIS-CONSIN	TOTAL
Virginia	13,889	1,106	2,074	1,193	213	18,475
North Carolina	2,820	1,354	594	417	62	5,247
Kentucky	9,748	9,371	4,405	1,044	127	24,695
Tennessee	1,786	678	3,502	343	155	6,464
Alabama	406	155	969	96	96	1,722
Mississippi	516	189	929	52	55	1,741
Six-state total	29,165	12,853	12,473	3,145	708	58,344
State of residence	29,192	9,811	8,387	3,860	611	51,861
Other states	4,530	1,853	7,689	3,683	749	18,504
U.S. total	62,887	24,517	28,549	10,688	2,068	128,709

SOURCE: U.S. Census Office, *The Statistics of the Population of the United States* (1872), 328–35.

Commission and who taught school at Camp Nelson, Kentucky, brought a large number of blacks from the camp to Springfield, Ohio, where they took work as servants. Describing the scene at the Springfield depot just before the arrivals detrained, the *Ohio Statesman* said the station was filled with "ladies waiting to conduct their unseen and untried servants to their homes."[27] Needless to say, the importation of servants by soldiers and others returning from the war was not uncommon, and by the end of 1866 the North was dotted with such black migrants.

Still, their movement was a trickle, not a stream, and it remained so for many years. As Table 4 shows, in neither the 1870s nor the 1880s did the net migration of southern blacks to the North exceed 67,000. That number was a tiny fraction of the total number of blacks in the nation at the time. The black population stood at about

27. Quoted *ibid.*, 131.

TABLE 4

Black Net Migration Gains and Losses of the States, 1870–1930

DECADE	NORTHERN AND WESTERN STATES		SOUTHERN STATES[a]	
	NET GAINS	NET LOSSES	NET GAINS	NET LOSSES
1870–1880	55,000	6,000	113,000	184,000
1880–1890	67,000	5,000	136,000	216,000
1890–1900	134,000	2,000	79,000	253,000
1900–1910	143,000	0	175,000	372,000
1910–1920	300,000	2,000	62,000	587,000
1920–1930	504,000	8,000	119,000	996,000

SOURCE: Hope T. Eldridge and Dorothy Swaine Thomas, *Demographic Analyses and Interrelations* (Philadelphia, 1964), Table A1.20, p. 260, Vol. III of *Population Redistribution and Economic Growth, United States, 1870–1950*, ed. Simon Kuznets and Dorothy Swaine Thomas.

Note: Net gains and losses are derived by treating the net migration figure for each state as absolute numbers and tabulating gains and losses separately.

[a] As defined in this table, the South conforms to standard census definitions and includes Oklahoma, the District of Columbia, and all the states where slavery was legal in 1860, except Missouri.

5,202,090 in 1870, and at 7,488,676 in 1890.[28] In this period most black migrants were moving within the South and not to the North. The pattern began to change in the 1890s, but it was not until the decade of World War I that the northward movement assumed truly significant proportions.

Of the southeastern states, Virginia, which felt the northern occupation especially intensely, ought to have sent significant numbers north, but it too contributed only a relative handful. In the immediate aftermath of the war, thousands of Virginia blacks congregated on the Lower Peninsula, where they had assurance of the protection of federal troops—and where many eked out a living serving the soldiers. In 1866, officials of the Freedmen's Bureau estimated that there were as many as thirty to forty thousand black refugees on the peninsula. Urgently the northerners sought to relocate as many as possible. In May, 1866, General Howard ordered his inspector general, Frederick

28. The figure of 5,202,090 is adjusted for the undercount in the census of 1870. On this, see Appendix A, "About Migration Statistics."

Sewell, to make a tour of the state, especially of places where the freedmen had gathered in the largest numbers. Howard instructed Sewell to devise the "best plan for reducing this aggregation, so that the negroes may be distributed over the State in comfortable homes and the direct supervision of the bureau reduced to the lowest point."[29]

Nothing worked very well, or so it seemed. Nine months later, Howard again sent Sewell to the peninsula with instructions to "see what can be done toward distributing the freedmen now collected there." He explained, "My purpose is to use every endeavor to induce these people to seek permanent homes and employment elsewhere." In pursuance of that goal the Hampton office of the bureau transported 522 freedmen to jobs in the North in 1866 and 1867. Half of the blacks placed, however, came not from the peninsula but from upcountry counties.[30]

The bureau was even less successful in persuading peninsula blacks to go south. The district superintendent met great resistance when he tried to get the freedmen to elect representatives to scout out Florida and Texas as potential migration destinations. Nor were the peninsula blacks particularly anxious to move to the Lower South. One party of thirty-one freedmen left Hampton for Arkansas in March, 1867, but it appears to have been an exception. A month earlier a functionary in the assistant commissioner's office blandly said in answer to an inquiry about the availability of labor for Arkansas that there were a number of unemployed freedmen on the peninsula "but as to their willingness to contract for service in Arkansas I am unable to furnish any information."[31]

Not enough is known about the resistance of the peninsula freed-

29. Robert F. Engs, *Freedom's First Generation: Black Hampton, Virginia, 1861–1890* (Philadelphia, 1980), 114–16; O. O. Howard to Frederick Sewell, May 8, 1866, in WD, LS, II, BRFAL, NA.

30. O. O. Howard to John M. Schofield, February 19, 1867, in Ascom, Virginia, LR, Box 18, BRFAL, NA; Engs, *Freedom's First Generation*, 117.

31. Headquarters, Ascom, Virginia, to C. H. P. Babcock, February 16, 1867, in Ascom, Virginia, LS, XV, Orlando Brown to Samuel C. Armstrong, March 5, 1867, in Ascom, Virginia, LR, Box 12, Henry M. Whittlesey, WD, to John M. Schofield, March 4, 1867, in Ascom, Virginia, LR, Box 18, all in BRFAL, NA; Engs, *Freedom's First Generation*, 116–17.

men to the relocation plans of the bureau, but many had reasons for staying where they were, even apart from the protection they enjoyed because of the presence of northern soldiers. Throughout the course of the war the area had been under Union control, and it had a well-developed system of freedmen's schools. Moreover, the economic condition of the freedmen may not have been quite so desperate as the persistent relocation efforts of bureau officials suggest. It seems likely that at least some blacks who were counted as unemployed by the authorities were supporting themselves through irregular work—a little woodchopping here, some oystering or fishing there, a temporary stint as a common laborer digging drainage ditches, and so on.[32]

In the end, most of the peninsula refugees did relocate, but whether as a result of the efforts of the Freedmen's Bureau is unclear. By 1870, the population of the four counties that the area comprises was down to 13,654, a figure only about 4,000 above its level in 1860. If there had been 30,000 refugees on the peninsula in 1866, over half were now gone. It seems certain that only a handful went to either the North or the Lower South. That part of the bureau's plan was clearly a failure. Many may have gone back to their home counties in Virginia. A substantial number probably found work at nearby cities like Norfolk and Portsmouth, where the black population more than doubled between 1860 and 1870.[33]

Initially loath to send blacks north, the Freedmen's Bureau overcame its hesitancy as it found that there was less to be feared from northern public reaction to black migration than from negative reaction to the agency's lack of success in ending black unemployment in the District of Columbia and other places. From 1865 through 1868, the Freedmen's Bureau sent over 9,000 District blacks north. At least another 522 freedmen were sent north from Virginia. Still, the migration the bureau arranged failed to inspire any further movement out of the South. Indeed, census data seem to suggest that many of

---

32. Engs, *Freedom's First Generation*, 115. See also the discussion of occasional and irregular work in Chapter 5 below.

33. U.S. Census Office, *The Statistics of the Population of the United States* (Washington, D.C., 1872), 281–82, Vol. I of *Ninth Census [1870]* (hereafter cited as *Ninth Census, Population, 1870*); *Eighth Census, Population, 1860*, 517; Engs, *Freedom's First Generation*, 118.

the blacks who went north at the bureau's prompting did not stay. The absence of continued migration to the North is almost certainly due to the disinclination of the region's employers to pay black workers competitive wages. Those who asked the Freedmen's Bureau about black labor expected to get it for a song. Hence it is hardly surprising that the freedmen did not flock to northern employers.

Available demographic data for the period 1850–1870 indicate that by and large the rate of movement was sluggish. An exception was the surge of relatively large numbers of blacks from Kentucky into Ohio, Indiana, and Illinois. Free transportation had become available to them just when the Midwest was experiencing a farm labor shortage. The combination of the need for labor and the means of moving it created the only South-to-North migration of significant proportions to occur in the years immediately after the war.

Migration is a process that feeds upon itself. One person moves and sends back word of plentiful jobs at good wages. Others follow, and the process repeats. Soon the migrants are sending transportation money back to those at home. If, however, conditions turn bad for those who have arrived, they write home warning off friends and relatives as they tell about layoffs and low pay.[34]

Certainly, it was the communication network among freedmen that was responsible for the low level of black migration from the South to the North all through the period from the end of the Civil War to World War I. What the evidence suggests, however, is less a dearth of jobs than an absence of jobs open to blacks. In the years after the Civil War, and especially after 1890, large numbers of European immigrants flooded into the North. Between 1870 and 1910, almost nineteen million came to the United States. As Table 4 shows, in this same forty-year period the North and West experienced a net migration gain of only about 386,000 blacks.[35] The sluggish pace of black movement to the North did not owe to a depressed demand for unskilled labor in the region. Rather, it reflected racism and history.

Long before the Civil War, northern blacks existed at the margins of economic life, and their position did not change with emancipation.

34. See the works cited in *n*21 above.

35. European immigrants are calculated from data in U.S. Bureau of the Census, *Historical Statistics,* I, 105–106.

Indeed, as Reconstruction was ending it seemed as though blacks were losing ground to immigrant competitors. In 1879, Henry Highland Garnet complained that in the cities of the North, where blacks once had a monopoly in such fields as barbering, whitewashing, calcimining, and catering, "they have been practically pushed out of these occupations in many localities."[36] The New York *Globe* saw a similar erosion in the occupational prospects of blacks when it remarked in 1884, "Time was when colored people largely monopolized such positions as coachmen, footmen, valets, chambermaids, chefs, and waiters; but they have slowly been superseded in these employments by foreign white help."[37]

In one respect, however, the demand in the North for black labor was increasing. In the 1870s, as industrialization gathered force, northern employers experimented with the use of black strikebreakers. In 1874, between four hundred and five hundred blacks were brought into Ohio's Hocking Valley to break a coal strike. They were recruited from Memphis, Richmond, Louisville, and other border and southern cities and were not told in advance that they were to serve as scabs. In the same year, blacks were used to break coal strikes in Freeburg, Illinois; Clay County, Indiana; and Massilon, Ohio. In the years that followed, the coal operators employed black labor as a tactic against strikers repeatedly, and their strategy was instrumental in breaking strikes at Braidwood, Illinois, in 1877; in Ohio's Tuscarawas Valley, in 1880; and in Pittsburgh, in 1880.[38]

In the late 1870s, black strikebreakers spread to the iron and steel industry, and in the 1880s, the Pittsburgh area saw blacks replace white strikers at the Black Diamond Mill, at the Moorehead Mill, and

---

36. Quoted by Leslie H. Fishel in "The North and the Negro, 1865–1900: A Study in Racial Discrimination" (Ph.D. dissertation, Harvard University, 1954), 153. See Leon F. Litwack, *North of Slavery: The Negro in the Free States, 1790–1860* (Chicago, 1961), 153–59 and *passim*.

37. Quoted by Fishel in "The North and the Negro," 478.

38. Sterling D. Spero and Abram L. Harris, *The Black Worker: The Negro and the Labor Movement* (1931; rpr. New York, 1968), 210; Herbert G. Gutman, "Reconstruction in Ohio: Negroes in the Hocking Valley Coal Mines in 1873 and 1874," *Industrial and Labor Relations Review*, October, 1962, pp. 256, 264; Herbert G. Gutman, "The Negro and the United Mine Workers of America," in *The Negro and the American Labor Movement*, ed. Julius Jacobson (Garden City, N.Y., 1968), 98.

at the Clark Mill. It has often been noted that in bringing in black strikebreakers, employers were following a policy of divide and rule. The point is valid, but it also needs to be said that, as in the South, white racism was not simply an attitude of the rich and powerful. It was a cultural outlook that cut across class lines. Racism was painfully evident in 1890, when four hundred of the five hundred employees at a Pittsburgh steel mill staged an eight-month strike "against working with colored men."[39]

By the early 1890s, it was clear that black strikebreakers posed a serious threat to the emerging labor-union movement. Essentially, white unionists had three options. They could open the doors of their unions wide to blacks and struggle for a labor movement that was united across racial and ethnic lines. They could insist on a continuation of the patterns of racial exclusion that had obtained up to that time. Or, they could take a middle path, admitting a token handful of blacks or segregating blacks in their own locals. Only a relative few unions chose the path of racial egalitarianism, and these tended to represent unskilled workers. More chose the middle road, but the majority simply wanted nothing to do with blacks.[40]

Foremost among the unions that opposed discrimination was the United Mineworkers of America. In the 1890s, that group mounted a successful organizing campaign, and its mode of operation is evident in the events that took place during a coal strike in Kansas in 1899. There the operators imported some six hundred black miners from Alabama. As usual, the blacks came without knowing that they would have to cross picket lines. When they reached Kansas, the striking United Mineworkers met them with pleas to come over and join the union. Some did, more did not. After the strike was settled, however, the union continued its organizing efforts among the blacks, and

39. U.S. Commissioner of Labor, *Tenth Annual Report . . . 1894* (Washington, D.C., 1896), Table 1, pp. 1082–85. See also, Charles H. Wesley, *Negro Labor in the United States, 1850–1925: A Study in American Economic History* (1927; rpr. New York, 1967), 237–38.

40. W. E. Burghardt Du Bois and Augustus Granville Dill, eds., *The Negro American Artisan,* Atlanta University Publications, XVII (1912; rpr. New York, 1968), 129. See also French Eugene Wolfe, *Admission to American Trade Unions* (Baltimore, 1912), 114–19.

many more crossed to the union side. Before long the area was a union stronghold.[41]

But the egalitarianism of the United Mineworkers was far more the exception than the rule. In 1912, W. E. B. Du Bois observed that "fully half of the trade unions in the United States . . . exclude Negroes from membership," with another fourth allowing only a handful of blacks to practice their trades. He concluded, "In only a few unions, mostly unskilled, is the Negro welcomed."[42] It was the unions in the steel industry that were representative of the mainstream racial attitudes of organized labor in the North. When the Amalgamated Association of Iron and Steel Workers came into being in 1876, its constitution proclaimed it a truly national union of iron and steel workers, embracing all workers in the industry. A year later, at its first annual convention, however, the union openly denied membership to blacks. Four years later, after it became clear that black strikebreakers threatened the union's effectiveness, the association reversed itself. At the same time, however, it treated blacks as second-class members, and the blacks quickly came to suspect that they were allowed in the union only to keep them from becoming strikebreakers.[43]

Events proved their mistrust well founded. In 1901, three black unionists honoring a strike at their own factory went to another union plant and asked for work. The superintendent where they applied agreed to give them jobs if the white workers did not object. But despite the urging of a union official, the white workers would not consent, and the blacks returned to the striking Carnegie steel plant from which they had come. Feeling that they were being used merely as pawns, they urged their fellow blacks to cross the picket lines and return to work.[44]

Blacks disagreed sharply on the value of the labor movement. Richard L. Davis was a founding member of the United Mineworkers

---

41. John M. Robb, "The Migration of Negro Coal Miners from Alabama to Southeast Kansas in 1899" (M.A. thesis, Kansas State College of Pittsburg, 1965), 69, 170–71; Gutman, "The Negro and the United Mineworkers," 49–52.

42. Du Bois and Dill, eds., *The Negro American Artisan*, 129.

43. Spero and Harris, *The Black Worker*, 249–50.

44. *Ibid.*, 251. See also Richard Robert Wright, *The Negro in Pennsylvania: A Study in Economic History* (Philadelphia, 1912), 96–98.

of America and had played a crucial role in organizing black miners in Ohio. Writing to his union paper, Davis spoke strongly about the need for solidarity. Rhetorically he addressed a white labor agent who had just come through his town in search of strikebreakers. He said: "We don't think you will get any [black strikebreakers] from this place. True our men are hard up but they will suffer a little longer before they will go to Raymond to blackleg the honest miners who have been so long struggling for their rights. . . . We are beginning to learn that an injury to one is the concern of all, and we cannot better our condition by running from place to place, taking the places of our fellow men." What is most remarkable about Davis' position is that he took his stance knowing that the white miners of Raymond would not allow union blacks to work side by side with them. Holding hard to the principle of solidarity, he at the same time asked the Raymond miners to treat black unionists as brothers and as men.[45]

Eloquent and idealistic as he was, Davis was in the minority. Faced with exclusions like those encountered at Raymond, most blacks in the era before World War I concluded that organized labor held nothing for them. D. A. Straker, an attorney in Detroit, probably spoke for them when he said that although the ostensible aim of the labor unions was "to protect labor against the oppression of capital," the "hidden purpose" of most unions was to "shut out and keep shut the doors of industry against a class of people on account of their race."[46]

More bitter than Straker was James Baylor, of Dayton, Ohio. A tailor by trade, he had personally experienced the kind of exclusion Straker described. In 1900, when he applied for passage to Africa, he complained that unions were denying him the right to make his living as he always had. He told of how, years earlier, he had come north from Paris, Kentucky, seeking work. He had settled in Dayton because he found employment there "at pretty fair wages." At that time, he said, there were "no trade unions to discriminate against color [and]

45. Stephen Brier, "The Career of Richard L. Davis Reconsidered: Unpublished Correspondence from the National Labor Tribune," *Labor History,* XXI (1980), 428–29; Gutman, "The Negro and the United Mine Workers," 54*n*, 56.

46. Quoted in David M. Katzman, *Before the Ghetto: Black Detroit in the Nineteenth Century* (Urbana, Ill., 1973), 124.

there was no back shops where nobody but white men could work[,] matters not how poore [a] workman he might be." The situation, however, had changed. "I cant hardly get any work sence they have so many unions thay dont want to give a black man any chance with his trade."[47]

Still, union discrimination against blacks was only a small part of a much larger problem. In the years before World War I, unionization affected only a fraction of the workers and businesses in America, whereas racial discrimination and exclusion could be found almost everywhere. Even college-educated blacks often had to content themselves with jobs as Pullman porters, janitors, and the like. Ten years after the Wilmington riot of 1898, Alex Manly, the former editor of the Wilmington *Record,* found work as a janitor in Philadelphia. Complaining of northern occupational discrimination in 1901, Straker wrote that a black man could be "a porter on a steam-car, but not a conductor; he may sweep the lawyer's office, but cannot become his law-partner, his typewriter or his stenographer." In 1910 1.2 percent of the population of Detroit was black, but of fifteen thousand male clerks, bookkeepers, cashiers, accountants, and commercial travelers in that city, only forty-six (0.3 percent) were black.[48]

Du Bois, in his 1899 study of Philadelphia blacks, listed as examples twenty men who had been denied a chance to practice their trade. A telegraph lineman from Richmond, Virginia, found on arriving in Philadelphia that he was barred from his craft because, as one prospective employer said, "We don't work no niggers here." A brush maker who sought to work at his trade was frankly told, "We do not employ colored people." A porter for a bookbinding establishment had learned to bind books by observation but was never given a trial by his employer.[49] Elsewhere the story was similar. In 1905, New York City had one black telephone operator. In 1890, Cleveland's

47. James Baylor to J. O. Wilson, February 21, February 27, 1900, both in Vol. CCXCII, Series IA, Domestic Letters Received, Records of the American Colonization Society, Library of Congress (hereafter cited as ACS, LC; unlesss otherwise noted, all citations are to Series IA, Domestic Letters Received).

48. Katzman, *Before the Ghetto,* 107, 62; W. E. Burghardt Du Bois, *The Philadelphia Negro: A Social Study* (1899; rpr. New York, 1967), 139.

49. *Ibid.,* 329–30.

burgeoning steel industry had only three blacks. In the early 1890s, a Bostonian observed that "of the thousands of clerks in Boston I do not know a single Negro behind the counter."[50]

Even those with jobs were not always secure. Du Bois ticked off a list of instances in which blacks in Philadelphia had been pushed out of work that had previously been theirs. A typesetter for *Taggart's Times* lost his job when the paper was taken over by an owner who did not share his predecessor's egalitarian views. A Philadelphia ink factory that had once employed many blacks began, upon the death of its owner, to replace its retiring black employees with whites. In New York in 1913, the Gimbel Brothers department store discharged its twenty black employees without notice, saying only that colored help was no longer desired.[51]

With discrimination and exclusion almost everywhere, it must sometimes have seemed as if the only opportunities blacks could find in the North were those that came when employers wanted to break strikes. Yet the reality was far more complex than that. In a time of rapid industrialization and urbanization, with much labor fluidity, racism was pervasive, but so was the need for cheap labor. If blacks were squeezed out of jobs as barbers, whitewashers, and coachmen, they were beginning to squeeze into important areas like coal mining, iron making, meat-packing, and municipal service, even if only at the bottom of the ladder.[52]

In essence, blacks were gaining and losing ground simultaneously, and ever so slightly the gains appear to have outweighed the losses. In the meat-packing industry, for example, blacks in Chicago made their appearance as scabs during the strike of 1904. Most of the perhaps two thousand blacks used to break the strike were eventually discharged, but in 1910 there remained 365 black stockyard and packinghouse

50. Kenneth L. Kusmer, *A Ghetto Takes Shape: Black Cleveland, 1870–1930* (Urbana, Ill., 1976), 66, 80; Elizabeth Hafkin Pleck, *Black Migration and Poverty: Boston, 1865–1900* (New York, 1979), 130.

51. Du Bois, *The Philadelphia Negro*, 341–42; New York *Age*, February 6, 1913.

52. For black gains in coal mining, see Gutman, "The Negro and the United Mine Workers," 51–52; and Spero and Harris, *The Black Worker*, 210–15. Regarding the iron industry, see Richard Robert Wright, *The Negro in Pennsylvania*, 93, 97. For meat-packing, see Alan Spear, *Black Chicago: The Making of a Ghetto, 1890–1920* (Chicago, 1967), 35–38.

workers in Chicago. The figure may not seem impressive, but it was equivalent to almost 1 percent of the black population of Chicago at the time.[53]

Virtually always the work that blacks obtained was of the dirtiest and most menial sort, but still it was work. In 1905, over 40 percent of the employed Negro males in Manhattan were in some form of domestic service, the greatest numbers as waiters, elevator men, and doormen. Another 15 percent were porters in stores, and 16 percent worked as laborers of one sort or another. Among women the range of opportunity was so narrow that 89.2 percent of the black working women in New York were in domestic service. The same general pattern could be found across the North.[54]

There was one relatively bright spot in the employment picture, and that was in the area of public service. In Chicago, where blacks were 2 percent of the population in 1910, they held 1.5 percent of the city's public-service jobs. Between 1900 and 1910, the percentage of blacks in the Chicago police department rose from 0.07 to 1.1 percent. At the same time, about five hundred blacks, or 1.1 percent of the city's Negro population, worked for the Chicago post office. In Detroit, the seven blacks in the police department were proportionate to their numbers in the city's population, and other blacks found job opportunities on the city's street railways. In Cleveland, which had a black population about a fifth as large as Chicago's, there were forty-two black postal employees in 1915. Black representation in the Cleveland police department amounted to about half the number one would expect in a world without discrimination.[55]

The marginal black job market that existed in the North in the years before World War I was fed by a migration stream very largely

53. Spear, *Black Chicago*, 35–38.

54. George Edmund Haynes, *The Negro at Work in New York City: A Study in Economic Progress* (New York, 1912), 74–76. See also Du Bois, *The Philadelphia Negro*, 99–109; Charles Wesley Burton, *Living Conditions Among Negroes in the Ninth Ward, New Haven, Connecticut* (New Haven, 1913), 9; Katzman, *Before the Ghetto*, 105–20; Pleck, *Black Migration and Poverty*, 124–29; Spear, *Black Chicago*, 29–35; and Kusmer, *A Ghetto Takes Shape*, 66–77, 84.

55. Harold F. Gosnell, *Negro Politicians: The Rise of Negro Politics in Chicago* (1935; rpr. Chicago, 1967), 253; Spear, *Black Chicago*, 35–36; Katzman, *Before the Ghetto*, 121; Kusmer, *A Ghetto Takes Shape*, 79.

from the Upper South. Often blacks in states like Virginia and Maryland learned of job opportunities in the North from employment agencies or recruiters for northern firms. Sometimes the agencies were based in the South, but many were in northern cities and did a lucrative business bringing women north. On February 17, 1900, there appeared in the Richmond *Planet* a notice signed by F. Z. S. Peregrino, of Albany, New York:

> I live right here in the north. I am in touch with those who need help and can find out who is unreasonable and unjust. I have a steady demand for good women as cooks, chambermaids and general servants, and often for good indoor and outdoor men servants. I pay your fare to which is added a reasonable amount for expenses and fees. I take no orders under any circumstances from disreputable houses and hells of that kind, and the best protection is afforded the respectable girl who respects herself.[56]

In 1905, Frances Kellor surveyed the operations of 732 such agencies. The firms she studied had offices in New York, Philadelphia, Boston, and Chicago. Sometimes they promised jobs when they had none to offer, and often they attempted to extract money from their impoverished clients through contracts permitting that an applicant's belongings could be held as security for payment of the agency fee and through the assessment of storage charges for the holding of that luggage.[57] Exploitative though many of the firms were, they clearly played an important role in bringing blacks north.

Sometimes the use of professional labor recruiters was unnecessary. The Midvale Steel Company in 1900 employed some eight hundred to a thousand black workers, who according to the company's president, C. J. Harrah, worked side by side with native whites, Irish, and Germans with no friction whatsoever. Explaining his hiring policies, Harrah said, "We do not take colored men from Philadelphia; we find the colored men we get here are accustomed to being brought up as waiters or in domestic capacities . . . so we prefer to get them from Virginia." He did not mean, though, that his firm sent labor agents

56. Richmond *Planet*, February 17, 1900.

57. Frances A. Kellor, "The Evils of the Intelligence Office System," *Southern Workman*, XXXIII (1904), 377–80; Frances A. Kellor, "Assisted Immigration from the South: The Women," *Charities*, XV (October 7, 1905), 11–14; Carl Kelsey, "Some Causes of Negro Emigration," *Charities*, XV (October 7, 1905), 15–17.

south, for he went on to explain, "They come through family influ- ence; they know somebody here, and he brings them."[58]   ·

Clearly there were some opportunities in the North for blacks, but equally clearly the number and quality of the openings were not great. If James Baylor, the discouraged tailor, still had family living in Paris, Kentucky, around 1900, he doubtless wrote to tell them of the grow- ing difficulties blacks had in finding work in his trade. Complaints like his must certainly have put a damper on the migration plans of all who heard them.

The statistics of black movement for the period from the Civil War to World War I confirm that some opportunities for blacks existed in the North but that the nature and extent of the opportunities were distinctly limited. As Table 5 shows, in the 1870s black net migration from the South amounted to only about 68,000. Successively, at the end of each of the next three decades, it rose to 88,000, to 185,000, and to 194,000. The increase that took place in the 1890s represented almost a doubling in the rate of black movement to the North. Still, black movement northward remained quite small. In the 1880s, the number leaving the South constituted 1.5 percent of the average Ne- gro population there for those years. In the 1890s, it was 2.6 percent, and in the next ten years, 2.4 percent. By contrast, in the 1940s, 16.7 percent of the average Negro population of the South for those years left that section.

Had the movement of the early years been in political protest against lynching, discrimination, and other forms of racial oppression, a considerable flight would have been likely from the Deep South, where the black population was densest and where conditions were most oppressive. In fact, the states of Georgia, Alabama, Mississippi, and Louisiana contributed almost nothing to the northward move- ment of the period 1870–1910. Rather, blacks who came north in that era tended to come from Upper South and border states like Virginia, North Carolina, Tennessee, and Kentucky.[59]

58. *On the Relations and Conditions of Capital and Labor Employed in Manufactures and General Business (Second Volume on This Subject),* Vol. XIV of *Report of the Industrial Commission,* 57th Cong., 1st Sess., House Doc. 183, p. 353.

59. Everett S. Lee *et al., Methodological Considerations and Reference Tables* (Phila- delphia, 1957), Tables P-1, P-3, Vol. I of *Population Redistribution and Economic Growth, United States, 1870–1950,* ed. Simon Kuznets and Dorothy Swaine Thomas, 3 vols.

TABLE 5

Net Migration and Net Migration Rates of Native Whites
and Negroes in the South, 1870–1950

DECADE	NET MIGRATION[a] (IN THOUSANDS)		RATE OF NET MIGRATION[b] (IN PERCENTAGES)	
	WHITE	NEGRO	WHITE	NEGRO
1870–1880	91	−68	1.1	−1.4
1880–1890	−271	−88	−2.6	−1.5
1890–1900	−30	−185	−0.2	−2.6
1900–1910	−69	−194	−0.4	−2.4
1910–1920	−663	−555	−3.3	−6.6
1920–1930	−704	−903	−3.0	−10.3
1930–1940	−558	−480	−2.0	−5.2
1940–1950	−866	−1581	−2.8	−16.7

SOURCE: Eldridge and Thomas, *Demographic Analyses and Interrelations,* Tables 1.27, 1.30, pp. 90, 99.

Note: As defined in the source and in this table, the South includes the Confederate South in addition to West Virginia, Kentucky, and Oklahoma.

[a]Net out-migration is indicated by negative numbers. Net in-migration is indicated by positive numbers.

[b]The rate of net migration is expressed as a percentage of the average Negro population of each state for each decade.

That pattern is reflected in contemporary studies of Negro households in New Haven, Philadelphia, and Chicago. A study in 1911 of 330 black households in New Haven's North Ward found that 45.1 percent of the household heads had been born in Connecticut or elsewhere outside the South. Virginia, North Carolina, Maryland, Delaware, West Virginia, and the District of Columbia accounted for 45.2 percent more. Only 8.8 percent came from other southern states. In a study of black women whom workers from the Philadelphia Association for the Protection of Colored Women met at the docks, only 2 out of 1,387 who gave information about their place of birth came from South Carolina; all the rest came from Virginia, Maryland, and the District of Columbia. In Chicago, a study of 100 fairly prosperous black families found that the heads of 77 had been born in the South.

Of them, 24 came from Kentucky and 19 more had been born in Tennessee.[60]

For southern blacks the period from 1890 to World War I was a time of extreme violence, and in these years stories circulated with some frequency about blacks heading north to escape southern barbarism. In the wake of the Atlanta riot, the press reported that many black families were preparing to leave the city and that if the violence continued, the "best element" among the Negroes was expected to leave. Richard R. Wright asserted that hundreds of blacks left North Carolina in the wake of the Wilmington riot.[61]

About 1907, Wright surveyed 512 Philadelphia blacks. He asked each to answer questions like "Why did you leave the South?" and "Why did you come to Philadelphia?" His results showed that 216 (42 percent) had come for higher wages, 22 (4.3 percent) had come for higher wages and travel, and 20 (3.9 percent) had come for higher wages and protection. Another 56 (10.9 percent) said they wanted to better their condition. Twenty-two more (4.3 percent) said they were "tired of the South." Still another 49 (9.6 percent) said they wanted to make a change. Sixty-nine (13.5 percent) said they had come with a parent or guardian, and 31 (6.0 percent) gave no reply.[62]

A few years later, a similar survey in New York City canvassed 210 blacks. Of these, 99 (47.1 percent) listed economic motives like the desire to find a job or to get higher wages as the main explanation of their coming. Sixty-eight (32.4 percent) said they came with a parent or that they came to join a family member who was already in New York. Another 16 (7.6 percent) gave reasons such as "just for a change" or "felt like traveling." Fifteen more (7.1 percent) cited the attractions of New York City, and six (2.9 percent) said they were tired of their previous place of residence. Another six gave varied answers that referred to matters like marriage or going to school.[63]

60. Burton, *Living Conditions*, 7–8; Wright, *The Negro in Pennsylvania*, 62; Louise DeKoven Bowen, *The Colored People of Chicago* (Chicago, 1913).

61. New York *Times*, September 9, 1906; Richard R. Wright, Jr., "The Economic Conditions of Negroes in the North: III, Negro Communities in New Jersey," *Southern Workman*, XXXVIII (1908), 385–93. See also New York *Age*, November 21, 1912.

62. Richard Robert Wright, *The Negro in Pennsylvania*, 55.

63. Haynes, *The Negro at Work*, 26–27.

Taken together, these surveys suggest that in the period 1890–1910 economic and family factors played the primary role in the decision to migrate from the South to the North. The period was marked by sharp rises in disfranchisement, in legal proscriptions, and in antiblack violence, but there is little to suggest that those ills had a major impact on black movement. The rate of black net migration in the 1890s rose by 73 percent in comparison with the previous decade, but the actual numbers remained minuscule.

It is possible to interpret many of the phrases used by the migrants to account for why they came north as indicating a desire to escape racial oppression. Still, even when we credit phrases like "tired of the South," "wanted to make a change," and "to better my condition" as reflecting racial motivations, the evidence still tells most heavily for economic and family factors as the determinants of movement.

In a variety of ways, conditions for blacks were better in the North than in the South. There was little segregation in public transportation. Blacks were free to vote and to hold office. Racial violence was far less frequent than in the South. Still, throughout the period from the Civil War to World War I there was only a trickle of migration from South to North.

Given the widespread racial oppression that existed in the South, sizable numbers might be expected to have come north, but that did not happen. Despite the freedoms and half-freedoms that it offered, the North remained an inhospitable haven for the blacks of the South. In freedom's midst, black job opportunities remained minimal or non-existent until World War I. Relative to the centrality of the need to earn a living, the advantages of northern life were mere fringe benefits that had to be measured against more important questions like whether work was available at all and whether the wages paid were high enough to justify taking the risk of migrating.

5

"A VERREY UNCERTIN BUISNESS"

With few real job opportunities in the North, the great majority of blacks had no alternative but to live out their working lives within the framework of the southern regional labor market. That meant that they were effectively cut off from the wage levels that applied to the rest of the country. Isolated within the post–Civil War South, a separate and autonomous unskilled labor market had developed. As in the North, market forces determined wage levels, but as Gavin Wright has shown, the southern market forces were largely independent of much that was going on in the rest of the country.[1] Still, these forces were strong enough to move labor to the places where it was in greatest demand.

For the freedmen, migrating to the high-wage areas of the South was not easy. No matter how discontented they were with their wages or living conditions, they generally lacked good information about distant job possibilities. Even when they had the knowledge they needed, the cost of transportation might prohibit migration. Because of their poverty, most simply could not move any significant distance unless an outside agency paid the fare.

At the same time, large numbers of planters in the Southwest and elsewhere urgently needed black labor. The occupation of the labor

1. Gavin Wright, *Old South, New South,* 64–70.

agent originated at the intersection of the interests of planters and laborers. It emerged first under the umbrella of efforts by the Freedmen's Bureau to get the blacks back to work, and it flourished during the time that the bureau was freely dispensing transportation, when labor agents could come to it as supplicants in pursuit of transportation orders. After the bureau ceased operations, the agents and the planters they served began to provide transportation, but the freedmen generally had to repay the cost of travel, which was counted as an advance against wages. By the late 1860s, the labor agents had come to play an important role in adjusting the distribution of southern labor.

Blacks were heavily dependent on outside agencies for long-distance moves, but they were able to assert considerable autonomy within the local economy. Over and over again whites bewailed the indolence and unreliability of the freedmen as blacks deserted an employer just when he needed them most. It was often the case, however, that the freedmen were leaving simply because they could make a good wage doing temporary work elsewhere. Just as the freedmen's quest for autonomy played a key role in shaping the labor system that emerged after slavery, their continuing insistence on regulating their own lives had a major impact on the way that that labor system worked and on the southern economy itself.

Early in 1867, a Richmond labor agent advertised railroad construction jobs in North Carolina for 150 "colored men." He offered twenty dollars a month with rations, or a dollar a day without rations.[2] One reason that it was necessary to import railroad workers to North Carolina from Virginia was that labor agents and planters from states to the southwest were picking the area clean of laborers. Indeed, many of those agents and planters themselves had to go up into southern Virginia for hands.

In February, 1867, Edward J. Gay, a wealthy Louisiana factor and planter, sent N. G. Pierson on a mission to procure hands in western North Carolina and southern Virginia. Not much is known about Pierson, but he was probably an overseer on one of Gay's several plantations. Pierson's first stop was Columbia, South Carolina, where he

2. Richmond *Daily Enquirer,* February 16, 1867.

110

found freedmen hard to get and "selling at ten dollars per head." From there he pressed on to Charlotte, North Carolina, hopeful that his chances would be "much better." A week later he was much discouraged and wrote Gay: "It is a verrey uncertin Buisness[.] after thay sine a contract it is verrey uncertin if they ar[e] go to [their] place of Destination[.]" Worse still was the competition. Pierson complained, "The [w]hole country is Fluded With Men From all parts of the South[,] hunting Freedmen and offering Fabules prises to get them." With no hands available in North Carolina, Pierson determined to go to Virginia, where he planned to "make out My Number."[3] But before leaving, he had one last piece of business to attend to in North Carolina. Having heard that the Virginia Freedmen's Bureau gave no transportation out of the state, he decided to make his transportation application at Charlotte, where for an initial bribe of twenty-five dollars and a later payment of sixty-five dollars, the bureau agent, Captain Ernest Hunter, was fully accommodating.[4]

While Pierson was in Charlotte, his employer's son, Andrew H. Gay, arrived, and the two joined forces. Gay learned the ropes quickly and sent his father a letter that was a virtual how-to-do-it manual for the labor-recruiting business. He explained that technically it was necessary to have all the hands assembled before one could get government transportation for them. At the same time, though, he noted that "after you have [the hands] it is hard to hold them if you do not start immediately." He told his father the way the problem was handled: "An assumed list of names is made out and presented to the Freedmens Agent[,] who for a consideration will make the papers out and approve them and sends them on to Washington for approval."[5]

Gay believed that there were still plenty of black laborers in North Carolina, but he was sure the opposition of the white community to their departure was having its effect. He thought that half the blacks took seriously the story that if they went south they would be sold into slavery. He probably exaggerated the impact of that tale and oth-

3. N. G. Pierson to Edward J. Gay, February 15, 1867, N.G. Pierson to Mr. Edwards, February 7, 1867, both in Gay Family Papers.

4. Pierson to Gay, February 15, 1867, in Gay Family Papers; "Expenses of N. G. Pearson [sic] for 27 Negroes from Virginia to Plaquemines for a/c of E. J. Gay from February 2, 1867 to March 15, 1867" (Gay Family Papers).

5. Andrew H. Gay to "Father," February, 1867, in Gay Family Papers.

ers like it, but he was certainly correct in remarking that it was virtually impossible to get hands without making use of black runners, "who are asking big pay to look for negroes." There was no alternative, for, as Gay claimed, "there is no use in trying to get hands without the assistance of these men."[6]

Like Pierson, Gay noted an intense competition for labor. In early 1867, the North Carolina–Virginia area was crowded with labor agents and planters from Louisiana and Mississippi. In addition to Pierson and Andrew Gay, there was David A. Barrow, who worked Edward Gay's Pecan Plantation, in Plaquemines Parish. When Andrew Gay found his hands, at least some of them were brought back home on transportation orders made out to Barrow. From Terrebonne Parish there were D. T. Towle and a Mr. Lolle. Whether Towle got his hands is unknown, but Lolle returned home to Louisiana "in Disgust with out Negro[s]." Also at Charlotte was a labor agent named Fullings, who acting for A. O. Cannon, of Holly Springs, Mississippi, was seeking transportation for forty-seven adults and five children.[7]

Though Pierson claimed transportation was not available in Virginia, he was wrong. (Perhaps he simply meant that it could not be easily purchased.) J. W. Bondurant, of Morehouse Parish, bypassed North Carolina and went to Lynchburg, Virginia, where he successfully recruited fifty-eight freedmen and their families. Acting through the assistant commissioner for Virginia he received transportation for "John Mitchell and (99) others, destitute Freedpeople."[8]

About this time, Pierson reached southern Virginia too. After

6. *Ibid.*

7. Pierson to Edward J. Gay, February 15, 1867, Andrew Gay to "Father," February, March 7, 1867, all in Gay Family Papers; Draft on the Account of David Barrow, September 14, 1867 (Gay Family Papers); assistant adjutant general, Ascom, North Carolina, to Col. J. R. Edie, March 11, 1867, in Ascom, North Carolina, LS, BRFAL, NA; Ascom, North Carolina, to Ascom, Louisiana, March 6, 1867 (forwarding contracts and copies of transportation order for the party of David Barrow and others), in Ascom, Louisiana, LR, Box 13, BRFAL, NA.

8. Henry M. Whittlesey (WD, BRFAL) to John M. Schofield, February 7, 1867, in Ascom, Virginia, LR, Box 18, BRFAL, NA; J. W. Bondurant to Ascom, Virginia (Telegram), February 9, 1867, in Ascom, Virginia, Regletrec, V, BRFAL, NA (parentheses in original); Alrutheus A. Taylor, *The Negro in the Reconstruction of Virginia* (Washington, D.C., 1926), 91.

making only a part of his number in Charlotte, he and Andrew Gay left in search of an area that had not been so picked over. Between them they made stops at Danville, Petersburg, Richmond, and points in between.[9] There is no evidence that they stopped in either Nottoway or Lunenberg County, but at the very time they were searching for hands, the agent of the Freedmen's Bureau in charge of those southern Virginia counties was observing that "quite a number of the most industrious and intelligent Freedmen of these counties have left and are now leaving here, for Kentucky, Tennessee, and Mississippi under contracts with gentlemen from those states, who come here looking for laborers, they offer from 12 to $15 per month and rations, and the Freedmen eagerly accept it."[10]

Why was it that southern Virginia blacks accepted the offers of Lower South planters with such alacrity while those from the Lower Peninsula showed resistance to going south? The answer would appear to be twofold. First, the northern soldiers and reformers who crowded into the peninsula reduced merely by their presence the power of the old master class. At the same time, these representatives of northern culture introduced a complex of northern attitudes about equality, human rights, and the nature of southern society, even though many of them were themselves more than a little biased against blacks.

Geographically, Nottoway and Lunenberg counties were less than a hundred miles from the Lower Peninsula, but in psychological terms the distance was more on the order of a thousand miles. True, there was a bureau presence in the area, but the comments of the local agent suggest his relative impotence. Describing the reaction of local farmers to the invasion of planters and agents from the Lower South, he said, "The farmers are becoming alarmed and complain of the loss of their best laborers, but as it will be a severe and necessary lesson to them, and fruitful of good results, I cannot say I sympathize with them in their loss." He went on to explain that "by reason of several employers driving off their laborers, without any compensation for their Services," he was forced to issue rations and clothing to some of

9. "Expenses of N. G. Pearson . . . to March 15, 1867"; Andrew H. Gay to "Father," March 7, 1867, in Gay Family Papers.

10. D. I. Connolly to Ascom, Virginia (Report), February 28, 1867, in Ascom, Virginia, Reports of Bureau Affairs, BRFAL, NA.

the discharged workers. Worse still, their number was "constantly increasing."[11]

In the end, Barrow, Pierson, and Gay took home over a hundred hands. Pierson had recruited twenty-seven laborers, for whom he received $125 in addition to reimbursement of $846 in expenses for hotels, food, railroad travel, and incidentals. Thus, Edward Gay spent almost thirty-six dollars apiece to import eastern blacks who would be paid less than eighteen dollars a month and who would technically be free to leave at the end of one year. The entire record of Gay's various plantations suggests that he never paid more than he needed to for labor or anything else. There is no way of avoiding the conclusion that in 1867 Gay was so hard pressed for labor that he was willing to spend very large amounts to get it.[12]

Expensive as it was to import laborers from the Southeast, it would have been a good deal more costly had it not been for the Freedmen's Bureau's footing of the transportation bill. Just after the war it cost about twenty-four dollars to transport black laborers from the Southeast to New Orleans. Certainly the availability of free transportation in early 1867 must have been a powerful force in drawing agents of the Lower South to Virginia and North Carolina.[13] And yet free transportation by itself was not what lured Louisiana planters to spend so much time searching for hands in North Carolina and Virginia. The urgency of their labor needs drove them to look far from home, but antebellum patterns and connections determined just where they looked. The Freedmen's Bureau's policy of issuing free transportation ended for the most part in the fall of 1867, but the Gay family continued to look to Virginia for hands for several years after that. In the fall of 1869, William T. Gay, Edward's brother, hired Joe Munn as overseer at his plantation in West Baton Rouge Parish. In December, William Gay sent Munn on a recruiting trip to Liberty, Virginia, in search of twenty-five or thirty new hands. The Gay family was originally

11. *Ibid.*

12. "Expenses of N. G. Pearson . . . to March 15, 1867"; Bill for Services Rendered, N. G. Pierson to Edward J. Gay, March 30, 1867, and Receipt, Pierson to Gay, April 2, 1867 (Gay Family Papers).

13. This estimate of the cost of transporting black labor is based on a report of the transportation costs charged by a labor agent named McDonald just after the war. See Samuel Cranwill to Edward J. Gay, December 14, 1869, in Gay Family Papers.

from Liberty, and it still had relatives in the area. Moreover, Munn himself was a Virginian, with family in the state. Expressing his confidence in Munn, Gay said, "[He] understands the Country & says he knows how & what to do and will bring them if possible to be had." [14]

By mid-January, 1870, three more representatives of the Gay interests were on their way to Virginia. They included Charles Dickinson—Andrew Gay's brother-in-law—and two plantation managers, Dr. Thomas Garrett and Roman Daigre. Along the way the trip turned almost into a nightmare. On January 19, Garrett telegraphed Edward Gay: "Prospects bad here[.] go to Mecklenburg county tomorrow[.] fear will not get hands enough for myself." On the twenty-fourth, Garrett was nearly euphoric, telegraphing from Danville: "Fair prospects getting all the hands needed this week[.] need more funds." From Danville, Dickinson headed home with about seventy hands and their dependents, but he lost twenty by desertion when he made the mistake of stopping in Mobile. In the meantime all contact with Munn was lost. With no place else to turn for hands, Garrett and Daigre resigned themselves to going to Richmond, where labor was both costly and oversophisticated. In early February, they returned home with twenty men and their families. Altogether, the mission of Dickinson, Garrett, and Daigre cost about $1,800, for a gain of approximately seventy hands. [15]

About then, Munn reappeared, bringing with him sixteen men and seven women, along with some boys and little children. The account of his travels suggests that the intensity of the competition for labor in Virginia was about as great as it had been three years earlier. Munn told William Gay that he "secured at various times parcels of negroes" with a view toward accumulating a sufficient number to serve the needs of all the Gay interests. So great was the demand on the part of other "contractors" and so strong was the opposition of the Virginians, however, that Munn found himself "unable to hold one lot until

14. William T. Gay to "Brother" [Edward J. Gay], December, October 12, 1869, Ann Phillips to "Edward," January 4, 1870, all in Gay Family Papers; William Seebold, *Old Louisiana Plantation Homes and Family Trees* (2 vols.; New Orleans, 1941), I, 338.

15. Thomas Garrett to Edward J. Gay (Telegrams), January 9, January 24, January 30, 1870, Samuel Cranwill to Edward J. Gay, January 11, February 3 (marginal notation), February 5, 1870, William T. Gay to "Bro." [Edward J. Gay], February 7, 1870, all in Gay Family Papers.

another could be secured." Finally, "in desperation," he headed home with the lot he had.[16]

If desperation led the Gay family to search for labor in faraway places, it also led them to try foreign labor. In 1871, Edward J. Gay, Jr., attempted to bring nineteen German laborers and a boy down from St. Paul, Minnesota, on the steamboat *Dexter.* At Memphis, the younger Gay had to sit up all night on guard against the same sort of desertion that had afflicted Joe Munn when he was trying to bring blacks from Virginia to Louisiana. Gay caught four trying to leave and sent them back to their berths, but to no avail: fourteen of the men escaped anyway. Why did they break their twenty-dollar-a-month contracts and run away? Probably for a better offer. Gay said that three men aboard the *Dexter* "offered to Employ all laborers who wished to work on the levees at $35.00 a month and board."[17]

It was hardly accidental that, in the period 1869–1871, Edward Gay was experimenting with foreign labor. Almost certainly, the costly labor expeditions to Virginia in 1867 and 1870 argued compellingly for a new approach. In August, 1870, his son Andrew suggested that importing Chinese laborers would be cheaper than sending to Virginia for blacks, "as they are so uncertain after you get them and it costs just as much."[18] Thus, in September, 1870, William Gay was dispatched to San Francisco to arrange for the importation of Chinese coolies. At about the same time, Edward Gay sent a man to Chicago to hire Scandinavian laborers. In late October, the Chicago agent firm of Johnson and Peterson, which specialized in emigrants, delivered thirty-five Scandinavians to Gay at the price of "nine dollars per head." Little is known of the fate of those workers, but they did not stay long. On December 4, Sue Gay complained to her brother: "If you knew how busy these old scandinavians keep us all you would wish yourself in Lexington or any other place."[19]

16. William T. Gay to "Bro.," February 7, 1870, in Gay Family Papers.

17. Edward J. Gay, Jr., to "Father," October 28, October 23, 1871, both in Gay Family Papers; Contract with Nineteen Laborers Made at St. Paul, Minnesota, October 16, 1871 (Gay Family Papers).

18. Andrew H. Gay to Edward J. Gay, August 13, 1870, in Gay Family Papers.

19. Sue Gay to John H. Gay, December 4, 1870, Major L. L. Butler to Edward J. Gay, October 15, 1870, both in Gay Family Papers; Receipt for $330.00 Paid by Ed-

The coolies must have been even more trouble. In October, 1870, Gay imported twenty-six men for the St. Louis Plantation, in Iberville, and twenty-six more for the Oaks Plantation, in Plaquemines Parish. It cost over $4,800 in gold to get them all, including perhaps $1,000 in advances. By March, 1871, the Chinese at St. Louis Plantation were attempting to desert, and the Gays began to play rough. William Gay promised that if the runaways came to the Oaks Plantation, he would turn them away, and he recommended having "the whole lot arrested and put in prison awhile on the ground of obtaining money under false pretenses." He explained that if they were permitted to leave "whenever they are compelled to do right & work satisfactorily," they would all soon disappear.[20] Within a short time three runaways were found and returned to the Oaks Plantation, but that was not the end of the conflict by any means. On April 27, 1871, Edward Gay brought Yu Choi and seven countrymen into parish court on charges of breaking their contracts. The judge ordered the defendants to pay the amounts owed for passage or to carry out the terms of their three-year agreements.[21]

It is no wonder, then, that, despite the expense, the Gays continued to use black labor and that they continued to import it from Virginia when necessary. In fact, at almost the same time that the labor troubles with the Chinese workers were coming to a head, Garrett was returning from another trip to Virginia. The process of getting hands had become easier for him since he was no longer trying to hunt up men himself. At the end of his luckless trip in 1870, he and Daigre had turned to the Richmond firm of Justis and McDonald for labor. In February, 1871, he ordered men in advance from that agency. He had

---

ward J. Gay to Johnson and Peterson for Labor, October 27, 1870 (Gay Family Papers); William T. Gay to "Brother" [Edward J. Gay], September 20, 1870, in Gay Family Papers.

20. William T. Gay to Edward J. Gay, March 20, 1871, Samuel Cranwill to Edward J. Gay, October 10, October 31, 1870, all in Gay Family Papers; Statement from Koopmanchap and Company to Edward J. Gay and Company, October 26, 1870 (Gay Family Papers).

21. Legal Document Stating Complaint and Disposition of the Yu Choi Case, April 27, 1871, Adonis Petch, Judge (April, 1871, Folder, Gay Family Papers). For an account of a strike of Chinese laborers in nearby St. Bernard Parish, see New York *Times*, April 22, 1871.

to shepherd them to Louisiana from Virginia, but Justis and McDonald took care of finding them in the first place.[22]

The firm to which Garrett had turned was a new one, but the reputation of one of its principals was already well established among the planters of southern Louisiana. McDonald (his first name is unknown) became a labor agent, just after the war, when a number of Louisiana planters contributed thirty dollars each to send him to Virginia in search of hands. His journey was the beginning of a regular business, and he made numerous trips back and forth, bringing on one occasion seventy hands for a Mr. Williams. The latter paid "$34 a head delivered," of which ten dollars was McDonald's commission and the remainder was a transportation fee charged against the account of the workers. Advertising his services in Louisiana in 1870, McDonald solicited orders for workers from Virginia and the Carolinas and gave an undertaking to supply transportation at a lower cost than the competition. He said he had no subagents in New Orleans, and he cautioned planters against the "numerous so-called labor agents who rely on floating vagabonds for their supply."[23]

Little is known of the early career of McDonald's partner, John P. Justis. The Richmond directory for 1869 lists him as a commission merchant, but later editions call him an employment agent or a labor agent. By late 1869, he was devoting himself mainly to the procuring of labor. On November 8, he advertised, "I wish to hire at once all the COLORED HANDS I can get at high wages." Almost three weeks later he was soliciting "500 COLORED HANDS to go south." By December 14, he was saying, "Five Thousand Colored Hands Wanted." He promised wages of eighteen to twenty dollars paid at the end of each month, and "good rations." In addition, there would be houses, he asserted, with plenty of land for a garden and with the privilege of raising fowl and pigs free of charge. Besides, the transportation would be free.[24]

22. Thomas Garrett to Edward J. Gay, February 8, 1871, Justis and McDonald to Thomas Garrett, February 11, 1871, J. P. Justis to Thomas Garrett, February 13, 1871, all in Gay Family Papers.

23. Samuel Cranwill to Edward J. Gay, December 14, 1869, in Gay Family Papers; New Orleans *Times,* January 20, 1870.

24. Richmond *Dispatch,* October 25, 1867, November 8, November 27, December 14, 1869; *Boyd's Directory of Richmond City . . . 1869* (Richmond, 1869), 132; *Boyd's*

Justis did not restrict himself to providing southerners with black farm workers. His advertisements also solicited domestic servants for New York City and Philadelphia, black miners for Illinois, railroad workers ("white or colored") for the Chesapeake and Ohio, and hands to build the Selma, Marion and Memphis Railroad.[25]

In dealing with an urban firm like Justis and McDonald, the Louisiana planters had to be concerned that they might be given hands "spoiled" by city life. Justis reassured Garrett on this point, saying, "I will not hire you any City Gents." Still another worry was that those recruited at great expense would work for one year and then leave. To avoid that, Garrett began to make contracts in which he agreed to pay the transportation of the laborers to Louisiana provided they stayed with him for at least two years. However easy it was to obtain hands from Virginia, it remained expensive. Thus, it must have been with relief that Garrett discovered in late 1871 that he could obtain some hands in Mississippi. In December, he brought back sixteen from that state.[26] After that the Gay plantations were able to get labor closer to home, and they do not seem to have used Justis and McDonald anymore.

Labor agents were not a very popular breed, especially among the farmers who stood to lose their hands, but they were the crucial link in the labor distribution system that came into being after the Civil War. Even though the agents served a function similar to that of the Negro traders of old, they were not simply slave dealers in new clothes. It appears that almost universally the full-time slave traders retired from handling black labor. Stopping in Knoxville in 1866, John Trowbridge stayed at a hotel that was falling apart from war damage and neglect. It was run by a former slave trader who apologized: "Hotel-keeping a'n't my business. Nigger-dealing is my business. But

---

Directory of Richmond City . . . 1870 (Richmond, 1870), 142; *Sheriff and Chataigne's Richmond City Directory . . . 1874–1875* (Richmond, 1875), 132; *Chataigne's Richmond City Directory . . . 1880* (Richmond, 1880), 164.

25. Richmond *Dispatch,* January 1, January 2, 1870, August 21, September 7, 1871, January 1, 1873, January 8, 1874, January 3, 1876, July 2, 1877.

26. J. P. Justis to Thomas Garrett, February 13, 1871, Thomas Garrett to Edward J. Gay, April 13, 1871, Thomas Garrett to "Sir" [Edward J. Gay], January 8, 1872, all in Gay Family Papers.

that's played out." With more than a trace of nostalgia, he boasted that in his day he had "sold over six hundred niggers," and he lamented, "Now I don't know what I shall turn my hand to."[27]

Whatever he decided to do, he almost certainly did not become a labor agent. Of eighty-three slave traders who were clearly described as such in the city directories of Memphis, Richmond, New Orleans, and Montgomery in the years just before the war, only one is known to have worked after the war as a labor agent. He was C. F. Hatcher, of New Orleans. In 1866, Hatcher described himself as the proprietor of a "General Intelligence Office for Labor." A year later he called himself a "Planters Emigrant Agent." After that, he disappeared from the directory. Nathan Bedford Forrest also recruited labor on a few occasions after the war, but that was no longer his main line of work.[28]

The lack of continuity in the personnel who dealt in black labor before and after the war was probably the result of two circumstances. First, it seems unlikely that black workers would have listened to the propositions of anyone who had been a slave dealer. Traders wishing to make the transition to dealing in free labor would have had to move far from their antebellum operations in order to avoid discovery. Fifty-three of the eighty-three slave traders in Memphis, Richmond, New Orleans, and Montgomery disappeared from the city directories without a trace, but there is no evidence that any of them turned up elsewhere as labor agents.

Even more important was the difference that freedom made for the task of recruiting labor. It must have taken a very different kind of

27. John T. Trowbridge, *The South*, 238.

28. For Hatcher, see *Gardner's Commercial and Business Guide of New Orleans [1860]* (New Orleans, 1860), 428; and *Gardner's New Orleans Directory for 1866* (New Orleans, 1866), unpaginated section headed "Too Late for Insertion." See *Gardner's New Orleans Directory for 1867* (New Orleans, 1867), 502. See also New Orleans *Times,* November 9, 1866; this contains an advertisement for the newly formed partnership of Hatcher and Trabue, commission merchants in tobacco. The eighty-three traders who were tracked include all the slave traders listed as such in the last directory before the Civil War in each of the four cities. This excludes many people who traded extensively in blacks but did not apply the occupational labels of "slave dealer," "slave trader," or "Negro trader" to themselves. An attempt was made to follow each in the directory of his city for the period 1866–1875. Needless to say, the information culled in this manner is hardly comprehensive. It is enough, however, to rule out the possibility that the slave traders played any kind of major role in moving labor about after the Civil War.

man to deal with blacks in freedom than to buy and sell them in slavery. One of the talents essential for agents after the war was the ability to persuade black workers that things would be better for them if they agreed to take the jobs the agents were offering. Needless to say, the art of persuading blacks about anything was little part of the work of a slave trader.

There is, however, one respect in which some of the old slave traders may have continued to be involved in supplying black labor to others, at least for a while. Ten of the eighty-three in the four cities did business after the war as auctioneers, commission merchants, factors, brokers, and the like. Four of them were listed in the directories only for 1866 or 1867, but most of the remaining six had listings that persisted into the 1870s.[29] There is no evidence that any of these ten slave dealers played a role during those years in supplying planters with labor, but there is the bare possibility that they did. When the Civil War ended, the South's commission merchants quickly tried to resume business as usual, conducting their affairs along the same lines as before the war. Many had assisted their clients in buying and selling slaves in the antebellum era, and it must have seemed natural that supplying free labor should become a part of their activity after the war. But, as Harold Woodman has shown, a quiet revolution in transportation and communciation was undermining the entire factorage business, thrusting the commission merchants into what would ultimately be a losing competition with locally based furnishing merchants.[30] In this environment of unwanted change, many commission merchants must have found the time-consuming work of providing labor for their clients a troublesome and unremunerative bother.

In 1869, when Thomas O. Moore, a former Louisiana governor, was seeking hands, he made heavy use of the commission-merchant

29. The traders with directory listings as auctioneers, commission merchants, and the like in 1866 or 1867 but not afterward were Bird Hill, of Memphis; John F. Johnson and Thomas Powell, of Montgomery; and Capt. George McCerren, of New Orleans. Those who persisted as commercial middlemen for a longer time include Anderson Delap, John Denie, and the firm of M. A. and A. S. Levy, all of Memphis; Mason Harwell, of Montgomery; and Solomon Davis and the firm of N. B. and C. B. Hill, of Richmond.

30. Harold D. Woodman, *King Cotton and His Retainers: Financing and Marketing the Cotton Crop of the South, 1800–1925* (Lexington, Ky., 1968), 254–94.

firm of Miltenberger and Pollock. Acting on Moore's behalf, the firm maintained contact with a number of labor agents, including C. H. L. Pierre, a labor broker from New Orleans and himself a black; Oran Dorsett, who had high hopes of bringing large numbers of freedmen out of Virginia or North Carolina; Captain Williams, the superintendent of the Jackson railroad, whose business gave him special access to black labor; and an E. Hall, who was in the "negro brokerage" business. It was Miltenberger and Pollock who located most of these contacts in the first place, it was they who checked up on the progress of the labor agents, and it was they who paid the fees and expenses when hands were obtained.[31]

Their efforts brought Moore some hands in 1869, but he needed still more in 1870, and his factors wrote him, "Should a chance offer to send you some negroes will do so." Perhaps the chance never came, perhaps Moore got a permanent supply of all the blacks he wanted, perhaps he rented out his lands. Whatever the reason, subsequent correspondence from his commission merchant said nothing more about supplying labor. It would not be surprising if Miltenberger and Pollock had simply decided that the whole thing was more trouble than it was worth.[32]

Another New Orleans factor, Richard Flower, surely found that it was. Acting on behalf of his client Albert A. Batchelor, he paid a labor agent for black laborers who never arrived. As a result, Flower and Batchelor ended disputing over who was responsible for the lost money, with Batchelor abandoning Flower and establishing a new account at Clapp Brothers. He must have asked them about credit for his black tenants, for in accepting Batchelor's business, they raised a caveat: "As to the negro business we could not take that unless you guarantee it[,] as our commissions are too small to justify our taking any risks."[33]

31. Miltenberger and Pollock to Thomas O. Moore, March 20, August 2, August 6, August 10, August 14, August 17, August 21, August 24, August 28, September 21, October 2, October 6, October 12, October 20, October 23, October 25, November 3, 1869, in Thomas O. Moore Papers, Troy H. Middleton Library, Louisiana State University.

32. Miltenberger and Pollock to Moore, March 5, 1870, in Moore Papers. The correspondence was followed through 1876.

33. Clapp Brothers to Albert A. Batchelor, February 2, 1872, in Folder 21, Flower

We know that those who became labor agents in the post–Civil War era tended to be neither former slave traders nor commission merchants, but there is little hard information about the people who entered this new occupation. Certainly a good number of the early labor agents were Union soldiers who had been attached to black units in the war. There is little to indicate, however, that many of these men made a lifetime career of the work. Likely, once the Freedmen's Bureau stopped giving free transportation, most moved on to other pursuits. Of those who worked as labor agents in the years after 1868, most tended to come from positions as clerks, grocers, salesmen, or insurance agents.[34]

Of the labor agents who listed themselves in city directories or who advertised in the newspapers, only a few were blacks. Pierre was a laborer who began supplying workers to others in 1867 and who, until 1875, appears to have shifted back and forth between laboring and brokering. From 1875 through 1887, the New Orleans city directories listed him as a labor agent. In 1881, his letterhead boasted that "at the shortest notice" he could furnish "Cane-cutters, Plough and Hoe Hands, Woodchoppers, Cotton Pickers, Levee and Rail-Road Hands and Mechanics of all Trades," and it ended with a postscript: "P.S.—I have made arrangements in different states for the emigration of Colored Families for the Sugar and Cotton Planters." By 1881, Pierre was handling Italian workers as well as blacks.[35]

Most blacks who were in the business of providing laborers for

to Batchelor, March 22, April 5, 1871, in Folders 17, 19, Batchelor to Flower, March 6, March 13, March 29, April 20, 1871, in Folders 17, 18, 19, all in Albert A. Batchelor Papers, Troy H. Middleton Library, Louisiana State University.

34. The generalization about the occupational antecedents of the labor agents is based on close study of the city directories of Memphis, Richmond, New Orleans, and Montgomery from 1850 to 1880. It is not, however, rooted in a systematic attempt to count the number coming from each occupation. For most of the agents there was simply no information available about previous occupations.

35. C. H. L. Pierre to J. H. Gay, February 5, 1881, September 26, 1881, both in Gay Family Papers. Pierre's 1881 letterhead says, "established in 1867." He is known to have provided laborers for the former governor Thomas Moore of Louisiana in 1869 and for Edward J. Gay in 1870. Still, the New Orleans directories listed him as a laborer in 1870 (p. 641) and in 1873 (p. 351). He was first listed as a labor broker in the directory for 1872 (p. 748). He appeared as a labor agent in 1875 (p. 750) and in all the following years through 1887 (p. 938). On his contacts with Moore and Gay, see Miltenberger

others kept a lower profile than Pierre. Working as subagents in the employ of white labor agents or planters, they were indispensable middlemen. In October, 1865, E. A. Fulton, a Memphis black who said he had orders for about a thousand hands, explained why such contact men were needed. He said that the freedmen in the city "don't want to go out into the Country because white folks treat them badly (as they say) so they stay in town and get day jobs." Fulton said that when whites approached these freedmen, "they think he is after Some tricksy and they dont care to have anything to do with them, while if a Colored man go to them he can get them to do almost anything he wants them to do."[36]

There was some exaggeration in this. Fulton was, after all, seeking the endorsement of the Freedmen's Bureau. Still, white labor agents and planters generally did have to act through black auxiliaries. A Missouri cooper who had acquired a plantation by speculating in cotton got his labor by going to Eufala, Alabama, with one of the black employees. He explained: "I sends my nigger out to talk to the people. They had nothin' to do; Georgians wanted to hire 'em for their board and clothes; and fifteen dollars a month seemed enormous." Within two days the former cooper left Eufala with sixty-five new employees. Even General Davis Tillson employed blacks in this way. In January, 1866, he told the bureau agent in Warren County, Georgia, that he had engaged a black man, William Jones, "to round up the hands for Cpt. Neely."[37]

More informally, some Upper South blacks functioned as labor agents when they returned home to visit after having gone to work in the Lower South. George Wiggins and Isham Johnson came to the Gay plantations from Virginia. In the summer of 1870, both went back home for a visit. As they were leaving, John A. Austin, the manager of Greenfield Plantation, where they worked, told them that "if any

and Pollock to Thomas O. Moore, August 14, 1869, in Moore Papers; and Contract Between Pierre and Edward J. Gay, July 27, 1870 (Gay Family Papers).

36. E. A. Fulton to O. O. Howard, October 11, 1865, in Ascom, Tennessee, LR, 1865, BRFAL, NA. It would be desirable, of course, to present evidence here that comes from the 1870s or the 1880s. Unfortunately, Fulton's testimony is the only known instance of a black labor agent's explaining why he was essential to the recruiting process.

37. Davis Tillson to P. H. Heath, January 15, 1866, in Ascom, Georgia, LS, II, BRFAL, NA; Whitelaw Reid, After the War, 563.

of their friends would come out with them I would pay good men $20 per mo & double their time when working at night." From Petersburg, Wiggins wrote: "There is a Great Menney people here working for 25 cts per day[.] those people cant live here[.] I can git some good hands[.] Some has said they Will Come When I Come home if I can git thir Way paid." From Balcony Falls, Johnson sent word that his family was ready to come and he could get more "if they new how to get out." [38]

What happened next is not fully clear, but it appears that, in consequence of the business policies and prejudices of Edward Gay, neither Wiggins nor Johnson produced any hands. Gay kept his plantation managers under a tight rein, and in order to pay the transportation of the Virginia blacks, Austin had to get his employer's personal authorization. In any case, Gay and his immediate subordinates were deeply mistrustful of blacks and were unwilling to place either money or tickets directly in their hands. As a result, communication was so delayed and garbled that the white firm of McDaniel and Irby, in Lynchburg, which was supposed to ship Johnson's family to Louisiana, had no record of Gay's instructions and sent the family instead to a plantation in Bolivar, Mississippi. [39] Nothing more is known of Wiggins' effort to procure hands in Petersburg. Still, the story of the trip that he and Johnson made to Virginia shows the potential for chain migration that existed between Virginia, where jobs were scarce and wages low, and Louisiana, where the pay was relatively high and workers scarce. It shows, too, that the arrangement of transportation was all-important, for unless a prospective employer paid the travel costs of the Virginia blacks, few were going anywhere.

Were Johnson and Wiggins labor agents? The answer is not easy. Narrowly defined, labor agents were those who made their living by providing workers for others; often but not always they took labor from one geographical area to another. But the eastern farmers who were losing their hands to planters from the Lower South rarely made such fine distinctions. To them there could have been little difference

38. John Austin to Edward J. Gay, August 11, 1870, George Wiggins to John Austin, August 3, 1870, Isham Johnson to John Austin, August 5, 1870, all in Gay Family Papers.

39. John Austin to Edward J. Gay, September 4, October 4, 1870, Edward J. Gay to L. L. Butler, September 2, 1870, all in Gay Family Papers.

between Andrew Gay, who came seeking labor for himself, and John Justis, who gathered it for whoever would pay his fee. Nor would they have been likely to discern much difference between Justis, on the one hand, and Joe Munn, George Wiggins, and Isham Johnson, on the other. The last three were not primarily labor agents, but they functioned as such when they tried to get hands for their employer.

For the sake of clarity, it is necessary to restrict the term *labor agent* to a person who made his living by acting as a labor middleman. But, it also needs to be remembered that when southern planters complained that their workers were being carried off by labor agents, they rarely bothered to distinguish between the professional labor suppliers and the quasi agents who came hunting laborers for themselves, their relatives, and their employers.

In all this there was a good deal of continuity with the past. If the slave traders accounted for many of the blacks brought from the Upper to the Lower South, there was also a strong tradition of planters and their relatives going to the Upper South in person to acquire new slaves without paying the middleman. In the postwar world, the direction of movement remained the same, and at first, Virginia continued to maintain its preeminence as a supplier to the Lower South.

With time, however, the southeastern labor glut began to ease, and Alabama joined the ranks of the sending states. In January, 1876, a Mississippi man observed four large railroad cars filled with Alabama blacks bound for the Vicksburg area. While the train was stopped, one of the blacks told him that they were going to "make cotton on the good 'fresh lands of Mississippi.'" He said Alabama was worn-out and that those who wanted hands could get as many as they liked by going there.[40] Still, the basic direction of movement remained the same as it had been in antebellum days.

Some of the continuities come out vividly in a comparison of the advertisements placed by slave dealers in New Orleans just before the war and those run by labor agents operating in that city in the 1870s. The offers of the slave traders frequently began, "Just arrived with a choice lot of VIRGINIA and CAROLINA NEGROES," and went on to say that fresh importations would be coming regularly. One advertisement asserted that the dealer would be "receiving fresh supplies dur-

40. *Hinds County Gazette* (Miss.), January 26, 1876.

ing the season." Often the notices of the postwar labor agents started with the phrase "Now on Hand," but there was the same stress on fresh arrivals coming in regularly. In March, 1873, C. C. Neally published a notice:

Now on hand
100 col'd cotton-sugar hands from Ala.-Ga.

Fresh arrivals of 50 to 100 by every trip of the steamer Creole, Tuesdays and Friday. The above hands are selected by reliable agents with great care and discretion, and none sent here except good field hands that are anxious and willing to engage for the season, for wages or share of the crop.[41]

The announcement was designed to evoke an image of the great slave-trading houses of old. It was an appeal to those who resisted the ways of the new order, and there were many who fit that description. In 1869, one of Edward Gay's clients wrote that he was going to manage the homeplace that year and that he wanted to "purchase my help before leaving the city."[42] Still, it is a mistake to assume that the new labor agencies were simply slave marts in disguise. Neally's advertisement itself suggests how much the world had changed, not only with its reference to wages and shares but also with its emphasis on the willingness of the blacks to engage for the season. The point was needed because, as Neally's customers knew all too well, there were still many blacks who were reluctant to lock themselves into a contract for an entire year. Under freedom, everything had changed even if older ways of viewing the world persisted.

To white planters, any sign of resistance by the freedmen to making contracts was another proof of black indolence and unreliability. In fact, the reluctance of blacks to enter into contracts was a rational economic response based on their ability to earn a good deal more at occasional jobs paying a daily rate than through an annual agreement. The southern black labor system had two principal components: a plantation subeconomy that required a year-round labor force and a

41. New Orleans *Times,* March 11, 1873. See also the advertisements of other agents at the same time, especially the notices of A. Hane, *ibid.,* September 10, September 26, 1873. To compare with advertisements by slave traders, see, e.g., the notices from the New Orleans *Picayune* supplement, January 4, 1860, reproduced in Frederic Bancroft's *Slave Trading in the Old South,* facing p. 316.

42. W. E. Edwards to Edward J. Gay, October 9, 1869, in Gay Family Papers.

"transient" subeconomy the labor needs of which were short-term but imperative. The blacks could earn more in the transient subeconomy, at short-term jobs in railroad construction, levee building, phosphate mining, coal mining, turpentining, lumbering, woodchopping, and other semi-industrial spheres, than they could in the plantation sub-economy, at farm work on an annual contract. The situation was comparable on the farms themselves, where extra hands, or day laborers, were paid more than those who worked side by side with them under annual contracts.[43]

The transient subeconomy was the functional equivalent of the economic subsystem that had existed in the time of slavery as the hiring system. Slave hiring had permitted the use of slave labor without capital investment, and it facilitated the transfer of labor to where it was most needed. That was just the sort of thing that happened within the transient subeconomy, except that there the blacks could bargain for themselves.

When the Civil War ended, the need for a geographically flexible work force was even greater than before. Railroads, levees, bridges, and buildings needed rebuilding and the pressures for industrialization, even though somewhat retarded in the South, created an ever-increasing demand for labor outside the agricultural sector. Too, all the jobs that had been done by hired slaves in the cities still needed to be done. There is no way of knowing how many of the "indolent" blacks who crowded into the cities just after the war were actually working, but since northern relief efforts could have aided only a small fraction of the urban-based freedmen, large numbers must have been participating in the transient subeconomy to one degree or another.

Railroad construction, in particular, drained labor from the farms. In July, 1865, B. K. Johnston, the provost marshal at Grenada, Mississippi, boasted that he had put all the extra blacks in his area to work for the railroad at wages of from ten to fifteen dollars a month. That this was not all due to his efforts is evident from his candid admission: "I was compelled to do this as it was impossible to get them back to the country where nearly every one will be Needed." Johnston was hardly a Negrophile, but like many bureau officials, he was glad to

43. Lorenzo J. Greene and Carter G. Woodson, *The Negro Wage Earner* (1930; rpr. New York, 1970), 31–34.

teach the planters a lesson about free labor. He explained to his superiors that since the planters insisted on mistreating their blacks, "it would be a good lesson to have to reason and entreat their Darkies to stay at work and raise their crops."[44]

Wherever there was railroad construction, the effect was the same as it was in Grenada. Two months after the war, twelve hundred freedmen were at work rebuilding the line between Jackson and Vicksburg. In May, 1866, the agent of the Freedmen's Bureau at Marshall, Texas, reported that the blacks in his area all wanted to leave the plantations to work on the railroads but that he had prevented a mass exodus. In Georgia, John T. Craxton asked General Tillson for two thousand blacks to work on a hundred-mile stretch of road. Tillson replied that Craxton would have no trouble finding workers.[45] By 1869, five thousand Georgia blacks were involved in building the Brunswick and Albany line alone. In 1870, when Edward Gay sought woodchoppers, one of his associates wrote, "The railroads are paying high wages for laborers and a number of Planters also require hands & therefore it is not easy to procure them, and they have to be picked up in small squads as they may offer."[46]

Visiting Eutaw, Alabama, in early 1871, Robert Somers found an area that once had been "dense" with slavery suffering from an acute labor shortage, which he attributed to the "roving" propensity of the blacks and to the lure of work on the railroads. He was certainly right about the railroads, but it seems doubtful that the blacks had any more of a roving propensity than other Americans of the time. When the Chesapeake and Ohio Railroad brought a force of perhaps five thou-

44. Lt. B. K. Johnston to Gen. Thomas, July 12, 1865, in Ascom, Mississippi, LR, Box 3, BRFAL, NA. That Johnston was hardly an egalitarian is suggested by his boast that he had "worked all the surplus stock of able bodied material off on the RR at $10 and 15 per month." What is intriguing, however, is that, despite such attitudes, he was trying to create a free labor system.

45. Wharton, The Negro in Mississippi, 124; Lt. J. M. Beebe to Ascom, Texas, May 26, 1866, in Ascom, Texas, Regletrec, I, John T. Craxton to Davis Tillson, November 5, 1866, in Ascom, Georgia, Regletrec, I, endorsement to Craxton to Tillson, November 5, 1866, in EB, I (378), November 12, 1866, all in BRFAL, NA (microfilm of endorsement M-798, roll 8).

46. Samuel Cranwill to L. L. Butler, July 30, 1870, in Gay Family Papers; C. Mildred Thompson, Reconstruction in Georgia: Economic, Social, Political, 1865–1872 (1915; rpr. Gloucester, Mass., 1964), 289.

sand blacks to work in West Virginia, it found that although the Negroes were the best and cheapest labor available, they had the disconcerting habit of going home at harvest time and again at Christmas.[47]

Clearly, blacks whose economic existence was marginal took every opportunity to supplement their income. They thereby produced a good deal of local and temporary movement. In August, 1881, James Tucker, a white farmer in Harrison County, Texas, noted in his diary: "Yesterday there was a general exodus of the nigger men from this vicinity to the railroad in the course of construction in Louisiana where they expect to remain at work a week or two[.] their wages are[,] for good hands[,] from 1 dollar to 1.25." He added, "Its a good thing for them if they can get employment . . . their crops being almost failures." Recording yet another movement in October, the same diarist said: "Nearly all the niggers in this Vicinity have gone to Redriver to pick cotton and others to Marshall. they go off pretending to hunt work but they never find it or if they do they make nothing of it."[48]

Tucker's deprecating skepticism was characteristic of the opinions of many white observers about black labor at the time. Even when making a routine report on the wages of black laborers, the *Daily Florida Union* injected a gratuitous note of derision. It said that black laborers and timber cutters working along the line of the railroad were getting from $1.00 to $1.30, and it correctly observed that the pay was far above the level of farm wages, but it added, "The 'trash gang' women and children stick to 'de old plantation.'" Stripped of its racist innuendos, the *Union*'s report accurately described a pattern whereby many a black farmer let his wife and children stay at home and tend the crops while he supplemented the family's income with railroad work and other semi-industrial jobs that paid more than he could earn on the farm.[49]

47. Robert Somers, *The Southern States Since the War, 1870–1* (New York, 1871), 159; Charles Nordhoff, "West Virginia: A Horseback Ride Through the Wilderness," *American Missionary*, XVI (1872), 1–24; Charles W. Turnerr, "The Chesapeake and Ohio Railroad in 1865–1873," *North Carolina Historical Review*, XXXI (1954), 165.

48. James Tucker Diary, August 1, October 14, 1881 (James Tucker Papers, University of Texas Library).

49. Jacksonville *Daily Florida Union*, March 4, 1882; Alrutheus A. Taylor, *The Negro in South Carolina During the Reconstruction* (Washington, D.C., 1924), 72.

The pattern went far beyond occasional work for the railroads. Across the South, black farm workers with annual contracts did what they could to supplement their meager farm earnings. Others took their chances and avoided annual contracts entirely, in the hope that occasional labor would provide a greater income than they would get by tying themselves to a farm agreement. Thus, blacks in the coastal areas of South Carolina rushed to work in newly opened phosphate mines. Others in North Carolina, and later in South Carolina and Georgia, took advantage of the chance to get jobs in turpentine manufacture. Lumbering and sawmilling operations existed in many parts of the South, and there too the blacks found an opportunity to supplement farm income or to replace it entirely. All over, too, there were temporary and sometimes seasonal jobs in woodchopping. Even though the railroads were beginning to use coal as fuel, many locomotives still burned wood, and so did the steamboats on the rivers.[50]

The entire transient subeconomy was very much a seasonal one. In Louisiana, for example, sugar manufacture required a massive amount of wood that had to be stockpiled by harvest time. It took two to three cords just to produce a single hogshead of sugar. In 1870, on just four of the plantations of Edward Gay, 1,802 cords of wood had been cut by mid-August. In Louisiana and Mississippi, blacks often took jobs in levee construction and repair, but in December, 1865, with the planting season at hand, it was almost impossible to find blacks available for that work. So bad was the shortage that in late 1865, Louisiana levee contractors were forced to import most of their laborers from St. Louis, Cincinnati, and Chicago.[51]

50. Alrutheus A. Taylor, *The Negro in South Carolina,* 72; George Brown Tindall, *South Carolina Negroes, 1877–1900* (1952; rpr. Baton Rouge, 1966), 126–27; W. McKee Evans, *Ballots and Fence Rails: Reconstruction on the Lower Cape Fear* (1966; rpr. New York, 1974), 198–99; Joe Gray Taylor, *Louisiana Reconstructed,* 385; Wharton, *The Negro in Mississippi,* 126; C. H. Howard, "Report of Inspection of South Carolina, Georiga, and Florida [December 30, 1865]," in HXD 70, p. 356. Richardson, *The Negro in the Reconstruction of Florida,* 69. In the summer of 1865, five thousand men were employed in cutting wood to fuel Mississippi River steamboats. In December of that year one New Orleans contractor was committed to delivering five thousand cords of wood to the New Orleans and Jackson Railroad. See Samuel Thomas to O. O. Howard, August 15, 1865, in Ascom, Mississippi, LS, IV, J. Benjamin Chandler to Ascom, Louisiana, February 3, 1866, in Ascom, Louisiana, Regletrec, II, both in BRFAL, NA.

51. J. Carlyle Sitterson, *Sugar Country: The Cane Sugar Industry in the South,*

Black farmers could often find supplementary work right next door, for in the effort to keep costs down and to cope with the labor shortage, many planters tried to squeeze by with only a few hands on .nnual contracts, who were assisted by day laborers at the busy seasons. The practice of using extra hands was not new. In antebellum times planters often enlarged their work force at peak periods with hired slaves. After cotton-picking time in Louisiana it was a regular practice to send excess hands down into the sugar-growing area. The sugar growers also imported temporary hands for the grinding season from Mississippi and from Louisiana rice plantations. After emancipation similar patterns were quick to reemerge. On a plantation near Franklin, Louisiana, freedmen who had accepted an annual contract complained in 1867 that they were being paid less than the extra hands who were working beside them for the grinding season. In 1875, McKeever's Grange Labor Exchange was advertising that it had available three hundred cotton pickers and four hundred sugar hands who had just "returned from rice farms and can be fully depended on."[52]

From the perspective of both planters and workers, the system of using extra hands had a good deal to recommend it. A Louisiana cotton planter boasted in 1867 that he had retained only two hands, whom he supplemented with an "extra one hired per day occasionally," and that in this way he was able to tend twenty-five acres of cotton and twenty of corn. In South Carolina, blacks who owned or rented small plots added to their income by working as day laborers "whenever they could." In 1868, a group of such freedmen approached the Reverend John Cornish while he was at breakfast, and he sent them into his fields at twenty to twenty-five cents a task. Using that kind of occasional labor and one full-time hand, the minister was growing over thirty acres of cotton.[53]

Larger operators did much the same thing. The payrolls of the vari-

---

1753–1950 (Lexington, Ky., 1953), 141; Statement Regarding Woodcutting, August 20, 1870 (Gay Family Papers); Ascom, Mississippi, to O. O. Howard, December 27, 1865, in Ascom, Mississippi, LS, XVI, BRFAL, NA.

52. New Orleans *Times,* November 7, 1875; Lt. James W. Keller to Ascom, Louisiana, October 31, 1867, in Ascom, Louisiana, Regletrec, VIII, BRFAL, NA; Joe Gray Taylor, *Negro Slavery in Louisiana* (Baton Rouge, 1963), 34, 73.

53. Joel Williamson, *After Slavery,* 135; Madison Batchelor to "Father" [Thomas Batchelor], July 25, 1867, in Folder 13, Batchelor Papers.

ous plantations of Edward Gay consistently show the use of extra
hands in significant numbers, and they show too that the pay of the
supplementary workers went to a higher scale than that of the regular
hands. In February, 1878, the payroll from the Shady Grove Plantation
listed twenty-four regular hands, who worked from sixteen to twenty
days and were paid at rates ranging from fifty to sixty-five cents a day.
The same payroll shows twenty-three extra hands receiving from fifty
cents to $1.50 a day for periods of from six to twenty days. That the
difference in pay rates did not simply reflect the differing abilities of
the individual workers is suggested by the concern of one of Gay's
managers that the added cost of using day laborers "will make my
labor expenses heavier for the next two months than I expected."[54]
Who were the extra hands? We know that in part they were black
farmers working under annual contracts who did day labor for the
extra cash it brought in. But there were others. A memorandum in
1869 from one of Edward Gay's managers or overseers said, "The
names here are children that I hired to go with old Austin Doan to
pick peas." With the seven names on the list appear wage rates ranging
from twenty to twenty-five cents a day. The children worked for four
and a half days. Both on the Gay plantations and elsewhere, women
too served as extra laborers. On the Sanfelasco Plantation, in Alachua
County, Florida, many of the laborers hired in 1873 to harvest the rich
cotton crop were women bearing the same last names as regular
hands.[55]

It all came down to the price of labor. In February, 1866, laborers
could be hired at Northampton, Virginia, for short periods but not
for a year. That was because they preferred to be free at harvest time,
when the demand for labor drove up wage rates. In January, 1870, the
Selma *Southern Argus* reported that in Perry County, Alabama, few
planters had hands, and that there was no probability that they would

54. Roman O. Daigre to Edward J. Gay, February 27, 1872, in Gay Family Papers;
Payroll for the Shady Grove Plantation, February, 1878 (Gay Family Papers).

55. Memorandum on a Scrap of Paper, in Folder for October, 1869 (Gay Family
Papers); David A. Barrow to Edward J. Gay, December 20, 1872, in Gay Family Papers;
Edward K. Eckert, "Contract Labor in Florida During Reconstruction," *Florida His-
torical Quarterly,* XLVII (1968), 44, 48. See also South Carolina Board of Agriculture,
South Carolina: Resources and Population, Institutions and Industries (Charleston, S.C.,
1883), 83.

get any soon. It explained that a good many freedmen were working on the railroad and that others were either renting lands or hiring themselves out as day laborers. In Coweta County, Georgia, a planter who had been using wage hands under an annual contract complained that the hands worked well enough in winter but that when grass began to spring up in the cotton and day laborers were in demand, three-quarters of them left to work for one of his neighbors for a dollar a day plus food and drink. As a result, he had to meet those "outrageous prices" or turn his crop out to grass.[56]

Outrageous prices sums it up. Eleven years after emancipation, many white southerners were still not reconciled to the idea that the blacks were free laborers whose wages were determined by the economic marketplace. At the same time, the remarks of this farmer suggest that market forces were indeed determining black wages. Even so, the black labor market was not quite as free as it sometimes seemed. The postwar labor shortage may have given blacks an advantage in pay in many parts of the South, but the freedmen operated in a highly circumscribed labor market where they were relegated to the heaviest and dirtiest jobs and where their chances of moving upward were remote. Although blacks were not kept to the plantation alone, it appears that, by and large, the tasks they performed were those that had been theirs since antebellum times.[57] In this was one of the greatest constants between slavery and freedom.

The great majority of the slaves were hardly prepared to become doctors, lawyers, or captains of industry in one swift jump. Southern whites, however, were also unprepared to look favorably on the idea of a long slow crawl toward black middle-class respectability. Little is known with certainty about the extent of black occupational mobility during the Reconstruction era, but it is clear that by 1890 southern blacks were virtually barred from all forms of clean work except in black-owned businesses serving the black community alone. They were not permitted to be salesmen or clerks; they were not allowed to work in clean industries like textiles. At Richmond, they worked in

56. *Southern Cultivator,* April, 1876, pp. 134–35; O. S. Pride to A. S. Flag, February 1, 1866, in Ascom, Virginia, Reports of Bureau Affairs, XXXVII, BRFAL, NA; New York *Times,* January 6, 1869; Selma (Ala.) *Southern Argus,* January 3, 1870.

57. Compare Starobin, *Industrial Slavery,* 129–31, with Greene and Woodson, *The Negro Wage Earner,* 31–34.

the manufacture of flour, tobacco products, and iron, but they had done that in slavery too.[58]

Blacks had also performed much of the skilled work of the antebellum South. When emancipation came, they held most of their section's jobs as blacksmiths, carpenters, barbers, masons, and plasterers. By 1890, however, the only skilled occupations in which they were represented in numbers that were at all consonant with their proportion in the southern population were bricklaying and plastering. To some extent, the decline in the representation of blacks in skilled occupations was a natural consequence of the end of slavery, since it became socially acceptable for whites to work with their hands too. The problem was not so much that whites were entering skilled occupations that had previously been dominated by blacks as that blacks were not allowed to move up in the occupational hierarchy. They were very largely barred from entry into the more prestigious and higher-paying skilled crafts, like those of the machinist and the printer, and with only a handful of exceptions, such as in the catering business, they could function as professionals or businessmen only within the impoverished black community.[59]

It is, then, a mistake to see the southern labor system as a truly free one in which the price of labor was governed solely by market forces. Even as the labor shortage acted to enhance black bargaining power, prejudice and discrimination pulled in an opposite direction, excluding blacks from the most desirable jobs and circumscribing their economic universe. The cumulative impact of the barriers that kept blacks from competing for the better jobs was to increase artificially the size of the black agricultural work force and thereby to hold wages down. Thus the real advantages that blacks gained from the overall southern labor shortage were substantially undermined by the closed system that denied them the right to all but the most limited forms of upward mobility.

In theory, of course, blacks were free to move north, where wage rates were higher than in the South. But for reasons that have already become apparent, they did not do that to any significant extent until

58. Howard N. Rabinowitz, *Race Relations in the Urban South, 1865–1890* (New York, 1978), 63–69.

59. Wesley, *Negro Labor*, 142; Spero and Harris, *The Black Worker*, 14–15, 159–60; Higgs, *Competition and Coercion*, 59.

the twentieth century. Gavin Wright has argued that until the eve of World War II, the southern labor market was isolated from the labor market of the North. He notes especially the impact of social and historical forces in shaping the isolation. Early on, he says, slavery had the effect of insulating the South from foreign and northern labor flows. Then, just when mass immigration from Europe was getting started, "the South was consumed by the turbulence of war and Reconstruction." By the time Reconstruction was over, it was too late, since a pattern of transatlantic labor flows had been thoroughly established.[60]

Although Wright is clearly correct that the southern labor market was isolated from the national labor market, it seems doubtful that the turbulence of the era of Civil War and Reconstruction had much to do with that. Just after the Civil War, the Freedmen's Bureau did take steps to send over nine thousand blacks to work in the North, and there was a migration of Kentucky blacks into the Midwest. Still, neither influx triggered any further movement of consequence, and it seems clear that the isolation of the southern labor market was an established fact before the Civil War. By 1866, northerners perceived black labor as far more alien than European labor, and they were simply not willing to pay blacks enough to lure them out of the South.

Black migration in the Reconstruction era in many respects extended antebellum trends. Under the direction of the slave traders, blacks had "migrated" from the Southeast to the Southwest. After the traders were gone, whites continued to play a major role in organizing long-distance movement, with the Freedmen's Bureau, the labor agents, and the planters themselves leading the way. What enabled the whites to have so much influence over black movement was the matter of transportation. It simply cost too much to get from Virginia to Arkansas for the impoverished freedmen to pay their own way, particularly for those who had the greatest need to go where jobs were plentiful. It was only when the Freedmen's Bureau offered free transportation or when planters and labor agents offered travel on a "go now, pay later" basis that large numbers of blacks were able to take advantage of the labor scarcity in the Lower South. Labor agents

60. Gavin Wright, *Old South, New South,* 74–75.

played a crucial role in all this, for it was they who brought the information—or sometimes, misinformation—about jobs in distant places, and it was they who arranged to transport blacks to their new jobs.

If white involvement was often essential for long-distance movement, it was hardly needed when the jobs were nearby. Almost immediately after the war, there developed a pattern in which blacks moved back and forth between their farm homes and work in semi-industrial jobs or as extra hands on nearby farms. That pattern had much in common with the slave hiring system of an earlier day. What was new was simply that the blacks made their own decisions about when to leave home and when to come back.

6

THE AFRICAN DREAM

Up to this point, black migration has been considered almost exclusively in its economic dimension. From a numerical standpoint, there is good reason for that: the great majority of those who moved did so primarily for economic reasons. Nevertheless, there were always some who sought to leave the South because they despaired of ever being treated as equals in a white man's world. This chapter describes migration movements that arose more from this sort of motivation than from economic considerations.

Blacks who dreamed of escaping from the South often spoke of colonization as holding for them the promise of freedom and independence. *Colonization* was an umbrella term sheltering a number of different but not always distinct objectives. It referred, first of all, to organized efforts to emigrate to a foreign land. The destinations most frequently focused upon were Liberia, in particular, and Africa, in general, but occasionally there was thought of establishing a black homeland in places as divergent as Central America and Cyprus. But the term could also embrace the idea of setting up a black homeland on government lands in the American West. Thus, the project of establishing black settlements in Kansas and Nebraska was also considered colonization. Sometimes the term meant all these things at once, for at its core the word denoted a black effort to escape oppression and go where it would be possible to live without white interference.

From the standpoint of quantitative results, politically motivated colonization efforts were relatively insignificant. Still, they are an essential counterpoint in the story of black migration within the South. For the inability of southern blacks to carry out their plans for colonization illustrates the way their poverty limited their ability to migrate independently over long distances. At the same time, the widespread interest in colonization that emerged at the end of Reconstruction demonstrates how angry and hopeless blacks felt as white capital achieved a renewed hegemony over black labor.

The idea of sending American blacks to Africa had one of its earliest roots in the work of Paul Cuffe, a black sea captain who carried thirty-eight American Negroes to Sierra Leone in 1816. Almost immediately white reformers who wanted to abolish slavery and to expatriate American blacks to Africa perverted his dream into something quite different. The abolitionism of the reformers flowed not from concern for the rights of blacks but from the conviction that slavery and racial heterogeneity would ultimately destroy American liberty.[1] Their aim was an all-white United States, which they sought to achieve through the creation, in 1817, of the American Colonization Society, a group devoted to arranging the expatriation of all blacks, free and slave. The organization's activities were based on the twin premises that blacks were inferior beings and that the integrity of American civilization required racial homogeneity. To achieve its goals, the society established the colony of Liberia, and between 1820 and 1865 it transported 6,301 former slaves and 4,501 free Negroes there. In 1847, acting from expediency rather than upon principle, it transformed the colony into an independent nation. Even after that change, though, the American Colonization Society played a decisive role in the affairs of Liberia for many years.[2]

Fearful that colonization was a scheme to force them to move to Africa, antebellum northern blacks overwhelmingly opposed the con-

1. Sheldon H. Harris, *Paul Cuffe: Black America and the African Return* (New York, 1972), 64–69; Philip J. Staudenraus, *The African Colonization Movement, 1816–1865* (New York, 1961), 9–11, 17–22.

2. Statistics calculated from figures in *African Repository*, XLIII (1867), 225. Another 1,227 blacks were settled in Liberia by the Maryland Colonization Society (Staudenraus, *The African Colonization Movement*, 20–21, 29, 241, and *passim*).

cept. Still, it is an oversimplification to see prewar blacks as unanimously and unconditionally resisting it in all its forms. The idea of colonization originated with a black, Cuffe, and at first it had the support of Richard Allen and James Forten, two of the most prominent blacks of the day. Privately, Forten expressed the belief that blacks would "never become a people until they com [sic] out from amongst the white people."[3]

In view of the racism of the American Colonization Society, colonization appealed to only a few blacks, but in the 1850s, as their conditions in the North worsened, interest in emigration revived. At a series of conventions, blacks discussed the relative merits of Central America and various places in Africa for settlement. And as the Civil War approached, a short-lived enclave was established in Haiti, and Martin R. Delany returned from Africa bearing treaties that permitted American blacks to settle in the Niger region. Of the 1,094 northern blacks who went to Liberia between 1820 and 1865, 70 percent emigrated in the last fifteen years of the period.[4] With the Civil War and its implicit hope of emancipation and perhaps a measure of equality, black interest in emigration began to fade. For some whites, on the other hand, the growing possibility of emancipation made colonization more imperative than ever. Abraham Lincoln's government became involved with two plans for the voluntary expatriation of American blacks. One was never implemented and the other failed miserably.[5] By the war's end most whites realized that colonization could not cure America's racial ills.

The dedicated stalwarts who ran the American Colonization Society disagreed. For them, the end of the war was only the "beginning of the negro question." They believed that blacks were unassimilable and that colonization was the only practical solution. If the freedmen remained in the United States, argued the colonizationists, they would

3. James Forten to Paul Cuffe, January 25, 1817, in William Lloyd Garrison, *Thoughts on African Colonization* (1832; rpr. New York, 1968), ix, vii–viii.

4. Litwack, *North of Slavery,* 257–62; Staudenraus, *The African Colonization Movement,* 244; Phil Samuel Sigler, "The Attitudes of Free Blacks Towards Emigration to Liberia" (Ph.D. dissertation, Boston University, 1969), 19–20, 112; Howard H. Bell, "The Negro Emigration Movement, 1849–1854: A Phase of Negro Nationalism," *Phylon,* XX (1959), 132–42.

5. Staudenraus, *The African Colonization Movement,* 246–48, 251.

be doomed to extinction. In 1866, the society bluntly asserted a doctrine that had been with it since its inception: "The white is likely ever to remain the superior race and consequently the rulers. . . . The weaker [race] will find it to its interest to remove from out of the reach of the stronger."[6]

More to create a racially homogeneous America than to protect a "weaker" race, the society mounted a campaign to help the freedmen get beyond the reach of the whites. In the South, it circulated thousands of copies of a new pamphlet, *Information About Going to Liberia*. The colonizationists promised prospective immigrants free transportation from their homes to Liberia, six months' support while they adjusted to their new environment, and a grant of ten acres of farmland. More land could be purchased for a dollar an acre.[7]

It soon became evident that the society would have to mute its racism if it was to have any chance of persuading blacks to leave the country. Accordingly, although the organization's underlying beliefs remained unchanged, its rhetoric shifted from a focus on black inferiority to an emphasis on black nationality. The very same annual report that urged blacks to put themselves beyond the reach of the "superior race" indicated the shift when it said, "Repulsions here and attractions there [in Liberia] will lead the colored population to seek a nationality of their own, with actual homes, real title to the soil, and active dominion of the country where they reside."[8]

Still, it was an uphill battle. In early 1866, the society's traveling secretary made a tour of Virginia and found little enthusiasm for emigration. Reporting on his reception in Petersburg, the secretary complained of a black minister who gave an "incoherent, boisterous, untruthful, mischievous harangue on human rights and things in general."[9] Recognizing the limitations of white emissaries, the society began to employ black speakers. In April, 1867, the organization's corresponding secretary recommended appointing Alexander Crummell as one of them: "We must needs have a Liberian going among the

6. *African Repository*, XLII (1866), 41, XLI (1865), 36.

7. Willis D. Boyd, "Negro Colonization in the Reconstruction Era, 1865–1870," *Georgia Historical Quarterly*, XL (1965), 365–66.

8. *African Repository*, XLII (1866), 41; Boyd, "Negro Colonization in the Reconstruction Era," 360–82.

9. Quoted by Boyd in "Negro Colonization in the Reconstruction Era," 364.

members of his race in this country. . . . The negroes distrust more and more the motives of the white man and are more clannish than ever. Hence one of their own number can better reach and influence them than anyone belonging to the other race."[10] Crummell did not return to the United States for six years, but blacks like Clement Robinson, Henry Erskine, William Slatter, Joseph J. Roberts, and Richard Cain worked at communicating the society's viewpoint in the period just after the war.[11]

The key figure in the Colonization Society's effort to win the support of the black community was its white corresponding secretary, William Coppinger. In 1838, at the age of ten, Coppinger went to work for the Pennsylvania Colonization Society as an office boy. He remained a loyal paid servant of the emigration cause until his death in 1892. In 1864, he received his appointment as corresponding secretary of the American Colonization Society, and from that point on he increasingly became the organization's mainstay.[12] It was Coppinger who answered the inquiries about Liberia from blacks across the South, and it was he who tended to the business of sending colonists to Africa. He organized the sailing of the society's thousand-ton steamer, the *Golconda,* and he personally went south to escort emigrants to the ship, to head off last minute defections, and to seek new recruits.

In November, 1866, Coppinger received a letter from Cornelius Reeves, a black Baptist preacher from Mullens Depot, South Carolina, who wanted to know "when we can leave this country on any of your Ships bound for Liberia." He said a thousand persons longed "to leave this land of oppression and sorrow" and that their labor contracts would expire on January 1, 1867. After that they would again have to bind themselves under "slave contracts or be driven from the land that

10. William Coppinger to William McLain, April 14, 1867, in Vol. CLXXXVII (73), ACS, LC (hereafter, the volume number will appear in roman numerals and the letter number within parentheses).

11. Willis D. Boyd, "Negro Colonization in the National Crisis" (Ph.D. dissertation, University of California at Los Angeles, 1953), 310, 322, 332; Boyd, "Negro Colonization in the Reconstruction Era," 379–80; Richard Bardolph, *The Negro Vanguard* (New York, 1959), 64.

12. Edwin S. Redkey, *Black Exodus: Black Nationalist and Back-to-Africa Movements, 1890–1910* (New Haven, 1969), 77–78.

gave them birth." He asked Coppinger to relieve him and his people by sending a ship in January "to carry us to the land of our forefathers where we may nomore Hear the voice of the oppressor."[13]

Reeves first learned of Liberia when he was "chosen out from among three hundred men" to go to Charleston to ask Robert K. Scott, the assistant commissioner of the Freedmen's Bureau, "what was the Best way for them to get rid of their oppressors." Scott counseled the blacks to move to Liberia, or to government lands in Florida or the West. What led Reeves's group to decide on Liberia is uncertain, but given the poverty of its membership, the free transportation offered by the Colonization Society must have been important.[14]

At Coppinger's request, Reeves forwarded a list of 286 applicants who wanted to make the trip, and plans were made for the group to leave on the spring sailing of the *Golconda*. By January, 1867, however, trouble loomed. When the time for signing new labor contracts came, the applicants found that their employers would not make agreements covering only the period from January 1 to mid-May. As Reeves saw it, the whites were "Envious against those wishing to emigrate." Thus, most of the prospective emigrants were forced to sign annual contracts for 1867, and Reeves had to write Coppinger asking him to defer the sailing date until the end of the year.[15]

Seeing a threat to his spring expedition, Coppinger took a firm line. He promised to fulfill his pledge to send the applicants on the May sailing but warned that the society could not bind itself "as to what we will do for your party next year." Implicitly countenancing a violation by the blacks of their labor contracts, he urged: "If, as you profess, Liberia is so much superior to this country, why not go there as soon as you can? Now is the time."[16] His goading had some effect. In early February, eighty-five applicants from Mullens Depot agreed

13. Cornelius Reeves to William Coppinger, November 26, 1866, in CLXXXV (344), ACS, LC.

14. Cornelius Reeves to William Coppinger, April 5, 1867, in CLXXXVII (32), ACS, LC.

15. Cornelius Reeves to William Coppinger, January 5, 1867, in CLXXXVI (58), ACS, LC; Cornelius Reeves to William Coppinger, December 7, 1866, in CLXXXV (379), ACS, LC.

16. William Coppinger to Cornelius Reeves, January 21, 1867, in Series IIA, Domestic Letters Sent, Box 23, ACS, LC.

that they would leave for Liberia that spring regardless of their contracts. A few days later Reeves reported that the society's offer of free transportation had "taken Great place in the mines [minds] of those who wish to go to Liberia and have lost nearly all of last years earnings by fraud."[17]

Another crisis threatened in early April, as local whites tried to convince their laborers that the recruitment for Liberia was simply a cover for luring them into bondage in Cuba. Simultaneously, the whites dilated on the sickness and death that were common in Liberia. Reeves complained that the whites had turned many against him and that some blacks were even calling him a traitor to his race. He felt his followers were easily deceived because "they cannot Read for themselves[;] hence they believe all manner of falsehood and Scorn the truth which is so plain that no reader can mistake them."[18]

Coppinger must have had more than a few worries whether, in the end, there would be any emigrants from Mullens Depot. Worse, the case was similar with all the parties preparing to leave. Thus, in April, 1867, when he went south to arrange the spring sailing, he was as concerned with bolstering the morale of the possible emigrants as with taking care of the details of the projected voyage. He stopped first at Florence, South Carolina, where two hundred farmers were supposedly making preparations to leave. By the time he got there, most were saying they wanted to put off their departure until the fall. Hoping to save a few for Liberia, he promised to return in two weeks.[19] Reaching Mullens Depot, he found himself in an agricultural area where "the only approach to a southern town is a country store." He met with the leading men and was struck by their poverty. Reeves provided a chicken, and others donated Indian bread and coffee, but

17. Cornelius Reeves to William Coppinger, February 7, 1867, in CLXXXVI (145), ACS, LC; Cornelius Reeves to William Coppinger, February 11, 1867, in CLXXXVI (149), ACS, LC.

18. Reeves to Coppinger, April 5, 1867, in CLXXXVII (32), ACS, LC. Although the allegations about Cuba were out-and-out falsehoods, there was more than a little truth to claims that Liberia was an unhealthy place at this time. On mortality rates there, see Tom W. Shick, *Behold the Promised Land: A History of Afro-American Settler Society in Nineteenth Century Liberia* (Baltimore, 1977), 27–28.

19. William Coppinger to William McLain, April 10, 1867, in CLXXXVII (64), ACS, LC.

"butter and milk and even a table were invisible[,] the place being too poor to furnish either." Afterward, Coppinger addressed fifty potential colonists. When he finished, he reckoned his hearers were about as solidly committed as possible under the circumstances.[20]

He next traveled to Columbia, Winnsboro, and Aiken. Then he went on to Macon, Georgia. At each stop his mission was to strengthen the resolve of those who had said they wanted to emigrate, and discreetly to gather new recruits. At Columbia, he met for three hours with Beverly Nash, who later served in the South Carolina legislature. Coppinger described the black leader as a "warm friend of Liberia," and that is consistent with the little that is known about Nash. At Winnsboro, a disappointed Coppinger learned that most of the applicants had already left, not for Liberia but for the "more Southern states." In the meantime, Reeves sent worrisome news that the members of his party feared having "words" with their former masters and wanted to leave at night.[21]

Coppinger established his headquarters at Charleston, from where the *Golconda* was to depart. A short time later he met with one of the most powerful black leaders in the city, Richard Cain, pastor of the Emanuel A.M.E. Church. Born in Virginia, Cain had lived in Ohio and in Brooklyn, New York, before coming to Charleston after the war. In the antebellum era he had actively supported Liberian colonization, and he continued to do so after the war. Coppinger called him "our open and decided friend." At their meeting, Cain promised to provide replacements for any last-minute defectors.[22]

In late April, Coppinger returned to Florence, to find that the blacks there had abandoned plans of going to Liberia. He must have

20. William Coppinger to William McLain, April 12, 1867, in CLXXXVII (71), ACS, LC.

21. Cornelius Reeves to William Coppinger, April 20, 1867, in CLXXXVII (103), ACS, LC; Coppinger to McLain, April 14, 1867, in CLXXXVII (73), ACS, LC. Nash had a sharp dislike for mulattoes and took great pride in his African heritage (Thomas Holt, *Black over White: Negro Political Leadership in South Carolina During Reconstruction* [Urbana, Ill., 1979], 17, 60).

22. William Coppinger to William McLain, April 24, 1867, in CLXXXVII (120), ACS, LC; Boyd, "Negro Colonization in the National Crisis," 322; Williamson, *After Slavery*, 190; Francis B. Simkins and Robert H. Woody, *South Carolina During Reconstruction* (1932; rpr. Gloucester, Mass., 1964), 131–32.

been in poor spirits as he proceeded on to Mullens Depot, and what he found there cannot have improved his frame of mind. The freedmen were "all astir making ready to attend a 'Republican Mass Meeting.'" Certain that the meeting would further undermine his cause, Coppinger tried to "fortify them against what they might hear about their rights in this country and confiscation of the lands." Leaving Mullens Depot before the meeting, he worried that the gathering would do the cause of colonization no good.[23]

He was surely right. In April, Reeves had had 140 applicants firmly committed for Liberia, but when he arrived at the *Golconda* in mid-May, he brought with him only 116 persons. Reeves's group was joined by 205 others, and when the *Golconda* left Charleston on May 30, 1867, it carried 321 black colonists. The following November, it took another 312 to Liberia, bringing the total to 633 for the year. Despite the uncertainties and the last-minute defections, 1867 had turned into a banner year for the society. In its fifty-year history, there had been only three times when the organization transported more emigrants to Liberia in a single year.[24]

If 1867 was good, 1868 promised to be even better. The year started out with applications from a party in Eufala, Alabama, and from another group of 175 in Aiken, South Carolina. Additional applications came from Georgia, Tennessee, and North Carolina. As usual, the period preceding the sailing was marked by uncertainties and defections, but when the *Golconda* left in May, 1868, it carried 451 emigrants. The society saw that if the same success was possible in November, the year would mark an all-time high for the number of colonists it had sent.[25]

Suddenly the application rate slackened dramatically. The society did not send another shipload of black emigrants until November, 1869, when it could muster only 160 colonists. Moreover, in the im-

23. William Coppinger to William McLain, April 30, 1867, in CLXXXVII (144), ACS, LC.

24. Reeves to Coppinger, April 20, 1867, in CLXXXVII (103), ACS, LC; William Coppinger to William McLain, May 9, 1867, in CLXXXVII (191), ACS, LC; William Coppinger to William McLain, May 30, 1867, in CLXXXVII (261), ACS, LC; Boyd, "Negro Colonization in the National Crisis," 304, 307–308, 318–19, 322; Staudenraus, *The African Colonization Movement,* 251.

25. Boyd, "Negro Colonization in the National Crisis," 324–28.

mediately preceding years, a precipitous falling-off in white support had weakened gravely the financial position of the society. In the antebellum era the average annual receipts of the organization had risen from $8,672 a year in the 1820s to $85,325 a year in the 1850s. Then, in the period 1860–1864, the average annual income slipped to $71,316. The slide became steeper after the war, and during the years from 1865 to 1869 the average annual income fell to $49,686.[26]

It was just when receipts were declining that the society had large groups of emigrants to send to Liberia, and the cost of that was considerable. Coppinger spent over thirty-two thousand dollars on the sailing in May, 1867, that carried 321 persons to Liberia, and that does not take into account the twenty thousand dollars the *Golconda* cost in 1866. Just to match the society's 1867 record in 1868, it would have needed sixty-three thousand dollars. The money was not there, and it was not forthcoming. Annual receipts in the 1870s plummeted to an average of $21,076. They would drop still further in the 1880s and the 1890s.[27]

The decline in support was hardly a sign that racial prejudice was dying. What it showed was that the Civil War and Reconstruction had almost completely undermined white philanthropic support for the idea that expatriating the blacks could resolve the American race problem. Increasingly, the American Colonization Society had become an irrelevance manned by a hardy handful of aging partisans who could not let go of an idea whose time had passed.[28]

For blacks, too, emigration lost appeal as Reconstruction developed. Visiting Mullens Depot at the opening of Military Reconstruction, Coppinger contemptuously remarked, "The political carn[ival] is opening in all this region." He was certain that black political activity boded ill for the cause of Liberia, and he was right. Two years later he saw his worst fears confirmed. After traveling from Montgomery, Alabama, to Columbus, Georgia, and from there to Eufala,

26. *Ibid.*, 338. Average receipts are calculated from data in Staudenraus, *The African Colonization Movement*, 251.

27. Boyd, "Negro Colonization in the National Crisis," 313, 322. Average annual receipts for the 1880s were $14,983. The comparable figure for the 1890s was $9,495. The figures are calculated from Staudenraus' *The African Colonization Movement*, 251.

28. Boyd, "Negro Colonization in the Reconstruction Era," 373–74, 381–82.

Alabama, he regretfully concluded that there was "scarcely any hope" of recruiting emigrants at the places he had visited.[29]

Summarizing the reasons that blacks were giving in 1869 for their lack of interest, Coppinger said, "The colored people in this region of country are almost universally content with their present condition and prospects." Feelings between the races were, he said, "better than at any time since the war," and Ku Klux Klan outrages were "less frequent and violent than formerly." Besides, the prospects for good corn and cotton yields were better than for many years, and the blacks still cherished hopes of getting "land, tools and a mule from Congress." To make matters worse for his cause, unfavorable reports from Liberia and a lack of mail from friends and relatives who had gone there dampened enthusiasm. It must have been a combination of such causes that lay behind the letter one resident of Mullens Depot wrote to Coppinger saying that the society did not need to bother sending more pamphlets to that place since no one there would ever apply again.[30]

It boiled down to two things: attractions in the United States, and repulsions in Liberia. If Coppinger exaggerated the contentment of the blacks, there can be no doubt that the political "carn" he found so disgusting had given them the rights and privileges of citizens and a measure of protection for their rights. More than anything else, Liberia was the hope of the dispossessed and the desperate, and for the moment at least, goodly numbers of blacks had substantial reason for thinking they were on a road to freedom and equality of a sort that Coppinger could hardly envision.

In the years from 1820 through 1864, the Colonization Society sent 10,764 blacks to Liberia. From 1865 through 1869, it dispatched 2,394 more. Over the succeeding thirty years it sent only another 2,013. In a practical sense, the African colonization movement was almost dead by 1870, for it no longer had the resources to carry out its purpose. In the 1870s, the society sent an average of only ninety-eight blacks a year, and in the 1880s the figure dropped to seventy-four.[31]

29. William Coppinger to William McLain, August 9, 1869, in CXCVI (140), ACS, LC; Coppinger to McLain, April 12, 1867, in CLXXXVII (71), ACS, LC.

30. Coppinger to McLain, August 9, 1869, in CXCVI (140), ACS, LC; Calvin R. Gerrall to William Coppinger, February 11, 1869, in CXCIV (138), ACS, LC.

31. Figures are calculated from data in *Liberia Bulletin,* February, 1900, p. 28.

At first, the low figures reflected both the dwindling finances of the Colonization Society and the black community's overwhelming lack of interest in emigration, but that soon changed, at least a little. Although the financial health of the society continued to deteriorate, the end of Reconstruction brought an upsurge in black interest concerning Liberia. The society's early postwar activities had planted a hardy seed that would begin to germinate as whites regained power in the South.

As the Reconstruction governments collapsed, Liberia came to hold increasing appeal, especially for blacks at the very bottom of the socioeconomic order. Though the Colonization Society was moribund, its debility was hardly apparent to the poor blacks who eagerly wrote away for its tracts, its pamphlets, and its quarterly journal, the *African Repository*. In a very real sense, those publications, with their message of hope, were the American Colonization Society. Only in Liberia, they proclaimed, could blacks find refuge from racial oppression; only in Liberia could black manhood and black nationality flower.

Thus, ironically, a white racist organization, the American Colonization Society, nurtured black emigrationism and the protonationalistic attitudes associated with it. Even in reduced circumstances, the society remained important in incubating these ideas. The power of the organization stemmed from its ability to offer blacks information about Liberia and about transportation to that country. It was the only organized body, black or white, that could do that.

For the poor farmers who received the society's literature, the arrival of a personally addressed packet of information had a strong impact. When J. A. Holloway, of Houston, Texas, got his materials, he wrote Coppinger, "I cannot Rest for Being ask questions about Liberia and the People a Round me Call a meeting at my House to Know all about the matter." He said that if the society had the right men in Texas "to tend to this Business . . . they would have a mighty host to Leave Texas as soon as they Could leave. i know for it is all the talk since i receive my Package."[32]

Equally important was transportation. If free transportation was essential for black movement into the Lower South, it was even more clearly so for those who wanted to go to Liberia. Bluntly, no trans-

---

32. J. A. Holloway to William Coppinger, December 20, 1883, in CCLIII (256), ACS, LC.

portation, no emigrants. In the years immediately after the war, the society had assisted virtually all the blacks it could find who were willing to go. Long after it lost the capacity to send all who would go, blacks remembered it as the group that had given free transportation. In April, 1875, with the volume of applications for Liberia rising sharply, the society announced that it would give preference to those who could pay part or all of their own expenses. A notice to that effect appeared in most subsequent issues of the *African Repository,* but to the desperate blacks who read the magazine seeking a way out, what counted was the offer of aid, not the qualification.[33]

Though the Colonization Society played a major role in disseminating ideas about emigration, Liberia, and black nationality, others also played a part. From Forten to Delany and Cain, there had always been those in the black community who felt that only exodus could bring freedom. After the war, emigrationists continued to be a minority among black leaders, but Cain and Delany, as well as others like William Whipper and Henry M. Turner, were important within that minority.[34]

Cain and Turner are especially noteworthy. Both became bishops in the A.M.E. church, and both used their church positions to get their message across to large numbers of blacks. Cain's newspaper, the *Missionary Record,* reached a large audience, and by the late 1870s it carried a standing editorial entitled "Ho for Africa! One million men wanted for Africa." As a United States congressman, Cain pressed for the establishment of a regular steamship line between the United States and Liberia to carry mail and emigrants.[35]

But Cain's contributions to the cause of colonization pale by comparison with those of Turner. Born a South Carolina free Negro in 1834, Turner became a traveling evangelist in his early twenties. A highly talented and ambitious man, he early on chafed at the racial barriers that stood in the way of his advancement. In the years just before the Civil War, he, like a number of other gifted blacks of the

---

33. *African Repository,* L (1874)–LVI (1880).

34. *African Repository,* XLV (1869), 264–65; Theodore Draper, *The Rediscovery of Black Nationalism* (New York, 1969), 38–39.

35. Bardolph, *The Negro Vanguard,* 88; *Congressional Record,* 45th Cong., 2nd Sess., 1646; 45th Cong., 3rd Sess., 77. Cain's editorial is quoted by Tindall in *South Carolina Negroes,* 156.

time, became convinced that emigration was the only answer. Then, in 1862, a speech by Crummell brought him to believe that Africa was the place blacks should go.[36]

For some years, Turner blew hot and cold on emigration. During the Civil War, he served as a chaplain for black troops, and it seems that, as the conflict gave promise of bringing equality, his interest in colonization waned. It revived again, though, after the war, as a result of his experiences as a chaplain with the Freedmen's Bureau in Georgia. Even in that organization he found discrimination. On July 18, 1866, he wrote Coppinger, "I became a convert to emigration five weeks ago. I expect to advocate it hereafter as much as I can."[37]

The record is murky, but it does not seem that Turner was very vigorous in his advocacy of emigration for the next few years. Rather, he turned his efforts to organizing the Republican party in Georgia and to building the A.M.E. church. For a time his political efforts were markedly successful. He became the most powerful black leader in Georgia and was elected, first, as a delegate to the constitutional convention of 1867 and, then, as a member of the state legislature. But his strength with the voters came to naught. In September, 1868, the Georgia legislature voted to bar black officeholding, and it expelled all black legislators, including Turner.[38]

As had happened before, Turner found racial prejudice standing squarely athwart the road to success and recognition. As a result, he became, in the words of Edwin S. Redkey, a "bitter disillusioned man." Certain that whites would never permit blacks to share in American society equally, he threw himself back into his church career and into the work of creating an emigration movement with a black nationalist outlook. His skill in building the A.M.E. church led to his rapid rise within the denomination. In 1876, he was given charge of the church's publishing concern, and four years later he was elected one of its twelve bishops. Not enough is known about his election to suggest that his popularity was rooted in his advocacy of emigration and black nationalism, but Cain, who held similar views, was elevated to the rank of bishop at the same time as Turner.[39]

36. Redkey, *Black Exodus*, 24–28.
37. *Ibid.*, 28, 26–27.
38. *Ibid.*, 26–27; Conway, *The Reconstruction of Georgia*, 166–67.
39. Williamson, *After Slavery*, 190; Redkey, *Black Exodus*, 29–30.

In church and at public meetings, in his church paper and in the pages of the *African Repository,* Turner trumpeted a message of anger, despair, and hope. Always outspoken, he never tired of denouncing racial injustice, and he harbored no hope that this wrong could be changed by appeals to fairness and right. "So long as we are a people within a people vastly our superiors in numbers, wealth, & c., having no government of our own," he said, "we shall be nothing, and be so treated by the civilized world." In the land where blacks had been slaves, they could only remain as serfs and second-class citizens, he believed. Nothing, not even the eloquence of a Demosthenes, could change that until blacks themselves won distinction "in manipulating and running the machinery of government." Only nationality would bring "large prosperity and acknowledged manhood to our people," and the nationality that was necessary could be achieved only in a place where blacks were free to rule themselves, a place like Liberia.[40]

Turner fully understood the impracticality of sending any large portion of the black population back to Africa. That was not his purpose. Rather, he sought to send out the best and most skilled to build a "city" upon an African hill, a city that would serve simultaneously as a base for the Christian evangelization of all of Africa and as a homeland where blacks might create a nation that would gain the respect of the world. In the pages of the *Christian Recorder,* he curtly denied that he was advocating a general black exodus from the United States: "Two-thirds of the American Negroes would be of no help to anyone anywhere."[41]

Ironically, it was precisely blacks who "would be of no help to anyone" that were most taken with his message. When Turner said, "If the Colonization Society were able to send them, shipload after shipload might leave every month for Liberia," those people thought he was speaking about them rather than about the most prosperous and skilled members of the black community. Unfortunately for Turner's dream, the very people whose property and talent qualified them as colonists for Liberia were the ones least inclined to go. However much discrimination they suffered, they had some stake in America. The unskilled masses who owned nothing, on the other hand, had less

40. *African Repository,* LII (1876), 85.
41. Quoted by Redkey in *Black Exodus,* 37.

to lose by going, and it was from among them that Turner drew his strongest support.[42]

But the poorest and the least educated were not the only blacks interested in Africa. The violence and repression that accompanied white efforts to end Reconstruction and to put the blacks back in their place were not reserved for the poor and sometimes had the effect of making converts for emigration among property-owning blacks. So it was with the Reverend Elias Hill, of York County, South Carolina, and his followers. Crippled from childhood, Hill was an active Republican supporter who in September, 1871, was interrogated and beaten by a party of Klansmen who accused him of inciting other blacks to commit arson. In consequence of that experience, Hill and sixty families who followed his leadership emigrated to Liberia.[43]

Even before being beaten by the Klan, Hill had been searching for escape from the violence-ridden area in South Carolina where he and his followers lived. He wrote, first, to his congressman, asking about opportunities for blacks in the American West. From the reply, he concluded that "those Western States toward which I had looked are worse plagued than we are," and he sought out information about Liberia. Seven months later he and 165 followers sailed for Africa.[44] As they departed, a local paper commented that the group was "made up of the most industrious negroes in that section of the country, many of whom, since their emancipation, have shown themselves to be thrifty and energetic, and not a few of them had accumulated money."[45]

Whatever the original source of Hill's knowledge about Liberia, it is clear that by the early 1870s the idea of Liberian emigration had developed a life of its own within the black community. Once dependent for its vitality upon the all-white Colonization Society, it now had the support of a handful of influential blacks like Turner and Cain. In addition, discussions of emigration appeared in church papers like the

42. *African Repository,* LII (1876), 86. One of the main conclusions of Redkey's *Black Exodus* is that in the period 1890–1910 the Liberia movement very largely involved the poorest class of blacks. That conclusion appears to hold for the earlier period as well.

43. Trelease, *White Terror,* 362–72.

44. Ku Klux Report, V, 1412; *African Repository,* XLVII (1871), 356–60.

45. Yorkville (S.C.) *Enquirer,* November 2, 1871, quoted by Trelease in *White Terror,* 372.

Christian Recorder and the *Missionary Record*. By the early 1870s, some itinerant preachers and circuit riders were helping to spread word about it. Writing from Elizabeth City, North Carolina, in 1871, a black minister told Coppinger that he had been "holding meetings & addressing the Colered people in parts of Virginia and this state without any authority except [as] I have obtained from my god." The minister reported that at Elizabeth City some blacks had organized themselves into a society "in order to aid each other to emigrate." He had fifty names from Elizabeth City, and he expected to have five hundred from his circuit within six months.[46]

It was, above all else, the collapse of Reconstruction that revitalized the idea of emigration within the black community. Always a minority movement, black emigrationism gained impetus from fears that the end of Reconstruction would bring heightened oppression and perhaps even reenslavement. From 1871 through 1875, the Colonization Society received an average of eighteen letters of application a year. Over the next five years, the annual average was fifty-nine. These figures are more impressive than they seem at first glance, for like Cornelius Reeves in 1866, the great majority of writers spoke on behalf of organized colonization clubs. These ranged in size from five, ten, or fifteen people up into the hundreds.[47]

Sentiment in favor of resettlement in Liberia was especially strong in North and South Carolina at the end of Reconstruction. In 1877, Coppinger received sixteen letters of application from North Carolina and nineteen from South Carolina. A year later the figures were twenty-seven and two respectively.[48] The decline in requests from South Carolina reflects only that South Carolina blacks had begun to organize their own exodus movement.

In 1877, Edgefield County, South Carolina, was one of the most violent places in the South, and blacks there showed a particularly strong desire to go to Liberia. In 1874, local whites had determined to regain full power in the county. They organized themselves into rifle clubs, and nothing less than the arrival of federal troops averted a con-

46. Thomas White to William Coppinger, March 27, 1871, in CCII (333), ACS, LC.

47. Tabulated from data in List of Applicants for Passage to Liberia, 1856–1889 (Series VI, Subject File, ACS, LC).

48. *Ibid.*

flict with an armed black militia. The governor, as a result, ordered the militia disarmed, and the whites were to turn in their guns too. In fact, both sides managed to retain at least a portion of their weaponry, and as later events proved, the whites had considerably more fire-power than the blacks. In July, 1876, at the town of Hamburg, in adjacent Aiken County, whites used a cannon to rout a group of black militiamen from the armory. They captured twenty-nine blacks and shot four of the most prominent in cold blood. Afterward, the rifle clubs in Edgefield, Aiken, and Barnwell counties conducted a campaign of terrorism to prevent black Republicans from participating in the election of 1876.[49]

Defeated at the polls by these tactics, Edgefield blacks found themselves subjected to a steady wave of harassment and violence as whites worked to drive them from public life entirely. On April 11, 1877, one day after President Rutherford B. Hayes withdrew the last federal soldiers from South Carolina, a young black lawyer virtually screamed for a way out. John Mardenborough, a former New Yorker, wrote Coppinger asking that the society aid him and seventy-five local blacks in getting to Liberia. Explaining why they wanted to leave, he said: "Colored men are daily being Hung, Shot and otherwise murdered and ill-treated because of their complexion and politics:—While I write a colored woman comes and tells me her husband was killed last night in her presence by white men and her children burned to death in the house; she says her person was outraged by these men and then she was whipped—such things as these are common occurrences." Then he pleaded, "In the name of God can not the Society send us to Africa or some where else where we can live without ill treatment?"[50]

The words *or some where else* are of crucial importance, for as will become apparent, almost always the goal of black political migration

49. Williamson, *After Slavery,* 267–69; Vernon Burton, "Race and Reconstruction: Edgefield County, South Carolina," *Journal of Social History,* XII (1978), 31–56. On violence in South Carolina, and particularly on violence in Edgefield County and the surrounding area, see *South Carolina in 1876: Testimony as to the Denial of the Elective Franchise in South Carolina at the Elections of 1875 and 1876,* 3 vols., 44th Cong., 2nd Sess., Senate Miscellaneous Document No. 48.

50. John Mardenborough to American Colonization Society, April 11, 1877, in CCXXVII (29), ACS, LC.

was escape in general rather than arrival at some specific place like Liberia or Kansas. Mardenborough worked actively in the weeks that followed his appeal in order to organize the movement. By April 30, he was predicting that he could "get nearly the whole of Edgefield County to leave." He asked for three hundred circulars to send to friends in adjacent counties. By early June, he had succeeded in getting 356 Edgefield blacks to sign up for Africa.[51] It was an impressive figure representing about 1 percent of the black population of the county.

Elsewhere in the county, at least one other group of blacks was considering emigration. In June, 1877, the Colonization Society received an inquiry from Bird Stevens, who lived "high up in the county . . . in a settlement very thick settled with colored people." Describing himself as a "leader of my race in this portion of the country," Stevens said that he had been instructed by the leading men "of our party" to find out about Liberia. He said that the people in his area were anxious to go there and wanted to know "what assistance the colonization Society will give them."[52]

By July, Mardenborough had left Edgefield County for Beaufort, and it seems a good guess that he fled in fear of his life. He had convinced Harrison N. Bouey, a black Edgefield probate judge, of the wisdom of emigrating, but with Mardenborough gone, Bouey was, according to his own description, the "only colored man who dares to say what he desires." Bouey asserted that "you rarely meet a color'd man that does not want to go" to Liberia, and he added that "they are likely to retain this disposition to go until they find that they cannot get off."[53]

It must have been precisely the desperate desire of blacks to move that alarmed local whites. In an effort to prevent the freedmen from leaving, planters began to pay them in certificates good at local stores

51. John Mardenborough to William Coppinger, April 30, 1877, in CCXXVII (86), ACS, LC; John Mardenborough to William Coppinger, May 15, 1877, in CCXXVII (122), ACS, LC; John Mardenborough to William Coppinger, June 6, 1877, in CCXXVII (176), ACS, LC.

52. Bird Stevens to William Coppinger, June 4, 1877, in CCXXVII (169), ACS, LC.

53. Harrison N. Bouey to William Coppinger, July 10, 1877, in CCXXVIII (21), ACS, LC; Harrison N. Bouey to William Coppinger, May 23, 1877, in CCXXVII (141), ACS, LC.

rather than in cash. Bouey tried to answer the white opposition to emigration by arguing that it was the duty of whites to contribute to the Christianization of Africa. He asked Coppinger to send the appropriate literature for making his case.[54] Given the climate of opinion in Edgefield, it is doubtful that Bouey persuaded many.

The judge may have had a genuine concern to Christianize Africa, or he may merely have been trying to ingratiate himself with the old colonizationist. He did say, "I do not sir, propose leaving with any bad spirit towards the white people of America, but to thank them for what they have done for me and my race." He expressed the opinion that the upheaval of the time was caused by the "political and general mistreatment" of blacks, "but I advise them to take it all quietly and Christianly, for I believe God is in the move."[55] On the same day that he wrote to Coppinger, he sent a very different letter to Turner. Maintaining that he would rather die than compromise with racial injustice, Bouey said: "You may not know me, but I have seen you, and know you too well to undertake to tell you, anything, of our humiliations socially and degradation politically, and our afflictions financially, in the South. We have no chance to rise from begars." Elaborating on the hopeless condition of the blacks, he wrote: "Men own the capital that we work, who believe that they have a right to either us or our value from the general government. Hence they believe that my race have no more right to any of the profits of their labor than one of their mules—the majority of colored men who work with these heartless democrats get just about what the mule gets of the profits of labor."[56] Bouey predicted that in five years the public schools of the South would be closed to blacks because "education makes unprofitable labor in the south—hence my people must, and will, be kept ignorant."[57] There was in all this not a word of concern for the heathen of Africa but, rather, deep bitterness toward southern whites. Indeed, it was the same sort of bitterness that Turner himself expressed and that rang so many chords among the poor blacks of the South.

54. Bouey to Coppinger, July 10, 1877, in CCXXVIII (21), ACS, LC.
55. Bouey to Coppinger, May 23, 1877, in CCXXVII (141), ACS, LC.
56. Harrison N. Bouey to Rev. H. M. Turner, May 23, 1877, in CCXXVII (142), ACS, LC.
57. Ibid.

Everywhere, the end of Reconstruction provoked blacks to ask whether they could survive and prosper under the new order created by the Redeemers. In the northern portion of South Carolina, June Mobley, a black from Union County, traveled from place to place arguing that the two races could not live as equals unless the freedmen were allowed to own land. Mobley's position was that since the whites would hardly allow that, the blacks had to consider emigration. As a result of these and other appeals, Coppinger received a spate of new correspondence from South Carolina. By the end of 1877, he had on hand communications from parties of blacks in Barnwell, Aiken, Union, Fairfield, Abbeville, Sumter, Laurens, Richland, and Chesterfield counties.[58]

About the same time, an autonomous, all-black Liberia front was developing in South Carolina. In July, 1876, J. C. Hazely, a Liberian agent of the American Colonization Society, spent the month delivering a series of lectures in Charleston. On July 26, with enthusiasm rising, four thousand of the city's blacks joined in a celebration of Liberian independence, at which the Reverend B. F. Porter proposed that a corporation be created for the purpose of transporting blacks to Africa. His suggestion led to the formation of the Liberian Exodus Joint Steamship Company. Serving with Porter as a sponsor of the new venture was Bouey, who, it appears, had been forced out of Edgefield County. The enterprise soon had the important support of Martin Delany and Henry Turner. The initial plan was to capitalize the company at $300,000, but the poverty of the South Carolina black community made that unrealistic. By January, 1878, despite considerable agitation, the sponsors of the project had sold only six thousand dollars' worth of stock.[59]

In the meantime, enthusiasm for Liberia continued to grow, and up-country blacks began arriving in Charleston ready to leave at once. Money or not, the directors of the corporation had to act if they were to maintain their credibility. In February, 1878, they purchased the bark *Azor*. A month later the ship was consecrated at ceremonies at-

58. Tindall, *South Carolina Negroes*, 158–59; List of Applicants for Passage to Liberia, ACS, LC.

59. Tindall, *South Carolina Negroes*, 154–56.

tended by five thousand blacks, including such notables as Delany and Turner.[60]

Unlike the agitation in the countryside, the speeches at this affair emphasized black nationalism and missionary work among the heathen of Africa more than domestic persecution. Turner pledged that the work begun at Charleston "would never stop until the blaze of Gospel truth should glitter over the whole broad African continent." The voyage of the *Azor* was, in his view, a first step toward developing a sense of nationality for blacks. Negroes, he said, were the only people "who had imbibed enough of the prejudices of those among whom [they] lived to despise and deny [their] own race."[61] Nevertheless, the people leaving for Africa were going more to escape southern persecution than to light either the lamp of the gospel for the heathen or the lamp of nationality for the blacks they left behind.

In April, 1878, the *Azor* sailed for Liberia carrying 206 emigrants. Another 175 were told they had to await the next sailing, but that voyage never came off. Plagued by insufficient funds and inexperienced management, the Liberian Exodus Joint Steamship Company became a disaster for all concerned. On the first and only voyage of the *Azor,* the ship's physician proved to have no medical training. He had assumed the title simply to get the boat through customs. Twenty-three persons died on the trip without competent medical attention. Short of funds, the company cut corners everywhere. On board ship, food was scanty and barely edible. Once in Monrovia, the emigrants found that they had supplies for three weeks rather than for the six months they had counted on.[62]

By December, 1879, nineteen emigrants had returned to the United States. Some declared that none of the *Azor* party would remain if they could afford the cost back to the United States. There was probably exaggeration in that. Certainly, some of the *Azor's* passengers achieved considerable success in Liberia. On the whole, though, the expedition was a terrible failure. The company's managers immediately began to lay plans for a second trip, but as they did, they were

60. *Ibid.*, 160.
61. Charleston (S.C.) *News and Courier,* March 22, 1878.
62. Tindall, *South Carolina Negroes,* 161–63.

deluged with bills from the first voyage. In November, 1879, the *Azor* was sold at auction to meet the company's debts.[63]

Whenever it becomes known that conditions at a destination may well be worse than at home, migration there stops. Few will travel long distances if there is a good chance that their movement will worsen their lot in life.[64] The return of some of the *Azor* emigrants and the discouraging letters from others did much to dampen for some years the ardor of blacks in South Carolina for Liberia.

In South Carolina, the Liberia cause was led by prominent blacks like Cain, Delany, and Turner. Elsewhere in the South, however, it tended to be a grass-roots interest arising out of the discontent of the poorest segment on the black community. That seems to have been especially true in the region around Shreveport, in northwestern Louisiana, where Henry Adams, a laboring man who became a prominent figure in local black affairs and the Republican party, led the emigration cause.

Testifying before a Senate committee, Adams told of how in December, 1870, he and other black former soldiers had organized a secret group to find out about the conditions under which southern blacks were living and to determine "whether we could remain in the South . . . or not." Focusing on those who labored in the fields rather than on more privileged members of black society, the organization operated on the premise that "you can't find out anything until you get amongst [ordinary working people;] you have got to go right into the field with them and sleep with them to know all about them."[65]

---

63. *Ibid.*, 163–65. The auction sale was intended only as a temporary expedient, but as a result of the duplicity of the white merchant who bought the *Azor*, the ship was lost permanently.

64. The literature of migration is vast. Some articles with a theoretical thrust that have been valuable in shaping my understanding of this subject: E. G. Ravenstein, "The Laws of Migration," *Journal of the Royal Statistical Society*, XLVIII (1885), 167–227, LII (1889), 241–301; Larry A. Sjaastad, "The Costs and Returns of Human Migration," *Journal of Political Economy*, LXX (1962), 80–93; Everett S. Lee, "A Theory of Migration," *Demography*, III (1966), 47–57. See also the less theoretical migration articles cited above in Chapter 4, *n*21.

65. *Report and Testimony of the Select Committee of the United States Senate to Investigate the Causes of the Removal of the Negroes from the Southern States to the Northern States,*

According to Adams, the secret committee had 500 members and, of these, 100 or 150 had spread across the South to learn how other blacks were faring in freedom. Their findings were uniformly discouraging. Despite emancipation, blacks were still oppressed everywhere in the South.[66] It is difficult to know just how much credence to give Adams' account of what the committee had discovered. The cheating of blacks and the violence toward them that he complained of were certainly real enough, but in the light of subsequent events it is difficult to credit his organization with having the skills and resources needed for an accurate survey of the conditions that it was investigating.

Be that as it may, blacks in northwestern Louisiana had good reason for grave concern about the direction of events in 1874, for white conservatives were becoming ever more aggressive. In March, 1874, sensing that the time was right for a reassertion of control, whites began organizing locally based White Leagues, with the aim of driving Republicans from government and intimidating the black population. By August, the White League in the Shreveport area was fairly strong, and at the end of the month the infamous Coushatta Massacre took place in adjoining Red River Parish.[67]

By mid-September, 1874, Adams and his associates had reacted to the epidemic of violence with a mass meeting, where they called into being a new organization, the Colonization Council. In a petition signed by one thousand blacks, the Louisiana freedmen asked President Ulysses S. Grant to remove them to a territory "where they could live by themselves." They said it was "utterly impossible to live with the whites of Louisiana" and expressed a willingness to go to Liberia "if no better place could be given them."[68]

All along, the Grant administration had been vacillating in its re-

---

3 parts, 46th Cong., 2nd Sess., Senate Report No. 693, II, 101–102 (hereafter cited as Senate Report on the Exodus).

66. *Ibid.,* II, 102, 103.

67. Joe Gray Taylor, *Louisiana Reconstructed,* 279–91.

68. New York *Herald,* September 19, 1874; Senate Report on the Exodus, II, 104, 105, 127, 158–59. The petition was received by the House on January 15, 1875, and was then sent to the Committee on Freedmen's Affairs (*Congressional Record,* House, 43rd Cong., 2nd Sess., 517).

sponse to southern violence. It faced a dilemma. It was inconceivable that the general government could fail to protect its citizens against the kind of violence that had taken place at Coushatta. It was also inconceivable that American democracy could long endure if military rule remained a permanent condition of life. Grant was disturbed by the direction of events. He was concerned, too, by the political reality that in Louisiana, lawlessness had reached the point where the conservatives were on the verge of taking forcible control of the state government.[69]

On September 15, 1874, the governor of Louisiana wired the president for federal troops to put down the violence. Grant responded immediately, and by the end of September the 7th Cavalry was establishing itself in the northern part of the state. A little later, the president sent General Philip Sheridan on an inspection tour, instructing him to take personal command where he felt it necessary. That Sheridan did in early January, 1875, when the conservatives moved to seize control of the legislature. The next day, he told the secretary of war that the situation in the South was so bad that Congress should declare the white terrorists in Louisiana, Arkansas, and Mississippi "banditti" who could be arrested, tried, and punished by the military authorities.[70]

For Adams and the blacks of the Shreveport area, the publication of Sheridan's sentiments must have seemed a vindication of their faith in the federal government. For southern whites, on the other hand, it seemed almost a declaration of war, and pretending that violence against blacks was quite exceptional, they protested mightily at an abuse of their constitutional rights.

Sheridan's letter to the secretary of war brought an important issue into relief: To what extent were Americans willing to see traditional constitutional liberties set aside in order to protect the rights of the black minority? Reconstruction had dragged on for ten years, and in

---

69. William S. McFeely, *Grant*, 416–18; Joe Gray Taylor, *Louisiana Reconstructed*, 287–94.

70. Joe Gray Taylor, *Louisiana Reconstructed*, 305–306; Lieut. Gen. P. H. Sheridan to W. W. Belknap, secretary of war (Copy), January 5, 1878, War Department Communications to the Department of Justice, Box 67, in Department of Justice, Source-Chronological Files, National Archives, Washington, D.C., Record Group 60 (hereafter cited as DJ Source-Chron Files, NA).

the North as well as the South there was a growing feeling that unlimited martial law—and that is what Sheridan seemed to be asking
for—was an unacceptable solution to America's racial problems.[71]

Stung by the storm of criticism that followed the publication of his
letter, Sheridan set out to document the full extent of political and
racial violence in Louisiana. He ordered his subordinates to prepare a
list, with specific detail, of the outrages that had occurred in the state
in the years since 1868. The orders from his headquarters intimated
that the accuracy of the list was less important than its length and the
speed with which it was compiled, and they suggested the "intelligent
negroes" of the community as the best sources of information. That
is how, in March, 1875, Adams came to be a spy for the army.

Concentrating his effort largely in Caddo, Bossier, and DeSoto
parishes, Adams appears to have gone from one place to another gathering accounts of outrages and occasionally taking sworn affidavits
from the victims. He submitted his final report on July 12, 1875, and
it consisted largely of the raw notes he took as he moved from one
cabin to another. The form and content of the notes show that he was
adhering closely to the reporting guidelines that Sheridan's headquarters had set in January. For each incident, he tried to give the names of
victim and assailant, as well as the date, place, and nature of the occurrence. Typical of the many incidents Adams reported were these
from DeSoto Parish:

> 1. Lewis Woods, shot by white men on Dr. Alleson's place, 1874. 2. Simms
> Gilling, shot by white men on Frank Williams's place, about voting a Re-
> publican ticket, 1868. . . . 14. Sam. Dales killed by white men on Wiley
> Frankes' place, 1868.[72]

71. For an excellent discussion of the practical limits of using military force for the
protection of civil rights in a democratic nation in the 1870s, see LaWanda Cox, *Lincoln
and Black Freedom: A Study in Presidential Leadership* (Columbia, S.C., 1981), 165–69.
The role of the army is described in detail by Joseph G. Dawson III in *Army Generals
and Reconstruction: Louisiana, 1862–1877* (Baton Rouge, 1982).

72. *Use of the Army in Certain of the Southern States,* 44th Cong., 2nd Sess., House
Executive Document No. 30, pp. 431, 409–50, 542–46 (hereafter cited as HXD 30);
Senate Report on the Exodus, II, 192–214. In both these government documents, the
format of Adams' reports makes little sense unless the reports are understood as a tran-
scription of his raw notes. Such an interpretation is confirmed in Senate Report on the
Exodus, II, 124, 155.

In 1876, the government published Adams' materials, and the hundreds of outrages and murders they catalog remain today a terrible indictment of southern brutality during Reconstruction. In a sworn statement, Adams attested to having received the names of 1,645 victims; his raw data, however, refer to only about two-thirds that many.[73] The discrepancy indicates Adams' unreliability in making numerical estimates, but it does nothing to alter the picture of horrendous violence which the case histories he collected yield. Moreover, his data comport well with what is known independently of the nature and extent of the violence directed against blacks in northern Louisiana during the Reconstruction era.[74]

The experience of working for the army must have given Adams confidence that, bad as conditions were, the government really was trying to make them right. Imagine, then, his reaction once it became clear, in early 1877, that the soldiers who had come in 1874 were to be withdrawn and that Louisiana whites were to be free to arrange matters to their own liking. For the blacks of Shreveport who had been contemplating emigration in 1874, that was the last straw. It was then, Adams explained, that "we lost all hopes" and concluded "that there was no way on earth . . . that we could better our condition" in the South.[75]

In a series of meetings, Adams and his group went over and over the matter, but there was no escaping the fact that the whole South "had got into the hands of the very men that held us slaves."[76] Thus it was that on July 9, 1877, the group petitioned President Hayes for a "territory to our Selves." It was a document of desperation that claimed to speak particularly for the black laboring men of the South. At one point the petition said: "We are the tillers of the Soil. We Suffer all. We need friends."[77]

Twice the petitioners called for the government to give them either their rights or a territory to themselves, but it was rights, not territory, that they craved. They complained that blacks were cheated at

73. HXD 30, p. 416.

74. Joe Gray Taylor, *Louisiana Reconstructed*, 284–85, 297–99, 420–21.

75. Senate Report on the Exodus, II, 108.

76. *Ibid.*

77. Petition from Henry Adams and Others to President Rutherford B. Hayes, July 9, 1877 (Box 5, President, DJ Source-Chron Files, NA).

the ballot box and on the farm and that they were denied justice by the very men who had held them slaves. Only in the event that the government did not help them regain their rights, they asked it to "appropriate Money to Send us Back to our own land," that is, Liberia, or to give them a "Territory to our selves."[78]

The petition contained 3,186 male names, including that of Adams. Many of the names clustered together by surname, and it seems clear that those who signed did so in family groups. If one takes account of the women and children, whose names did not appear on the petition, the document can be seen as reflecting the feelings of perhaps ten thousand people. The petition claimed an even larger base saying, "We have 25,000 both men and women ready signed, ready to be forwarded to you."[79]

Adams and his group were in earnest about leaving the country, and on August 31 he applied to the American Colonization Society on behalf of sixty-nine thousand men and women who wished "to be colonized in Liberia or some other country." Of these, two-thirds wanted to go to Liberia. Speaking for the society, Coppinger replied that applications were so numerous that it would be "some time before your case will in turn be reached and acted upon." In the meantime, he counseled the Shreveport blacks to raise all the money possible for going to Africa and to petition Congress to appropriate money for Liberian emigration.[80]

On September 15, 1877, Adams' group held another mass meeting. The organization claimed the meeting was attended by five thousand persons representing "29,000 colored people in the South." Again the blacks petitioned the president for aid in escaping the South, and again they produced an ambivalent document showing that what they really wanted was a redress of their grievances in Louisiana and that emigration was a last resort in the event "that protection cannot be given."[81]

Sentiment in favor of settlement in Liberia peaked in northwestern Louisiana with the mid-September meeting. The blacks had writ-

78. *Ibid.*

79. *Ibid.*

80. William Coppinger to Henry Adams, September 10, 1877, in LS, XXVIII, Part 1, p. 148, ACS, LC; Henry Adams to John H. B. Latrobe, August 31, 1877, in CCXXVIII (170), ACS, LC.

81. Senate Report on the Exodus, II, 156, 155.

ten to the American Colonization Society hoping to get immediate transportation assistance. What they got instead was advice that they should collect dues, stay organized, and send out a few migrants every year. Adams wrote back that his society was doing well but that it was not collecting dues on a weekly or monthly basis because "this is A Herible [horrible?] Part of the country and our Race cannot get money for our Labor ever[y] week Nor ever[y] month."[82]

In the weeks that followed, Adams and Coppinger corresponded extensively. Adams spoke eagerly of sending a party of commissioners to Liberia to scout out the land. Coppinger responded with helpful suggestions about how the blacks might raise money. Always encouraging, he nonetheless made it clear that the Louisiana blacks would have to pay for sending their commissioners. By December, he must have known that the mission would never be. On January 6, 1878, the American Colonization Council, which claimed seventy-one thousand supporters, had a treasury of only two hundred dollars, and Adams was estimating that perhaps one-third were still firm for the cause.[83]

But Adams' numbers rarely reflected reality, and there is no reason to think that this estimate was any better. In 1880, he told the Senate committee on the exodus of 1879 that his emigration organization had ninety-eight thousand persons enrolled for colonization and that most came from Louisiana, with the rest from Texas, Arkansas, Mississippi, and Alabama.[84] Ninety-eight thousand was equivalent to one-fifth of the black population of Louisiana in 1880. Adams' count would be enormously impressive if true, for it would indicate the existence of a massive organization among the poor blacks of Louisiana. But it was not true. Adams appears to have taken the number out of

82. Henry Adams to William Carpenter [Coppinger], September 24, 1877, in CCXXVIII (251), ACS, LC; Coppinger to Adams, September 10, 1877, in LS, XXVIII, Part 1, p. 148, ACS, LC.

83. Henry Adams to William Coppinger, January 6, 1878, in CCXXX (26), ACS, LC; William Coppinger to Henry Adams, October 1, October 12, 1877, both in LS, XXVIII, Part 1, ACS, LC. See also Adams' letters to Coppinger dated October 8, November 5, December 10, and December 19, 1877, all of which are in Vol. CCXXIX, ACS, LC (Nos. 26, 149, 291, 340). The figure of 71,000 appears at the end of a petition Adams enclosed with his letter of January 6, 1878.

84. Senate Report on the Exodus, II, 110.

thin air. In letters and petitions, he had made a variety of claims concerning the number of people who had signed up for colonization: 25,000, on July 9, 1877; 69,000, on August 31, 1877; 29,000, on September 15, 1877; 33,000, on September 24, 1877; 71,000, on January 6, 1878; and 98,000, on March 12, 1880.[85] The pattern makes no sense, especially in view of the evidence that enthusiasm for emigration to Liberia began to wane after September, 1877. Moreover, Adams sometimes made numerical assertions that were patently false. At one point, he proclaimed personal knowledge that in 1865, after slavery ended, "over two thousand colored people [were] killed trying to get away," and the petition of July 9, 1877, contained the pronouncement that "nearly half a Million blacks" had been killed for their beliefs.[86] What can be said with some certainty is that if the petition of July 9, 1877, really represented all the persons whose names appeared on it, the group probably involved about ten thousand blacks when family members are included.

Although the Louisiana colonization enterprise was clearly much more modest than Adams' numbers would imply, it was a genuine cry of pain from poor blacks who had abandoned hope of finding freedom in the United States. The situation was the same in many places across the South, but only rarely did the colonization groups that arose in response to despair succeed in sending even a few hundred emigrants to Africa. Everywhere, blacks planning to leave the South found themselves stymied by organizational inexperience and by the hard fact that the great majority of them did not have enough money to go anywhere.

85. The figure of 33,000 is from Adams to Carpenter [Coppinger], September 24, 1877, in CCXXVIII (251), ACS, LC. The remaining numbers have been documented above.

86. Senate Report on the Exodus, II, 192; Petition from Henry Adams and Others to President Rutherford B. Hayes, July 9, 1877.

7

THE KANSAS DREAM

The despair that led some blacks to organize for emigration to Africa brought others to hope that they might find freedom in Kansas. In important ways the two colonization attempts were alike. Both involved a migration goal that was more political than economic, and both were doomed to founder on the poverty of their members. In addition, both movements came to naught because there was not enough economic opportunity at the destination to sustain a migration of impoverished farmers who were used to working under very different conditions. The two enterprises were similar also in appealing primarily to the poorest segment of the black community. Generally, those who opted for either Africa or Kansas had the idea that an exodus for any place was better than staying in the South. As a result, when one of the two havens appeared unreachable, some who were interested in settling there simply chose the other destination as their goal.

The story of the Kansas exodus may appear simple enough, but it is in fact sufficiently tangled that evidence that some blacks wanted to leave the South for Kansas sometimes gets transmuted into the impression that a large migration from the Lower South actually occurred. As enthusiasm for emigration to Kansas gathered strength, it captured the attention of planters who feared losing their labor, of black leaders who saw an opportunity to show the nation the extent of white oppression in the South, and of politicians from both parties who sensed a chance to push toward their own ends. By and large, then, the historical record is weighted heavily with the opinions of people seeking to interpret and deal with an event that their wishes or fears magnified into an emerging mass migration from the Deep South.[1]

As Table 6 suggests, however, the migration itself was not very large. The total black influx into Kansas *throughout the 1870s* can hardly have numbered much more than twenty-five thousand, and it appears that most of the blacks who made it to Kansas came from Kentucky, Tennessee, and Missouri, rather than from the Deep South. Louisiana looms large in the traditional story of the exodus, but figures concerning states of birth show that in 1880, after the exodus had peaked, there were only 1,300 Louisiana-born blacks in Kansas.[2]

To the extent that there was a significant population movement to Kansas at this time, it came from the western border states, not from the Deep South. And yet, most accounts of the Exodus of 1879 pay relatively little attention to the specifics of the border-state migration, preferring instead to assume that whatever was pushing blacks out of the Deep South was causing them to flee the border states as well.[3] There has been some justification for focusing on the Deep South. Although few blacks left that region, a wave of sentiment favoring colonization did touch it in 1879, and it is worth asking why the mood for exodus developed just then and why it abated before it fairly got started. Of special interest is the question of whether the migration

---

1. For the purposes of this chapter the Deep South is defined as including the states of Mississippi, Louisiana, Texas, Arkansas, and Alabama.

2. A host of questions can be raised about the meaning of the census data. Some blacks may have come to Kansas and then returned to Louisiana before the census of 1880 was taken. Some migrants from Louisiana may not have been counted as such because they had been imported into Louisiana as slaves from places like Virginia and Maryland and were listed by the census as natives of those states. Such issues are discussed in Appendix B, "The Extent of the Exodus to Kansas, 1870–1880," but no matter how one juggles the numbers in Table 6, they show that the overall migration was rather small and that movement from Louisiana and other Deep South states was even smaller.

3. This lack of attention to the western border states is a consequence of the fact that there are very few local studies of the exodus from those states. A monograph concentrating on this subject is badly needed.

TABLE 6

State or Region of Birth of U.S.-Born Blacks
Living in Kansas, 1870, 1880, and 1890

STATE OR REGION OF BIRTH	1870	1880	1890
Kentucky	2,360	6,985	7,220
Tennessee	696	5,418	6,235
Missouri	5,924	6,488	6,925
Subtotal	8,980	18,891	20,380
Alabama	168	854	793
Mississippi	132	2,776	1,780
Louisiana	98	1,300	846
Texas	178	2,464	1,565
Arkansas	893	768	572
Indian Territory/Oklahoma	352	355	519
Subtotal	1,821	8,517	6,075
Delaware	5	10	7
District of Columbia	23	29	32
Maryland	121	214	224
Virginia	1,142	1,844	1,643
North Carolina	420	842	760
South Carolina	74	384	349
Georgia	127	532	480
Florida	4	33	31
West Virginia	—	32	47
Subtotal	1,916	3,920	3,573
Unknown	10	0	670
Southern total	12,717	31,328	30,028
North and West[a]	532	1,550	1,542
Kansas	3,797	10,921	17,425
U.S. total	17,056	43,799	49,665

SOURCES: U.S. Census Office, *The Statistics of the Population of the United States* (1872),
328–35; U.S. Census Office, *The Statistics of the Population of the United States at the Tenth Census,
June 1, 1880* (Washington, D.C., 1883), 488–91, Vol. I of *Tenth Census [1880]*; U.S. Census Office,
Compendium of the Eleventh Census, 1890 (Washington, D.C., 1897), III, 32–37.

[a] United States citizens born abroad or at sea are included here.

was in any way the result of Republican machinations. The Democrats charged as much, but they had a political agenda of their own, being concerned to show that all was sweetness and light between the races and that southern blacks were not terrorized or oppressed. This chapter will be concerned with exploring the roots of a migration that never really took hold but that had large political implications.

Well before 1879, Kansas was a focal point for discontented blacks. As early as 1869, handfuls of blacks here and there across the South had been championing the land of John Brown as a place to escape oppression. Kansas came to mind in that respect both because of the state's antebellum history and because railroad building there drew black laborers from Tennessee who spread word of the rich western lands available for settlement. What is more, the railroads and land promoters were boosting the area in their search for white settlers. It was natural that the stories of rich land available on easy terms would appeal to blacks as well as whites.[4]

As early as September, 1869, Randall Brown organized an emigration society at Nashville, Tennessee, to enable local blacks to seek freedom in Kansas, Nebraska, and the Indian Territory. In Alabama in early 1871, ninety-eight black farmers formed the Alabama Negro Labor Union to consider the plight of black workers in their state. Though most of the Alabamians were unenthusiastic about migrating, a vocal minority believed that the only cure for the economic and social inequities blacks faced was removal to the "broad and free West." In deference to that viewpoint, the group delegated its president, George F. Marlowe, to find out about opportunities for blacks in Kansas.[5]

When the organization met in January, 1872, Marlowe gave a glowing account. He said schools and railroads were everywhere and that blacks could get land for $1.25 an acre. The convention adopted his report, but the paucity of subsequent black migration from Alabama

---

4. Walter L. Fleming, "'Pap' Singleton, the Moses of the Colored Exodus," *American Journal of Sociology*, XV (1909), 64; Ray Allen Billington, *Westward Expansion: A History of the American Frontier* (4th ed.; New York, 1974), 614–16.

5. Alrutheus A. Taylor, *The Negro in Tennessee, 1865–1880* (Washington, D.C., 1941), 110; Senate Report on the Exodus, III, 136–37. The quotation is given by Loren Schweninger in *James T. Rapier and Reconstruction* (Chicago, 1978), 88.

to Kansas makes it appear that most of those present agreed with the delegate Robert H. Knox, of Montgomery, who urged them to "rest here a while longer," trusting in God and the federal government for the protection to which, "as citizens and *men,* we are entitled." He conceded, however, that if such protection was not forthcoming, it would be time to "desert the State and seek homes elsewhere."[6]

When white Kansans first learned that blacks were taking an interest in their state, some responded with words of welcome. In 1871, after hearing reports that four parties of southern blacks were organizing to establish colonies in the state, the Fort Scott *Monitor* endorsed their emigration, saying, "It is a very wise move on their part, and will be of great benefit to Kansas." The newspaper claimed that in Kansas they would face "no obstacle to impede their progress, or to seriously interfere with their happiness and prosperity," and it concluded, "For their own sake and ours we welcome them to Kansas." Only a few blacks can have seen these remarks when they first appeared, but the editorial got a far wider readership when it was reprinted in a Washington-based black newspaper, the *New National Era.*[7]

Three weeks later the *New National Era* wrote its own editorial, urging the "large number" of southern blacks who owned their own farm to "sell out . . . and strike for the West." There, like foreign immigrants, they could settle a quarter section and go to work, sending south for friends and relatives when they needed help. In the West, they would have freedom from Klan outrages and would no longer have to suffer the "blighting influence of the prejudice and hate now so wickedly brought to bear on the colored race of the South."[8]

These editorials may or may not have marked the first time blacks had been urged to go to Kansas. What is clear is that by 1871 Kansas was coming to occupy a place in black thought as a refuge from oppression. One black who may have been affected by the early news about Kansas was Benjamin ("Pap") Singleton, of Tennessee, who later credited himself with being the "whole cause of the Kansas immigration."[9] Born a slave in Tennessee in 1809, Singleton had run away to freedom in the North but returned to his native state after the

6. Senate Report on the Exodus, III, 138, 137.
7. *New National Era,* August 24, 1871.
8. *Ibid.,* September 14, 1871.
9. Senate Report on the Exodus, III, 382.

war. He settled at Edgefield, across the river from Nashville, and worked as a carpenter and coffin maker. Deeply concerned about the fate of his race, he, like Henry Adams, had little use for the established black leadership. He mistrusted educated black men and believed that landownership held the key to black happiness and prosperity.[10] In 1869, he formed the Tennessee Real Estate and Homestead Association, and a later testimonial from several Kansas notables holds that the work of fostering black emigration to Kansas began with that. Still, it is probable that Singleton's initial enterprise was created solely to encourage black landownership within Tennessee. But the price of land within Tennessee was simply too high for blacks to afford, and the plan did not get very far. At some time in the early 1870s, Singleton began to turn his attention to Kansas.[11]

The timing of Singleton's activities with regard to Kansas in the early 1870s is murky, but this much is certain: at some time early in the decade, he traveled to Kansas, and in September, 1874, he and several associates formed the Edgefield Real Estate Association. A short time later, Singleton planted the Baxter Springs colony in Cherokee County, Kansas. It was established in 1875 or 1876 and had a population of about three hundred.[12]

Superficially, Singleton's colonizing efforts resembled those of other western land promoters. He organized real-estate associations, publicized the virtues of the lands he was seeking to settle, and personally shepherded his colonists to their new home in the West. Still, there was a world of difference between Singleton and his white counterparts. There is no evidence that his associations were profit making or even that they were intended to be. His associations had the sound of other real estate speculations, but were in fact ventures in political migration. At meetings and picnics that were heavily laden with appeals to racial solidarity, he gathered recruits and solicited funds.[13]

By 1876, with momentum building among Tennessee blacks, Sin-

10. Nell Painter, *Exodusters: The Black Migration to Kansas After Reconstruction* (New York, 1977), 108–11.

11. *Ibid.,* 109–13; Fleming, "'Pap' Singleton," 63–65.

12. Painter, *Exodusters,* 113, 114; Senate Report on the Exodus, III, 391; Robert G. Athearn, *In Search of Canaan: Black Migration to Kansas, 1879–80* (Lawrence, Kans., 1978), 76–77, 288–89n.

13. Painter, *Exodusters,* 114–15.

gleton wrote the governor of Kansas that he could raise from one to three thousand colonists by the fall. He asked about the terms for acquiring land, and he requested help toward defraying the cost of transportation and resettlement. He said that his people were "bound to leave this state fast[,] as soon as we can get a Way[,] for Starvation is Staring us in the face."[14] Though he got no funds from the governor in 1877 or 1878, Singleton succeeded in founding the Dunlap colony in Morris County, Kansas. The new settlement had eight hundred inhabitants.[15]

Altogether, Singleton brought at least 1,100 blacks from Tennessee to Kansas in the years before 1879. Indirectly, he may have brought many more. He told the Senate committee on the exodus that he spent six hundred dollars "flooding the country with circulars."[16] He claimed that his broadsides urging emigration to Kansas had gone to "Mississippi, Alabama, South Carolina, Georgia, Kentucky, Virginia, North Carolina, Texas, Tennessee and all those countries." He put his circulars into the hands of "every man that would come into my country," and he gave them to "the boys that started from my country on the boats, and the porters on the cars."[17]

Still, Singleton and his associates were not the only ones encouraging black emigration to Kansas. Nicodemus, the most famous of the Kansas black colonies, grew out of a collaboration between W. R. Hill, a white land developer, and three Topeka blacks who had gone there from Kentucky in 1874. In July, 1877, one of the three, the Reverend Simon Roundtree, issued a circular inviting the "colored people of the United States" to settle in the "Great Solomon Valley of Western Kansas." In August, Hill, working closely with a number of black ministers, traveled through Scott and Fayette counties in Kentucky speaking before church groups and telling of the great opportunities available in Kansas.[18]

The mission was a success, and in early September three hundred colonists from the vicinity of Fayette went to Kansas. Before leaving,

14. Quoted *ibid.*, 114.
15. Athearn, *In Search of Canaan*, 77.
16. Senate Report on the Exodus, III, 380.
17. *Ibid.*, 382, 381.
18. Glen Schwendemann, "Nicodemus: Negro Haven on the Solomon," *Kansas Historical Quarterly*, XXIV (1968), 13–14.

they organized themselves into a colony, which they invited others to join. Their appeal began,

ALL COLORED PEOPLE

that want to

GO TO KANSAS

on September 5, 1877

CAN DO SO FOR $5.00.

Like most emigration handbills, the one bearing this message was completely apolitical, focusing simply on the opportunity to file for the "abundance of choice land now belonging to the government."[19] Altogether, Nicodemus attracted about six or seven hundred colonists in 1877 and 1878. Over 530 came from Kentucky. Caught up in the enthusiasm over the colony, 157 blacks from Fayette and Scott counties, in Kentucky, attempted to build the Morton City colony near Kinsley, Kansas. Their plans proved too ambitious, however, and they soon abandoned their effort.[20]

Thus, in the years before 1879, migrants from Kentucky and Tennessee had established no fewer than four black colonies in Kansas. The total population of the colonies was about two thousand. Of course, a parallel migration of settlers who came to Kansas on their own, responding, perhaps, to some of the broadsides, accompanied the colonization. The exact magnitude of that migration is unknown.[21]

What is certain is that in the spring of 1879, the volume and character of the migration to Kansas changed drastically. Before then, the movement had been predominantly of self-sufficient black farmers from Kentucky and Tennessee. They were not as well-off as the white immigrants pouring into Kansas, but they were not destitute either. They came prepared to look after themselves, and if they suffered, their sufferings were not unlike those of the whites. As a result, their arrival drew relatively little attention.[22]

19. *Ibid.*, reproduction of circular facing p. 16.

20. *Ibid.*, 13–15; Painter, *Exodusters*, 149–50; Athearn, *In Search of Canaan*, 77.

21. The only hard quantitative information about migration to Kansas comes from the censuses of 1870 and 1880. Because the population counts took place ten years apart, there is no way of distinguishing between blacks who arrived in 1879 and blacks who arrived earlier in the 1870s.

22. Athearn, *In Search of Canaan*, 75–79.

In 1879, the stream of blacks from Kentucky and Tennessee was joined by an intense but brief surge from the Lower South. It seems certain that the flow from Kentucky, Tennessee, and Missouri expanded markedly as well. What made the Exodus of 1879 different from the migration that preceded it was not only increasing numbers, but also a dramatic change in the character of those who were going north. Many were so desperately poor that they required relief aid from the moment of their arrival. Whereas the earlier black migration to Kansas had been relatively orderly, like the movement of white Americans to the West, the Exodus of 1879 had elements of mass hysteria and precipitous flight.[23]

Suddenly, in the spring of 1879, the Deep South was pulsating with the potential for a significant black exodus. Especially in the Mississippi River areas of Louisiana and Mississippi, blacks in large numbers were talking about going to Kansas. At one level, that was simply a continuation of earlier trends. Throughout the 1870s, blacks had been talking about going to Liberia or the American West. But worsening political and economic conditions and the dawning recognition that Liberia was not a viable alternative, made Kansas ever more attractive.

And yet the Exodus of 1879 was more than the culmination of earlier trends. In 1879, the movement to leave the South developed a dramatic new dimension that contemporaries called Kansas Fever. Their term was derisive, designed to capture the irrationality and naïveté of the would-be migrants. Suddenly thousands of blacks had become convinced that if only they could reach the banks of the Mississippi or if only they could get to St. Louis, the federal government would give them free transportation to Kansas. In addition, some believed that once they reached this new promised land, the government would give them free land, and even subsistence for the first year.[24]

It all seemed ludicrous, especially to white onlookers. But it was not quite so absurd as the skeptics liked to believe. For both blacks and whites there was land in Kansas that was almost free. As everyone knew, for a filing fee of ten dollars, an adult citizen could claim 160 acres of the public lands under the Homestead Act of 1862. After liv-

23. *Ibid.*, 78–79.
24. Painter, *Exodusters*, 177–78, 205; Athearn, *In Search of Canaan*, 6–7, 10, 189.

ing on the land or working it for five years, the homesteader could, upon the payment of a few more small fees, gain title to it. True, speculators had taken the best ground, but the prospect of free land remained.[25]

Nor was the idea of government-supplied transportation and subsistence simply plucked from thin air. On January 16, 1879, Senator William Windom, a Republican from Minnesota, presented the Senate with a resolution proposing that a committee of senators investigate the feasibility of "encouraging and promoting by all just and proper methods the partial migration of colored persons" from states where they were denied their rights as citizens to "such Territory or Territories of the United States as may be provided for their use and occupation."[26]

Windom's resolution did not pass and anyway it said nothing about free land or free transportation, let alone subsistence. Yet there were good reasons that blacks might conclude from it that the federal government would provide those things. First, they knew that, in view of their impoverishment, no large-scale migration could succeed without aid. Appealing to President Rutherford B. Hayes in November, 1878, J. T. Brewington, a black schoolteacher from Mississippi who had recently moved to Kansas, sought assistance to bring his Mississippi friends and neighbors north. He told Hayes, "We are in the first place entirely unable to reach those lands [in Kansas], secondly to raise means to subsist the first year, thirdly to raise means to get implements with which to commence labor to get sheltering."[27]

If blacks knew they lacked the resources for a large-scale migration, they also had some historical reason for believing that the national government might help them. Had not the Freedmen's Bureau provided rations, blankets, and even shelter in the first months after the war? Had not that agency provided transportation for thousands of black migrants? Was it not true that the bureau had provided assistance

25. Billington, *Westward Expansion,* 606–608.

26. *Congressional Record,* 45th Cong., 3rd Sess., 483. See also Rayford W. Logan, *The Betrayal of the Negro: From Rutherford B. Hayes to Woodrow Wilson* (New York, 1965), 135–38.

27. J. T. Brewington to President Rutherford B. Hayes, November 6, 1878, quoted by Painter in *Exodusters,* 179.

to some who migrated to Florida under the terms of the Southern Homestead Act? "Forty acres and a mule" had proved to be a chimera, but the idea was not a figment of black imaginations. It began with white northerners associated with the federal government.

In addition, there was the American Colonization Society. For years it had offered to pay transportation and six months' subsistence to those who would go to Liberia, where land was available for a song. The offer had been sharply amended in 1875, but it is likely that more knew of the original terms than of the change. The mere knowledge that such an offer existed rendered more plausible the word that the federal government was giving similar terms for Kansas. The Windom resolution made no promise of free land, but it is not hard to imagine blacks beset by poverty, violence, and fears of reenslavement reading the idea into it.

In the month after Windom introduced his resolution, news of his proposal spread through the Deep South, and increasingly the press carried stories that dwelt on the possibility of a black exodus to the western states. On January 22, 1879, the Jackson *Weekly Clarion* made passing mention of Windom's "scheme for keeping up the agitation." Three weeks later the same newspaper was showing mild concern at the "proposed negro migration to the western states." Sadly but philosophically, it concluded, "It is perhaps to be regretted that such a [migration] movement has been agitated among the negroes, who compose in a large measure the laboring class." The newspaper's editorial went on to acknowledge that there was no way to stop the movement and that any effort to do so would merely "add to the negro's desire to leave."[28]

Meantime, a private letter from a black in Port Gibson, Mississippi, appeared in the *National Republican,* a newspaper in Washington, D.C., that had a direct connection to the Republican party. Written to a "fugitive citizen" of Mississippi, the letter had been passed on to the paper. In it, the writer praised Windom's resolution for giving blacks an opportunity "to remove to some State where our rights will be protected." He claimed that if transportation and reliable information about the West could be had, "Mississippi would be depopulated . . . in two years." The "fugitive citizen" was probably the former con-

28. Jackson (Miss.) *Weekly Clarion,* January 22, February 12, 1879.

gressman John R. Lynch, of Mississippi, who arrived in Washington, D.C., just at that time.[29]

There is no telling how many southern blacks saw the letter in the *National Republican,* but what counted more was that southern white papers picked it up and spread it for all to read. In Jackson, Mississippi, the *Weekly Clarion* quickly copied it. At about the same time, the Port Gibson *Reveille* denounced those who were encouraging blacks to leave the South as "enemies to both races and enemies to society." Needless to say, black readers may have held different views from those of the editors of the *Reveille.*[30]

Simultaneously, a group of blacks in Washington, D.C., met to organize a conference on the situation of blacks in the South. Among the participants were Lynch, of Mississippi, Francis L. Cardozo, of South Carolina, and P. B. S. Pinchback, of Louisiana. All had been prominent southern black Republicans, and all had become, in effect, refugees. News of their organizational meeting appeared in the press in mid-February, along with other accounts of rising black interest in an exodus from the South.[31]

In short, in the weeks just after the announcement of Windom's resolution, black migration became an increasingly mentioned subject in public discussion. Until that time, blacks seeking to leave the South had pleaded for aid, hoped for aid, demanded aid, but had not acted as though they believed that aid was on the way. Suddenly, just as news of Windom's resolution began to circulate through the South, poverty-stricken blacks began encamping along the Mississippi River, acting in the full belief that federally funded steamers would soon pick them up. What brought about the change? Why did they now assume they were to get federal aid? The most plausible explanation is that as the newspaper accounts of the resolution were translated into word-of-mouth accounts and as the story moved farther and farther from its source, dreams and wishful thinking elbowed reality to the side.[32]

On this point the petitions of the Shreveport blacks (pp. 161–65 above) are instructive. Taken collectively, they show a group of poor

29. *National Republican,* February 10, February 11, 1879.

30. Port Gibson (Miss.) *Reveille,* quoted in *National Republican,* February 17, 1879.

31. *National Republican,* February 12, 1879; Jackson (Miss.) *Weekly Clarion,* February 19, 1879.

32. For a different interpretation, see Painter, *Exodusters,* 178–80.

blacks, driven by fears of violence and reenslavement, who wanted a place of their own so badly they could almost taste it. The petitions show too that the freedmen were acutely aware that transportation and subsistence costs posed an insuperable barrier to migration. With desire and desperation so strong, an atmosphere existed where any ray of hope was likely to be magnified many times over. It is easy to see how Windom's phrase "encouraging and promoting [black migration] by all just and proper methods" might have been just such a ray.

The Senate debated Windom's resolution on February 7 and 24. The measure then went to a quiet death, from inaction. It is likely more than a coincidence that the first indication that some blacks of the Deep South had come to believe that they would receive federal aid to migrate to Kansas appears in newspaper reports dated February 26 and February 28, 1879. By early March, some blacks in Mississippi were giving credence to a rumor that on or about March 15 a steamboat or a through train would depart from Vicksburg carrying all blacks to Kansas who wanted to go.[33]

The free transportation never materialized, but at first that did little to diminish enthusiasm. As spring came, hundreds of blacks made their way to steamboat landings along the Mississippi. Before the exodus excitement spent its force, thousands more joined them. They went, certain that if only they could get to a boat headed toward St. Louis, all their troubles would be over. Many were so poor that they lacked even the four or five dollars needed for boat passage to St. Louis. Others had passage money, but little more. If they made it to Kansas, they would be just about penniless on arrival. But none of that seemed to matter. Those who came to the banks of the Mississippi were supremely confident that God or the federal government would see to their needs.[34]

It did not happen so. Those without money quickly found that the steamboats would not take them. Still, they did not give up. By April, encampments of impoverished would-be migrants were at steamboat landings on both sides of the river. At first, those with passage money fared better, but then the planters began to worry that the exodus

33. *Congressional Record,* Senate, 45th Cong. 3rd Sess., 1077–82, 1808; Painter, *Exodusters,* 185–86.

34. Painter, *Exodusters,* 185–99; Athearn, *In Search of Canaan,* 9–11.

would deprive them of their labor supply. Planters and St. Louis merchants prevailed upon the steamboat companies not to accept black
passengers even if they could pay full fare. The refusal of service began
in mid- or late April and lasted about a month or two.[35]

The policy of denying passage ended in late spring, apparently as a
result of the intervention of Thomas W. Conway, the former Freedmen's Bureau official. He threatened to charter a fleet of steamers,
arm them, and sail to the rescue of the blacks. Making it appear as if
he had the approval of President Hayes for his project, Conway
persuaded the steamboat companies to rescind voluntarily their ban
against black passengers.[36]

Even so, the restrictions did not end totally. Before the exodus
began, the companies had been carrying blacks to St. Louis at rates of
from $2.50 to $4.00. In the months from June to September, they
insisted on $5.00. Moreover, one steamboat captain was quoted as
saying that there were two places along the river where he dared not
land a boat carrying black passengers. In Natchez and Vidalia, the
captain said, "they have armed every white man . . . to mob the first
captain that lands a boat . . . with colored people on board."[37]

In the main, though, blacks with money could get passage north
after mid-May or early June. But it was too late; the back of the exodus had been broken by the interdiction. Poverty-stricken to begin
with, the blacks had used up the few resources they had in waiting by
the river for the boats. Once the boats would take them, few had the
passage money. Perhaps more important, the sustained interruption
appears to have undermined the myth that the government was going
to provide transportation, land, and subsistence.[38]

But what explains the strength of the myth in the first place? Why
had the belief that the government would provide those benefits taken
such a powerful hold on so many? Nell Painter tries to explain the
irrational side of the response of the "exodusters" by calling them
millenarians. She argues that, from a psychological perspective, Kan-

---

35. Painter, *Exodusters,* 197–99.

36. Senate Report on the Exodus, III, 438, 442; Athearn, *In Search of Canaan,*
144–46.

37. Senate Report on the Exodus, II, 149.

38. Painter, *Exodusters,* 200–201.

sas Fever allowed blacks to deny the hard reality that for the foreseeable future, the end of Reconstruction doomed them to second-class citizenship. Within the mythology of Kansas Fever, she says, the national government "played a salvationist role" as an imagined provider of land, transportation, and subsistence.[39]

It is an interesting argument, but more is needed before it can be wholeheartedly accepted. *Millenarism* is a term for "religious movements that expect imminent, total, ultimate, this-worldly collective salvation,"[40] but the evidence is simply too scanty to conclude that Kansas Fever was primarily a religious movement. Two white accounts from the period stress the "religious frenzy" of the participants, but black sources are remarkably silent on the point.[41] Painter notes the frequent use of metaphors like the Negro Canaan and the promised land, but on that basis one would have to describe both the organized antebellum flight of runaway slaves to the North and the Great Migration of World War I as millenarian, since similar imagery occurred in connection with them.[42]

Perhaps the most critical similarity between Kansas Fever and millenarian movements lies in the nature of the conditions behind them. Yonina Talmon says that, on the whole, millenarism is the religion of the lower class and of persecuted minorities. Often, she says, it is found where there is multiple deprivation, that is, where the effects of poverty, low status, and powerlessness are combined. Particularly relevant to the abortive Exodus of 1879 is Talmon's observation that sudden and dramatic crises that aggravate existing deprivation (for example, the end of Reconstruction) can precipitate millenarism even as they symbolize and highlight the existence of long-term deprivation.[43]

By June, 1879, the intense emotional power of Kansas Fever was spent. Millenarian movements always face a moment of truth when the time appointed for salvation passes uneventfully. When the steam-

39. *Ibid.*, 177–78n.

40. Yonina Talmon, "Millenarism," in *International Encyclopedia of the Social Sciences,* ed. David A. Sills (18 vols.; New York, 1968), X, 349.

41. Wharton, *The Negro in Mississippi,* 116; *Appleton's Annual Cyclopedia,* 1879, XIX, 634.

42. Painter, *Exodusters,* 195–96.

43. Talmon, "Millenarism," 354.

boats refused to stop, Kansas Fever faced a similar crisis. At first, the believers held fast, loyally remaining at the landings week after week. Painter contends that they gave up only when their money ran out. Economic resources were no doubt part of the story, but many must have given up in disillusionment as well. Had it been otherwise, the migration should have resumed in force once the steamboats began picking blacks up again.[44]

Despite all the obstacles, there were blacks in the Deep South who made it to Kansas. Once there, however, they often had difficulties finding food, shelter, and work. Facing many hardships, some of those who participated in the Exodus of 1879 concluded before long that Kansas was not the haven they had imagined and began looking for another promised land. Some began to write the American Colonization Society inquiring about the availability of passage to Liberia. In the years from 1882 to 1885, the society received 352 letters of application for Liberia from blacks across the country. Of them, 53 came from Kansas and 9 from adjacent Nebraska.[45]

G. Hardy, writing for himself and twenty-four others from Parsons, Kansas, explained that his group had emigrated from Texas in 1879, "but we find that our Case are not bettered at all." Destitute, he asked for aid in getting to Liberia, because "we can-not obtain the labor it seeme in the united State. it seemeth that we are in the Way. in all occupation. Even in the [s]Chool House."[46]

Brewington, the black schoolmaster who, in November, 1878, had asked President Hayes for help in bringing his neighbors in Mississippi to Kansas, asked for information about going to Africa. "Many of us wish to go there," he said, "if we can only benefit our children by going." Writing for another group of blacks from Emporia, Kansas, R. C. Coleman told something of their hopes and dreams when he asked: "Tell Me[,] so do the Colord man Run the Relrods [railroads] and do they Belong to Him[?] if so tell me now about How Large is Liberia." Even in the all-black communities that had been established in Kansas there were some who wanted to go to Liberia. Writing from

---

44. Painter, *Exodusters*, 200.
45. Tabulated from List of Applicants for Passage to Liberia, ACS, LC.
46. G. Hardy to William Coppinger, June 15, 1882, in CCXLVII (154), ACS, LC.

the Dunlap colony, Abraham Powell said that he wanted to go "as soon as I can."[47] But by and large these discontented blacks had little more success in getting to Liberia than did the members of the Colonization Council established by Henry Adams.

One of the most intriguing aspects of the black movement to Kansas is the recurring interconnection between it and the movement to Liberia. Many of those who were involved with the Exodus of 1879 had earlier considered going to Liberia, and once in Kansas, some of the migrants began corresponding with the American Colonization Society about going to Liberia. Indeed, it is probably best not to see the attempt to settle in Liberia and the attempt to settle in Kansas as separate enterprises. The two can be understood as dimensions of a larger political impulse whose focus was on escaping from racism and poverty rather than on reaching a particular destination.

This point emerges clearly when we consider the movement initially led by Henry Adams. By the spring of 1878, interest in Liberia was waning sharply in northwestern Louisiana, but a new form of colonization was gaining attention. On April 27, at Shreveport, Dr. R. J. Cromwell presided over a meeting of Adams' Colonization Council and introduced a new organization, the Negro Union Association, which was devoted not to emigration to Africa but to the establishment of black colonies on government lands within the South.[48] Following the pattern of its predecessor, the new group held a public meeting and sent a petition off to Washington. What was different was the leadership of the association and the central goal of its petition. None of its leaders had been officers of the Colonization Council, and none of its aims touched on Africa. Instead, it asked that Congress create a freedmen's colonizing commission charged with

47. J. T. Brewington to William Coppinger, May 8, 1882, CCXLVII (90), ACS, LC; R. C. Coleman to William Coppinger, August 28, 1883, in CCLII (111), ACS, LC; Abraham Powell to William Coppinger, March 2, 1884, in CCLIV (195), ACS, LC.

48. Henry Adams to William Coppinger, enclosing minutes of the general Colonization Council meeting, April 27, 1878, in CCXXXI (83), ACS, LC; Petition from the Negro Union Cooperative Aid Association of Shreveport, Louisiana, May or early June, 1878 (U.S. House of Representatives, Records of the Committee on Education and Labor, 45th Cong., 2nd Sess. [H. R. 45-H8.5, Colonization of Liberia by American Negroes], National Archives, Washington, D.C., Record Group 233).

surveying southern public lands and breaking them up into twenty-acre plots for distribution to the freedmen.[49]

The petition carried the names of three hundred persons. Adams was not an officer of the new association, but his name appears first on the list of rank-and-file signers of the petition. And its wording gave a small nod to those who still favored the African alternative, by making passing reference to the "best and most worthy of our race" who were preparing to "breast the ocean and diseases of Liberia." Clearly these blacks were very much in touch with the arguments for and against going to Africa.[50]

In the six months that followed the group's petition, conditions worsened in northern Louisiana as whites assured themselves of a clean sweep in the voting of November, 1878. Violence and fraud were everywhere. After the election, Adams sent a letter of complaint to the United States attorney at Shreveport, and Cromwell wrote President Hayes asking that black troops be sent to Louisiana. At the same time, Cromwell, acting in his capacity as president of the Negro Union Cooperative Aid Association—as his group was now named—issued a call for a convention of delegates from black organizations for the purpose of devising a "general plan whereby we may become united as a race." Listed as an officer and director of the coming convention was "H Adams, President Liberia Council."[51]

The convention was scheduled for December 5, 1878, but Adams did not attend. He left Shreveport a day earlier to answer a subpoena from a federal grand jury in New Orleans that was looking into violations of the federal election laws. As far as is known, he never returned to Shreveport, and Painter aptly calls him an exile in New Orleans. For a while, at least, he remained in contact with the blacks of Shreveport. In April, 1879, when the push to go to Kansas was reaching its strongest, he wrote William Coppinger, of the American Colonization Society, trying to arrange for a ship to come to New Orleans

49. Petition from the Negro Union Cooperative Aid Association of Shreveport, Louisiana, May or early June, 1878.

50. *Ibid.*

51. Call for a convention to be held on December 5, 1878, enclosed with Henry Adams to William Coppinger, November 16, 1878, in CCXXXIII (122–23), ACS, LC; Painter, *Exodusters,* 97–99.

to pick up the blacks from the Shreveport area and take them to Liberia.[52]

His letter sheds light both on the fears of the Louisiana blacks and on the relationship of Adams' Colonization Council to the Exodus of 1879. Writing at the height of the exodus to Kansas, Adams said that many leaving the South were going to Kansas "just to get out of the Southern States" before the whites shut the door on attempts to flee. "We believe," he said, "that if we Stay here untell 1881 that the Democrates, as the Slave Holder[s] of the South, will fix it So we can never get from South to the north unless we Run away." The Colonization Council was consequently advising its followers to "Leave the South and get Some Whaere we would be able to Leave for Liberia in the time to come."[53]

To the end, Adams remained a partisan of settlement in Liberia, and it is ironic that he is sometimes viewed as a prime figure in the exodus to Kansas. His reputation in that regard arises simply from the lengthy and dramatic testimony he gave before the Senate committee investigating the Exodus of 1879. His testimony, as well as the corroborative materials he provided, shows clearly that he played almost no direct role in the Kansas enterprise itself.[54] He did indeed help popularize the idea of leaving the South, but from start to finish, his goal was Liberia. Months before the enthusiasm for Kansas began to surge, Louisiana blacks began defecting from his organization. It seems doubtful that many were much affected by the Colonization Council's belated advice that they leave the South for the North before emigration became impossible.

Confirmation that the colonization efforts in Louisiana played little role in the exodus to Kansas can be found in the census data cited earlier which show only 1,300 Louisiana-born blacks in Kansas in 1880. Clearly, there had been some movement from Louisiana to Kansas, but even if all of it came from northwestern Louisiana, it was a trickle, not a flood.

52. Painter, *Exodusters*, 96–97; Henry Adams to William Coppinger, April, 1879, in CCXXXV (78), ACS, LC.

53. Adams to Coppinger, April, 1879, in CCXXXV (78), ACS, LC. See also Henry Adams to William Coppinger, May 27, 1879, in CCXXXV (179), ACS, LC.

54. Senate Report on the Exodus, II, 101–214.

Though neither Mississippi nor Texas had a Henry Adams to speak for it, these were the two states in the Deep South that sent the greatest number of black migrants to Kansas. Each contributed roughly twice as many as Louisiana, but even so, the absolute numbers are strikingly small considering the racial oppression that existed and considering the Kansas Fever that was so widely reported at the time.[55]

There is simply no escaping the conclusion that, regardless of the oppression in the South, extensive black political migration was a near-impossibility owing to the poverty of the blacks and the lack of economic opportunity in the North. What is striking is not that so few went north but that the exodus to Kansas captivated the imaginations of so many. It is certain that the underlying cause of the exodus was the sense of desperation that blacks had about their economic and political future, but it seems equally obvious that the immediate trigger for Kansas Fever was Senator Windom's resolution, which gave blacks reason to hope that the federal government would come to their rescue.

In North Carolina, too, there developed a colonization effort upon which national politics had a major impact. There, however, the original impulse toward colonization was distorted into a politically manufactured migration whose sole purpose was to strengthen the Republican party in the election of 1880. Indiana had gone Democratic by a narrow margin in 1876, and three years later it seemed possible that the in-migration of a few thousand Republican voters might tilt the state in the opposite direction.[56]

At the start, however, the situation in North Carolina had strong similarities to that elsewhere in the South. The potential migrants were poor rural blacks, and as was the case elsewhere, enthusiasm for colonization had both a Liberia dimension and a Kansas dimension. Like Adams and Singleton, Sam Perry, the leader of the North Carolina effort, had little use for the established black leadership. He testified, "I had not much to do with the big professional negroes, the rich men. I did not associate with them much, but I got among the workingmen."[57]

---

55. See Table 6 above.
56. Athearn, *In Search of Canaan,* 206–207.
57. Senate Report on the Exodus, I, 180, 184; II, 102, 105, 109; III, 380, 381.

The group that Perry led centered in Lenoir County and reached into the surrounding area. Their activity began in the early 1870s, and they were especially strong along that portion of the Southern Railroad line that ran between Goldsboro and Kinston.[58] On Sunday evenings, Perry and other black workingmen met to discuss colonization and to read railroad promotional literature about the West. After a while interest flagged, but in late 1876 it reignited. As a result, the North Carolina blacks petitioned their legislature "to ask Congress to set us apart a territory in the West."[59]

As in Louisiana, some of the intending colonizers favored Liberia rather than the West. The leader of the contingent that looked toward Liberia was Peter C. Williams, a widely respected minister and schoolteacher. It was probably no coincidence that just when the disputed Hayes-Tilden election threatened to give the nation its first Democratic administration since the Civil War, Williams began seeking information about taking a group to Liberia.[60] Perry, however, vigorously "opposed going to any foreign country." But even he had to admit that in 1876, "everybody was going to Liberia." By early 1877, though, interest in emigration was subsiding, and Perry later explained, "That was the time they gave us the schools and that stopped the movement." Perhaps equally important, the Liberia partisans were stymied by news that the American Colonization Society was unlikely to provide free transportation.[61]

For a while after that, the North Carolina blacks lost interest in colonization schemes, but by early 1879 they were again seeking to leave the South. Williams had abandoned hope of going to Liberia. Instead, he and Perry were joint leaders of a venture aimed at resettlement in Kansas. Some time in mid-September the two men petitioned the National Emigrant Aid Society, in Washington, D.C., to help them get to Kansas.[62]

It was a fateful decision, for the organization to which they applied

58. *Ibid.*, I, 280, 284, 294, 296, 298, 299.

59. *Ibid.*, 281, 280, 294; Athearn, *In Search of Canaan*, 214.

60. Senate Report on the Exodus, I, 287; P. C. Williams to President Ulysses S. Grant, November 14, 1876, in CCXXV (110), ACS, LC; P. C. Williams to William Coppinger, November 20, 1876, in CCXXV (130), ACS, LC.

61. Senate Report on the Exodus, I, 287; William Coppinger to P. C. Williams, November 17, 1876, in LS, XXVII, Part 2, p. 262, ACS, LC.

62. Senate Report on the Exodus, I, 281; Athearn, *In Search of Canaan*, 215.

was a creation of the Republican party, and the North Carolina blacks soon found themselves shunted off to Indiana as part of a plan to build Republican strength in that state. The National Emigrant Aid Society formed in Washington, D.C., in March, 1879, in direct response to news of the arrival in St. Louis of the first contingents of the exodus. Its founders established the group, they said, for the purpose of "regulating immigration from the South to the West." Senator Windom was the organization's first president, and an early report listed three other Republican senators, six Republican congressmen, and the editor of the *National Republican* as members. With the possible exception of one person who could not be further identified, all the members had patronage connections to the Republican party.[63]

At the organization's first meeting, H. W. Mendenhall, a white first secretary at the Treasury Department, remarked that since most blacks voted Republican, he would very much like to see them go to Indiana, where their votes were needed.[64] He was vigorously opposed by Charles N. Otey, a black editor, who protested that his people had

63. New York *Times,* April 7, 1879; *National Republican,* March 22, 1879. The *Times* article lists nineteen members. A careful perusal of the testimony given before the Senate committee on the exodus yields five additional names. The membership of the organization known from the two sources included Senators William Windom, Hannibal Hamlin, Zachariah Chandler, and Henry M. Teller, and Congressmen John Garfield, William E. Chandler, George C. Gorham, Joseph Jorgansen, Joseph H. Rainey, and Charles E. Williams. Among the white members of the group were A. M. Clapp, editor of the *National Republican;* H. W. Mendenhall, an employee at the Treasury Department; Thomas Tullock, a former employee at this agency and in 1880 the assistant postmaster for the city of Washington, D.C.; and J. W. Rankin, pastor of Washington's Congregational church. Among the blacks were J. W. Cromwell, W. G. Fearring, and Milton Holland, all employees at the Treasury Department. Other blacks involved with the society were John R. Lynch, Merrimon Howard, Richard R. T. Greener, O. S. B. Wall, and Sayles J. Bowen, all of whom had or would have patronage connections with the Republican party. J. M. Adams, a black man who was to become secretary of the society, has not been otherwise identified. The only member totally unidentified is J. M. Edwards. See, besides the New York *Times* article cited above, Bardolph, *The Negro Vanguard,* 117 (Greener); *National Republican,* February 12, 1879 (Howard); and Senate Report on the Exodus, I, 173 (Adams), 21, 77 (Bowen), 34–35 (Clapp), 4 (Cromwell), 93 (Fearring), 279 (Holland), 80 (Mendenhall), 3 (Rankin), 1–3 (Tullock), 21 (Wall).

64. *National Republican,* March 22, 1879; Senate Report on the Exodus, I, 83. For other accounts of the founding meeting, see Senate Report on the Exodus, I, 40–41, 277.

been "used long enough as tools." Mendenhall's position was not formally adopted, but neither was it rejected. Otey, who quit the organization at this meeting, was the only one to oppose the plan.[65]

Just about this time, Mendenhall wrote E. B. Martindale, the Republican editor of the Indianapolis *Journal,* asking him "what advantages could be offered colored emigrants" to Indiana. At the same time, Thomas Conway began to take an interest in the exodus venture. A former Freedmen's Bureau official who had gone on to serve as superintendent of education in Louisiana, Conway had deep commitments to the Republican party and to the cause of the freedmen.[66]

En route to St. Louis and Kansas, Conway stopped in Indianapolis, where he met with several prominent Republicans "to see what could be done regarding these laborers as to getting employment for them [in Indiana]." The men he spoke with told him that Indiana could provide employment for five or ten thousand blacks.[67] Returning to the East in late May, he stopped again in Indianapolis, where he told leading Republicans that he "thought it advisable not to send any more to Kansas—that many of them were wanted in Indiana, Illinois, and other States, and . . . it [was] advisable for them to go there."[68]

As far as can be determined, nothing more was done or said about bringing blacks to Indiana for the next several months. Then, in late August, J. M. Adams, who had become the secretary of the National Emigrant Aid Society, gave a newspaper interview in which he claimed that a great exodus was in the making. He said that he was constantly receiving letters from southern blacks and that several had assured him that blacks wanted to go "where they may vote and have their votes counted." Mendenhall wrote the chairman of the executive committee of the Republican state central committee in Indiana proposing that southern blacks be colonized in Indiana in order to increase the Republican vote in the coming election. About two weeks later, Perry and Williams went to Washington carrying a petition addressed to the National Emigrant Aid Society.[69]

65. Senate Report on the Exodus, I, 102, 101, 83.
66. *Ibid.,* II, 35, III, 433, 435, 440.
67. *Ibid.,* III, 441.
68. *Ibid.,* 441, 440; *National Republican,* May 26, 1879.
69. New York *Times,* August 31, 1879; Senate Report on the Exodus, II, 11–12, I, 282, 85.

By the time they arrived, big changes had occurred in the society. The prominent Republicans originally associated with the group were gone, and as far as can be determined, Republican patronage workers constituted the organization's entire membership, both black and white.[70] Perry and Williams spent several weeks in Washington, during which they went from one member of the society to another seeking help and advice.[71]

Not surprisingly, Mendenhall told them that many in Kansas were suffering because of the size of the black influx and pointed out that Ohio, Indiana, and Illinois were nearer and cheaper. He particularly favored Indiana, where he had lived for four years and where, he thought, jobs could easily be found. About a week later, the North Carolinians agreed to go to Indiana. Mendenhall wrote to Martindale asking if they "could be furnished with employment if they stopped there."[72]

Still, the National Emigrant Aid Society was not ready to give money to Perry and Williams, and the two had to beg funds at a Washington church in order to pay their way to Indiana to look over the land. Once in that state, they trekked from one prominent Republican to another searching for opportunities for their followers. It was disheartening. The kind of work that was available in Indiana involved hiring-out, and Perry and Williams knew that their people "wanted to farm and not to hire out."[73]

No one in Indiana really cared about the blacks themselves. A black minister, John H. Clay, of Greencastle, Indiana, would not allow Perry and Williams the use of his church to raise money to continue on to Kansas, but he did provide them with a batch of circulars inviting black laborers to Indiana. The handbills announced that homes were available for ten thousand blacks and that the black population of Putnam County would provide newcomers with fifteen or twenty dollars a month, as well as with a cow, a calf, a garden, and wood to

70. The only persons known to have been active in the society in the fall of 1879 or later were J. M. Adams, A. M. Clapp, J. W. Cromwell, W. G. Fearring, Milton M. Holland, H. W. Mendenhall, and O. S. B. Wall.

71. Senate Report on the Exodus, I, 283, 11–12, 34, 85–86.

72. *Ibid.*, 86, 85, II, 29. Simultaneously, J. M. Adams sent a similar letter to the acting treasurer of the Indiana Republican state central committee (II, 29).

73. *Ibid.*, I, 283.

burn.[74] Perry must have known that to be untrue, but he was in a predicament. Apparently he decided to sacrifice the interests of his followers to the wishes of the Republicans he had met in Washington and Indiana. With little money and with his followers waiting for him to return with news of how they might get to Kansas, he headed home in mid-October carrying Clay's circulars. He held meetings and distributed leaflets, whipping up enthusiasm. Perry later testified that his knowledge of Indiana was "too shallow to advise anybody to go there," and he claimed that he merely passed out the circulars and told the people "what the men told me." Confronted in 1880 with some of the more extravagant claims in the circulars, Perry protested: "The circular says that. . . . I do not vouch for the truth of it."[75]

But he had indeed vouched for the truth of it. Mingo Simmons was an early follower of Perry and his vivid, if embittered, account corresponds to everything that is known in the case. The project began, according to Simmons, with Perry's claiming that he had learned from a flyer that blacks going to Kansas would get land and plenty to do, "that the government wanted us to go out there." Perry held meetings, and despite the skepticism of some blacks, "they kept up the meetings and at last we started Perry out to Kansas, . . . to pick out somewhere for us to go." Simmons recalled that Perry wrote home "to know whether we would [still] like to go there, to Kansas." Next, he said, Perry wrote that "Indiana was a better place." Perry asserted "that in Kansas we would starve out; and he said how we would like it in Indiana."[76] Perry assured his followers that "all is fixed for you, and [George J. Langsdale, editor of the Greencastle (Ind.) *Banner*, and Clay] want you out there." He told them that they could not go farther than Indiana, they could not go to Kansas. Langsdale and Clay had furnished the money to get to Indiana but "they won't furnish the money for you to go to Kansas."[77]

Money was the crux of the matter. When Perry and Williams first approached the National Emigrant Aid Society, it would not subsidize them even as far as Indiana. But that all changed. In November, 1879, when Perry brought his first group, numbering fifty-one migrants, to

74. *Ibid.*, 284, 288.
75. *Ibid.*, 288, 287.
76. *Ibid.*, 374.
77. *Ibid.*

Washington en route to Indiana, the society spent $170 to assist those who could not pay their own fares. Over the next five weeks, it spent a total of $1,708.65 on the transportation of emigrants. The net cost to the society of sending one migrant from North Carolina to Indiana was eight dollars.[78]

In testimony before the Senate exodus committee, the president of the National Emigrant Aid Society tried to leave the impression that his group was willing to send fleeing southern blacks wherever in the North they wanted to go. But all the money it spent on transportation was for those going from North Carolina to Indiana. Nor, it appears, was this group the only source of funds for the project. Once during the exodus from North Carolina to Indiana, Perry found himself in Washington without enough money to cover the transportation of his charges. He sent a telegram to Indianapolis, and within twenty-four hours he had about $620.[79] Generosity like that toward impoverished blacks, even within Republican ranks, was more than a little unusual, especially from Indiana, a state notorious for its unfriendliness to nonwhites.

There is no way of knowing precisely how many blacks Perry guided from North Carolina to Indiana. O. S. B. Wall, the president of the National Emigrant Aid Society, guessed that perhaps 2,500 or 3,000 had gone. Those numbers are far too high. The number of Baltimore and Ohio Railroad tickets the National Emigrant Aid Society supplied for Perry's party is 763. Census figures concerning states of birth suggest that the number of migrants in Perry's group cannot have been much greater than 1,000 or 1,500.[80]

Virtually all the Democrats from Indiana who testified before the Senate committee on the exodus said that there was no demand for

78. *Ibid.*, 36, 42.

79. *Ibid.*, 24, 25, 37, 73, 290–91.

80. *Ibid.*, 32, 36–37, 42, 73. The census of 1870 listed 1,354 North Carolina–born blacks living in Indiana. In the census of 1880, the comparable figure was 3,167. The net gain was 1,813, and this, therefore, is the lower limit for black migration from North Carolina to Indiana in the period 1870–1880. The theoretical upper limit to the migration flow is 3,167, but for the total to reach that number, all black North Carolinians living in Indiana in 1870 would have had to die or leave the state by 1880. All things considered, it is highly unlikely that the migrants who were part of Perry's movement were fewer than 763 or more than about 1,500. See *Ninth Census, Population, 1870*, 332; and *Tenth Census, Population, 1880*, 490.

black labor in Indiana and that the migrants were faring badly. Indiana Republicans generally disagreed, and Langsdale, of the Greencastle *Banner,* presented a compilation of migrant testimonials that the newcomers were generously welcomed and that they had good work at decent wages.[81]

Blacks who had gone to Indiana and returned to North Carolina told a different story. As early as November 15, 1879, Perry totally reversed himself and wrote Hemer (?) Bergen that "if I owned a lot in Indiana and one in hell I would rent out the one in Indiana and live in hell before I would live there." Simmons, who felt badly misled, told a congruent story. He said that after going to Indiana he had worked for a wage of fifty cents a day but that when he left, at the end of three weeks, he received not a cent, the charges for room and board having equaled the wages he had earned.[82]

Perhaps Perry and Simmons were selected to testify because they would bolster the Democratic version of events, but the Republicans did not present any black migrants as witnesses with an opposite story. Figures concerning the states of birth of blacks living in Indiana are fully consistent with the conclusion that conditions for blacks were miserable in the state. In 1870, there were 1,354 blacks who had been born in North Carolina living in Indiana. In 1880, just after the exodus from North Carolina, the number rose to 3,167. In 1890, it was down to 1,995. Other explanations may be possible, but the figures suggest that after the migration of 1880 many migrants returned home or went elsewhere and that migration from North Carolina slowed to a crawl. Had conditions in Indiana been as attractive to blacks as the Republicans of the state maintained, that would not have happened and the statistics would have been quite different.[83]

The migration of the North Carolina blacks, rooted in a desire to find a place where they would not be oppressed, was transformed by workers for the Republican party into a political expedient for winning Indiana in 1880. These Republicans—both black and white—

81. Senate Report on the Exodus, I, II. See especially the testimony of Langsdale in II, 302–19.

82. *Ibid.,* I, 287, 295, 371–72, 375.

83. *Ninth Census, Population, 1870,* 332; *Tenth Census, Population, 1880,* 490; U.S. Census Office, *Compendium of the Eleventh Census, 1890* (3 vols.; Washington, D.C., 1897), III, 33.

showed extraordinarily little concern for the people they were manipulating. Just how callous they were emerges in the testimony of
Wall, the president of the National Emigrant Aid Society. When asked
who was receiving the emigrants at the Indiana end of the line, he
testified: "I have no further interest in the matter in the world than
that I, as a humanitarian, meet these people here, desire very much to
do all that I can to help them go west, get good homes there. I have
no connection with any organization or anybody [in Indiana], and
hope and believe that the people there are imbued with the same spirit
that I am, and will welcome them and take care of them, which I hear
that they do; but when it comes to particulars, I cannot tell you defi-
nitely."[84] In short, Wall sent the North Carolina blacks on to Indiana
without concern over their probable fate.[85]

The Senate inquiry that heard Wall's testimony was itself highly
political. When the exodus to Kansas gained national attention in early
1879, Republican senators sought an investigation as a way of publi-
cizing the violence and disfranchisement that were occurring in places
like Louisiana. Throughout most of 1879, the Democratic majority
turned a deaf ear, however, to requests for an investigation. Then, as
it began to appear that the Republicans were importing black voters
into Indiana, the Democrats changed their mind. Thus was born
the Select Committee of the United States Senate to Investigate the
Causes of the Removal of the Negroes from the Southern States to the
Northern States.[86]

The committee looked into the exodus for three months, and at the
end, each side produced a report vindicating its initial position. The
majority report of the Democrats took the evidence that Republicans
sent black voters into Indiana to imply that the entire exodus to Kansas was a Republican plot. At the same time, they dismissed stories of
southern violence and intimidation as political rhetoric. Accounts of
violence, they held, were "all hearsay, and nothing but hearsay." What
was impressive, they found, was the "extraordinary spectacle of two

84. Senate Report on the Exodus, I, 25.

85. Wall may well have been trying to conceal his contacts in Indiana, but even so
the totality of the evidence indicates that neither he nor any of the Republicans who sent
blacks on to Indiana cared what happened to them after their arrival.

86. Athearn, *In Search of Canaan*, 208–209.

people[s] attempting to reconcile themselves in spite of the interference of outsiders."[87] The majority report was a specious account that ignored central realities in southern life.

The minority report was only slightly more honest. It ignored the evidence that Republicans had imported blacks to Indiana for political purposes and focused attention on Kansas. It argued that the "real origin of the exodus movement" was to be found in the conditions of racial oppression under which blacks had to live. The Republicans emphasized Henry Adams' assertion that around 1877 he and his followers "lost all hopes." The Republicans traced the black discontent that produced the exodus to political violence, disfranchisement, discrimination in the courts, and economic dissatisfaction.[88]

They were right to ascribe the migration to racial oppression, but their view was too simplistic and self-interested to explain very much. Although violence and racial oppression seem to have been greatest in Deep South states like Mississippi and Louisiana, the movement to Kansas from Missouri, Tennessee, and Kentucky was larger than that from all the Deep South states combined.

It is true that interference by the planters with steamboat transportation may have kept the number of migrants from the Deep South down. But there is no evidence that in places away from the Mississippi River—like northern Louisiana, the area from which Adams came—transportation avenues were closed to blacks. Rather, there is some evidence that black migrants traveling by rail could move about as they chose.[89] Even with that freedom, few went to Kansas.

Judged as an episode in migration history, the exodus to Kansas was just too small to be significant. Only a minuscule part of the black population went north at that time, and most of those who did came from the border states. Still, the story of the Kansas venture, and of the larger colonization scheme of which it was a part, is significant because it represents the reaction of the most bitter and alienated segment of black opinion to the end of Reconstruction. Race-conscious blacks had lost all hope of getting equality or justice in the South.

87. Senate Report on the Exodus, I, vii, v.
88. *Ibid.*, x–xi, xiii–xxv.
89. *Ibid.*, II, 513, 578, 588, III, 244.

The desire to establish colonies in Kansas or Africa showed the wish of the participants to find a place where they could be masters of their own world without white interference.[90] That is why Kansas and Africa became so interwoven in their thinking. For the blacks who supported colonization, it was escape rather than the particular destination that mattered. In searching for a place of their own, the advocates of colonization contributed to the development of the ideas of black nationalism and black separatism that became particularly significant in the twentieth century. Still, there is no escaping the conclusion that in 1879, when employment opportunities for blacks were minimal in the North, political migration was an unrealistic objective for the poverty-stricken blacks of the South.

90. The same desire to find a place where one could be one's own master would emerge in the black migration to Oklahoma of 1889–1910 (see Chapter 9 below), but that was a migration in which the political impulse to move was supported by a modicum of opportunity in the destination area.

PART TWO

BLACK MOBILITY AND THE REASSERTION

OF WHITE HEGEMONY

8

REINVENTING THE BLACK CODES

Reconstruction was over. The stalemate between white capital and black labor was broken. Throughout the years just after the Civil War, planters had complained constantly of their inability to command their labor as before. Other whites too bemoaned their loss of racial control. Once they dominated the machinery of state government again, they could move to regain mastery of the black work force and to reassert power in all spheres of southern life. They had to do that cautiously, though, so as not to provoke northerners into reversing their tacit decision to let southerners handle southern problems.

In the first half of the twentieth century, works about the South often portrayed the overthrow of Reconstruction, the disfranchisement of blacks, and the establishment of segregation as virtually simultaneous. Their view was of a near-monolithic white South rising up in the 1870s to overthrow corruption and northern oppression and to establish white supremacy. More by implication than by direct statement, the works left the impression that, Reconstruction aside, segregation and disfranchisement were part of the natural order of things. Then, in the mid-twentieth century, as segregation was coming under attack, C. Vann Woodward pioneered a different version of southern history. He perceived the period just after Reconstruction as an era of "forgotten alternatives," when the races lived together, however uneasily, in a society that still allowed many blacks political rights and in which segregation was far from the rule. He envisaged that, just possibly, southern history might have gone from there toward greater egalitarianism.[1] But, according to Woodward, that was not allowed to happen. In the 1890s, southern farmers, white and black, revolted under the banner of Populism, and those with power responded to the threat by engineering segregation and disfranchisement. Their aim, in Woodward's view, was to ensure that ordinary whites and blacks could never again make common cause against the rich and the powerful. By playing on the racism of ordinary southern whites, he argued, they contrived an artificial black threat that had to be met with total repression and complete white unity. Thus was born the "solid South," thus was born segregation.[2]

Woodward's is an exciting view that has shaped our understanding of southern history, but it tends to treat 1877 to 1890 as years when not very much happened. During this time, as in Reconstruction, suggests Woodward, blacks continued to vote in significant numbers and to move about in a society not yet rigidly segregated. Despite the withdrawal of northern troops, there was continuity with the past. For Woodward, the big discontinuity came only in the 1890s: that was when the whites with power established segregation and brought about disfranchisement.[3]

But the evidence of this chapter points in a somewhat different direction. It suggests that the racial events of the 1890s were, to a large extent, intensifications of processes that had been at work at least since the end of Reconstruction. To show that clearly, however, it is necessary to broaden the focus to include the entire spectrum of attempts to put the blacks "in their place" again and not just efforts to immo-

1. C. Vann Woodward, *The Strange Career of Jim Crow* (3rd ed.; New York, 1974), Chapter 2.

2. *Ibid.*, Chap. 3. See also C. Vann Woodward, *Tom Watson: Agrarian Rebel* (New York, 1953), 216–43; and C. Vann Woodward, *Origins of the New South, 1877–1913* (Baton Rouge, 1951), Chap. 12, esp. pp. 327–39.

3. For discussions of Woodward's views and of the historiographical tradition he fathered, see John W. Cell, *The Highest Stage of White Supremacy: The Origins of Segregation in South Africa and the American South* (Cambridge, Eng., 1982), Chapter 4; Joel Williamson, ed., *The Origins of Segregation* (Lexington, Mass., 1968), v–ix; Rabinowitz, *Race Relations in the Urban South*, 331–34; and Numan V. Bartley, "In Search of the New South: Southern Politics After Reconstruction," *Reviews in American History*, X (1982), 150–63.

bilize black labor. At this juncture the story of black movement becomes inseparable from the larger story of black freedom. The two must be told together in order to set the effort to limit black mobility in its context.

When Reconstruction ended in 1877, there was reason to fear that total black disfranchisement would quickly follow. One of the central goals of Redemption had been white control of state government, and almost everywhere, the process of Redemption had been accompanied by fraud, intimidation, and violence. It stood to reason that the Redeemers would try to ensure the permanence of their victory through the disfranchisement of the voters most threatening to their aims. And yet there was also reason to hope that things would not turn out that way. Reconstruction ended to the accompaniment of white promises to protect black citizenship rights under the new order. President Rutherford B. Hayes promised; Governor Wade Hampton, of South Carolina, promised; Governor Francis R. T. Nicholls, of Louisiana, promised.[4] Equally important, southern whites of all political persuasions knew that in close contests, black voters might be useful allies. Besides, the whites had no sense of how the North would react to a blatant bid to destroy black freedom openly and all at once. No wonder the history of black suffrage in the South is murky.

Still, the main outline is clear. In one state after another whites moved with deliberate speed to enact laws that would reduce or eliminate the black vote without making mention of race. As Table 7 indicates, in the years from 1871 through 1889, all the former Confederate states passed statutes to restrict suffrage. Poll taxes came to Georgia, in 1871 and 1877, and Virginia, in 1877. In 1881, under Readjuster rule, Virginia repealed the tax, but three years later the commonwealth adopted the Anderson-McCormick election law, which the Richmond *Dispatch* candidly described as an act "operat[ing] to perpetuate the rule of the white man in Virginia."[5] Election laws of the same ilk were enacted in Mississippi, in 1876; North Carolina, in

4. Frenise A. Logan, *The Negro in North Carolina, 1876–1894* (Chapel Hill, N.C., 1964), 27; Williamson, *After Slavery,* 408; Joe Gray Taylor, *Louisiana Reconstructed,* 494–95.

5. Quoted in Charles E. Wynes, *Race Relations in Virginia, 1870–1902* (Charlottesville, Va., 1961), 40. See J. Morgan Kousser, *The Shaping of Southern Politics: Suffrage*

TABLE 7

Southern States Passing Laws to Deny Suffrage to Blacks, 1871–1889

YEAR	POLL TAX	REGISTRATION	MULTIPLE BOX	SECRET BALLOT	APPORTIONMENT	OTHER
1871	Georgia					
1872						
1873						
1874		Texas				
1875	Virginia	Alabama				
1876		Mississippi, Texas				Alabama
1877	Georgia	North Carolina				
1878						
1879				Alabama, Texas		
1880	Virginia					
1881	(repealed)					
1882		South Carolina	South Carolina		Texas	
1883						
1884		Virginia				
1885						
1886						
1887		Florida				
1888						
1889	Florida	Tennessee, North Carolina	Florida	Tennessee		

SOURCES: Allen Going, *Bourbon Democracy in Alabama: 1874–1890* (University, Ala., 1951), 34–35; Vernon Lane Wharton, *The Negro in Mississippi, 1865–1890* (1947; rpr. New York, 1965), 199–200; Frenise A. Logan, *The Negro in North Carolina, 1876–1894* (Chapel Hill, N.C., 1964), 55–58; Lawrence D. Rice, *The Negro in Texas, 1874–1900* (Baton Rouge, 1971), 130–32; J. Morgan Kousser, *The Shaping of Southern Politics: Suffrage Restriction and the Establishment of the One-Party South, 1880–1910* (New Haven, 1974), 85–87, 98–99, 171–72, 210–11, 239.

TABLE 8

Reduction of the Black Electorate:
Proportion of Blacks Voting in Three States in the 1880s

STATE	1880	1884	1888	DECLINE FROM 1880 TO 1888
Florida	88%	86%	64%	27%
Georgia	39	38	19	50
South Carolina	70	35	26	63

SOURCE: Kousser, *The Shaping of Southern Politics*, Tables 3.3, 4.4, pp. 68, 92. Used by permission of Yale University Press.

Note: Florida, Georgia, and South Carolina are the only southern states for which voting-turnout figures by race are available for 1880, 1884, and 1888.

1877; South Carolina, in 1882; and Florida, in 1888. South Carolina made both registration and voting itself more difficult, especially for illiterates.[6]

Precise statistics are hard to come by, but the figures that are available suggest the effectiveness of early efforts at disfranchisement. Table 8 shows the drop in voting participation for three states that collectively accounted for 28 percent of the black population of the South in 1890. In Georgia and South Carolina, more than half the blacks who voted in 1880 were no longer going to the polls in 1888. In Florida, the drop was less dramatic, but it still reflected a 27 percent decline in an eight-year period. What is known of the experience of other states suggests that drops in Florida, Georgia, and South Carolina were all too representative of the southern black experience in the 1880s.

But there were places where the black political presence remained vital. From 1869 to 1891, every session of the Virginia legislature had Negro members, and blacks played a vital role in Tennessee politics until the late 1880s, when they were crushed by lily-white Republi-

---

Restriction and the Establishment of the One-Party South, 1880–1910 (New Haven, 1974), 171–72, 210–11, 239.

6. Kousser, *The Shaping of Southern Politics*, 85–87, 98–99; Frenise A. Logan, *The Negro in North Carolina*, 55–58; Wharton, *The Negro in Mississippi*, 199–200.

cans. In the years from 1879 to 1901, blacks served fourteen terms in Congress.[7] Such numbers can be misleading, however. Of the fourteen congressional terms, two involved disputed elections, in Mississippi and Virginia, in which the black was declared the loser locally but granted office by a Republican Congress. In the absence of northern interference, neither man would have served in Congress. The remaining twelve terms involved representatives from just two congressional districts, which were unusual in having overwhelming black majorities. In North Carolina's Second Congressional District and in South Carolina's Seventh Congressional District, blacks held real political power. Paradoxically, however, the very existence of these districts showed the weakness and political isolation of black Republicans. Both districts came into being only because conservative whites engaged in a deliberate gerrymander aimed at quarantining black political power.[8]

In the 1880s, significant numbers of Black Belt Negroes continued to go to the polls, especially in Alabama, Mississippi, and Louisiana. Still, in these places they were not generally functioning as independent electors. In Alabama, where blacks amounted to almost half the population, no black was sent to the legislature after 1876, and Horace Mann Bond calls the black vote after 1885 in the state a "fictitious entity manipulated by Democratic politicians." Fraud was endemic in Louisiana, too, where in 1888, Black Belt parishes gave the Democratic gubernatorial candidate truly remarkable percentages of the eligible voters: Madison Parish, 104 percent; Tensas Parish, 112 percent; and Concordia Parish, 115 percent. In the Mississippi counties with the densest black population, the races reached an accommodation called fusion, under which they shared the offices, with the whites dominating and getting the most powerful positions. Elsewhere in the state the election statute of 1876 or outright intimidation and violence

---

7. Woodward, *The Strange Career of Jim Crow,* 54; Joel Williamson, *The Crucible of Race: Black-White Relations in the American South Since Emancipation* (New York, 1984), 227–28. Names of black congressmen can be found in Bardolph's *The Negro Vanguard,* 84. Terms of office appear in *Biographical Directory of the American Congress 1774–1971* (Washington, D.C., 1971).

8. Eric Anderson, *Race and Politics in North Carolina, 1872–1901: The Black Second* (Baton Rouge, 1981), 3–5; William J. Cooper, Jr., *The Conservative Regime: South Carolina, 1877–1890* (Baltimore, 1968), 103–107.

did the job. By 1880, only 34 percent of Mississippi's eligible black voters were going to the polls.[9]

Although some blacks continued to vote in many parts of the South, Joel Williamson is correct that "the great mass of blacks had not voted since Reconstruction" and that the period from the end of Reconstruction through 1889 witnessed a large-scale curtailment of black suffrage.[10] Black voters were not yet banned from the polls, but from the perspective of most white southerners, the end was in sight.

It is against this background that the disfranchisement actions of the 1890s must be understood. In 1890, Mississippi became the first state to call a constitutional convention for the purpose of ending black suffrage. Opponents of black voting argued that ever since 1875, fraud and violence at election time had become a way of life, and that they were eating away at the integrity of the state. One white argued for barring blacks from the polls because "the old men of the present generation can't afford to die and leave their children with shot guns in their hands, a lie in their mouths and perjury on their souls in order to defeat the negroes."[11]

A great majority of white southerners would have been happy to amend their state constitutions to include the provision "No Negro in this state shall ever again have the right to vote." But it was universally understood that anything that straightforward would conflict with the Fifteenth Amendment's restriction against the abridgment of the right to vote on grounds of race. Hence, although the pressure for disfranchisement in the 1890s arose in part from the feeling that the time had come to be "honest" about black voting, there was no way to escape a continuing need for at least some dissembling.[12] Consequently, the

9. Horace Mann Bond, *The Negro in Alabama: A Study in Cotton and Steel* (1939; rpr. New York, 1969), 141; Allen Going, *Bourbon Democracy in Alabama, 1874–1890* (University, Ala., 1951), 37–40; Kousser, *The Shaping of Southern Politics*, Table 1.2, pp. 130, 154; Wharton, *The Negro in Mississippi*, 199–204.

10. Williamson, *The Crucible of Race*, 229.

11. Quoted by Wharton in *The Negro in Mississippi*, 207, 206. See Albert D. Kirwan, *Revolt of the Rednecks: Mississippi Politics, 1876–1925* (1951; rpr. Gloucester, Mass., 1964), 58; and William Alexander Percy, *Lanterns on the Levee: Recollections of a Planter's Son* (1941; rpr. Baton Rouge, 1973), 68–69.

12. Francis Butler Simkins, *Pitchfork Ben Tillman: South Carolinian* (Baton Rouge, 1944), 296–99; Kirwan, *Revolt of the Rednecks*, 66–67; Wharton, *The Negro in Mississippi*, 212.

disfranchisers had to continue the pre-1890 practice of fashioning devices that might appear racially neutral but could exclude blacks from the franchise. Poll taxes, property tests, and literacy tests all filled the bill, and all took hold in one state or another. Such methods, though, carried the risk that poor or illiterate whites might also lose their vote.

Some of the disfranchisers felt that to be less a risk than a benefit. Alexander W. Terrell, who headed the forces for disfranchisement in Texas, proposed a poll tax to eliminate the "thriftless idle and semi-vagrant element of both races."[13] Whites outside the Black Belt tended, for their part, to suspect sentiments like Terrell's to be what disfranchisement was all about. The great majority of southern whites had no affection for the idea of black suffrage *per se*, but many held inflexibly that not one white man should lose his vote in order to keep blacks from the polls.[14]

The issue of white exclusion arose at once at the Mississippi constitutional convention. The franchise committee proposed that voters be limited to local residents of at least one year who had paid their poll tax and who had not been convicted of certain specified crimes. In addition, any voter had to be able to read on demand any section of the Mississippi constitution or "understand the same when read to him, or give a reasonable interpretation thereof." The unspoken assumption was that the understanding clause would be used to ensure that no white man was deprived of suffrage by virtue of illiteracy, but many Mississippians felt misgivings. Even so, the franchise committee's proposal became the governing law of the state, and according to Vernon Wharton, the fear that the literacy clause would be used later to eliminate white opponents "proved to be largely unjustified."[15]

Although there were variations from state to state and although only four other states held disfranchising conventions, Mississippi plainly served as a model for most of the South, particularly for states where the black population was densest. At the heart of Mississippi's approach were four elements: a registration procedure designed to eliminate blacks on grounds of residence, criminal convictions, and the like; a poll tax; a literacy test; and an understanding clause meant

13. Quoted by Kousser in *The Shaping of Southern Politics,* 202.

14. Simkins, *Pitchfork Ben Tillman,* 295; Kirwan, *Revolt of the Rednecks,* 66–68; Wharton, *The Negro in Mississippi,* 215.

15. Wharton, *The Negro in Mississippi,* 213–15.

to enable whites to evade the literacy requirement. Although most states substituted a grandfather clause for the understanding clause, the basic strategy of providing an escape hatch for white illiterates was there. The states that followed Mississippi's lead were South Carolina, in 1894–1895; Louisiana, in 1897–1898; North Carolina, in 1899–1900; Alabama, in 1901; Virginia, in 1902; and Georgia, in 1908.[16]

Arkansas, Florida, Tennessee, and Texas held no disfranchising conventions, they did not amend their constitutions, and they did not adopt literacy tests. Rather, they relied largely on poll taxes, secret-ballot legislation, and the white primary to exclude blacks. It was no accident that in three of the four states the proportion of blacks in the population was significantly lower than in the other southern states. The strength of the white counties in these states doubtless accounts for their ability to resist planter pressure for more stringent measures.[17] Forty or fifty years later, Tennessee and Texas were the southern states where blacks voted most freely. Even so, only a small fraction of the eligible black population actually got to the polls.[18]

It is certainly true that Black Belt planters played a major part in ending black suffrage. Still, throughout the broadly based Democratic party in particular, and throughout southern white society in general, there was a wide consensus on the desirability of such a step. Blaming disfranchisement entirely on the planters, by suggesting that they duped the white farmers of the South into acting against their own interests, makes the planters into all-powerful villains and ordinary

16. *Ibid.*, 213; Simkins, *Pitchfork Ben Tillman*, 297; Kousser, *The Shaping of Southern Politics*, 239; V. O. Key, Jr., *Southern Politics in State and Nation* (New York, 1949), 538, 556.

17. The proportions of blacks in the total population of the southern states in 1890 were Texas, 21.85 percent; Tennessee, 24.37 percent; Arkansas, 27.41 percent; North Carolina, 34.71 percent; Virginia, 38.38 percent; Florida, 42.49 percent; Alabama, 44.87 percent; Georgia, 46.75 percent; Louisiana, 50.04 percent; Mississippi, 57.68 percent; and South Carolina, 59.86 percent. The proportions are calculated from figures in U.S. Bureau of the Census, *Negro Population*, 44.

18. Figures on the extent of black voting after disfranchisement are scanty. Working in the late 1930s, Ralph Bunche and his assistants estimated black voting in the southern states: Mississippi, a few hundred; Alabama, 1,500; South Carolina, 1,500; Louisiana, 2,007; Arkansas, 8,000; Florida, 10,000; Georgia, 10,000; Virginia, 20,000; North Carolina, 50,000; Tennessee, 50,000; and Texas, 50,000. See Gunnar Myrdal, *An American Dilemma: The Negro Problem and Modern Democracy* (2 vols.; New York, 1962), I, 486–88.

whites into virtuous fools. It presumes that ordinary white farmers could not think for themselves, and it forgets that one hardly needed to be a wealthy planter to employ black hired hands and to identify with others who used black workers. It also fails to acknowledge that, however large the gap between rich and poor whites, in important ways the two shared a culture. Tragically, the culture was deeply imbued with racist ideas.[19] Unfortunately, the realities of southern life determined that there was never a significant chance that a coalition between blacks and ordinary whites might work. As Lawrence Goodwyn has commented, Populism came into being in an "American environment suffused by the cultural values of white supremacy." Here and there blacks and whites made brief alliances with each other, but the alliances were never based on a genuine white commitment to racial equality. Although black and white farmers confronted many of the same economic ills, they had different political priorities. Writing on coalition politics in Kansas, William Chafe persuasively argues that their differences posed a major obstacle to any alliance between the two groups. He notes that "the primary concern of the white person was economic," whereas "the primary concerns of the Negro . . . were prejudice and violence."[20]

Just as disfranchisement was an outgrowth of events in the 1880s and earlier, so too with lynching. Although this kind of mob murder is mainly associated with the years after 1890, it was part of southern life by the early 1880s.[21] As Table 9 shows, the second half of the decade witnessed a massive increase in the frequency with which the crime occurred. In the years from 1885 to 1889, the number of lynchings of blacks increased by about 63.5 percent over what it had been in the previous five-year period. Never again did the rate rise quite so steeply, not even in the early 1890s.

19. The view that ordinary farmers were used and misled is associated with the larger conviction that Populism had the potential for creating an interracial coalition of mudsills and bottom rails that might have transformed the South. See Woodward, *Tom Watson*, 216–43; and Lawrence C. Goodwyn, "Populist Dreams and Negro Rights: East Texas as a Case Study," *American Historical Review*, LXXVI (1971), 1435–56.

20. Lawrence Goodwyn, *Democratic Promise: The Populist Movement in America* (New York, 1976), 276, 285–91, 299; William H. Chafe, "The Negro and Populism: A Kansas Case Study," *Journal of Southern History*, XXXIV (1968), 418. See also Barton C. Shaw, *The Wool-Hat Boys: Georgia's Populist Party* (Baton Rouge, 1984).

21. Williamson, *The Crucible of Race*, 184.

TABLE 9

Lynchings in the United States, 1880–1968

PERIOD	NUMBER	CHANGE FROM PRIOR PERIOD
1880–1884	233[a]	
1885–1889	381	63.5%
1890–1894	611	60.4
1895–1899	500	−18.2
1900–1904	456	−8.8
1905–1909	335	−26.5
1910–1914	291	−13.1
1915–1919	278	−4.5
1920–1924	208	−25.2
1925–1929	73	−64.9
1930–1934	77	5.5
1935–1939	42	−45.4
1940–1944	19	−54.8
1945–1949	12	−6.8
1950–1954	2	−83.3
1955–1959	4	100.0
1960–1964	3	−25.0
1965–1968	0	00.0
Total	3,525	

SOURCE: Robert L. Zangrando, *The NAACP Crusade Against Lynching, 1909–1950* (Philadelphia, 1980), Table 2, pp. 6–7.

Note: The overwhelming majority of the lynchings took place in the South. The former Confederate South accounted for 3,099 lynchings, the border South for 314, and the rest of the nation for 112. See Zangrando, *The NAACP Crusade,* Table 1. The estimates described in note *a* were allocated proportionately.

[a]Figures for 1880 and 1881 were extrapolated from the data for 1882–1889 by means of a trend analysis. The extrapolated numbers were 37 for 1880 and 43 for 1881.

It is necessary to distinguish between the sort of mob violence en-demic during Reconstruction and lynching as it developed a few years later. In Reconstruction, mob violence most often stopped short of murder, and when killing was involved, it happened without cere-mony. Moreover, the violence tended to take the form of political intimidation or of a response to some real or imagined incident in which whites supposed that a black had stepped out of his place.[22] By contrast, lynching was "ritualized murder" conducted under the claim that the mob was dispensing justice. It had been around throughout most of American history, but in the post-Reconstruction South it took on an especially savage character, with hundreds of men, women, and children from wide areas participating in brutal ceremonies in which torture, mutilation, and burning sometimes preceded the killing.[23] One of the primary defenses of lynching was that it was necessary to protect white womanhood, but almost three-quarters of the lynchings did not involve charges of rape or attempted rape at all.[24]

Clearly, blacks of the 1880s knew about lynching. Tuskegee Institute was founded in mid-1881, and the lynching statistics that the school kept begin with 1882, when forty-nine blacks and sixty-four whites died by this sort of mob violence. In August, 1887, Jesse B. Duke, the editor of the Montgomery *Herald*, a black newspaper, editorialized against lynching, suggesting that some alleged rapes were cases where the white woman had willingly consented to sex with a black partner. In consequence of the indiscreet remark, Duke had to flee Montgomery to avoid becoming a lynch victim himself. A year later an instructor at Tuskegee was forced to resign after publishing an attack on lynching, in a Mississippi paper.[25]

The incident with Duke suggests that lynching was a fully developed phenomenon by August, 1887. Still, that he ventured to be so indiscreet may imply that the phenomenon was brand-new and that blacks did not yet fully appreciate the situation they faced. If that is so, however, what explains that in 1898 a black editor in Wilmington, North Carolina, made precisely the same sort of allegation as Duke, sparking the riot there?[26]

In 1892, lynching reached a monstrous all-time high, with 161

---

22. *Ibid.*, 183.

23. Robert L. Zangrando, *The NAACP Crusade Against Lynching, 1909–1950* (Philadelphia, 1980), 4, 8; Williamson, *The Crucible of Race*, 183–89. Between 1882 and 1885, the number of whites lynched in any year exceeded the number of blacks lynched. Then came a great reversal. See Table 2 in Zangrando's book.

24. Zangrando, *The NAACP Crusade*, 8.

25. *Ibid.*, 6–7; Louis R. Harlan, ed., *The Booker T. Washington Papers* (13 vols.; Urbana, Ill., 1972), II, 326, 474–75.

26. Harlan, ed., *The Booker T. Washington Papers*, IV, 459–60.

blacks murdered by mob action. After that the numbers began to drop, but the decline was agonizingly slow and it took over seventy years before lynching ended. The weight of the evidence suggests that lynching was not a class phenomenon. If lower-class whites often made up a disproportionate part of the mob, the defenders of their action included senators, governors, planters, professionals, and business people. In 1893, the infamous lynching of Henry Smith, in Paris, Texas, drew a crowd of ten thousand. People came by special trains arranged for the occasion. Present at the torture, mutilation, and murder of Smith were men of social and business standing and women "whose culture entitled them to be among the social and intellectual leaders of the town."[27]

Even though the great majority of lynchings had nothing to do with sexual crimes, white southerners apparently believed that lynching was, first of all, a defense of white womanhood. At the nub of this connection, according to Joel Williamson, was the white myth of the "black beast rapist" who had to be held in check at all costs. Whatever the roots of that myth, the long history of the miscegenation laws seems to show that from colonial times onward, whites had been preoccupied over interracial sex.[28] Clearly, the idea of the "black beast rapist" had strong links to the fears that led earlier generations of whites to erect elaborate legal barriers against miscegenation.

Indeed, as Table 10 demonstrates, the generation preceding 1890 had done its work so well that by the time the lynching fever reached its zenith, the South was blanketed with miscegenation statutes. By the end of 1866, at least five former Confederate states had adopted new laws or constitutional provisions banning racial intermarriage or penalizing those who sanctioned such unions. Moreover, it seems certain that the states that neglected to enact such measures did so only because they already had miscegenation laws on the books from the antebellum era.

In the years from 1868 to 1871, with Reconstruction at high tide,

27. Quoted by Williamson in *The Crucible of Race*, 186, 185. See Zangrando, *The NAACP Crusade*, 6.

28. Williamson, *The Crucible of Race*, 306–309; Joel Williamson, *New People: Miscegenation and Mulattoes in the United States* (New York, 1980), 10–12; Winthrop D. Jordan, *White over Black: American Attitudes Toward the Negro, 1550–1812* (Chapel Hill, N.C., 1968), 164–72, 469–71.

TABLE 10

School Segregation and Miscegenation Laws in the South, 1865–1915

Year	ALABAMA	ARKANSAS	FLORIDA	GEORGIA	LOUISIANA	MISSISSIPPI	NORTH CAROLINA	SOUTH CAROLINA	TENNESSEE	TEXAS	VIRGINIA
1865	Mc			M		M		M			
1866	Mx	MS						M	S	Sc	
1867											
1868	S				*S*			*MS*	S		
1869											
1870					*M*				MMcSSc		S
1871						*Mx*					
1872				S							
1873		S						M	S		Mx
1874											
1875	Sc				*S*		McSc				
1876		SSc									M
1877				Sc							
1878	S					S					
1879					So				M	Mx	
1880						Mx					
1881			Mx						S		S
1882											
1883											
1884		Mx									
1885			Sc						S		
1886											
1887			Sc								
1888											
1889											
1890						McSc					
1891											
1892											
1893											
1894					M						
1895		S						McSc			
1896						S		S			
1897		S									

TABLE 10

(continued)

YEAR	ALABAMA	ARKANSAS	FLORIDA	GEORGIA	LOUISIANA	MISSISSIPPI	NORTH CAROLINA	SOUTH CAROLINA	TENNESSEE	TEXAS	VIRGINIA
1898					Sc						
1899											
1900											
1901	McSc						S		S		
1902											Sc
1903			M				S				
1904											
1905											
1906											
1907	Mx										
1908					M						
1909											
1910											
1911											
1912				S							
1913		S									
1914											
1915											

SOURCE: Summaries of statutes given by Franklin Johnson in *The Development of State Legislation Concerning the Free Negro* (1918; rpr. Westport, Conn., 1979).

Note: Included in the table are state laws and constitutional provisions dealing with miscegenation and school segregation. In a handful of cases, particularly in the years from 1868 to 1870, the laws tabulated here barred segregation or made miscegenation permissible. The listings of those laws are italicized. Abbreviations: M = miscegenation measure; S = school segregation measure; c = constitutional provision; x = change in state code without a separate session law; o = action by omission in state constitution.

Louisiana, Mississippi, and South Carolina had repealed their miscegenation laws. The countertrend did not last long. Between 1870 and 1884, nine of the eleven southern states took action—or further action—to ban miscegenation. Tennessee enacted both a constitutional prohibition and a law. Virginia and the Carolinas passed bills banning intermarriages. In Alabama and Texas, the supreme courts upheld antebellum statutes prohibiting blacks and whites from intermarrying. Arkansas, Florida, and Mississippi quietly resurrected antebellum miscegenation statutes that had been dropped from the books or become dormant during Reconstruction. Between 1870 and 1884, only Louisiana and Georgia failed to act on miscegenation, and in the case of Georgia the inaction appears to have been due to satisfaction with a statute of 1866.[29]

Table 10 reveals that even in the hysterical years from 1890 onward, there was little rush to rewrite the miscegenation laws. When Mississippi, South Carolina, and Alabama held their disfranchising conventions, they took the opportunity to write antimiscegenation provisions into their fundamental laws. Beyond that, only Louisiana and Florida enacted miscegenation statutes after 1884. Although the myth of the "black beast rapist" was a new and ominous development, it was in tune with old fears. In particular, from emancipation onward there was a concern with prohibiting any sexual relationship that carried with it the hint that whites and blacks might be equal.[30]

At bottom, the miscegenation acts were the ultimate segregation laws. They embodied the very essence of the beliefs southern whites held about race: that whites were racially superior to blacks and that any mixing of the two groups was bound to sully the whites. They were, besides, among the racial laws most frequently enacted in the post–Civil War era.[31]

Still, as Table 10 discloses, school-segregation laws were even more popular. Just after the war, at the time of the black codes, Tennessee and Arkansas prohibited blacks from attending white schools. Then, as Reconstruction began to crumble, there came a deluge of such measures. In 1869, Virginia established a constitutional ban against school

29. Here and below the information about state miscegenation and segregation laws is from Franklin Johnson's *The Development of State Legislation Concerning the Free Negro* (1918; rpr. Westport, Conn., 1979). This work is a comprehensive compilation of statutes making reference to race. Because it is organized by states and by chronology within states, page references are omitted here and below. See also Charles S. Mangum, Jr., *The Legal Status of the Negro* (Chapel Hill, N.C., 1940), 241.

30. Johnson, *State Legislation.*

31. *Ibid.;* Williamson, *New People.* See also George M. Frederickson, *White Supremacy: A Comparative Study in American and South African History* (New York, 1981), 126, 129, 130.

integration. Similar constitutional prohibitions followed in Tennessee, in 1870; Alabama and North Carolina, in 1875; Texas, in 1876; Georgia, in 1877; and Florida, in 1885 and 1887. By simple statute, Arkansas and Mississippi banned racial integration in the classroom in 1873 and 1878 respectively.[32]

Louisiana acted by omission. The state's fundamental law of 1868 contained an unequivocal ban on school segregation, but a new constitution in 1879 was totally silent on the matter. South Carolina's constitution of 1868 said that every public school was to be open to all, "regardless of race or color," but its *Revised Statutes* of 1873 contained no legislation addressing segregation in the schools. In 1874, the New York *Times* reported segregation in the South Carolina public schools everywhere except in remote places with white schools only.[33]

By the late 1880s, state school-segregation laws were fully in place almost everywhere in the South. It is hardly surprising then that from 1890 to 1915 the pace of legislation slowed despite the heated racial climate. Between 1868 and 1888, the eleven southern states had adopted eighteen such statutes. From 1889 to 1915, they added thirteen more. The later laws were often redundant assertions of the mood of the white South rather than remedies against specific vestiges of equality.[34]

Although the laws of school segregation and miscegenation were fully in place prior to the 1890s, most of the state laws segregating transportation, public accommodations, and the like came later. Even there, however, the legal groundwork was established by 1890. Just after the Civil War, Florida, Mississippi, and Texas passed bills requiring segregation on the railroads, but Reconstruction negated them. Then, in a brief moment just before the collapse of Reconstruction, seven states adopted civil-rights statutes prohibiting, or appearing to prohibit, discrimination on the railroads (see Table 11). In 1875, the United States Congress adopted a civil-rights act of its own.

Responding to the passage of this federal law, Tennessee devised legislation that protected hotels, railroads, restaurants, and places of amusement from legal suits charging discrimination. In 1881, the four blacks in the Tennessee legislature made a valiant fight to repeal that act, or at least to eliminate its coverage of railroads. They lost, but the

32. Johnson, *State Legislation.*
33. *Ibid.;* Williamson, *After Slavery,* 222.
34. Johnson, *State Legislation.*

TABLE 11

Railroad and Streetcar Segregation Laws in the South, 1865–1915

Year	Alabama	Arkansas	Florida	Georgia	Louisiana	Mississippi	North Carolina	South Carolina	Tennessee	Texas	Virginia
1865			R			R					
1866										R	
1867											
1868											
1869					C*c*			C			
1870				C*c*							
1871										C*c*	
1872											
1873		C	C		C	C					
1874											
1875									Cx		
1876											
1877	M										
1878											
1879											
1880											
1881									R		
1882									Rf		
1883											
1884									Rf		
1885											
1886											
1887			R								
1888						R					
1889										R	
1890					R						
1891	R	R		R					R	R	
1892											
1893		R									
1894					RD						
1895											
1896											

TABLE 11

(continued)

YEAR	ALABAMA	ARKANSAS	FLORIDA	GEORGIA	LOUISIANA	MISSISSIPPI	NORTH CAROLINA	SOUTH CAROLINA	TENNESSEE	TEXAS	VIRGINIA
1897											
1898								R			
1899				R			R				R
1900								R			
1901											S
1902					S						S
1903	S							R	S		
1904						S					R
1905			S					S	S		
1906						RD					S
1907			DS				S			RS	
1908											
1909			R								
1910											
1911											
1912											
1913											
1914										R	
1915											

SOURCE: Summaries of statutes given by Franklin Johnson in *The Development of State Legislation Concerning the Free Negro.*

Note: Included in the table are state laws dealing with segregation on railroads and streetcars. Abbreviations: C = broad civil-rights act applying to public carriers, public accommodations, and the like; Cc = civil-rights act limited to public carriers of one sort or another; Cx = law protecting businesses *against* civil-rights suits; D = law segregating railroad depots or waiting rooms; R = law segregating railroads; Rf = law requiring that passengers paying first-class rates be carried in a first-class car; S = law segregating streetcars. Italics mark laws that ran against the trend toward segregation.

legislature did pass a supposed compromise requiring the railroads to provide blacks with "separate but equal" facilities. Legislation in 1882 and 1884 ordered first-class passengers to be accommodated in first-class cars, but that simply meant that blacks paying the first-class fare were entitled to their own segregated section.[35]

Tennessee's compromise of 1881 appears the point of departure for other states' laws that aimed at segregating transportation in the South. As Table 11 shows, in the years from 1887 to 1894 there occurred a wave of lawmaking to segregate the railroads. Virtually all of the new laws incorporated the principle of "separate but equal." Florida, Mississippi, and Texas were the first states in the new wave, and in an interesting coincidence, they were precisely the three states that had enacted the short-lived railroad segregation laws of 1865 and 1866.[36]

By the time this crest of railroad legislation subsided in 1894, all the southern states except Virginia and the Carolinas had passed laws. Then, beginning in 1898, a more powerful wave brought these states into the fold. At the same time, many of the old laws were strengthened, and nine states added statutes mandating streetcar segregation.[37]

A few state segregation laws of the post-1890 period did go beyond earlier statutes. In 1906, Mississippi decided that in cities of over three thousand residents the city commission had to establish separate toilets by both race and sex. In 1912, Louisiana and Virginia passed cumbersome residential segregation laws. Even so, the number of such state laws is surprisingly small when compared with the extent of segregation in the fabric of everyday southern life. As Howard Rabinowitz has observed, the southern segregation system was the result more of custom and local ordinance than of state statutes.[38]

It is clear that the drive to white domination in the South occurred on many fronts simultaneously and that disfranchisement, lynching, segregation, and the opposition to miscegenation were linked to one

35. Ibid.; Woodward, The Strange Career of Jim Crow, 23–24; Joseph H. Cartwright, The Triumph of Jim Crow: Tennessee Race Relations in the 1880's (Knoxville, Tenn., 1976), 102–104.

36. Johnson, State Legislation.

37. Ibid.

38. Ibid.; Rabinowitz, Race Relations in the Urban South, passim; John Hope Franklin, "History of Racial Segregation in the United States," Annals of the American Academy of Political and Social Science, CCCIV (1956), 6–9.

another in the white determination to put blacks back "in their place." The laws and practices that southerners accepted in order to achieve that end bespeak a society in which the ideology of white supremacy reigned almost unchallenged. The world without slavery was also to be a world where white hegemony was complete.

In it, laws pertaining to convicts, prisons, and punishment played a central role. Emancipation created the need for a vastly enlarged prison system, but the funds for expansion were not available. Across the South, whites resisted spending money on their former bondsmen, even money for prisons.[39] At the same time, they constantly demanded strict controls to keep the blacks "where they belong." From that perspective, what was needed was a self-supporting penal system capable of controlling blacks. The South drew on the experience of slaveholders and on developments in nineteenth-century penology to come up with systems that shifted the cost of punishment to the convicts themselves. In antebellum and northern experiments, convicts had been worked both inside and outside prison walls and had been employed both by states and by private contractors. Almost always, however, they remained under the direct supervision of prison officials.[40] What sharply distinguished the postbellum convict labor system in the South from the early experiments is that, taking a leaf from the slave hiring system, it permitted the lease of prisoners for unsupervised use outside the prison walls. At both the state and the county level, convict labor became a commodity as governments hired out prisoners to railroads, corporations, and farmers.[41]

Convict labor laws were an integral part of the effort to create a new legal structure to deal with emancipation on white terms and, hence, should be seen as part of the black codes. In 1866, Florida permitted counties to hire their convicts out to individual contractors. North Carolina established county chain gangs to work on the roads

39. Fletcher M. Green, "Some Aspects of the Convict Lease System in the Southern States," in *Essays in Southern History Presented to Joseph Gregoire de Roulhac Hamilton,* ed. Fletcher M. Green (Chapel Hill, N.C., 1949), 112–13.

40. *Ibid.,* 113–14; Edward L. Ayers, *Vengeance and Justice: Crime and Punishment in the Nineteenth-Century American South* (New York, 1984), 185–222.

41. The best accounts of the leasing system are in Ayers' *Vengeance and Justice* and in Dan T. Carter's "Prisons, Politics, and Business: The Convict Lease System in the Post–Civil War South" (M.A. thesis, University of Wisconsin, 1964).

and made it legal for counties to hire their convicts out to railroads and other corporations. In the same period, Arkansas, Tennessee, and Virginia legislated provisions for hiring out state convicts. Four states— Alabama, Georgia, Mississippi, and Texas—legalized the hiring-out of prisoners at either the state or the county level. Alabama authorized counties to lease prisoners to persons or corporations anywhere within the state "as may be determined by the court of county commissioners." It appears that Louisiana and South Carolina got started late, but by 1873 they too were leasing out prisoners.[42]

Ironically, some of the worst aspects of the southern prison labor system originated with the Republican governments of Reconstruction. Operating in a world of scarce tax dollars and crumbling prisons, the Republicans turned to leasing as a temporary expedient. In the process, they discovered that hiring out convicts relieved the state of custodial responsibilities at the same time that it brought in revenue.[43]

The engagement of Republican governments in leasing appears to have been almost exclusively for reasons of state economics, fortified sometimes by the lures of greed and corruption. The same reasons impelled the Redeemers, when they came to power, but for them there were racial motives as well. Though no one said so directly, the Redeemers were committed to using black convicts for internal southern development. Beyond that, many saw the convict labor system as a means of disciplining the black labor force.

In 1868, expressing widely held white attitudes, a newspaper in Milledgeville, Georgia, applauded the sending of two hundred state convicts to work on the Macon and Brunswick Railroad. On the

---

42. Alabama, *Penal Code*, 1866, secs. 218, 220, 265; Arkansas, *Acts*, 1866–67, pp. 76–84; Florida, *Acts*, 1866, p. 13; Georgia, *Acts*, 1865–66; p. 37; Mississippi, *Laws*, 1865, pp. 166–67, 1866–67, p. 735; Tennessee, *Acts*, 1865–66, p. 48; Texas, *General Laws*, 1866, pp. 119, 192–93; Virginia, *Acts*, 1865–66, p. 217; Jesse F. Steiner and Roy M. Brown, *The North Carolina Chain Gang: A Study of County Convict Road Work* (Chapel Hill, N.C., 1927), 21, citing North Carolina, *Public Laws*, 1866–67, Chap. 30, 1872–73, Chap. 174, sec. 10, 1874–75, Chap. 113; James C. Bonner, "The Georgia Penitentiary at Milledgeville, 1807–1874," *Georgia Historical Quarterly*, LV (1971), 320–21; Mark T. Carleton, *Politics and Punishment: The Story of the Louisiana Penal System* (Baton Rouge, 1971), 17; Tindall, *South Carolina Negroes*, 266.

43. Carter, "Prisons, Politics, and Business," 46–53; Ayers, *Vengeance and Justice*, 188–90.

grounds that placing petty criminals in "comfortable quarters . . . where they are well-fed, clothed and doctored, amounts to no punishment at all and almost a dead expense to the taxpayers," the newspaper endorsed putting minor offenders to work upon the railroads, thereby making them "pay their own expenses." [44] Focusing less on crime than on race, the paper went on: "The revolution in Southern society calls for a revision of our whole criminal code. The city for instance pays fifty dollars every day to support a lazy good-for-nothing set of vagabonds who infest her guard house. . . . Our people are sick and tired of it and unanimously demand the formation of these rascals into working squads for the improvement of our streets." [45] White southerners wanted a cost-free method of punishing black misdeeds, but they also wanted to make blacks perform public services that the poverty-stricken South could not otherwise afford.

The Georgia editor began by praising convict leasing but ended with a proposal for putting petty convicts to work on public projects. What counted was not who worked the prisoners but that they be set to compulsory labor of benefit to the community. In the period from the Civil War to the 1890s, the emphasis was upon the hiring-out of prisoners, but when the evils of leasing became too obvious to ignore, the leasing states shifted to other forms of compulsory labor without missing a beat. [46]

As the Redeemers took power in one state after another, convict leasing grew ever stronger. In 1874, Redeemers in Georgia expanded the power of the governor to lease out convicts and provided also that prisoners could be hired out to any private citizen. Their statute even sanctioned convicts' hiring themselves out. It said, "It shall be lawful for such convict to hire himself or herself to any citizen who pays the amount of said sentence." [47]

Little is known about the extent of county leasing during Recon-

---

44. *Southern Recorder* (Ga.), November 17, 1868.

45. *Ibid.*

46. Carter, "Prisons, Politics, and Business," 96–102.

47. Georgia, *Supplement to Code,* 1874–77, p. 94, citing Georgia, *Acts,* 1874, p. 29; Bonner, "The Georgia Penitentiary," 324. In 1894, in *Walton Co. v. Franklin,* the Georgia Supreme Court ruled against the hiring-out of county convicts to individuals (95 Ga. 538).

struction, but it is clear that the victory of the Redeemers brought a sharp rise in plans to put local convicts to work. In March, 1877, the Vicksburg *Daily Commercial* strongly criticized the condition of local roads, which it charged was due either to negligence or to the inefficiency "of our system of working the roads." Addressing the county board of supervisors, the paper noticed: "In some other counties of the State the jail prisoners are being successfully worked on the roads at small expense, and the experiment might be tried in this county. We all know the usefulness of our city 'chaingang.' "[48] The editorial proposed that the board of supervisors direct Sheriff Flanagan "to employ this labor on the county roads." It concluded, "Once let the work be started, let the necessity for good roads be once realized and appreciated, and Vicksburg will gain an advantage which she will be slow to lose."[49] Three weeks later, the *Daily Commercial* reported that its idea had received endorsement from the influential Cotton Exchange and that the board of supervisors had approved the plan. With satisfaction, it announced, "As soon as this court adjourns[,] Capt. Flanagan will be out upon the road with his force doing great good where so little has heretofore been done."[50]

This incident illustrates the way southern localities learned from one another in their effort to reassert white domination. A second notable example of that is the adaption by South Carolinians of the "Mississippi plan" to their own uses in 1876. They invited a former South Carolinian who lived in Mississippi to return to his native state "to give practical instruction in the 'Mississippi plan' of carrying elections in [the] face of a hostile majority."[51] The same sort of emulation led Dallas County, Alabama, to decide in 1886 to work its convicts on the county roads; its decision came only after its commissioners went to see how the system worked in Georgia.[52]

Nowhere is the link between the end of Reconstruction and the development of leasing sharper than in South Carolina. Federal troops

48. Vicksburg (Miss.) *Daily Commercial*, March 29, 1877.

49. *Ibid.*

50. *Ibid.*, April 17, 1877.

51. Alfred B. Williams, *Hampton and His Red Shirts: South Carolina's Deliverance in 1876* (1935; rpr. Freeport, N.Y., 1970), 65–66, 31–32.

52. Montgomery *Daily Advertiser*, December 24, 1886.

left the state in April, 1877, and within two months the legislature had enacted a bill to "Utilize the Convict Labor of this State." It provided that, except for those convicted of the most heinous crimes, state convicts could be hired out. Apparently, the state never permitted leasing at the county level, but in 1885 it joined the move to work county convicts on the streets and roads.[53] Thus began the South Carolina chain gang, an institution that persisted long after leasing was abandoned as barbaric.

Chatham County, Georgia (which includes the city of Savannah), sits along the Georgia coast in a lowland area dense with swamps. One of the major uses of its convict labor was to drain those areas. The work was hard, dirty, and unhealthful, and almost all of it was done by blacks. Because nearby Liberty County had no sizable project on which to work its convicts, it hit upon the notion of sending them to help on Chatham's Cuyler Swamp Canal. Thus, said the local newspaper, "Chatham will secure the labor of these convicts and Liberty will be relieved of the expense of feeding and caring for them."[54]

The precise means by which Chatham County got its own work force is apparent from a tribute that was part of a small ceremony in 1892 in the Savannah City Court, presided over by Judge William D. Harden. The jurist had announced his retirement, and the grand jury answered with a homage to the judge. It said that he had "shown favor to none and [had] been absolutely fearless and impartial in his rulings." Then it focused on his central achievements: "His system of imposing long periods of penal servitude on persons guilty of crimes involving moral turpitude and not imposing fines, besides appreciably lessening the number of crimes committed, first made it possible for the great work of draining the country to be undertaken and successfully carried out by the county commissioners, a work which has increased the value of the taxable property of our county by hundreds of thousands of dollars."[55]

Some states even adjusted their laws in order to build up the convict pool that could be leased out. Mississippi's infamous "pig law" of

53. Tindall, *South Carolina Negroes,* 267.
54. Savannah *Morning News,* August 30, 1882, February 12, 1881, August 31, 1886, January 4, January 24, 1890.
55. *Ibid.,* January 12, 1892.

1876 defined the theft of any property valued at over ten dollars or of any cattle or swine as grand larceny. In 1874, the state had 272 state convicts. By 1877, the number was 1,072. In 1887, when the law was repealed, the number was 966. Fourteen months later it was only 484.[56]

All across the South, conditions for convicts were horrendous. Between 1877 and 1880, 285 South Carolina prisoners were sent to build the Greenwood and Augusta Railroad. Of these, 128, or 44.9 percent, died in the three-year period. Tennessee supposedly had a better record than most southern states, but in the biennium 1884–1885, when its prison population averaged 600, there were 163 deaths. In the years from 1880 to 1885, the death rate in Mississippi for white convicts averaged 5.3 percent a year. The comparable figure for blacks was 10.97 percent. By contrast, annual mortality at six midwestern prisons in the period 1884–1886 averaged from 0.51 percent to 1.08 percent a year.[57]

Those who dealt in convict labor were never so indelicate as to own to the resemblance between their system and antebellum slavery. Still, as Dan Carter has noted, "they used the same methods of classifying their labor. Lessees divided convicts into first, second, third, fourth, and fifth class hands, much as slave-owners did before 1860." In some respects, convict labor was worse than slavery. Under slavery, chains and shackles were used only by slave traders and for discipline. In the postbellum era, they were standard equipment for prisoners who labored outside the prison walls. In the early 1880s, Georgia's "General Notice to Lessees" specified, however, that "in all cases of severe illness the shackles must be promptly removed."[58]

On a visit to the United States in 1878, Sir George Campbell met with former and current members of a Georgia convict leasing concern. One of these men admitted that he quit the company "because he could not stand the inhumanity of it." On the other hand, one partner talked gleefully of all the money he was making. Campbell

56. Green, "Some Aspects of the Convict Lease System," 120–21; Wharton, *The Negro in Mississippi,* 237.

57. Cohen, "Negro Involuntary Servitude," 56; Wharton, *The Negro in Mississippi,* 240–41. See also George W. Cable, "The Convict Lease System in the Southern States," *Century,* n.s., V (1884), 589.

58. Quoted by Cable in "The Convict Lease System," 592 (italics added by Cable have been removed); Carter, "Prisons, Politics, and Business," 63.

concluded, "This does seem simply a return to another form of slavery."[59]

The southern convict labor system had many faces by the late 1880s. In some places, it was a leasing system that gave the lessees total control over the prisoners. Elsewhere, as in Alabama, the state was beginning to take at least some responsibility for guarding and caring for its prisoners. Beyond that, many states and counties used the public-account system, under which government itself worked the prisoners on public projects like roads and bridges. The most popular form of public-account system was the county chain gang. By 1886, all the former Confederate states except Louisiana, South Carolina, and Virginia had some sort of law permitting that employment of county convicts.[60] Often, at the county level, leasing existed side by side or in alternating sequence with the publicly operated chain gang. How the alternating sequence might operate is illustrated by the situation in Monroe County, Mississippi, in 1883, when the county had trouble leasing out its convicts. On February 7, the board of supervisors ordered its clerk to "re-advertise for the hire of the county prisoners," with the contract to go to the highest bidder. Several weeks later the county was still trying to lease the convicts out, but since the contractor for the Canton, Aberdeen and Nashville Railroad had just declined to hire them, the situation looked bleak. On March 3, the board voted to employ a guard to work the county prisoners on the roads. At the same time, however, it reserved the right to rescind its order any time an acceptable bid for the prisoners came along.[61]

By the 1880s there was in the South a convict labor system designed to deliver a maximum of punishment at a minimum of cost to the taxpayers. Targeted against blacks, it rested on the assumptions that they were innately criminal and that whites were entitled to appropriate their labor for the common good. As white southerners struggled to regain racial control at the polls and in the social sphere, the omnipresent convict labor system threatened the liberty of any black who might challenge the new order. Equally significant, it stood

59. Sir George Campbell, *White and Black: The Outcome of a Visit to the United States* (London, 1879), 365.

60. Steiner and Brown, *The North Carolina Chain Gang,* 16.

61. Aberdeen (Miss.) *Examiner,* February 15, March 8, March 15, 1883.

as a powerful potential sanction against laborers who might break their contracts or question an employer's method of accounting.

As the convict labor system took form, planters continued their effort to reshape the labor system the North had imposed. Although they had adjusted quickly to the principle of free labor that enabled them to discharge unneeded workers, they found it harder to accept that blacks had a corresponding freedom to change jobs when they pleased. Thus, apprehensive post-Reconstruction planters set to weave a fabric of law that would limit black movement. In that, however, they advanced somewhat more slowly than in matters like disfranchisement, miscegenation, and school segregation. The whites were more divided on questions of black labor than on other issues involving race. The planter with a full work force might well favor a stringent law against labor agents, but the farmer several counties off who desperately needed hands probably had other ideas. Moreover, whites who never used black workers had different opinions on mobility than planters whose livelihood depended on black labor.

Despite the crosscurrents, post-Reconstruction planters continued trying to fashion a world very much akin to what the black codes of 1865 had envisioned. Almost all the labor-control measures they favored were either replications or extensions of measures first conceived just after emancipation.

Tennessee was the only former Confederate state that had not adopted an enticement law immediately after the war. In 1875, though, it made up for the omission by simultaneously enacting an enticement law and a vagrancy law. The enticement law forbade employers to hire anyone "under contract or in the employ of another." Willful violators were liable for damages to the original employer. Those who unknowingly hired someone already under contract were liable for damages unless, upon knowledge, they discharged the worker in question.[62] The Tennessee law was conjoined with a contract enforcement statute that penalized workers who broke their labor agreements "without good and sufficient cause." They were to forfeit "all sums due for service already rendered, and be liable for such other damages [as] the employer may reasonably [claim]." On the day this bill was signed into law, the governor also approved a vagrancy measure that

---

62. Tennessee, *Acts,* 1875, pp. 168–69; Cohen, "Negro Involuntary Servitude," 37.

gave judges broad latitude in sentencing. Blacks were certain that the bill was aimed at them.[63]

Legislation does not always achieve its purpose, but the passage of restrictive laws in the South sheds light on the kind of world postbellum employers wished to build. In addition, the up-and-down history of some of the statutes is a good historical barometer. Arkansas adopted its enticement law in 1867 but repealed it a year later under the pressure of Reconstruction. Then, in 1875, the state reenacted precisely the same law.[64]

In the years from 1880 to 1882, South Carolina, Alabama, North Carolina, and Georgia all adopted enticement measures. South Carolina's black code of 1865 had included such a provision, which had been lost, however, when Union authorities invalidated the entire code. In 1880, the state imposed a substantially similar regulation penalizing anyone who "by any means whatsoever" enticed or persuaded any tenant, servant, or laborer to violate a labor contract.[65] Because the language Alabama employed was racially neutral, its enticement law survived Reconstruction. But by 1881 the original wording was not strong enough to suit state legislators, so a clause was added making the mere attempt to entice a laborer a criminal offense. The story was similar in North Carolina, where an amendment in 1881 made the law of 1866 applicable to oral contracts as well as written ones. Georgia acted by greatly increasing the penalties for enticement.[66] Thus, as Table 12 makes clear, the end of Reconstruction brought a small wave of enticement legislation in more than half the Confederate South between 1875 and 1882.

The number of states enacting or stiffening such laws would have been even larger except for veto by the governor of Mississippi in 1884. Four years earlier, Louisiana had debated one too, but little is known of how or why it failed. Both states came into the fold in 1890;

63. Tennessee, *Acts,* 1875, pp. 168, 188–89; Cartwright, *The Triumph of Jim Crow,* 18.

64. Arkansas, *Acts,* 1866–67, p. 300; Arkansas, *Digest of Statutes,* 1873, Chap. 87, pp. 740–42; Arkansas, *Acts,* 1874–75, p. 281.

65. South Carolina, *Acts,* 1879–80, p. 423; Williamson, *After Slavery,* 77.

66. Alabama, *Acts,* 1865–66, pp. 111–12, 1881, p. 42; Georgia, *Laws,* 1865–66, pp. 153–54, 1882–83, pp. 57–58; North Carolina, *Public Laws* (Special Sess.), 1866, pp. 122–23, *Public Laws,* 1881, p. 540.

at about the same time, Florida replaced its enticement law with a stronger one.[67] By 1890 all the former Confederate states save Texas and Virginia had adopted or amended enticement acts in the years after Reconstruction (see Table 12). A quiescent period lasted from 1891 through 1900, but in the years after that there was a veritable flood of such legislation.

Enticement laws were specialized statutes governing the behavior of employers. They did nothing directly to prevent workers from leaving the farm. To fill the gap, southern planters devised a new kind of contract enforcement statute that made it a crime to take advances in cash or goods with the intention of later breaking one's contract. Louisiana planters had been using the concept of "false pretenses" since at least as early as 1871 (see p. 117 above). Sixteen years later a Mississippi newspaper praised the ingenuity of local justices of the peace who had forged restrictions against taking advances under false pretenses, using the common law.[68] The first state false-pretenses act came in Alabama in 1885. Then, in 1889, North Carolina provided for a maximum ten-dollar fine or ten days' imprisonment for laborers who took advances under false pretenses. Two years later it raised the penalty to fifty dollars or thirty days. In 1891, Florida decided that anyone who entered into a written contract with the "intent to defraud" and abandoned his employer "without just cause" and without repaying his advances was to be punished by a fine of from five to five hundred dollars or imprisonment of from thirty days to a year.[69]

A major shortcoming of the false-pretenses statutes lay in the matter of intent. Did the laborer enter the contract with a plan to take advances and then abscond? Or did the worker leave simply because he was dissatisfied or because he knew of a better offer elsewhere? In 1891, the Alabama Supreme Court held that to win a conviction for false pretenses, the prosecution had to prove that an intent to defraud existed when the contract was made.[70]

67. For Louisiana, see Senate Report on the Exodus, II, 223; and Louisiana, *Laws,* 1890, p. 178. For Mississippi, see *Appleton's Annual Cyclopedia . . . 1884* (New York, 1885), 528; and Mississippi, *Laws,* 1890, p. 69. See Florida, *Laws,* 1889, p. 156.

68. Wharton, *The Negro in Mississippi,* 95.

69. Alabama, *Acts,* 1884–85, p. 142; Florida, *Laws,* 1891, pp. 57–58; North Carolina, *Laws,* 1889, pp. 423–24, 1891, pp. 98–99; Cohen, "Negro Involuntary Servitude," 42.

70. Cohen, "Negro Involuntary Servitude," 43.

In August, 1903, as the wave of southern racial legislation was reaching its crest, Georgia came up with a form of false-pretenses law that aimed to eliminate the ambiguity of intent. It stipulated that when money advanced on a labor contract was not repaid, the existence of the contract was in itself "presumptive evidence" of an intent to defraud. Later that year, Alabama adopted a similar strategy: it made the refusal to work or repay advances "prima facie evidence of the intent to injure or defraud." Comparable laws took hold in North Carolina, in 1905; in Mississippi, in 1906; in Arkansas and Florida, in 1907; and in South Carolina, in 1908.[71]

In *Bailey* v. *Alabama* (1911), the United States Supreme Court struck down the Alabama statute as a violation of the Thirteenth Amendment and the Federal Peonage Act, but many southern states were loath to accept the ruling. The Arkansas *Digest of Statutes* of 1916 and the Mississippi *Code* of 1917 continued to carry false-pretenses acts without any indication that they had been undermined by the highest court in the land. Appropriate changes finally came in the new codes of 1921, in Arkansas, and 1930, in Mississippi. Florida passed provisions that aimed at preserving the status quo while making it appear that the objections of the court had been met. In Georgia and North Carolina, the state supreme courts managed to salvage the unsalvageable, and the laws lived on into World War II.[72]

Louisiana did not have a false-pretenses act, but did not need one, either. Eschewing subterfuge, in 1890 that state enacted a patently unconstitutional law that simply made it a crime to break a labor contract upon which advances had been made and not repaid. Two years later, the act was amended to apply only to contracts covering a year or less. In 1906, the state supreme court upheld the statute; at the same time, the legislature broadened it to include tenant contracts as well as share contracts. Finally, in 1918, the state supreme court struck down the contract law.[73]

71. *Ibid.*

72. Daniel, *The Shadow of Slavery*, 65–81; Cohen, "Negro Involuntary Servitude," 43–44. Later, it will be argued that the fact that Arkansas and Mississippi ultimately removed the false-pretenses laws from their books was a sign of progress. Both things are true. That it took ten to twenty years for the laws to be erased indicates heavy resistance, but the removal of the laws was a sign of movement.

73. Louisiana, *Laws*, 1890, p. 178, 1892, pp. 71–72, 1906, pp. 87–88; *State* v. *Murray*, 116 La. 655 (1906); *State* v. *Oliva*, 144 La. 51 (1918).

In 1900, Alabama and Mississippi adopted breach-of-contract laws every bit as unconstitutional as the one in Louisiana. These states barred a laborer who had broken a contract from entering into a second contract without the permission of the first employer. The Alabama statute was quickly struck down, but Mississippi's law survived until 1913.[74]

Emigrant-agent laws were a less obvious intrusion on the rights of the individual, but they too aimed at limiting black movement. First imposed just after Reconstruction, these enactments targeted the labor recruiters who transported workers from one state to another. Performing essentially the same economic function as the slave traders of antebellum days, the agents nevertheless operated in a very different world. To the extent that the North had imposed a free labor system on the South, the agents represented that system in operation.[75]

Testifying in 1883 about the disturbing impact of the labor agents, Robert B. Kyle, a planter and lumber-mill owner from Gadsden, Alabama, said: "You have your farm and your supplies, and your calculations made, and your labor engaged, and think you are going to get along all right, but suddenly some man comes and says to your laborers, 'I want so many men to build a railroad; I will pay $1.50 a day, and pay every Saturday night;' and your laborer says to his wife, 'Sally, I am going off to work on the railroad,' and off he goes, leaving his wife and family behind him." Kyle argued that only stringent contract enforcement legislation could cure the problem.[76] But another way was by curbing the labor agents. Perhaps the first effort to do that was in Mississippi's enticement law of 1865. It did not mention labor agents but included a proviso setting heavier fines for enticers taking laborers outside the state than for local offenders.[77] Another early reaction occurred in Virginia, where recruiting activity was heavy in the

74. Alabama, *Laws, 1900–1901*, p. 1208; *Toney v. State*, 141 Ala. 120 (1904); Mississippi, *Laws*, 1900, p. 140; *State v. Armstead*, 103 Miss. 790 (1913).

75. The literature on labor agents and labor agent laws is skimpy. See William F. Holmes, "Labor Agents and the Georgia Exodus, 1899–1900," *South Atlantic Quarterly*, LXXIX (1980), 436–48; Leo Alilunas, "Statutory Means of Impeding Emigration of the Negro," *Journal of Negro History*, XXII (1937), 148–62; Alfred W. Reynolds, "The Alabama Negro Colony in Mexico, 1894–1896," *Alabama Review*, V (1952), 243–68.

76. U.S. Senate Committee on Education and Labor, *Report on the Relations Between Capital and Labor* (Washington, D.C., 1885), IV, 31–32.

77. Mississippi, *Laws*, 1865, p. 85.

late 1860s. In February and March, 1870, the Virginia General Assembly dealt with four resolutions to control the recruiters. One deplored the "suicidal" policy of permitting the best class of agricultural laborers to leave the state and asked for laws to stanch the outflow. The house adopted the resolution, but, anticlimactically, passed only a tepid measure charging labor agents twenty-five dollars for a license.[78] Why Virginia did not take more drastic action is unknown, but there is reason to suspect that many nonplanter whites would have been happy to see the state denuded of blacks.

In 1873, a Georgia lawmaker proposed to obligate each county in the state to impose a license tax on "immigrant brokers." His bill died quickly, but three years later the legislature voted for an "act to prohibit Emigrant Agents from plying their vocation . . . without first obtaining a license." The law defined emigrant agents as persons engaged in hiring Georgia laborers for employment outside the state, and it levied a hundred-dollar license tax on them in each county where they operated. A year later, the amount was raised to five hundred dollars.[79]

Alabama offers a glimpse of the complex interplay of forces that pulled for and against restrictions on emigrant agents. Demands for antiagent laws were in the air at least as early as January, 1874. Then, in December, 1876, the legislature considered a proposal that would have imposed a license tax of five hundred dollars on agents in each county where they were active. The bill was defeated, but its supporters tried again a month later. That time, they set the fee at a hundred dollars a county, and they restricted the effect of the statute to fourteen specified Black Belt counties. Thus weakened, the bill passed.[80] Two years afterward, an amendment provided that violators were to be fined not less than three hundred dollars and that they could also be given up to twelve months in jail. Six counties were dropped from the list of places requiring the license, and seventeen were added. Again

---

78. *Virginia House Journal,* February 12, February 19, March 9, March 14, 1870; Virginia, *Code,* 1873, pp. 341, 359.

79. *Georgia House Journal,* January 31, 1873; Georgia, *Acts,* 1876, p. 17, 1877, p. 120.

80. Going, *Bourbon Democracy,* 96n; Mobile *Daily Register,* February 3, 1876; Montgomery *Daily Advertiser,* January 30, 1876; Selma (Ala.) *Southern Argus,* December 15, 1876; Alabama, *Acts,* 1876–77, p. 225.

in 1880, the legislature strengthened the law, raising the tax to $250 per county. Between 1879 and 1880, the list of counties to which the law applied remained virtually unchanged.[81]

The shifting response of state legislators to the emigrant-agent law, as well as the changing provisions of the law itself, is symptomatic of the revolution taking place in Alabama's politics at this time. The initial defeat of the law in December, 1876, reflected both the opposition of black counties where Republicanism was still strong and the opposition of predominantly white counties where antipathies toward blacks were strong. By recasting the law to apply only in specified counties, the proponents of the bill won the white opposition to its side. The law was to apply only to places where those in power wanted to limit black mobility.

During Reconstruction, Radicalism had been strong in heavily black cotton-producing counties like Dallas, Autauga, and Perry, and in some of those places blacks and their allies kept a tenuous hold on local power as late as 1877. Those counties uniformly opposed laws to limit black mobility. But two years later, everything had changed. In the emigrant-agent laws of 1879 and 1880, these places joined the counties with the licensing requirement, and they were among the counties voting to enact the law. It seems clear that in the meantime, political power had shifted and that the planter class was back in charge.[82]

In North Carolina, the minor black exodus led by Sam Perry in late 1879 provoked considerable alarm, and it may have been part of the reason that the state senate passed an emigrant-agent bill in January, 1881, much like the laws in force in Alabama and Georgia. Still, the house refused to go along, and the measure died.[83] It was ten years before North Carolina ratified an emigrant-agent law, but during those years the state took other steps to control black labor, including the adoption of its enticement law.

Neither the emigrant-agent laws nor the enticement laws made

81. Alabama, *Acts, 1876–77*, p. 225, 1878–79, p. 205, 1880–81, pp. 162–63.

82. *Alabama House Journal*, 1876–77, p. 243, 1878–79, pp. 199–200. For the changing political complexion of Alabama counties, see maps in Going's *Bourbon Democracy*, 222–25, and in John W. DuBose's *Alabama's Tragic Decade: Ten Years of Alabama, 1865–1874* (Birmingham, Ala., 1940), 413.

83. Frenise A. Logan, *The Negro in North Carolina*, 132–33.

mention of race, but everyone knew that the aim was to limit *black* movement. In January, 1891, the Atlanta *Constitution* worried about a "New Exodus," which, it claimed, had in the previous two years drawn perhaps 100,000 blacks from the Carolinas to Mississippi, Louisiana, and Arkansas. Its figure was a bit high, but the movement was real enough to lead a North Carolina landlord to plead for government action against the agents. He said, "We are bothered by people from other states persuading away our laborers, which ought to be a criminal offense."[84]

Agreeing, the North Carolina legislature imposed a license fee of a thousand dollars per county on emigrant agents and penalized violators with fines of up to five thousand dollars and jail terms of up to two years. Like Alabama's agent law, the North Carolina statute specified the counties in which the law was to be effective. For all practical purposes, it applied only where there was a high ratio of blacks to whites.[85]

In 1891, South Carolina enacted a similar law, which, however, applied to all counties in the state. Two years later, the license fee was lowered from a thousand dollars to five hundred dollars and a curious new provision almost welcomed employment brokers to the state. It laid down that between July 1 and December 31 of each year, "nothing in this Act shall be construed to prevent emigrant agents from operating in this State without a license."[86] Clearly, the white community was not of one mind on the desirability of limiting black mobility.

Encapsulated in South Carolina's emigrant agent statutes of 1891 and 1893 were the two poles of southern white thought on the proper place of blacks in society. Virtually all white southerners agreed that the United States was a white man's country. Divisions arose, however, over the status blacks were to have in the white nation. Seeing them as essential to the economic life of the South, planters argued for a kind of control that would keep blacks in their place while rendering them more useful to white employers. Others simply wanted blacks to go away, and as quickly as possible.

A debate in the Georgia Senate in 1889 illustrates the practical ramifications of that difference of opinion. The state senator Thomas P.

---

84. Quoted *ibid.,* 133. See Atlanta *Constitution,* January 31, 1891.
85. North Carolina, *Laws,* 1891, p. 77.
86. South Carolina, *Acts,* 1891, p. 1084, 1893, pp. 429–30.

Gibbs, a physician from Morgan County, spoke in favor of repealing the state's emigrant-agent law, on the grounds that it would be good public policy to facilitate black emigration from the state. The blacks in their emancipated condition were unfit for laboring, he said. They had lapsed into barbarism, and there existed a large number of vagabond blacks who were a "continual menace to property, to peace, and to virtue." Gibbs predicted that "the time would come before long, when the white people would rise as one man and demand emigration or extermination." Nonetheless, at the vote those who argued that black workers were particularly fit for laboring prevailed, and the repeal effort failed.[87]

The division between southerners who wanted blacks to leave and those who wanted to bind them ever more firmly to their employers had deep roots. Since the early nineteenth century, a segment of white opinion had held that blacks should be encouraged to leave the United States. That point of view persisted into the postbellum era, when some planters hoped to replace their laborers with foreigners (see pp. 38–40 above). Most quickly saw that the wish was a chimera. Not much is known about what the "plain folk" of the white South preferred concerning black labor, but such evidence as there is suggests that they generally favored plans to remove the black people from their midst.

In 1867 and 1868, Hinton Rowan Helper, renowned for his prewar attack on the planting class, published two vitriolic racist works demanding black colonization. In the preface to the first of these, he said, "The primary object of this work is to write the negro out of America, and . . . the secondary object is to write him . . . out of existence." Elsewhere, Helper asserted that "the whole Negro race is a weak and worthless race" and that providence had "an indestructible plan . . . for exterminating the Negro." He desired that blacks vanish from the face of the earth, and he believed that that would occur if only the Negroes were colonized somewhere and left strictly to their own devices. Without white assistance, he believed, the blacks would simply die out. Helper claimed to speak for the poor southern whites, who, he asserted, were held down by the very existence of the blacks.[88]

87. Quoted by W. Laird Clowes in *Black America: A Study of the Ex-Slave and His Late Master* (London, 1891), 139–40.

88. Hinton Rowan Helper, *Nojoque: A Question for a Continent* (New York, 1867),

Ideas like Helper's were part of the climate of opinion in the South in the late nineteenth century, and in the white mind they were interwoven with a variety of schemes for the colonization, emigration, and voluntary deportation of blacks. It seems certain that plans like his were especially popular among the people who were his special preoccupation, the plain folk of the white South who did not depend heavily on Negro labor and who had nothing to lose by the disappearance of the blacks. Thus it was that in 1889 the *Progressive Farmer*, a Populist journal in North Carolina, asserted that the black was and would remain, "so long as he stays, a running festering sore on our body politic." It added, "We would hail with delight and rejoicing his peaceful departure."[89]

White support for the idea of sending blacks out of the country rose sharply around 1890, especially in South Carolina. Both senators from the state endorsed the idea of providing government funds for voluntary expatriation; Senator Matthew C. Butler proposed a bill to that effect. At the same time, an editorialist for the Charleston *News and Courier* published a tract elaborating on the necessity that the races be geographically separate. In 1903, the socially prominent editor of the Atlanta *News* wrote that a full separation of the races could be achieved by colonizing the blacks in a state that would be all their own.[90]

For some whites the idea of black emigration created tension between the dictates of the heart and the demands of the head. Racism drew them toward ridding the land of blacks entirely, but economic calculation pulled them in the opposite direction. The chief manager of the Farmer's State Alliance in South Carolina candidly admitted that he opposed Senator Butler's emigration bill out of economic self-interest, but he went on to say that he supported the idea "from a patriotic point of view." It appears that in such contests self-interest generally won out. Thus it was that in 1897, when the sole black in

v, viii; Hinton Rowan Helper, ed., *The Negroes in Negroland; the Negroes in America; and Negroes Generally* (New York, 1868), 238–39, 240–41, 249–50.

89. Quoted by Frenise A. Logan in *The Negro in North Carolina*, 129. See also Thomas D. Clark, *The Southern Country Editor* (Indianapolis, 1948), 193.

90. Tindall, *South Carolina Negroes*, 180; Redkey, *Black Exodus*, 59–65; Mark Bauman, "Race and Mastery: The Debate of 1903," in *From the Old South to the New: Essays on the Transitional South*, ed. Walter J. Fraser, Jr., and Winfred B. Moore (Westport, Conn., 1981), 183, 186.

the South Carolina legislature tried to secure the repeal of the emigrant-agent law, his motion was defeated by a vote of 80 to 34.[91]

The fate of emigrant-agent legislation was also affected by doubts about its constitutionality. In 1882, Alabama's high court struck down the agent law of 1879. In North Carolina, the statute of 1891 lasted only about two years. Certainly, planters in those states would have had it otherwise. What thwarted them, for a time at least, were decisions on the constitutionality of the laws, as well as tensions and ambivalences about the place of blacks in southern life. But in 1900 the constitutional reservations melted away, as the United States Supreme Court upheld Georgia's licensing law.[92]

That opened the floodgates. In 1903, Alabama, Florida, North Carolina, and Virginia all passed emigrant-agent statutes. In 1907, South Carolina added a license fee of two thousand dollars per county to the five hundred dollars that agents were already supposed to pay. Mississippi joined the states with such laws in 1912. Then, as black migration to the North threatened the southern labor supply, still tougher laws were enacted in Alabama, in 1915, 1919, and 1923; in Florida, in 1917 and 1923; in North Carolina, in 1917; in Georgia, in 1918, 1920, and 1923; and in Virginia, in 1924. Tennessee and Texas adopted their first emigrant-agent laws in 1917 and 1923 respectively.[93]

Along with the wave of emigrant-agent, enticement, and contract enforcement laws at the beginning of the twentieth century, there came a spate of vagrancy measures. As with the contract provisions, there had been a rush to enact these laws just after the Civil War. Only Tennessee and Arkansas failed to pass vagrancy acts in the period 1865–1867. There followed a time of legislative inactivity. As Table 12 shows, from 1870 to 1902 new vagrancy statutes were few and far between. Moreover, most of these were of minor significance.

91. Tindall, *South Carolina Negroes*, 180–81.

92. *Joseph* v. *Randolph*, 71 Ala. 499 (1882); *State* v. *Moore*, 113 N.C. 697 (1893); *Williams* v. *Fears*, 179 U.S. 270 (1900).

93. Alabama, *Laws*, 1903, pp. 344–45, 1915, pp. 501, 527, 1919, p. 691, 1923, p. 208; Florida, *Laws*, 1903, p. 135, 1917, pp. 25–26, 1923, p. 329; Georgia, *Acts*, 1918, p. 56, 1920, pp. 87–88, 1923, p. 38; Mississippi, *Laws*, 1912, p. 73; North Carolina, *Laws*, 1903, pp. 347–48, 1917, p. 421; South Carolina, *Acts*, 1907, p. 543; Tennessee, *Acts*, 1917, p. 189; Texas, *General Laws* (2nd Called Sess.), 1923, pp. 93–95; Virginia, *Acts*, 1902–1904, p. 211, 1924, p. 679.

Two exceptions were South Carolina's vagrancy law of 1893 and a Georgia statute of 1895. South Carolina, after the voiding of its black code in 1866, had fallen back on an antebellum vagrancy law that punished idlers with up to a year at hard labor. The amendment of 1893 softened the penalty considerably. Vagrants were to pay fines of up to one hundred dollars or spend thirty days in jail. The reasons behind the relaxation are unclear, but it certainly seems inconsistent with the general trend of events in the South. Nothing like it occurred in Georgia, which in 1895 stipulated that "any person may arrest a vagrant and have him bound over to some person for a time not longer than one year."[94]

With those two exceptions, however, the southern states in the 1890s were simply not intent on vagrancy legislation. Then, in the years from 1903 to 1909, Alabama, Arkansas, Florida, Georgia, Mississippi, North Carolina, Texas, and Virginia all put stringent laws on the books. A standard feature was a new definition of vagrancy, but the definition varied from one state to another. The South was struggling to make the definitions of vagrancy at once both broader and more precise. There is nothing equivocal, however, about the change that took place regarding the penalties for the crime. Alabama's old law punished offenders with fines of from ten to fifty dollars. The new law provided fines of up to five hundred dollars and jail terms of up to six months at hard labor.[95]

Some states gave the appearance of moving toward a more mod-

94. South Carolina, *Revised Statutes*, 1872, Chap. lxxi, p. 384; South Carolina, *Acts*, 1893, p. 521; South Carolina, *Code*, 1952, sec. 16-565; Georgia, *Code*, 1895, p. 453.

95. The vagrancy laws of the southern states as they stood before and after 1903 were Alabama, *Code*, 1886, sec. 4047; Alabama, *Laws*, 1903, pp. 244–45, 1907, pp. 453–55; Arkansas, *Statutes*, 1884, secs. 1871–77; Arkansas, *Acts*, 1905, pp. 702–703, 1907, pp. 948–49; Florida, *Revised Statutes*, 1892, secs. 2642–43; Florida, *Laws*, 1905, pp. 97–98; Georgia, *Code*, 1895, secs. 453–55; Georgia, *Laws*, 1903, pp. 46–47, 1905, pp. 109–11; Louisiana, *Revised Laws* (Wolff), 1896, secs. 3877–83; Louisiana, *Laws*, 1902, p. 164, 1908, pp. 308–309, 1912, pp. 511–12; Mississippi, *Annotated Code*, 1892, secs. 1322–23; Mississippi, *Laws*, 1904, pp. 199–205; North Carolina, *Criminal Code and Digest*, 1899, sec. 638; North Carolina, *Laws*, 1905, pp. 412–13; 1915, Chap. 1; South Carolina, *General Statutes and Code of Civil Procedure*, 1881–82, secs. 1604–1609; Tennessee, *Code Annotated*, 1965, sec. 39–4701; Texas, *Criminal Statutes* (Willson), 1889, Chap. 7, secs. 634–35; Texas, *General Laws*, 1909, pp. 111–12; Virginia, *Code*, 1887, secs. 884–86; Virginia, *Acts*, 1902–1904, pp. 876–77.

TABLE 12

Labor Control Laws in the South, 1865–1915

YEAR	ALABAMA	ARKANSAS	FLORIDA	GEORGIA	LOUISIANA	MISSISSIPPI	NORTH CAROLINA	SOUTH CAROLINA	TENNESSEE	TEXAS	VIRGINIA
1865	V		V		ECV	ECV		ECV			
1866	EV		EC	EV				EV		V	V
1867	E	EC						E			
1868			V					C			
1869					V						
1870											A
1871											
1872											
1873		C		E							
1874				S			V				
1875		EC							ECV		
1876				AV							
1877	A			A							
1878											
1879	A			V			V				
1880	A							E			
1881	EV						E				
1882				E							
1883	S	C									
1884											
1885	C										
1886											
1887											
1888											
1889			E				C	C			
1890					EC	E					
1891			C					CA	A		
1892					EC						
1893									AV		
1894					A						
1895											
1896											

TABLE 12

(continued)

YEAR	ALABAMA	ARKANSAS	FLORIDA	GEORGIA	LOUISIANA	MISSISSIPPI	NORTH CAROLINA	SOUTH CAROLINA	TENNESSEE	TEXAS	VIRGINIA
1897								C			
1898								A			
1899							A				
1900						EC					
1901	C			E			A		E		
1902				A							
1903	CAV		A	ECV			A				A
1904						V		C			V
1905		EV	V	V				ECCV			
1906				E	EC						
1907	ECV	V	CV	S				ECV	CA		
1908					V			C			
1909		C								V	
1910											A
1911	C										
1912					V	A			C		
1913			C					V	E		
1914											
1915		A						V			

SOURCE: The session laws of the eleven former Confederate states, 1865–1915.

Note: Abbreviations: A = emigrant-agent law; C = contract enforcement law (including any false-pretenses law); E = enticement law; S = criminal-surety law; V = vagrancy law.

erate penalty structure, but by and large the appearance was deceptive. Consider Arkansas. Late-nineteenth-century vagrants landed in the county jail for from thirty to ninety days and were on a diet of bread and water for half of their time. The act of 1905 set fines of from ten to thirty dollars in addition to costs, but it also provided that in default of payment, the vagrant passed into the custody of the sheriff, "to be worked on the public roads of the county." An amendment in 1907 makes the intention of the act of 1905 still clearer. It allowed that in any county "having a contract with any [convict] contractor for working its prisoners," persons convicted of vagrancy "may in the discretion of the county judge of such county, be sent to such contractor to work out the fines, costs and imprisonment imposed, upon the same terms and conditions as other county prisoners."[96]

Perhaps the most important feature of the vagrancy laws of the early twentieth century was an innovation making it the duty of peace officers to supply local prosecutors with the names of suspected vagrants. Alabama's act said, "It shall be . . . the duty of the sheriff and constables of every county . . . to give information under oath to any officer now empowered by law to issue criminal warrants for all vagrants within their knowledge or who they have good reason to suspect as being vagrants." Similar clauses appeared in the statutes of Alabama and Georgia, in 1903; of Mississippi, in 1904; of Florida, in 1905; of Arkansas, in 1907; and of Texas, in 1909. They seemed to have the purpose of facilitating vagrancy roundups whenever local officials felt them necessary.[97]

Such roundups were hardly new. They had occurred occasionally just after the Civil War, as the army and the Freedmen's Bureau struggled to put the new labor system into service. There is also fragmentary evidence of some roundups occurring as Reconstruction came to an end. On August 17, 1877, the Vicksburg *Daily Commercial* noted that "the majority of the loafing 'cullerd populations' have gone to the country to pick cotton." Five days later it enjoined: "Cotton pickers will soon be wanted in the country. Bring up the idlers and those who are without employment."[98] Still, the roundups by no means occurred everywhere, nor did they focus only on blacks. In 1875, the Elberton *Gazette* reported that there had been no little excitement in its town as a result of the "action of the Town Council in ordering the Marshall to arrest all vagrants irrespective of creed or

---

96. Arkansas, *Acts*, 1905, pp. 702–703, 1907, pp. 948–49.

97. Alabama, *Laws*, 1903, pp. 244–45. For citations to the other acts mentioned, see *n*95 above.

98. Vicksburg (Miss.) *Daily Commercial*, August 17, August 22, 1877.

color." Moreover, "a goodly number both white and black were arrested."[99]

There has never been a systematic study of local newspapers of the South to determine the nature or frequency of vagrancy roundups. Nevertheless, what seems clear from the material that has been encountered is that roundups did occur in the years after Reconstruction and that some had mainly the aim of finding laborers whereas others had the primary purpose of cleaning up the towns. Raids of the latter sort sometimes targeted whites as well as blacks. It appears that in the period from Reconstruction to the turn of the century, the vagrancy laws were not a major tool of racial oppression. Blacks who testified in 1880 before the Senate's committee on the exodus came with a long list of the tactics used against them, but not a single one mentioned the vagrancy laws. Indeed, in all the testimony the Senate committee heard, the only reference to vagrancy acts was by a white planter who said that leaders of the exodus in the area of Macon, Mississippi, had suffered arrest on a vagrancy charge.[100]

In 1884, the Savannah *Morning News* lamented the "rapid increase in the number of idle negroes, principally boys from 12 years and upwards." It charged them with committing depredations on white people, and it claimed that "every southern city is affected in the same way as Savannah." The solution, as it saw it, was simple: "The enforcement of the vagrancy laws is all that is necessary." Those arrested, it ventured, could be put to good use "in draining the county and building good roads." What is interesting is the implication that the vagrancy laws were not already being used as a means of curing black "idleness."[101]

It seems clear that the wave of vagrancy laws that swept across the South in the years between 1903 and 1909 represented both a departure from and a continuation of past practices. Vagrancy roundups, even vagrancy roundups for the sole purpose of securing labor, were not unknown in the nineteenth century, but at least in the 1880s they do

---

99. Elberton (Ga.) *Gazette,* April 5, 1875. A similar story appears in the *Teche Pilot* (La.), June 29, 1889.

100. Cohen, "Negro Involuntary Servitude," 49.

101. Savannah *Morning News,* September 11, 1884.

not appear to have been very frequent, either. They became much more commonplace in the first decade of the twentieth century, as the spirit of the new vagrancy laws spread across the South.[102]

Linking the laws of vagrancy and contract enforcement was a criminal surety system under which persons arrested on certain minor charges might be released into the custody of someone who paid their fines and court costs. The one who paid the costs was usually a planter, and what he got in return was the prisoner's labor for an agreed period of time. There was some appearance of a choice in this, for the prisoner could always elect to remain in jail, or on the chain gang, instead of accepting the offer of surety. The system existed across the South, but by and large it appears to have had roots in the common law rather than in the laws of the states. As far as has been determined, the only states to enact statutes dealing with the subject were Georgia, in 1874, and Alabama, in 1883 and 1907.[103]

The workings of the surety system come out plainly in the case of Ed Rivers, a black Alabamian convicted of petty larceny. For his offense, the judge sentenced him to pay a fine of $15.00 and court costs of $43.75. Discharging his obligation in jail would have taken Rivers sixty-eight days on the chain gang. Instead, on May 4, 1910, he entered into a surety contract that committed him to serving his new employer for nine months and twenty-four days. Rivers worked until June 6 and then refused to labor further. When his employer had him arrested for violating the surety contract, the judge set a fine of one cent, in addition to court costs of $87.75. Rivers at that point signed another surety agreement promising to work fourteen months to pay off his growing debt.[104]

The surety system was the nexus between the penal system and the agricultural system. Blacks who were charged with any of a host of minor crimes, ranging from vagrancy or petty larceny to breach of contract or obtaining advances on false pretenses, could choose to be recycled back to the agricultural system as obedient laborers. There, they were at the mercy of their sureties for as long as it took to pay off the debt, for the surety could always return recalcitrant prisoners

---

102. Cohen, "Negro Involuntary Servitude," 50–52.

103. Georgia, *Acts,* 1874, p. 29; Alabama, *Code* (Mayfield), 1907, secs. 6846–47.

104. *U.S.* v. *Reynolds,* 235 U.S. 133, 139–40 (1914).

to the authorities. With few exceptions, going with the planter was preferable to going on the chain gang, but the nature of the choice reveals the surety system to be part of a larger system of labor control that aimed to limit black mobility and to render potential trouble-makers docile.

Georgia was the first state to give the surety system statutory sanction. Its convict law of 1874 made it lawful for prisoners convicted of misdemeanors to hire themselves to any citizen who paid their fine. In 1894, the state supreme court ruled that the law had been repealed by legislation of 1878, but in the interim it had functioned as good law.[105] Alabama's surety law of 1883 punished prisoners, like Rivers, who failed to live up to their surety agreements. As a protection for the convict, the law specified that the agreements had to be signed in open court. An amendment in 1907, however, made that unnecessary if the agreement was signed in the presence of a mayor or city recorder. As with the vagrancy acts, the trend was toward the creation of a legal structure that enlarged the white control of black labor.[106]

The invention of legal devices to limit black mobility began with emancipation and regained vigor as soon as Reconstruction came to a close. As Table 12 suggests, the legislation occurred in four waves. The black codes constituted the first wave, but many of those statutes were undone early in Reconstruction. As that era came to a close, however, a second wave began. The southern states were feeling their way—trying to see what worked, trying to find laws suited to their circumstances. Alabama and Georgia were especially hard hit by black migration to the West, and they led in writing emigrant-agent laws and laws that compelled the enforcement of contracts by one strategy or another. For reasons not fully clear, the second wave tailed off in the middle eighties. Then, in 1889, came a third wave, slightly weaker than the one that preceded it. That lasted until 1894, and in it most of the states that had not legislated after Reconstruction remedied their inaction. Another quiescent period followed, but the turn of the century brought a fourth wave of such ferocious intensity that it dwarfed the three that preceded it. In the first decade of the twentieth century almost all the southern states passed laws dealing with enticement,

105. Georgia, *Acts,* 1874, p. 29; *Walton County* v. *Franklin,* 95 Ga. 538.
106. Alabama, *Code,* 1907, secs. 6846–47.

breach of contracts, labor agents, and vagrancy. Especially in view of the collateral surge of legislation regarding segregation, it is clear that a dramatic change had occurred. It was as though a dam had burst and the restraints that previously kept planters, and white southerners generally, from ordering matters as they chose were washed away. Still, one must remember that some of the repressive legislation of the time was a response to court decisions striking down or limiting the impact of earlier laws. That was especially so in the case of the false-pretenses statutes.[107]

The effort to bring the black labor force under control was in keeping with broader efforts to reassert white hegemony over the political process and, ultimately, to drive blacks from the political arena. It was also consistent with legal efforts to keep the races separate in the home and at school. In short, though the planter elite certainly had a very special interest in limiting black movement, the laws of labor control were also part of a broader attempt to reestablish white dominance in all areas of southern life. That attempt was simply an extension of the drive to destroy Reconstruction.

The 1890s have been seen as a watershed dividing the "solid South" and the world of segregation from an earlier time of "forgotten alternatives" when southerners might have chosen a path toward racial equality. That is an appealing view, but this chapter suggests that the continuities with the past were far too strong for such a thing to have happened. The most common manifestations of racial oppression and segregation were fully evident long before the 1890s.

And yet it must also be said that there was change aplenty in the years from 1890 to 1915. The change is reflected especially in the way the white South dealt publicly with matters of race. For there was a willingness not just to disfranchise but to do so without any apology save for the fig leaf required by the Fifteenth Amendment. There was a willingness not just to lynch blacks publicly but to defend such behavior as just and moral. There was an insistence not just on the separation of the races but on formalizing and codifying the separation. Certainly one of the most significant developments of the period from 1890 to World War I was the enactment of a host of labor-control laws.

107. See Chapter 10 below.

All the statutes had roots in the era before 1889, but in the years that followed there was a sharp increase in the frequency with which such measures were enacted and in their severity. Indeed, it is difficult to avoid concluding that by 1907 southern legislators had come remarkably close to reenacting the black codes. By then the southern legal system was laden with vagrancy laws, enticement acts, contract-enforcement measures, and convict laws that, taken together, certainly look like the framework for a comprehensive system of involuntary servitude. Whether that system was truly effective in preventing black movement is the next question.

9

BLACK MOBILITY AFTER

RECONSTRUCTION

It was one thing to design and erect a structure of laws to prevent people from moving. It was quite another to make the laws work. A central paradox of the era from the end of Reconstruction to World War I is that, even as the laws of labor control and racial proscription constricted black freedom, southern planters continued to find the kind of labor control they sought beyond their grasp. In one place and then another they stopped black workers from moving, but always there were other places where the net was not so fine and where migration went on. Ultimately, black movement proved to be the stuff of freedom, for as long as blacks could respond to economic opportunity by voting with their feet, their employers were forced into at least a limited competition with one another.

This chapter and the one that follows will explore black movement in the post-Reconstruction era against the backdrop of mounting efforts to destroy black rights. Although blacks lived in a world of shrinking freedoms, the tensions and contradictions within southern white society, within the nation, and within the southern economic system made it impossible to bring black movement to an end. Indeed, the successful immobilization of the black population would have required reinventing slavery itself, and the South had come too far for that.

In the 1870s, while southern newspapers carried dramatic news of the struggle over Reconstruction, they also published more prosaic stories dealing with the travels of ordinary black laborers. In December, 1872, the Mobile *Daily Register* reported that 170 emigrants from northern Alabama had passed through Montgomery en route to Texas.[1] Seven weeks later it printed a letter from "A Colored Man Advising Against Emigration." In it, D. W. Echols, of Columbus, Georgia, noted that the Constitution gave blacks the same rights in Georgia as elsewhere and asked: "Why leave our old homes? Why sacrifice our present comforts and advantages for those that we know not of?" Approvingly, the *Daily Register* added, "This is sound advice from our colored friend."[2]

A year later, the *Daily Register* reported that so many Alabama blacks were traveling through Meridian, Mississippi, that the railroads could hardly keep up with the demand. The newspaper professed not to be alarmed, however; it reasoned that those who were leaving were "simply drones in the bee hive who bring no mite of honey to add." Their departure would actually be a blessing, it supposed, for "as the negroes leave the garden spots . . . where land is as rich as cream and literally 'as cheap as dirt,' white labor will fill their places."[3]

A little later, the *Daily Register* was bemused by the crosscurrents of black migration. Migrants from Marengo County who had gone to Mississippi were returning home "quite disenchanted with their paradise on the great river." Meanwhile, blacks from Union County, Alabama, were reportedly hiring themselves to railroads and farmers in Georgia. "The whole thing," commented the *Daily Register*, "shows a nomadic and roving temperament in these people, and the need of a permanent industrious and thrifty white rural population."[4]

Many did not share the newspaper's equanimity, and planters soon were demanding action against the emigration agents before they

1. Mobile *Daily Register,* December 7, 1872.
2. *Ibid.,* January 28, 1873.
3. *Ibid.,* January 13, January 6, 1874.
4. *Ibid.,* January 24, 1874.

denuded the state of its labor. In the legislature the white counties resisted such pleas, and the exodus continued. In 1875, Charles Nordhoff related how thousands of migrants, especially from Georgia and Alabama, were bound for the Yazoo Bottom, in Mississippi, and for the cotton regions of Arkansas, Louisiana, and Texas.[5]

To stem the tide, some newspapers contrived articles to dissuade blacks from leaving. A Georgia paper presented a purported conversation that, according to it, occurred after labor agents took a group of local Negroes off to Mississippi with the promise of wages of two dollars a day. In the dialogue, the wiser of two blacks said: "Dey tried to stuff dis nigger wid dat two dollar bizness but, I knowd dem folks out dar warn't settin' poor black niggers up in de bankin bizness, no, suh! . . . When yer git too far away from de old marster and de old home you's away from de only freedman's bank whar de nigger is got left now."[6] There were good reasons for skepticism about the blandishments of the labor agents, but this discourse did not present them. It was blatant antimigration propaganda by the planters to slow the exodus.

Newspapers in areas receiving the migrants had a sharply different perspective. A letter to the editor of the *Hinds County Gazette* in Mississippi told of an abundant supply of labor pouring out of Alabama as blacks headed for the rich new lands near Vicksburg. A year later the Vicksburg *Daily Commercial* noted the heavy migration to the Arkansas Valley and asked, "Couldn't we do something to induce the tide to roll this way?"[7]

The dominant migration was from southeast to southwest, but not all the out-migration was from places like Georgia and Alabama and not all the in-migration was to places like Mississippi and Arkansas. Migration occurred within states as well as across state lines. In Mississippi, for example, there developed a sort of migratory pecking order. At the top of the hierarchy were the Delta counties, which sent

5. Going, *Bourbon Democracy*, 96; New York *Times,* February 6, 1874; Charles Nordhoff, *The Cotton States in the Spring and Summer of 1875* (New York, 1876), 21, 93, 108.

6. Elberton (Ga.) *Gazette,* August 4, 1875.

7. Vicksburg (Miss.) *Daily Commercial,* April 10, 1877; *Hinds County Gazette* (Miss.), January 26, 1876.

their emigrant agents to the Mississippi hinterland as well as to distant states. Blacks flowed into the Delta from adjacent, less fertile counties. At the same time, laborers from still poorer regions of the state moved in to fill the places of those who had just left. As Negroes from Hinds County flowed into the Delta, their places were taken by others from more impoverished localities, like Pike, Amite, and Lincoln counties.[8]

Economic development did much to shape migration patterns. In 1882, Collis P. Huntington and a partner purchased the franchises of several Mississippi railroad companies and gained 774,000 acres of Yazoo land. Immediately, they began constructing the Louisville, New Orleans and Texas Railroad. By 1892, the road had 807 miles of track. The project generated an immediate need for heavy labor, and more important, it opened up new areas to cotton cultivation. This project was but a small part of the economic development taking place in Mississippi in the late nineteenth century.[9]

The migration of blacks to the Southwest was one skein in a general American movement to settle the West. In Indiana just after the Civil War, a black and several southern white refugees joined in hiring Addison Coffin to go to North Carolina to fetch their families. In carrying out his assignment, Coffin realized that many North Carolinians wanted to go west, and he decided to make his living as an emigrant agent. In 1866, he made ten trips from North Carolina to the West carrying about 4,850 white emigrants and about 150 blacks. Although the pace of movement slowed after that, Coffin continued to carry emigrants from North Carolina to the West all through the 1870s.[10]

It is hardly surprising, then, that black migrants who left Columbus, Georgia, in the 1870s went alongside a good many white migrants. In early February, 1876, the local agent for the Western Railroad at Columbus remarked that since December 1, 1875, he had sold some six hundred tickets to emigrants going to Alabama, Mississippi,

8. Wharton, *The Negro in Mississippi,* 109–10.

9. Robert L. Brandfon, *Cotton Kingdom of the New South: A History of the Yazoo Mississippi Delta from Reconstruction to the Twentieth Century* (Cambridge, Mass., 1967), 68–75 *passim.*

10. Addison Coffin, *Life and Travels of Addison Coffin* (Cleveland, 1897), 15, 128–29, 134–42.

Louisiana, and Texas. Of the passengers, four hundred were blacks and two hundred were whites.[11]

The movement of blacks from Georgia and Alabama to the southwestern states elicited patterns of newspaper reportage that persisted through the years up to World War I. The articles that described the movement fell into three types. One sort took the stance of "Go and good riddance; we'll be better off without you." Pieces of this type generally observed that the departure of the blacks would make room for white farmers to till land that the freedmen had used. A second type viewed the migration with alarm, frequently describing proposals to prevent emigrant agents from "making off with our labor." A third type did its best to dissuade potential migrants from leaving, often citing the opinions of disillusioned migrants.

Implicit in most of the newspaper stories was the conviction that labor agents of one sort or another organized and directed the long-distance black movement. That fitted with white racist ideas that blacks were incapable of acting without direction. Still, there were good reasons for associating late-nineteenth-century long-distance black migration with the agents. Because so many blacks were too poor to go very far without aid and because they lacked ready access to information about opportunities in distant places, they had little choice but to rely on those who came to them in search of labor.

Some blacks did migrate on their own, though. Two of the most notable instances were the movement of perhaps three thousand to five thousand blacks from Edgefield County, South Carolina, to Arkansas in 1881 and 1882 and a major migration of almost 100,000 blacks to Oklahoma in the years between 1890 and 1910.[12] Like the exodus to Kansas, both movements had a political dimension. Unlike that venture, however, both had destination areas holding genuine economic opportunity.

Edgefield County was at the time noted for its bloody race relations. During Reconstruction, black Republicans and white Democrats contended openly for power, and violence was endemic. Edgefield was the place from which John Mardenborough and Harrison

11. New York *Times,* February 5, 1876.

12. Contemporary sources estimated the Arkansas movement at five thousand, but given the census figures discussed below, it seems likely that the number was smaller.

Bouey made their agonized pleas to the American Colonization Society.[13] After Reconstruction, the whites of Edgefield steadily circumscribed black political activity. By 1881, the blacks were complaining that they had been pushed from the ballot box and had a "hostile political party" in charge of their rights.[14] They felt that despite their hard work over the previous ten years, they had less than when they began. Most of the black farmers in the Edgefield area were tenants who paid their rent in cotton. They were sensible that, at year's end, after paying their rent, they had virtually nothing to show for their efforts. Later some observers would blame the tenant system for the black exodus, since in adjacent areas untouched by the exodus, sharecropping prevailed.[15] That may be so, but the same evidence can be better read to opposite effect, given that the migrants were able to pay their own way to Arkansas. Whatever the defects of the tenant system, it provided greater opportunity than sharecropping.

The movement from Edgefield began in the fall of 1881 with the organization of a number of local emigration societies. The most prominent was led by John Hammond, a black Baptist minister. His group met twice a week and charged dues of a dollar. It was sufficiently prosperous and well organized to send a three-man party to look over the land in Arkansas. The committee returned with news that wages beyond Little Rock were from twelve to twenty dollars a month and that government land could be had almost for the asking.[16]

Acting on the information the scouts had obtained, Hammond's society decided to go. It assessed its members to cover the cost of train fare and Hammond arranged for the trains to pick up his people at the Augusta station on December 26. Just before Christmas, the migrants started for Augusta by wagon and on foot. The first train was almost a day late, and the newspapers made much of the delay. Yet, the entire migration appears to have received careful planning and to have gone off without a serious hitch. It would be interesting to know what befell these South Carolinians once they arrived in Arkansas.[17]

13. Burton, "Race and Reconstruction," 31–56.
14. Tindall, *South Carolina Negroes*, 170–71.
15. *Ibid.*
16. *Ibid.*, 171–72.
17. *Ibid.*, 172; Huntsville (Ala.) *Gazette*, January 7, 1882.

Almost a decade later, blacks began moving to the Oklahoma Territory in one of the most significant migrations of the post–Civil War era. For whites and blacks alike, Oklahoma was a prime attraction. In 1889, the federal government had divided the Indian Territory and opened a portion called the Oklahoma District to settlement by non-Indians. At once there came a massive rush of "Oklahoma boomers" who wanted to stake their claim to free land under the terms of the Homestead Act. Like the whites, black boomers came seeking economic opportunity, but many came also hoping that they might be able to live without white interference.[18]

One black politician who cherished such a hope was Edwin P. McCabe, who had been associated with the all-black town of Nicodemus, in Kansas. In 1882, he had become the state auditor, and the highest black official in Kansas, but four years later he was forced out of his position because of race. Chafing, he developed a plan to take advantage of the opening of Oklahoma to create an all-black state. He set out to become a land promoter who would attract enough members of his race to the area so that they could gain control of the territory at the ballot box.[19] As a first step, he became a founder of the town of Langston, forty miles from Oklahoma City, where he established the McCabe Town Company. His firm dispatched agents into the southern states to attract settlers to a "New Eldorado" in which blacks might govern themselves unhindered. He published the Langston *Herald*, featuring handsome pictures of the town. He did not explain that the illustrations were artists' renderings of how the place would look when completed and that the town consisted then of one general store, a cluster of shacks, and a tent city. As a consequence of the publicity McCabe had spread and of the general enthusiasm the Oklahoma boom inspired, the black population of Oklahoma rose from 21,609 in 1890 to 55,684 in 1900.[20]

18. Redkey, *Black Exodus*, 99–100.

19. Mozell C. Hill, "The All-Negro Society in Oklahoma" (Ph.D. dissertation, University of Chicago, 1946), 27–28; Alfred Theodore Andreas, *History of the State of Kansas* . . . (Chicago, 1883), 229–30; William H. Chafe, "The Negro and Populism: A Kansas Case Study," *Journal of Southern History*, XXXIV (1968), 406; Norman L. Crockett, *The Black Towns* (Lawrence, Kans., 1979), 19.

20. Hill, "The All-Negro Society in Oklahoma," 30–31; U.S. Bureau of the Census, *Negro Population*, 43–44. During the period 1890–1900, the white popula-

Anyone who came with the hope of establishing an all-black state soon met disappointment. From the start, whites far outnumbered blacks. In 1890, the ratio of whites to blacks was eight to one; by 1990, it was twelve to one; in 1910, it was over ten to one.[21] There was not much of a planter elite to dominate society in Oklahoma, but racial hatred and discrimination were everywhere. Indeed, whites often tried to drive blacks away entirely. In 1891, the El Reno *News* said, "Negroes have been ordered to leave the country and are objects of terror." In 1893, when McCabe tried to establish a town called Liberty in Noble County, the white residents of nearby Perry reacted so violently that he abandoned the project. In 1896, the *Kingfisher Press* claimed that "in the southern portion of the Oklahoma Territory, white cappers are running the Negroes out of the country. At Norman, not one Negro remains."[22]

Only within the all-black towns could these nonwhites find safety from the fires of hatred. Only there could they find any security and self-respect. It was on the development of such towns that efforts to bring blacks to Oklahoma hence focused. Seeking to attract settlers to Boley, Oklahoma, around 1905, T. M. Haynes sent representatives to southern churches to tell about his new town and to talk about the race question. Simultaneously, he mailed circulars encouraging southern blacks to come and invest themselves in Boley. One notice exulted that Haynes had "solved the Race Problem by Proving to the World that the Negro is Capable of Self Government. Boley is the largest Negro city in the whole world."[23]

There were many promoters and many claims in the years from

---

tion of Oklahoma rose from 172,554 to 670,204. From 1900 to 1910, the black population increased from 55,684 to 137,612; that of the whites went from 670,204 to 1,444,531. The figures for 1900–1910 represent a net-migration increase of 68,000 for the blacks and 479,000 for the whites. Comparable net-migration figures are not available for the decade 1890–1900. See Eldridge and Thomas, *Demographic Analyses and Interrelations*, 260.

21. Ratios are calculated from figures in U.S. Bureau of the Census, *Negro Population*, 43–44.

22. Both Oklahoma papers are quoted by Hill in "The All-Negro Society in Oklahoma," 25–26. See Crockett, *The Black Towns*, 25. Sometimes Indians too tried to drive the blacks out (Redkey, *Black Exodus*, 101).

23. Hill, "The All-Negro Society in Oklahoma," 32–35; the quotation is on p. 33.

1890 to 1910, and by the end of that period, all-black towns were established at Langston, Boley, Rentiesville, Foreman, Taft, Vernon, Tatums, and Clearview. With a population of about four thousand in 1911, Boley was the largest and most successful of these places.[24] Some towns never got much beyond their planning, and most of those that survived faced a lifelong battle with the hostile society surrounding them. These places may have been poor, even shabby, but for the people living in them they provided a haven from the white world, a setting in which it was possible to nurture the self-respect and dignity of children.

The existence of the black towns highlights the political and racial dimensions of the migration. Settlers there appear to have come from the most restless and politically dissatisfied segment of the southern black population. Often they were people who had moved before in search of a place where they might be free in America. They had gone from South Carolina to Arkansas or from North Carolina to Louisiana to Texas, but they had not found freedom. Finally they tried Oklahoma, only to discover that conditions in their new home were at least as bad as anywhere else. The all-black towns did, however, offer a haven of the spirit from the ravages of the rampant racism that was all around.[25] But the towns just could not provide effective insulation from the surrounding white world. Oklahoma became a state in 1907, and in the succeeding years it disfranchised most blacks and segregated the railroads. On top of that, the black towns were "dying economically." As a result, some of the Oklahoma migrants began to think of moving on. In 1908, McCabe went to British Columbia, and a year later two hundred blacks from Oklahoma arrived in Saskatchewan. In 1910, a number of families from Clearview moved to Canada.[26] Then, in 1913, Chief Alfred Sam launched a campaign to lead American blacks back to their natural "fatherland" in Africa. He started his work in Oklahoma, where it drew special strength from some of the resi-

24. Crockett, *The Black Towns,* 29, 36, 110, 152; Hill, "The All-Negro Society in Oklahoma," 33.

25. Jimmie Lewis Franklin, *Journey Toward Hope: A History of Blacks in Oklahoma* (Norman, Okla., 1982), 17–18; letters from Oklahoma blacks to the American Colonization Society, in CCXCII–CCXCV, Domestic Letters Received, ACS, LC.

26. Crockett, *The Black Towns,* 168–70.

dents of the all-black towns of Boley and Clearview. Like any number of other emigration schemes, however, this one failed, but the allure it held for some Oklahoma blacks testifies to the bitter disappointments they had experienced. By that time, in matters of race Oklahoma had become just another southern state. Some blacks were still going there for economic opportunity, but the dream that it might be a place of freedom was dead.[27]

In the migrations to both Oklahoma and Arkansas, blacks moved on their own, without the assistance of labor agents. In the main, though, large-scale long-distance movement in the era before World War I required the agents' participation. The migration from Edgefield Country to Arkansas was only a small part of a massive movement to that state, and it seems clear that most who went had the backing of labor agents. Like Mississippi, Arkansas was rapidly expanding the area of cotton cultivation, and it had an almost insatiable appetite for labor. The black population of Arkansas rose from 210,666 in 1880 to 309,117 in 1890. Of the increase, about 56,000 has to be attributed directly to migration. Many of the newcomers came from the Carolinas. In 1880, there were 5,700 South Carolina–born blacks living in Arkansas. By 1890, the figure was 12,700. The numbers for North Carolina, though a bit smaller, were similar.[28]

One of the blacks taken to Arkansas by the labor agents, William Pickens, later became a prominent official of the NAACP. Looking back to his childhood, he described how in 1888 the labor agent had told his parents of land beyond the Mississippi that was a balmy paradise with coconuts, oranges, lemons, and bananas for the picking and with enormous yields of corn and cotton. His unlettered parents must have found the pitch all the more convincing because they had long debated going to Arkansas, "where the soil was fertile and the wages high." They decided to take a chance and signed a labor contract binding them to work for their new employer until their transportation

27. *Ibid.*, 170–74; Redkey, *Black Exodus,* 292–93. See also William E. Bittle and Gilbert Geis, *The Longest Way Home: Chief Alfred C. Sam's Back-to-Africa Movement* (Detroit, 1964).

28. U.S. Bureau of the Census, *Negro Population,* Table 13; Everett S. Lee *et al., Methodological Considerations and Reference Tables,* Table P-3, p. 301; Eldridge and Thomas, *Demographic Analyses and Interrelations,* Table A1.20, p. 260.

debt was paid.[29] When they got there, they saw the deception at once. Instead of tropical fruit and clement weather, they were met with snow, ice, and cold. Penniless, they had no choice but to work for the man who had paid their transportation. A year later, they were farther in debt than when they started. A year after that, they owed more yet. In desperation, the elder Pickens went to Little Rock on a pretext, to see if he could find a better situation. There he contracted with another farmer, who advanced transportation money for the family. Breaking the first agreement, Pickens' father stole away with the family to the new place at Galloway. Within a year he had managed to pay off the new transportation debt.[30]

During this period, blacks from North Carolina were also moving to Arkansas, and labor agents played a significant role in their migration too. In 1890, stung by accusations that blacks were leaving the South because they were oppressed, the Tarboro *Southerner* insisted: "Short crops [and] bad treatment, politically or otherwise, had nothing to do with the movement. The glowing accounts of other localities and the seductive promises of the agents who received many dollars per head did the work." The newspaper went on: "As long as the Negroes can be persuaded to leave in paying quantities, the agents will come for them. If the people do not want them to leave, the agents must be kept away."[31]

In focusing so exclusively on the labor agents, the *Southerner* was both right and wrong. It was wrong to discount economic misery and political discontent as forces underlying the migration. As will become clear, the agents were successful precisely because they went about their work in just the places where conditions were bad and because they offered the hope of better things to come. The newspaper was right, however, in believing labor agents were hard at work in the state.

Given the attitudes that the white southerners represented by the *Southerner* had toward blacks, they were not going to try to protect

29. William Pickens, *Bursting Bonds: The Heir of Slaves* (Enl. ed.; Boston, 1923), 3, 8, 21–22.

30. *Ibid.*, 23–35.

31. Tarboro *Southerner*, April 3, 1890, quoted by Frenise A. Logan in *The Negro in North Carolina*, 133.

their labor supply by alleviating the sources of black discontent. Rather, they concentrated on stopping the agents. That meant trying to break the chain of communication on which migration depended. Migration occurs with a sense that conditions *here* are worse than conditions *there*. Potential migrants always know about conditions at home. What they need is information about distant places where the situation might be better. That was precisely the job of the labor agents. However much they may have exaggerated the quality of life at the destination they were promoting, they always brought with them one indisputable truth: that in the place they were trying to sell, labor was so scarce that planters were willing to spend extra money to get it.

One of the prime movers in the exodus from North Carolina that gave the *Southerner* so much concern was Robert A. ("Peg Leg") Williams, a flamboyant one-legged Confederate veteran who made his living as a labor recruiter. A native Mississippian who had served in the cavalry under Nathan Bedford Forrest, Williams claimed that in the period from about 1883 to 1890, he had moved some eighty thousand blacks from the South Atlantic states to Texas and the Mississippi Valley. His business records were said to list the name, age, place of origin, and place of destination of each migrant he had shipped. The Atlanta *Constitution* once characterized him as the "King of the labor agents." A few days after that it described him as the "Moses of the Carolina exodus, the Brer fox of his profession, the luckiest, pluckiest, spryest labor agent [in the] south."[32]

If Williams' activities made good copy, they were also profoundly disturbing to anyone who employed black labor. Thus it was that in February, 1890, he was arrested in Raleigh, North Carolina, on a charge of abducting two Negro boys to Mississippi. North Carolina did not have an emigrant-agent law at the time, and the charge was simply a police expedient to prevent Williams from carrying on his work. (Twenty-four years earlier, Addison Coffin had suffered a simi-

---

32. Holmes, "Labor Agents and the Georgia Exodus," 439; Clark, *The Southern Country Editor*, 196; *Atlanta City Directory, 1901*, 1483; Atlanta *Constitution*, February 25, March 1, March 9, 1890. It is hard to resist the speculation that Williams himself was the author of the *Constitution*'s hyperbolic description.

lar kind of harassment while he was assisting white emigrants. He was arrested for aiding debtors to abscond from the state.)[33]

Undaunted by the harassment, Williams boasted that by the next day he would move three hundred Negroes out of Scotland Neck. Things did not go as he predicted, however, and he remained in jail for several days. Once free, he returned to his occasional home base in Atlanta, where bantering with a reporter about his recent brush with the law, he joked: "I broke jail. Rescued by the niggers. Never had such a time." In fact, he appears to have been out on bond, but the subsequent disposition of his case is not known.[34]

Even as Williams was extricating himself in North Carolina, he was announcing a scheme to export black labor to the North. He said he planned to use the New York *World* to advertise his readiness to solve the North's labor shortage by supplying an unlimited number of black workers. He vowed that "if they really want negroes I'm going to send them. I'm going to keep on sending them until they say 'stop!' " One person present when he said that teased, "There are enough republicans up there [in the North] now." Williams answered, "That's all right . . . a few thousand negroes would make lots of white democrats." He went on to describe a scheme to import "thrifty white labor" from the North or from Europe to take the place of the southern negro. Consistently, Williams portrayed himself as serving white interests by reducing the size of the southern black population.[35]

Williams' plan to carry blacks to the North never got very far, and throughout the early 1890s he continued to make his living transporting blacks to the Southwest. Then, in late 1894, he became involved with a scheme to colonize thousands of blacks in Mexico. The plan originated with W. H. Ellis, a young black from San Antonio who was seeking the main chance, and with the Agricultural, Industrial, and Colonization Company of Tlahualilo, a corporate entity that owned 2.5 million acres in Mexico. The company had attempted to introduce cotton production into Mexico but had met with scant success. Someone, possibly Ellis, persuaded it to import sixty black cot-

33. Atlanta *Constitution,* February 25, 1890; Coffin, *Life and Travels,* 137.
34. Atlanta *Constitution,* February 25, March 1, 1890.
35. *Ibid.,* March 9, 1890.

ton growers.[36] That worked well and made the company want to re-
peat its experiment on a larger scale. Ellis and the company entered
into an elaborate agreement whereby he would supply black colonists
and keep them at work. The contract specified that the laborers were
to get 50 percent of the crop, with the other half divided between the
company and Ellis in the proportion of four to one. The company was
to advance passage money and was to have control over the sale of the
crop until the debt had been liquidated. Despite the 50-percent split,
the contract was a recipe for peonage. It was dated December 11, 1894,
and was to go into effect only if Ellis delivered the first hundred families by February 15, 1895.[37] Ellis turned to Williams for help. On December 29, the two announced an agreement according to which Williams would furnish five thousand black laborers within a year and
Ellis would pay ten to twenty dollars a head for them, the exact commission being "graded by the value of the emigrant as a laborer." The
two proclaimed that within a year they would take 100,000 blacks
from the American South to Mexico. The number was clearly for
publicity purposes, and Ellis later said that only ten thousand were
expected in the first year.[38] Williams set about organizing the migration. Through the press, he proclaimed himself ready to "solve the
race problem by sending all the negroes to a colony in Mexico."[39] He
probably said that in the hope of blunting white opposition.

At the same time, he issued circulars to excite blacks about Mexico.
One of these began, "Get ready at once!—Mexico! Mexico! Mexico!"
It proclaimed that five hundred country farmhands in families were
wanted to take advantage of the "greatest opportunity ever offered to
the colored people of the United States to go to Mexico, which is
better known as the country of 'God and Liberty.' " Williams pledged
to advance railroad fare, clothing, provisions, and other necessities.[40]

36. New York *Times,* November 14, 1889; Reynolds, "The Alabama Negro Colony in Mexico" (1952), 243–44.

37. Reynolds, "The Alabama Negro Colony in Mexico" (1952), 244; *Failure of the
Scheme for the Colonization of Negroes in Mexico,* 54th Cong., 1st Sess., House Document
No. 169, pp. 46–47 (hereafter cited as *Failure of Mexican Colonization*).

38. Reynolds, "The Alabama Negro Colony in Mexico" (1952), 247–48.

39. Atlanta *Constitution,* January 2, 1895.

40. *Failure of Mexican Colonization,* 59.

The circular waxed eloquent about the location, quality, and price of the Mexican lands. So rich were they that one could "easily raise a bale to the acre." It also said that the company would provide "comfortable houses to live in." It failed to say that the colonists were expected to build those dwellings.[41] Still, the notice did lay out the basic terms the company was offering. For a second time, it made discreet reference to the racial freedom blacks could expect to find in Mexico: "We wish to impress on your minds that the great Republic of Mexico extends to all of its citizens the same treatment—equal rights to all, special privileges to none." Potential migrants were warned to "send in your lists of families at once or you will get left."[42]

Black subagents who carried the circulars into the black community played a crucial role in validating their content. As the departure time neared, Williams made his headquarters in Birmingham, at the Afro-American Labor and Benevolent Association. When he arrived on January 26, 1895, a goodly number of blacks were already waiting at the railroad depot. The first train left three days later. A month afterward, Williams himself escorted 350 migrants to Mexico. Altogether he sent 816 persons in 145 family groups to Mexico.[43]

Upon arrival the colonists discovered that the conditions were far different from the promise. By March 5, southern newspapers were reporting that twenty-five destitute refugees had passed through San Antonio as they struggled back to Alabama. Their narrative was only the first of a string of horror stories.[44]

Soon the Mexican venture drew sharp fire from an unexpected quarter. When Williams escorted the last group of colonists to Mexico, he remained for about fifteen days. Then he went directly to San Antonio, where he publicly denounced the entire scheme, even issuing a notice headed, "Statement of Facts Regarding the Movement of Negroes to Mexico." In it he charged that "the inducements offered by W. H. Ellis . . . are far from being carried out." The colonists had been promised that temporary living quarters would be ready for their arrival and that they would have houses within sixty days. In fact, there were no quarters of any sort and the emigrants "were forced to

41. *Ibid.*, 46, 59; Reynolds, "The Alabama Negro Colony in Mexico" (1952), 251*n*.
42. *Failure of Mexican Colonization*, 59.
43. Reynolds, "The Alabama Negro Colony in Mexico" (1952), 249, 250, 253.
44. *Ibid.*, 261–62.

camp out around their wagons." Worse still, they had to live and work under the supervision of armed guards.[45]

Williams' behavior is startling. Exaggeration was, after all, essential to a labor agent's work, and Williams was not given to understatement. He explained that his sudden turnabout came "on account of the erroneous statements made to me by W. H. Ellis and friends of his. . . . I found that they were all interested in the scheme of getting the handsome commission of $5 or $6 on every one that he induced to locate on this ranch."[46] In short, Williams seems to have foreseen a major fiasco. He was doing what he could to protect his reputation as a fair-dealing, honest labor agent.

He was certainly right to feel uneasy, for as matters developed, accusations of censorship, of the beating of "stubborn youngsters," and even of the murder of escaping colonists were added to those already leveled.[47] As the months passed, the situation worsened. Some colonists were starving, some were sick with smallpox. On July 20, most fled the colony, scattering along the railroad "without friends, funds or food, living on mesquite beans and branch water." At this point, the American consul at Coahuila asked for State Department intervention. The Cleveland administration was hardly enthusiastic, but when it became clear that colonists were really sick and starving, it provided medical aid, rations, and ultimately, transportation back to Alabama.[48]

The Mexican colonization venture was a minor episode in the story of black mobility, but it is significant because it gives a rare glimpse of a labor agent at work. It shows Peg Leg Williams trying to soften up white public opinion by promising that emigration would solve the race problem. It shows him using black subagents to carry his circulars to those he might induce to migrate. It shows him shepherding his flock to its destination in much the same manner that emigrant agents like Coffin carried white people to the frontier.

It is worth noting also that no one made a serious effort to stop the blacks in Alabama from leaving. Indeed, many whites mocked the

45. *Ibid.,* 262; Atlanta *Constitution,* March 9, 1895.
46. Atlanta *Constitution,* March 9, 1895.
47. Reynolds, "The Alabama Negro Colony in Mexico" (1952), 264, 267.
48. Reynolds, "The Alabama Negro Colony in Mexico," *Alabama Review,* VI (1953), 31–58.

naïveté and credulity of the blacks at the same time that they welcomed their departure. The *West Alabama Breeze,* of Northport, in Tuscaloosa County, said it had "not a particle of objection to this move . . . in fact we are inexpressibly proud of it." Of the 816 emigrants, about 170 were from Eutaw, Alabama, and in March, 1895, one paper from that place commented: "Poor deluded things! They have abandoned their humble houses, sold their little stock for almost nothing, sacrificed all the ties of nativity and are eager to go to the land of milk and honey."[49]

As the movement progressed, however, some white citizens of Eutaw lost their smiles. A dispatch to the Birmingham *Age Herald* said that "much excitement exists here amongst the landowners," and it went on to note that "owing to the excited condition of the white people it is not probable that further efforts will be made by the railroad people or paid immigration agents to induce the Negroes to emigrate to Mexico." The movement to Mexico took place without overt violence, but it is an open question whether the tranquillity would have continued had the exodus lasted into March, 1895.[50]

Little is known of Williams' activities over the following few years, but in January, 1899, he was again carrying black laborers from North Carolina to the cotton fields of Mississippi and Arkansas. The Atlanta *Constitution* said that "money to move labor has been placed on deposit for Mr. Williams" and that he already had two hundred families en route to the Mississippi Valley. It reported that he planned in the coming days to send 250 more to the Little Rock and Pine Bluff areas.[51] A month later he was still at work, personally escorting a "car load" of blacks from Columbus, Georgia, to Arkansas. Whether he carried on his business through the year is not known, but by the fall the Illinois Central Railroad was using him to take blacks to Mississippi. He was by then operating in the Georgia Black Belt, where labor conditions made his appeal especially powerful. In Morgan County, in particular, a summer drought had devastated the cotton crop, bringing desperate poverty in its wake.[52]

49. Both papers are quoted by Reynolds in "The Alabama Negro Colony in Mexico" (1952), 255, 258.

50. Quoted *ibid.,* 255.

51. Atlanta *Constitution,* January 15, 1899.

52. Birmingham (Ala.) *News,* February 20, 1899; Holmes, "Labor Agents and the Georgia Exodus," 438.

In November, 1899, Williams' cousin and business associate, Mary E. LaVette, began recruiting labor in Morgan County. LaVette was a powerful speaker who painted a glowing picture of Mississippi as a land of Canaan, where the pay was higher and the racial conditions better than in Georgia. One press account had her promising sixty acres and a mule. In late November, she was arrested for operating without an emigrant-agent license. She refused to pay the fee, insisting that she had won a similar contest in Columbus, Georgia. Williams paid her bond, and her arrest made her a heroic figure in the eyes of local blacks. According to the white press, the exodus at that point became a "craze," with LaVette a Moses figure.[53]

Shortly after that, with the hostility of local farmers mounting sharply, LaVette dropped out of sight. But the agitation continued, spreading beyond the confines of Morgan County. Operating out of Greensboro, in Greene County, Williams took center stage. Before he began recruiting, he approached some of the leading white citizens of the town with a proposition. As the Greensboro correspondent for the Atlanta *Constitution* described it, "He was ready and willing to solve what promised to be a perplexing problem, viz: 'What to do with the idle and destitute.' If the whites were willing and would use their influence to prevent his arrest. [*sic*] He agreed to stop soliciting whenever the gentlemen who had been invited to consult with him asked him to do so."[54]

The deal was struck, and it seems probable that one of the men with whom Williams consulted was the editor of the Greensboro *Herald*. That newspaper vigorously supported the idea of reducing the black population, arguing that "in the long run the county would greatly benefit even if Williams convinced a majority of Greene's blacks to leave." There was in all this more than a little similarity with the start of Williams' involvement with the Mexican venture, which included the promise to solve the race problem.[55]

If it is a good guess that the editor of the Greensboro *Herald* was a member of the group that met with Williams, it is an even better guess that another member of the group was Jim Davison, the Greene

53. Holmes, "Labor Agents and the Georgia Exodus," 439; Atlanta *Constitution*, November 26, 1899, January 17, 1900; *Atlanta City Directory, 1901*, 1014, 1483.
54. Atlanta *Constitution*, January 17, 1899.
55. Holmes, "Labor Agents and the Georgia Exodus," 440.

County prosecutor. Davison made no secret of his support for Williams, and when local farmers badgered him to prosecute Williams for violating the emigrant-agent act, he simply refused to bring a case. In mid-December, however, the planters successfully appealed to the state comptroller for an arrest warrant charging Williams with operating without an emigrant-agent license.[56]

Like LaVette, Williams declined to purchase the license. Instead, he retained Davison as his lawyer and posted a thousand-dollar bond, the money for which was supplied by thirty-one white citizens of Greensboro. Davison then secured an injunction allowing the agent to continue his work. On December 22, Williams sent another hundred blacks to Mississippi. As in the case of LaVette, excitement mounted in the days following his arrest.[57]

It would be interesting to know the precise sociological makeup of the group that put up the bond money for Williams. Davison and the editor of the Greensboro *Herald* were certainly among them, and it seems highly likely that most who contributed were urban folk whose living did not depend primarily on black labor. Whoever they were, they could not afford to be oblivious to the growing concerns of the planters who were their neighbors, customers, and clients. As the new year opened, the men who had conferred with Williams when he first came to town requested another meeting.[58] The Atlanta *Constitution*'s Greensboro correspondent was either a member of the group or very close to someone who was present at the meetings. He reported that up to then, Williams' supporters had not been worried by how much Williams was exciting the blacks. Now, however, the Negroes were so thoroughly stirred up that they were making "unreasonable" demands. Contracts were being broken. The group told Williams that his activity was "injuring the county," and it reminded him "of his promise to quit when requested to do so." The labor agent presented his side of the matter, underlining how he had been arrested despite the assurance that he would not be molested. He argued that he should be permitted to make two trips more, and a deal was reached to that effect.[59]

56. *Ibid.*
57. *Ibid.*; Atlanta *Constitution*, December 26, 1899, January 17, 1900.
58. Atlanta *Constitution*, January 17, 1900.
59. *Ibid.*

Those who participated in the agreement did not reckon with the mounting anger of the planters. Within a short time, persons who were not parties to the understanding had Williams arrested for his failure to secure an emigrant-agent license for the new year, that is, 1900. Acting on the advice of Davison, Williams paid the $500 tax under protest. In consequence of the arrest, the labor agent felt relieved of his promise to stop soliciting labor after two trips. At the same time, the white country folk became ever more perturbed.[60]

In the middle of all that, Williams wrote a long letter to the Atlanta *Constitution* defending himself against attacks in the paper. His eloquent statement helps explain why he was so effective in persuading blacks to move west and whites to let them go. Contradicting the picture of the labor agent as someone who operated in secret, he said, "I am the man moving the people," and he proclaimed, "My business is advertised to the world; I inclose you one of my circulars, which you are at liberty to publish if you desire." He said he was a "democrat" and an honest businessman simply trying to help his fellowmen along the way. If his critic took a trip into the countryside of Morgan, Greene, or Oglethorpe County, Williams submitted, "he would not need an explanation of why the negroes are leaving Georgia." At bottom, he suggested, "is a bread and meat problem—in the first place, very little work, if any; two to three years failure in crops and the starvation prices paid them for farm labor—15 to 25 cents a day and they board themselves."[61] He explained that whites as well as blacks were suffering and that the whites could not afford to furnish the blacks with rations for the winter season when there was not work for them: "Hence the Negroes have to go west where there is work the year round at $12 to $15 per month and board, and cotton to pick at 50 cents per hundred and day work at 75 cents. Mississippi, Arkansas, Texas and Louisiana have work for 10,000 laborers now and are willing to pay their transportation from Georgia out." He invited the attention of the public "to the condition of these people as they pass through Atlanta." They are, he said, "half clad and starving. I have to feed them from the time they start until they arrive at their destination."[62]

60. *Ibid.*
61. *Ibid.*
62. *Ibid.*

Williams appears to have written his letter in early January, but it was not published until January 17, four days after a dramatic series of events had begun. Even if his letter had appeared earlier, however, it probably would not have changed many minds. Williams described himself as "doing missionary work on the request of the citizens of Greensboro," and he estimated that "four out of five" whites favored his work.[63] That is perhaps so, but the white farmers of central Georgia had too much to lose through black emigration to give him their support.

Matters came to a head on January 13, 1900. By that time, Williams was said to have sent about 2,500 Negroes from Morgan County alone to Mississippi and Arkansas. In Greensboro, "a few hot-headed gentlemen" made threats, but "cooler people took the matter in charge and arranged a basis of settlement with Mr. Williams." The agreement was essentially that a new and lower bond would be set for his violation of the emigrant-agent law in the previous year. Since his bond then had been posted by his supporters in Greensboro, that would effectively free up the five hundred dollars that Williams had spent out of his own pocket when he reluctantly paid the emigrant-agent tax for 1900. In addition, there was the understanding that if Williams acted in good faith, an effort would be made to prevent his indictment by the grand jury. For his part, Williams was to get out of town immediately, taking no Negroes with him.[64]

That same day, Williams boarded a westbound train with only an assistant accompanying him. Once the train crossed the Greene County line and was five miles into the adjoining Morgan County, it stopped at Buckhead, where it took on a party of black recruits. Also boarding the train at Buckhead was Sheriff Oliver Fears, who arrested Williams straightaway on charges of not having paid the Morgan County emigrant-agent license tax. When the train pulled into the town of Madison, a hostile mob of citizens from Greene, Morgan, Jasper, and Newton counties was waiting to prevent Williams from removing blacks from the area. The arrest obviated their mission. Without Williams to buy tickets, few of the emigrants could go on. At Madison, railroad agents unceremoniously threw all the blacks

63. *Ibid.*
64. *Ibid.*, January 15, January 17, 1900.

without tickets off the train. Then, waiting until the train was moving out of town, they threw their baggage off too, strewing it along a mile-long path.[65]

In the hands of the authorities, with mob violence threatening, Williams took the advice of his attorney. He issued the statement that there would be no further transportation to Mississippi and urged the blacks to enter into contracts for the year. On January 16, he appeared in Ocmulgee Circuit Court arguing that he should be released from jail because the emigrant-agent law was unconstitutional. The court denied his motion and scheduled his trial for the spring but allowed him to return to Atlanta. The news dispatch from Greene County commented, "This will probably end labor agitation in this section."[66]

The prediction came two months early. In mid-January, Williams went underground. Quietly he sent his white assistants and black subagents into the Georgia Black Belt and let them do their work. One of the assistants, a white named Porter Woodson, worked in Newton County until he was arrested for soliciting emigrants without a license. William F. Holmes remarks that after Woodson's arrest, the migration from Newton County collapsed because there was no one to pay the transportation costs of the migrants.[67]

In Oglethorpe and Clarke counties, Williams' emissaries were black subagents, who proved less visible to the authorities than Woodson. But there another sort of problem arose, since Williams did not trust the subagents enough to give them money to pay the railroad fares of the migrants. Instead, he entered into an arrangement with the Seaboard Railroad for it to carry black migrants to Atlanta without tickets. By March, the subagents had been extremely successful and a mass exodus was under way. At that point, however, subjected to heavy pressure from planters in the affected communities, the railroad refused to carry any more blacks without tickets.[68]

On the day after the railroad's new policy became public, the station at Athens, Georgia, was the scene of unusual activity. Many of

65. *Ibid.;* Holmes, "Labor Agents and the Georgia Exodus," 441–42.

66. Atlanta *Constitution,* January 17, 1900; Holmes, "Labor Agents and the Georgia Exodus," 442.

67. Holmes, "Labor Agents and the Georgia Exodus," 443–44; *Woodson* v. *State,* 40 S.E. 1013 (1902).

68. Holmes, "Labor Agents and the Georgia Exodus," 443–44.

the blacks had sacrificed everything for the exodus. They remained at the station with nowhere to go, perhaps still hoping to leave. Throughout the day, the bitterness of their disappointment flashed in incidents of violence. In the meantime, James Monroe Smith arrived. Smith was one of Georgia's largest convict lessees and a man who allowed no one to trifle with his labor. In 1895, he had stopped a train to prevent labor agents from making off with some of his workers. On this day, he was at the station overseeing the arrest of sixteen hands who, he said, had broken their contracts. On the following day, police dispersed the remaining crowd by reading aloud the state vagrancy law and warning that anyone who did not go at once would be arrested.[69]

About a month later, in April, 1900, Williams' case reached the Georgia Supreme Court, which upheld his conviction. His appeal went to the United States Supreme Court. Represented by Davison, he argued that the Georgia emigrant-agent law restricted the "right of the citizen to move from one State to another" and hence abridged his privileges and immunities as a citizen of the United States. He argued also that his business was a form of interstate commerce and therefore not subject to regulation by Georgia law.[70]

The Court rejected both arguments. It held that limiting labor agents could "only incidentally and remotely" affect the freedom of laborers to leave a state or to enter into contracts. Ignoring the actual history of the Georgia law, the Court ruled that "the intention to prohibit this particular business cannot properly be imputed from the amount of the tax payable" by labor agents. Moreover, the Court was of the opinion that if the state wanted to discriminate against a business whose manifest tendency was to induce the laboring population to leave, that would not be unreasonable. The Court also denied the argument that Georgia was interfering with interstate commerce, holding that "labor contracts were not in themselves subjects of traffic between the States."[71]

69. Ibid., 444; E. Merton Coulter, James Monroe Smith: Georgia Planter, Before Death and After (Athens, Ga., 1961), 36. On Smith, see also Charles R. Koch, "All the Land That's Next to Mine," Farm Quarterly, Autumn, 1958, pp. 103–106.

70. Williams v. Fears, 179 U.S. 270 (1900).

71. Ibid., 275, 278.

Anticipating legal vindication, Williams had rented "handsome offices" on Wall Street in Atlanta. The day after he lost before the United States Supreme Court he put on a brave face and told the county tax collector that he expected to take out an emigrant-agent license. Whether he actually bought the license is uncertain, but the Court's decision unquestionably marked the end of his career as a public labor agent. Ray Stannard Baker takes the view that legal prosecution drove Williams out of business and quotes him as saying that within a hundred miles of Atlanta there were counties "where it's worth more than a man's life is worth to go in to get Negroes to move to some other state. There are farmers that would not hesitate to shoot their own brother were he to come from Mississippi to get 'his niggers,' as he calls them, even though he had no contract with them."[72]

In Mississippi, too, white planters stood ready to use force against those who tried to take their labor. In 1908, as the boll weevil began to reach the state, planters in the Natchez area saw black migrants from Louisiana fleeing the infestation by moving up the Mississippi River to the Delta, which was still free of the insects. As the planters of the Natchez area soon learned, it was a very reasonable action, since the need for black labor decreased dramatically once the weevils hit with full force. For the time being, however, the planters' only thought was how to protect their labor supply. They were particularly worried because their area had recently "been drained of all its superfluous negro labor by labor agents from Birmingham, Ala[.], and other parts of the mineral belt." Their concerns were heightened when a steamboat from the Black River section of Louisiana headed upriver toward the Delta carrying five hundred migrating blacks. Soon after, the steamer *America* landed at Natchez carrying blacks on their way to the Yazoo. A large party of local Negroes were waiting at the wharf to join them, and more still were gathering at Sycamore Point and at other places along the river.[73]

At that juncture, white opposition crystallized, and the "money interests of the town and [Adams County] got together and organized the Bankers and Merchants Labor Agency for the purpose of keeping

72. Quoted by Ray Stannard Baker in *Following the Color Line: American Negro Citizenship in the Progressive Era* (1908; rpr. New York, 1964), 80.

73. Charleston (S.C.) *News and Courier*, December 27, 1908.

the negroes at home and encouraging immigration." The thirteen white labor agents and two black labor agents in Natchez were told "they must git." All left town on the first train. In addition, a ten-member committee of the Bankers and Merchants group visited the blacks at the wharf. Rather mildly, the correspondent covering the events described the intimidation that followed: "Their methods were so emphatic that the negroes concluded to abandon their idea of leaving." The labor agent in charge advised the blacks to remain, and he promised to depart. After that, another committee "waited upon" the editor of a local black newspaper and warned him to leave town. The delegation relented, however, after the editor committed himself to writing against emigration.[74]

A year later, the weevil having made sharp inroads into the cotton crop in southern Mississippi, white attitudes had greatly changed. A headline in the Vicksburg *Herald* proclaimed, NEGROES FLOCK TO DELTA[,] LABOR AGENTS NOT MOLESTED. Datelined Fayette, Mississippi, November 30, the article under the headline recounted that many Negroes from the area around Jefferson County were moving to the Delta. Most were leaving debts behind, but surprisingly neither planters nor business interests were trying to stop them from going. The paper said that labor agents were operating freely on the streets of Fayette, a "thing that would have incited mob violence two years ago."[75]

The change did not mean that local whites had had second thoughts about the limits of black freedom. Rather, it signaled temporary and more lasting shifts that were taking place in the local economy because of the spreading boll weevil. As it became clear that the weevil had come to stay, local farmers began to see the virtues of crop diversification. The article in the Vicksburg *Herald* stated that most of the large planters were going to be giving considerable attention to stock raising and forage crops. It concluded that "cotton acreage will be reduced to a minimum."[76] Accordingly, planters in Jefferson County were not the least bit preoccupied with protecting their blacks from the labor agents. Indeed, the proprietary attitudes of the past seemed

74. *Ibid.*

75. Clipping from Vicksburg (Miss.) *Herald,* December 2, 1909, in Boll Weevil Clipping Files, Selected Boll Weevil Clippings, U.S. Department of Agriculture, Bureau of Plant Entomology and Quarantine, National Archives, Record Group 7-60.

76. *Ibid.*

completely dispelled. When whites a few years before had spoken of not permitting their blacks to be taken away, they were expressing attitudes that were a legacy of slavery, yet the inheritance was hardly undiluted. The proprietary attitudes of antebellum planters had included a generous dose of paternalism, and that was largely absent in the late nineteenth and early twentieth centuries.

The attitude in Georgia when Williams was recruiting and again in Natchez in 1908 reflected little more than naked economic self-interest and the memory that whites had once owned blacks. The proprietary impulse prevailed only so long as it seemed that black movement would create labor shortages or would lead to demands for higher wages. When conditions turned so bad that planters faced the prospect of supporting their blacks for months at a time, free labor attitudes born in the days of Reconstruction became ascendant. Blacks had to fend for themselves, and for the time being at least, the planters came to share the outlook of the many whites who did not depend on black labor and who had never objected to the work of the labor agents.

Labor agents faced increasing hostility in the early twentieth century. That is evident in the events that befell Peg Leg Williams in Georgia and in the mob action that took place in Natchez in 1908. Though there were times when the agents worked unencumbered, the trend was toward stopping organized black movement. The case of *Williams* v. *Fears* legitimated the southern license laws that could hobble labor agents, and in the years from 1903 to 1912 six of the eleven former Confederate states adopted new emigrant-agent legislation. With increasing openness, planter interests employed mob violence to stop the work of the agents. The data are too fragmentary to prove that that sort of violence was on the increase, but the pattern of the laws speaks for itself.

10

THE PARADOX OF BLACK MOBILITY AND
INVOLUNTARY SERVITUDE

Clearly, black movement was occurring regardless of laws, court decisions, and even the threat of mob action. The crucial question, however, is whether coercive measures were affecting the nature and extent of black movement in a significant way. More broadly, the issue is whether the legal structure of involuntary servitude that had been created in the years after Reconstruction was in fact immobilizing the black labor force. Passing restrictive laws was one thing; effectively limiting freedom of movement may have been something quite different.

The situation in the South was changing over time, and it differed from place to place as well. In the first months after emancipation, cases of slaverylike abuse were commonplace, but by the time of Reconstruction, they were becoming rare.[1] The realities of Reconstruction simply did not allow white southerners to continue living in the

---

1. Roark, *Masters Without Slaves,* 134–35; Litwack, *Been in the Storm,* 183–85; Daniel, "The Metamorphosis of Slavery," 88–89. In the last two of these works, evidence is given of the reluctance of planters to conform to emancipation, but the great majority of examples of that reluctance come from the period 1865–1866. The Meridian (Miss.) *Mercury* of December 20, 1879, carried one of the rare stories of slavery persisting years after emancipation.

past to that extent. Even after Reconstruction ended, public charges that blacks were held in involuntary servitude or peonage remained rare until the twentieth century.

It is, of course, impossible to demonstrate the negative hypothesis that peonage and involuntary servitude were minor phenomena until the twentieth century. It is significant, however, that George Washington Cable, who wrote about matters of race from the mid-1870s until about 1894, never referred directly to either subject. The closest he came was in discussing topics like convict labor and the crop lien laws of the South. When he wrote of the lien laws, he made it clear that he thought they were responsible for the exodus of 1890 from the Carolinas to Mississippi and Arkansas. He would hardly have made the assertion if he had believed that statutes were immobilizing the black population.[2]

The situation must have been changing with some speed in the 1890s, for simply to judge from appearances, a new system of involuntary servitude emerged full-blown in South Carolina, Georgia, Florida, Alabama, and Mississippi just at the turn of the century. The system probably reached its mature form around 1901, nourished both by the new laws of involuntary servitude and by the increasing virulence of antiblack sentiment in the South. Almost simultaneously with the emergence of this forced labor system came efforts to destroy it. Indeed, within a four-year span of time, lawyers in Georgia, Florida, and Alabama independently discovered that the long-dormant federal peonage act of 1867 might be used against the new slavery.[3]

In 1901, Fred Cubberly, an attorney from Levy County, Florida, witnessed the arrest at gunpoint of a laborer by a naval-stores operator who claimed that the worker had deserted his service owing forty dollars. Horrified, Cubberly knew the arrest had to be illegal, but he could think of no statute that obviously covered the case. Then he recalled the federal peonage law of 1867, an act that had never been successfully used to deal with labor exploitation in the South. Although it had been enacted during Reconstruction, its origin and history were totally unrelated to the condition of blacks and to events in the South. It had been created solely to end debt servitude in the New

2. Arlin Turner, ed., *The Negro Question: A Selection of Writings on Civil Rights in the South by George W. Cable* (Garden City, N.Y., 1958), 230–31.

3. Daniel, *The Shadow of Slavery*, 3–7, 6–7n, 43–47.

Mexico Territory, and it lay dormant until the twentieth century. Cubberly, a United States commissioner, told John Eagan, the United States attorney for the Northern District of Florida, of his idea of invoking the statute, and Eagan encouraged him to bring a test case.[4]

A short time afterward, James Dean, a naval-stores operator, visited Cubberly and told how Samuel Clyatt and two other armed Georgians had come to his place in search of four blacks working at his camp. They claimed the laborers owed them money, and Dean then offered to pay off their debts. Clyatt accepted payment for two of the men but insisted on taking the others back home "to make an example of them."[5] That became Cubberly's test case. The law of 1867 targeted the "system known as peonage," and the lawyer set out to prove that the practices of people like Clyatt were part of a broader system involving collusion between employers, law enforcement officials, and judges. The centerpiece of the system in Florida was the false-pretenses law of 1891, which was invoked whenever employers used debt to hold their workers in thrall. Attacking this vicious system, Cubberly in 1902 launched the case of Clyatt on its journey to the Supreme Court.[6] In the end, that case would test the applicability of the peonage act of 1867 to conditions in the South. Before that happened, however, federal district judges in other southern states would summon the peonage law to fight other injustices against blacks.

As the case of Clyatt was moving through the courts, a patrician judge in Alabama mounted his own campaign against the emerging peonage system. A former governor, Thomas G. Jones, was appointed federal district judge for the Middle District of Alabama in 1901. He had the strong support of Booker T. Washington. Shortly after taking office, Jones requested the United States Secret Service to investigate peonage in his district, and when its report came in April, 1903, Jones immediately impaneled an investigating federal grand jury. Under Jones's close direction, the grand jury uncovered a pattern of peonage that involved the collaboration of wealthy landowners, local constables, justices of the peace, and plantation overseers.[7]

---

4. *Ibid.*, 3–4; Howard Devon Hamilton, "The Legislative and Judicial History of the Thirteenth Amendment" (Ph.D. dissertation, University of Illinois, 1950), 171–74.

5. Daniel, *The Shadow of Slavery*, 4–5.

6. *Ibid.*, 6–7; Florida, *Laws*, 1891, pp. 57–58.

7. Daniel, *The Shadow of Slavery*, 43–44. In light of the secret but major role that

The grand jury discovered that blacks were often arrested on base-less charges and tried by a justice of the peace who sentenced the of-fenders to pay fines they could not afford. In accordance with the criminal surety system, the offenders were given the opportunity to work out their time. Usually a planter just happened to be in court. Once an agreement was signed and a black was taken to his job, he was supervised by plantation overseers who functioned as guards.[8]

Responding to a request of the grand jury, Judge Jones spelled out the boundaries of peonage as a federal offense. He said that to have a system of peonage, it was not necessary to have formal state sponsor-ship. He held that the law covered the acts of individuals as well as governments. At the same time, he explained that no form of forced labor, no matter how heinous, could be considered peonage unless the laborer was forced to work in order to satisfy a debt.[9]

Jones argued for the unconstitutionality of Alabama's law of 1901 prohibiting persons who jumped their labor contracts from entering into a second contract unless they notified the previous employer of the new agreement. "What is this," he asked, but declaring that a contract breaker "shall not work at his accustomed vocation for others without permission of the creditor?" He asserted that everyone knew that farm laborers were "men of very little means" who had to rely upon advances or had to have work to support themselves. "To a man in this condition," he said, "a dispute or difference with his employer, resulting in the abandonment of the service . . . is calamitous in the extreme." Unless the worker broke the law, he had to choose between staying where he was and starving. The whole "scheme and purpose" of the law was to use the coercive power of the state to force laborers and renters to pay their debts or remain with their employers.[10]

Since only laborers and renters came within the scope of the law, Jones ruled it to be unconstitutional class legislation that violated both the constitution of Alabama and the Constitution of the United States.

Booker T. Washington later played in initiating legal efforts to undermine peonage, one must wonder whether or not he played a role in stimulating Jones to look into it. See Louis R. Harlan, *Booker T. Washington* (2 vols.; New York, 1972–83), I, 300–302, 308–310, II, 249–51.

8. Daniel, *The Shadow of Slavery*, 46–47.
9. *Peonage Cases,* 123 F. 671 (M.D. Ala. 1903).
10. *Ibid.,* 685–87.

Still, he upheld the constitutionality of Alabama's false-pretenses law, which penalized anyone who made a contract "with the intent to injure or defraud his employer." [11]

Judge Jones was a genuine foe of peonage. Before the investigation was over, it had uncovered evidence of an extensive system of forced labor in Coosa, Tallapoosa, and Lowndes counties. But Jones also operated on the principle that public exposure was enough for vanquishing evil. After his herculean steps to bring the problem into the open, he levied minimal jail terms and fines on those who were convicted. In many cases, he went back and set aside even the token punishments. When all was said and done, the net punitive result of Jones's crusade was that four persons spent a combined total of five months in jail, while others paid a total of five hundred dollars in fines. [12]

At about the same time, Emory Speer, the federal judge of Georgia's Southern District, presided over the indictment of Thomas J. McClellan and Edward, William, and Frank McCree on peonage charges. McClellan, the sheriff of Ware County, was charged with causing John Wesley Boney to be held in peonage by selling him to the McCrees. According to the indictment, the McCree brothers then held Boney in peonage to work off a supposed debt. Edward McCree was a leading member of the Georgia legislature, with influential well-wishers. [13]

Ruling against a motion to dismiss the case, Judge Speer took the highly unusual step of noting the distinguished supporters of the accused peon masters. He said:

> That a chairman of a penitentiary committee of the Georgia Senate appeared for the prisoners; that a member of the House judiciary committee in Congress, from the district of the prisoners, contributed a brief in their behalf; that a solicitor general of the state court in their state judicial district, charged with the prosecution of such offenses under the state law, sat with the prisoners and their counsel during the hearing—taken altogether is somewhat persuasive of the conclusion that if there is no system of pe-

---

11. *Ibid.*, 690–91.

12. Daniel, *The Shadow of Slavery*, 58, 59, 63.

13. *United States* v. *McClellan* et al., 127 F. 971–72 (S.D. Ga. 1904). On the McCrees, see New York *Times*, May 6, 1903, August 6, 1904.

onage de jure, to which the statute applies, there is yet a de facto system of some equivalent sort.[14]

The defendants claimed that the peonage act was unconstitutional and that even if it was constitutional, it applied only to abolishing the overall system of peonage and not to specific acts of selling and imprisoning a human being. Speer ruled against them, saying that the Thirteenth Amendment was full and sufficient warrant for the adoption of a law abolishing peonage. As to whether the law reached to specific acts of individuals, Speer cited the opinion of Judge Jones, in Alabama, saying that the term "a condition of peonage" used in the statute "should be broadly construed in favor of the liberty of the citizen."[15]

As these events were unfolding in Georgia, the case of Clyatt was working its way toward the Supreme Court, where the constitutionality of the federal peonage law was to be decided. The case was important because the statutory arsenal of the federal government included only two laws bearing directly on forced labor. One was the peonage act; the other was the portion of the Civil Rights Act of 1866 that made it a crime to kidnap a person in order to sell the victim into slavery or involuntary servitude. The weakness of the latter statute was that most who endured forced labor in the South were not kidnapped in the literal sense of the term.[16]

For the Justice Department to be able to act effectively against forced labor, the peonage act had to pass muster with the Supreme Court. It did. Speaking for the Court, Justice Brewer upheld its

14. *United States* v. *McClellan* et al., 127 F. 972–73.

15. *Ibid.*, 972, 973, 975.

16. *Revised Statutes of the United States, 1875, secs.* 5525–26. In addition, Assistant Attorney General Charles W. Russell argued that a portion of the Ku Klux Klan Act of May 31, 1870, prohibiting conspiracies to deprive persons of rights guaranteed under the Constitution, might also be used against involuntary servitude. It was a plausible suggestion by modern standards, but Russell should have realized that *Hodges* v. *United States,* 203 U.S. 1 (1906), indicated that the Supreme Court was extremely unlikely to support such an interpretation. See *Revised Statutes of the United States, sec.* 5508, and "Report of Hon. Charles W. Russell, Assistant Attorney-General, Relative to Peonage Matters, October 10, 1907," in *Annual Report of the Attorney-General of the United States for 1907* (2 vols.; Washington, D.C., 1907), I, 207–208 (hereafter cited as Russell, "Peonage Matters").

constitutionality, saying peonage was a species of involuntary servitude banned by the Thirteenth Amendment. Therefore, the court concluded, the peonage act applied not only to the system of debt servitude that had existed in New Mexico but to that which existed in the South.[17] Brewer defined peonage as a "status or condition of compulsory service, based upon the indebtedness of the peon to the master. The basal fact is indebtedness."[18] That was a realistic definition, rooted in the history of peonage, but it was to have unfortunate consequences. Because there were no other laws aimed at implementing the Thirteenth Amendment, the decision created the absurdity that forced labor to satisfy a debt was a federal crime but outright slavery in the absence of a debt was no federal offense at all.

As if to underscore the limitations of the victory in the case of Clyatt, Brewer went on to hold that Clyatt had been improperly convicted, because his indictment charged him with *returning* Will Gordon and Mose Gridley to peonage. Nowhere did the evidence show that the two blacks had earlier been held in peonage. Thus, although Clyatt was certainly guilty of holding the men in a condition of peonage, he was not guilty of *returning* them to peonage, and the conviction was overturned.[19]

A short time later, South Carolina joined the list of states in which determined federal judges had condemned peonage. In 1897, the state had adopted a new contract law providing that any laborer working for a share of the crop or for wages who took advances "and thereafter willfully and without just cause fail[ed] to perform the reasonable service required of him" could receive a fine or imprisonment. Amendments in 1904 stiffened the penalties and provided that even conviction and time in jail would not release the worker from the unpaid debt that had landed him in jail in the first place.[20] In 1907, both the South Carolina Supreme Court and a federal district court ruled that statute unconstitutional. Speaking for the federal court, Judge William H. Brawley first summarized South Carolina's defense, saying that, from the perspective of those who supported the law, it was "part of a

17. *Clyatt* v. *United States*, 197 U.S. 215–17 (1905).
18. *Ibid.*, 215.
19. *Ibid.*, 218–21.
20. Cohen, "Negro Involuntary Servitude," 46.

system of local administration in matters of great concern to the industrial life of the state" and that "under our system of local self-government the power of the state in that sphere is supreme; and . . . the white people of the state, now charged with the responsibility of its government, being better acquainted with the negro, his capacities and limitations, can determine better than those outside of it what policy will best subserve his interest and their own."[21] Like Jones and Speer, Brawley had impeccable southern credentials. He was a Confederate veteran who took great pride in his aristocratic heritage. Moreover, his summary of the state's position showed that he fully understood the stance of those who dominated affairs. Still, his response was short and unequivocal: "The one sufficient answer to the argument is that the question of human liberty is not one of merely local concern. It rests upon the Constitution of the United States." The courts, he said, had no higher duty than to construe liberally the parts of the Constitution that protected personal security and liberty. Besides, he argued, efforts to attract foreign white immigrants would fail "so long as our statute books hold legislation tending to create a system of forced labor."[22]

Also in 1907, the assistant attorney general Charles W. Russell wrote a report, "Peonage Matters," in which he argued that the federal peonage law needed amendment in such a way as to make the legal definition of the crime "broad enough to include the holding of persons in servitude whether in liquidation of an indebtedness 'or otherwise.'" He mentioned that one of the United States attorneys in Alabama had noticed that the definition of peonage in the decision on Clyatt was influencing the people in his district to avoid the element of indebtedness while maintaining involuntary servitude.[23]

It was a needed proposal but one unlikely to succeed in the heavily racist environment of the early twentieth century. Indeed, the opposition in the South to such ideas is clear from the way that in the years immediately following the Alabama peonage trials of 1903, all the southern states except Tennessee, Texas, and Virginia revised their

21. *Ex Parte Drayton* et al., 153 F. 996 (1907); Cohen, "Negro Involuntary Servitude," 46.

22. *Ex Parte Drayton,* 996.

23. Russell, "Peonage Matters," 207–208.

contract or enticement laws to strengthen the hands of employers in preventing their black workers from leaving.[24] Analysis of the statutory changes suggests that many were intended to get around unfavorable court decisions.

The legislative activity sprang not so much from a willful desire to thwart the federal courts as from a deep conviction about the racial order of things. Explaining the roots of southern contract laws, Judge Brawley said, "One of the legacies of . . . slavery is that there are a number of people who believe that the negro will not work unless he is forced to work, and there is a strong disposition towards legislation of a kind that would compel work in payment of a debt."[25] From such a perspective, it stood to reason that if the federal government upset one contract law, another had to be fashioned to gain the same end.

In 1910, the attorney general asked each of the United States attorneys to submit a special report on peonage. His letter requested particulars about recent cases and any prosecutions that had been instituted. He wanted information, as well, about state laws that lent themselves to attempts to "produce a condition of involuntary servitude." The attorney general offered the thought that cases of involuntary servitude that could not be reached by the peonage law might come under Sections 19 and 20 of the United States Criminal Code of 1909 "relating to the deprivation of Federal civil rights . . . on account of race, color or alienage."[26]

The responses to Washington's request for information revealed a good deal about both the extent of involuntary servitude and the enforcement attitudes of the various United States attorneys. The United States attorney for the Eastern District of North Carolina gave the details of a case from 1907 in which the accused had been acquitted

24. See Table 12 above.

25. *United States* v. *Clement,* 171 F. 979 (1909).

26. Attorney general to Herbert Seawell (Copy), October 31, 1910, in Central Files of the Department of Justice, Classified Subject Files Relating to Peonage, National Archives, Record Group 60 (doc. no. 150153-5, file no. 50-0; hereafter the collection is cited as DJ Peonage Files, NA). It seems likely that there was a connection between the request of the attorney general and the preparation of the government's brief as *amicus curiae* in the case of *Bailey* v. *Alabama.* Most of the correspondence between the United States attorneys and the attorney general was actually handled by William R. Harr, who was involved in preparing and presenting the government's position on the Bailey case.

even though he was clearly guilty. He explained that "there was existing at the time considerable prejudice against this class of prosecutions and this prejudice went into the jury box." Still, he concluded, "It is my opinion . . . that peonage as embraced in the statutes of the United States does not exist in the Eastern District of North Carolina."[27]

The report from neighboring South Carolina was as reassuring—and as disquieting—as the word from North Carolina. Ernest Cochran, the United States attorney for South Carolina, detailed his prosecutions of two major peonage cases, one involving R. Lebby Clement and the other Joshua Ashley, a prominent political figure. In both cases, sympathetic juries acquitted the defendants, but even so, Cochran was sure that the prosecution had had an "immense influence in stopping peonage in this state." He concluded, "While I believe that there are in South Carolina cases existing of peonage here and there, yet I am satisfied that whatever peonage there may be is of a mild type and as a rule unaccompanied with brutalities."[28]

The United States attorney for the Southern District of Alabama reported on thirteen peonage cases. Six had resulted in the acquittal of all defendants. Three brought in fines of $1,075 assessed against eight individual defendants. Four were still pending. Expressing a common view among the attorneys, he said, "It is extremely difficult to secure convictions, but at the same time vigorous prosecutions with the attendant anxiety and the expense to which [the defendants] are put have a very good effect, and even though convictions will, in most instances not be secured, at the same time I propose to prosecute such cases as vigorously as possible."[29]

Some government lawyers were even more sanguine. In the Eastern District of Arkansas, William Whipple observed that a few years before, the crime of peonage was "ripe"—rife?—in some of the southern counties of his state "but of late years very little complaint has been made, the prosecutions heretofore conducted seeming to

27. Herbert F. Seawell to attorney general, December 2, 1910, in DJ Peonage Files, NA (doc. no. 150153-29).

28. Ernest F. Cochran to Attorney General, November 11, 1910, in DJ Peonage Files, NA (doc. no. 150153-18).

29. U.S. attorney for the Southern District of Alabama to attorney general, January 26, 1911, in DJ Peonage Files, NA (doc. no. 150153-44).

have had a salutary effect." A similar story came from the Southern District of Florida, where J. M. Cheney averred that in consequence of the convictions of the general manager of the Prairie Pebble Phosphate Company, who had received a fine of three thousand dollars, of the superintendent of the Barker Chemical Company, whose punishment he did not give, and of two others, who had faced fines of a thousand dollars each, "the practice of peonage has been entirely abandoned." In fact, Cheney assured, after these prosecutions many employers in the district took "great pains to advise themselves as to what constituted peonage, and have very carefully avoided making themselves liable under the statutes."[30]

The United States attorney for the Southern District of Mississippi described a particularly heinous instance of peonage in which a black man and his family twice abandoned their contract and ran away from their employer after being mistreated. After their second capture, they were "stripped naked, tied with ropes, and were most unmercifully whipped." Though the government had a strong case, the grand jury failed to return an indictment. The attorney concluded: "It is almost impossible to get a Grand Jury to find an indictment against white men for holding negroes in Peonage in this district. The Grand Jury is generally composed almost entirely of white farmers, who have negroes in their employ, and who are well acquainted with labor conditions as they exist in Mississippi, and they seem to be prejudiced against finding indictments for peonage."[31]

In December, 1910, William D. Frazier, who had charge of the Northern District of Mississippi, painted a benign picture of conditions in his area, but a year later he changed his mind. Writing to the attorney general in 1910, he sounded like many of his colleagues. "Up until a few years ago," he said, peonage existed "more or less throughout the Delta section of our State." Then the conviction in 1908 of a wealthy planter from Tunica County made the difference: "Planters throughout the Delta who are personal friends of mine, assure me that since the conviction, the practice of forcing labor has been almost

30. William G. Whipple to attorney general, November 8, 1910, in DJ Peonage Files, NA (doc. no. 150153-15); J. M. Cheney to attorney general, November 21, 1910, in DJ Peonage Files, NA (doc. no. 150153-24).

31. R. C. Lee to attorney general, November 28, 1910, in DJ Peonage Files (doc. no. 150153-28).

abandoned." [32] Frazier did concede that the investigations of his office occasionally showed a "condition existing that does not constitute the crime of peonage, because of the fact that there is no indebtedness due . . . which is simply a case of involuntary servitude, or slavery pure and simple." Responding to the attorney general's query about state statutes that could be used to produce a condition of peonage, he listed Sections 1146, 1147, and 1148 of the Mississippi Code of 1906. He added that most members of the bar deemed those laws unconstitutional but that owing to the "peculiar labor conditions existing in our Delta section," the supreme court of Mississippi had always dodged the issue. [33] Then, in August, 1911, in responding briefly to another request from Washington for information about peonage conditions, Frazier blurted out, "In my opinion, Sections 1147 and 1148, Mississippi Code of 1906 are taken advantage of constantly in the holding of parties in involuntary servitude and peonage." [34]

It was an exceptional moment of candor, for with varying degrees of sincerity, most of the United States attorneys had been telling Washington what it wanted to hear. Peonage, most seemed to be saying, had been a very serious matter but was now on the way out. True, defendants were often acquitted, even in the face of compelling evidence against them, but the prosecutions themselves were having a good effect, warning southern employers away from the crime. Here and there, as in the reports of Cheney and in Russell's account of his conversation with a United States attorney in Alabama, one gets a glimmering that although peonage was indeed declining, this was partly because employers were learning to skirt around the edges of the crime, taking advantage of the technicality that holding an individual in involuntary servitude was not a crime so long as it was not done to satisfy a debt.

One comes away from most of the reports of the United States attorneys with the feeling that the concerns of the government's legal officers were narrow and procedural. Most would enforce the peonage statute in cases where individuals were held to labor to satisfy a debt,

32. William D. Frazier to attorney general, December 31, 1910, DJ Peonage Files (doc. no. 150153-32).

33. Frazier to attorney general, December 31, 1910, in DJ Peonage Files.

34. William D. Frazier to attorney general, August 17, 1911, in DJ Peonage Files (doc. no. 150153-80).

but they were hardly interested in devising imaginative ways of protecting blacks against the broader forms of involuntary servitude that, according to the decision regarding Clyatt, were not embraced in the peonage law of 1867.

A significant exception to the norm was Alexander Akerman, the assistant United States attorney for Georgia's Southern District. If there was one attorney in all of Georgia who might defend helpless black laborers against their oppressors, it was natural that it should be this man. His father, Amos T. Akerman, had moved to Georgia from New Hampshire in 1854. The elder Akerman opposed secession but fought for the South in the Civil War. Afterward, he became a Republican, serving first as a United States attorney in Georgia and then as attorney general of the United States. In both capacities, he was an outspoken opponent of the Klan and a dedicated supporter of equal rights.[35] The son was as committed to the rule of law as his father. At a time when almost all Georgians took white domination for granted, he simply assumed that blacks were entitled to the full protection of the laws.

That supposition permeated his peonage report to the attorney general, which he filled with concrete details about the cases of forced labor handled by his office. One involved O. B. Jarmen, a turpentine operator in Turner County who employed seventy-five to a hundred hands. According to Akerman, Jarmen juggled his accounts to keep his hands in perpetual debt. When a worker deserted him, he went before a justice of the peace to get a warrant "charging the man with any offense known to the Penal Code of Georgia." Often acting in person, he arrested the runaway, took him back to his place, whipped him, and put him back to work. Akerman's office had Jarmen indicted for peonage and for conspiracy to intimidate witnesses. Later, however, Jarmen received a continuance because of illness, and it is uncertain whether the case ever came to trial.[36]

Akerman described at length the system of involuntary servitude that existed in the Southern District of Georgia, emphasizing the way it was organized around debt, labor contracts, and the false-pretenses

35. McFeely, *Grant*, 367–74.

36. Report of Alexander Akerman, assistant U.S. attorney for the Southern District of Georgia, to attorney general [November, 1910] (DJ Peonage Files, NA, doc. no. 150153–12).

act of 1903.[37] Having made a contract with a worker, the employer attempted to keep the laborer in perpetual debt the way Jarmen did. When a worker tried to break out of the system by running away, the employer tracked him down and brought him before a court on the charge of violating contract law or on some other offense. The court then fined the runaway, and the employer offered to pay the fine. The unsuccessful runaway thus bound himself more tightly to the farmer than before, since his fine increased his debt. Sometimes a runaway was hunted down and returned to the farm without even the semblance of a trial.[38]

Akerman held that it was "largely through the administration of the 'Labor Contract Law' that the farmers [could] compel laborers to work for them." That, he said, was because in the more rural parts of the state the juries that dealt with cases arising under the contract law were "largely made up of men who either operate farms themselves or are interested in their operation, hence it can be understood that convictions are almost a matter of course." Some cases went on appeal to higher courts, but Akerman remarked, "Considering the number of cases brought under the 'Labor Contract Law,' the number of cases carried beyond the trial courts are insignificant."[39] Convictions that were appealed were "almost invariably" reversed, but never on constitutional grounds, "the courts presumably preferring to declare the law valid, but to reverse the cases upon other grounds." Akerman seems to be implying that the higher courts of Georgia were following a deliberate strategy to prevent an appeal to the federal courts. The reversal would satisfy the grievance of the litigant while preventing him from making a constitutional stir by appealing the matter further.[40] That strategy would be consistent too with Frazier's comment that because of the "peculiar labor conditions existing in our Delta section," the Mississippi Supreme Court had always avoided tests of the constitutionality of its labor-contract laws.

To protect black laborers against involuntary servitude, Akerman recommended that Congress be urged to adopt a short, simple statute that banned forced labor, using "as nearly as possible, the language of

37. *Ibid.*, 13–15.
38. *Ibid.*, 13.
39. *Ibid.*, 14.
40. *Ibid.*

the Thirteenth Amendment." He believed that the very word *peonage* had a foreign sound about it that made Georgia juries loath to indict or convict. He also proposed that the penalty for violating the statute be "much milder."[41] His purpose was not to make things easier for the guilty but to create a climate in which Georgians would be willing to convict lawbreakers. The adoption of Akerman's plan might have made a difference, but given the political realities of the time, it had little chance.

The situation was not entirely bleak, however. Although the reports of the United States attorneys tended to be far too optimistic, the federal courts had in the first decade of the twentieth century conducted a moderately successful first assault against peonage. That assault continued and broadened in *Bailey* v. *Alabama,* in 1911. A major consequence of the decision regarding Clyatt was that the false-pretenses laws had become the frontline defense of whites who wanted compulsory labor laws of some sort to keep blacks at work. When those statutes were struck down, the legal structure that supported peonage and involuntary servitude suffered a serious blow. The blow came in *Bailey* v. *Alabama.*

Alonzo Bailey was an Alabama farm laborer who in December, 1907, signed an annual labor contract with the Riverside Company. His wage was set at twelve dollars a month, and he was given an advance of fifteen dollars to be taken out of his monthly pay. When after working for just over a month, he left without refunding the advance, the Riverside Company had Bailey arrested and tried under the state's false-pretenses law. Since the law contained a prima facie clause, it was an open-and-shut case. Bailey was sentenced to pay fifteen dollars in damages, a thirty-dollar fine, and costs. Not having the money, he received instead 20 days of hard labor, for the fine, and 116 days, for the costs.[42]

In 1911, the case reached the Supreme Court. There, Bailey's lawyer argued that the real object of the statute was "to enable the employer to keep the employee in involuntary servitude by the overhanging menace of prosecution which he knows must be successful on account of the artificial presumption or rule of evidence making the

41. *Ibid.,* 15.
42. *Bailey* v. *Alabama,* 219 U.S. 228–31 (1911).

quitting prima facie evidence of the crime, which is practically conclusive because the defendant cannot testify in his own behalf as to his unexpressed intent."[43] The state of Alabama, for its part, maintained that the statute aimed simply at dealing with the common-law crime of cheating by false pretenses. Disingenuously, it argued that the prima facie rule did not "overcome" the presumption of innocence granted to all defendants, unless the jury was "satisfied from all the evidence of the guilt of the accused beyond a reasonable doubt."[44]

Dismissing all arguments to the effect that the false-pretenses law was aimed at black laborers, the Court noted that the law "on its face, makes no racial discrimination." At that time in American life the Court was not about to resurrect the Fourteenth Amendment as a shield for blacks. On the other hand, it was not willing to leave in place a statute that was the legal cornerstone of peonage. In a narrowly focused but strong ruling, Chief Justice Charles Evans Hughes found that "although the statute in terms is to punish fraud, still its natural and inevitable effect is to expose to conviction for crime those who simply fail or refuse to perform contracts for personal service in liquidation of a debt." Hughes went on that if one judged the purpose of the law from its effect, this was a law aimed at compelling the performance of labor contracts.[45]

The question, then, was whether such statutory compulsion was constitutional, and Hughes had little trouble concluding that it was not. Resting his reasoning exclusively on the history and content of the Thirteenth Amendment and of the federal peonage law of 1867, he argued that the Alabama law required compulsory service of a sort prohibited by both.[46] By restricting his inquiry in that way, he was able to strike a hard blow against peonage but leave intact the elaborate legal structure that, through separate-but-equal rulings and other devices, permitted a host of racial discriminations.

Three years later, in *U.S.* v. *Reynolds,* the Court employed an identical strategy to strike down Alabama's criminal-surety statute.[47]

---

43. Quoted by Daniel in *The Shadow of Slavery,* 75.
44. *Bailey* v. *Alabama,* 219 U.S. 226.
45. *Ibid.,* 231, 238.
46. *Ibid.,* 238–45.
47. *United States* v. *Reynolds,* 235 U.S. 133.

Speaking for the Court, Justice William Day explained that although it was perfectly proper for a state to impose prison sentences or fines upon those convicted of violating the law, it was not proper for it to enforce the labor demands of the surety, who was, after all, a private individual. Day saw that under Alabama's statute the private contract with the surety "must be kept under pain of re-arrest. . . . Thus, under pain of recurring prosecutions, the convict may be kept at labor, to satisfy the demands of his employer." Any law that allowed that was an unconstitutional violation of the Thirteenth Amendment and the peonage act.[48]

Taken together, *Bailey* v. *Alabama* and *U.S.* v. *Reynolds* demolished the legal foundation for peonage in Alabama. They could be expected to have done the same for the rest of the South, but for the next thirty years Georgia and Florida managed to hold on to false-pretenses laws that were substantively identical to the act ruled unconstitutional in the case involving Bailey. A full-scale exploration of how they did that is beyond my scope, but Pete Daniel has emphasized a lack of enforcement zeal in the Justice Department.[49] Georgia and Florida apparently followed as well the strategy, outlined by Alexander Akerman, in which higher courts ruled for the defendants in labor-contract cases but kept the peonage issue out of the federal courts by deliberately not reversing such cases on constitutional grounds.

We come now to the most difficult part of this inquiry into southern forced labor, and the reader is warned in advance that no precise answers will be found here. It is clear that the structure of involuntary servitude erected after Reconstruction immobilized some blacks. From the Great Migration of 1916–1917 and earlier movement as well, however, it is equally clear that many blacks had full freedom to travel where they wished. The question, then, is not whether blacks in the South were free to move where they wanted but rather to what extent they had such freedom. Instances of forced labor that illustrate the brutalities of the southern system of involuntary servitude are important indicators of the racist extremes to which the system could go, but no matter how horrendous the brutality in any individual instance, its details tell little of the extent of the system. Even in recent

48. *Ibid.*, 150.
49. Daniel, *The Shadow of Slavery*, 79–80, 180.

years, the newspapers have published occasional stories with headlines like "Three in Texas Charged With Using Slave Labor," telling how the victims were held as slaves. Such stories are accurate enough, but we know that in the present day they represent the rare exception. We know, too, that on the eve of the Civil War about 93 percent of all southern blacks were slaves.[50] The slavery of antebellum times had a great deal more impact than the slavery of today, and the difference is in the numbers. That is why it is so important that we have some sense of how big the numbers were with peonage and involuntary servitude. Unfortunately, to ask such quantitative questions is not to answer them. Extant statistics simply do not allow an even approximate estimate of the extent to which southerners had a free labor market.[51] On the extent of involuntary servitude, there is no alternative to a dependence upon traditional source materials. The best that is possible is a general sense of how pervasive the practice of holding blacks to labor against their wills was. Earlier in this work, it has been argued that, apart from the chain gangs, there is little evidence that from the end of Reconstruction into the 1890s, forced labor existed in the South on a significant scale. Paradoxically, this is true even though southern legislators in these years were taking the first steps toward creating a legal structure of involuntary servitude. The court cases and newspaper stories that one would expect to find if forced labor was rampant are absent. The first known peonage case to come before the federal courts was in 1899.[52]

Still, as has been shown, at about the turn of the century there was a sharp and dramatic rise in involuntary servitude. This appears clearly in 1903, when federal courts began to deal with a significant number of peonage cases. It might be argued that this rise was more a reflection of the reforming zeal of the Progressive era than of an actual increase in forced labor, but such an argument would not take account

50. U.S. Bureau of the Census, *Negro Population,* 55.

51. As described in Chapter 2 above, Stephen J. DeCanio tried to determine the extent to which freedom was limited in the southern labor market, but his study was fatally flawed by the assumption that the rural population was an adequate surrogate for the labor force. See p. 26 above, and DeCanio, *Agriculture in the Postbellum South,* 10–15, 262–64, 302–303.

52. *United States* v. *Eberhart,* 127 F. 252 (C.C. Ga. 1899); Daniel, *The Shadow of Slavery,* 6–7n.

of the rising tide of racism in the South. Had peonage and other forms of involuntary servitude been constant across the decades, it would be far more likely that white southern opposition would have surfaced earlier, rather than in 1903, when racism was at flood tide.

Daniel in his excellent study of peonage correctly says that only one reckoning of the extent of peonage in the early twentieth century survives from the time. It is the testimony of Special Agent A. J. Hoyt, of the Department of Justice, that with regard to the states of Georgia, Alabama, and Mississippi, "investigations will prove that 33 1/3 percent of the planters operating from five to one-hundred plows are holding their employees in a state of peonage." Hoyt was an experienced field investigator, and though there is not much to go on in assessing the validity of his estimate, the internal evidence of his assertion hints at a man who was trying to be as precise as possible.[53] He did not say peonage would be found everywhere but restricted himself to farms of from five to one hundred plows.

Another way of trying to get a sense of the extent of involuntary servitude is to ask how and when black forced labor in the South came to an end. In the past, I—and others—have held that involuntary servitude continued up to World War II and beyond. Certainly one can compile an impressive list of post–World War I forced-labor cases, ranging from the infamous peonage farm of John Williams in 1921 to the Work or Fight programs of World War II.[54] Still, it would be misleading to imply that little had changed in the South since 1865, or even since 1911. From the time of *Bailey* v. *Alabama*, and probably earlier, involuntary servitude in the South was in decline.

Evidence of that is necessarily circumstantial. There was, to begin with, the legal response of the southern states to the decision in favor of Bailey. If Georgia and Florida virtually ignored the decision until the 1940s, other states gave grudging acceptance somewhat sooner. In Alabama itself a false-pretenses act that passed in 1911 omitted the

53. Daniel, *The Shadow of Slavery,* 22. For other references to the extent of peonage, see pp. 38, 60, 107–109, 148 of the same book.

54. *Ibid.,* 170–91, esp. 190; Cohen, "Negro Involuntary Servitude," 59–60; Novak, *The Wheel of Servitude,* 71–74, 83. Speaking for myself, I can say that I certainly intended to leave the impression that involuntary servitude continued very common into the era of World War II. I ended with Jonathan Daniels' quotation in 1938 of a southern editor that "slavery is still in force . . . but not generally profitable."

objectionable prima facie clause. The Arkansas code of 1916 contained that state's false-pretenses law despite its unconstitutionality, but the state removed the offending provision five years later. Similarly, Mississippi's *Code of 1917* included such a statute, but the *Revised Code of 1930* did not. Neither Arkansas nor Mississippi attempted to supplant the statute with another having comparable effect.[55]

Almost immediately after Bailey's victory, the North Carolina Supreme Court found the state's prima facie clause unconstitutional. Still, the overturned section remained in the state code until 1943.[56] So long as it was there, it was susceptible of being used as if it were still good law by those who did not know or did not care about constitutional niceties. In that way, it served mainly to intimidate black laborers.

North Carolina also had a false-pretenses law that was applicable only to certain specified counties. It was much like the statewide false-pretenses law except that "final jurisdiction" was given to justices of the peace, who did not need law degrees and who were often local farmers with a natural sympathy for their white neighbors. They might easily not know the implications of the Supreme Court decisions that were relevant to the act they were enforcing. At first, in 1905, the law covered thirty-nine counties. Over the years, sixteen more were added, the last four in 1925, 1927, 1931, and 1953.[57]

The legislative evidence does not all point in one direction, but it certainly suggests that, however reluctantly, the South was moving away from the use of forced labor. Pointing in the same direction are data pertaining to the frequency of lynching. Lynching and peonage were separate phenomena, but an intense racism underlay both. As the twentieth century progressed, both came increasingly to appear to enlightened public opinion as barbaric atavisms. It is reasonable to expect that as lynching declined, the occurrence of peonage became rarer too. Table 9 shows the frequency of lynching in the South for the period 1880–1968. Those murders reached a horrendous peak in

55. Cohen, "Negro Involuntary Servitude," 44.

56. *Ibid.*

57. North Carolina, *General Statutes,* 1969 Replacement, sec. 14-358; North Carolina, *Public Local Laws,* 1925, p. 207, 1927, p. 631; North Carolina, *Public Laws,* 1931, p. 179, 1953, p. 343.

the early 1890s and declined thereafter. It is difficult to talk about numbers like 500 or 456 or even 12 or 2 as showing progress, for they represent human beings brutally killed by mobs for the crime of being black. But relative to the numbers of five years earlier, they were indeed an improvement. Over the years fewer and fewer people were murdered in lynchings, and however long the road ahead, that was progress.

This is not to propose a perfect correlation between the frequency of lynchings and instances of forced labor. To do so would be to abandon the argument that large-scale involuntary servitude was a relatively late phenomenon that did not emerge fully until the dawn of the twentieth century. Still, it is plausible to think that over the long haul the frequency of lynching and involuntary servitude declined in loose tandem. It would follow that by the early 1930s the number of blacks laboring against their will would have been dropping sharply.

Still, it sometimes seemed that nothing in the South had changed and that slavery had in practice persisted well into the twentieth century. In 1921, the nation was horrified by the gruesome details of eleven murders committed to conceal the fact that John Williams, of Jasper County, Georgia, had been running a peonage farm. Almost twenty years later, in 1939, William Cunningham, of Oglethorpe County, Georgia, went to Chicago on the almost unbelievable mission of rounding up four black runaways. He even attempted to enlist the help of the Chicago police.[58] But in spite of episodes like that, forced labor was dying long before.

The movement of the black population is the strongest evidence for the decline of involuntary servitude. As Table 5 shows, in the decade from 1910 to 1920 over a half million blacks left the South, amounting to about 6.6 percent of the black population of the South. In the decade of World War II, the number of blacks leaving the South came to 16.7 percent of the black population. Figures like that would not have been possible if large numbers of blacks had been held to labor against their wills.

Tables 13 and 14 show the extent of black migration by state for the period 1870–1950. Table 13 gives net migration estimates for each of the southern states over the period; Table 14 casts the same data in

58. Daniel, *The Shadow of Slavery*, 110–31, 175—77.

TABLE 13

Net Migration of Negroes in Selected Southern States, 1870–1950

STATE	1870–1880	1880–1890	1890–1900	1900–1910	1910–1920	1920–1930	1930–1940	1940–1950
Virginia	-48	-64	-74	-59	-32	-138	-44	-37
West Virginia	2	4	7	18	20	16	-4	-19
North Carolina	-11	-47	-49	-36	-36	-21	-72	-150
South Carolina	19	-23	-67	-87	-90	-244	-115	-193
Georgia	-25	15	-17	-20	-87	-298	-103	-223
Florida	2	19	32	51	6	66	59	9
Kentucky	-16	-27	-9	-25	-18	-19	-10	-25
Tennessee	-31	-23	-15	-39	-33	-16	10	-44
Alabama	-43	-7	10	-25	-82	-94	-73	-196
Mississippi	22	-17	-1	-37	-149	-83	-68	-309
Arkansas	32	56	-4	27	-2	-53	-38	-136
Louisiana	1	7	-14	-18	-57	-30	-10	-134
Oklahoma	[a]	3	[a]	68	1	2	-15	-45
Texas	27	16	18	-13	5	10	5	-79

SOURCE: Eldridge and Thomas, *Demographic Analyses and Interrelations*, Table A1.20, p. 260.

Note: Figures are in thousands. Net out-migration is indicated by negative numbers. Net in-migration is indicated by positive numbers.

[a] Figures were not given in the source because census data were nonexistent or because using the data given for the nonwhite category would have yielded a misleading picture of the size of the black population.

TABLE 14

Net Migration Rates of Negroes in Selected Southern States, 1870–1950

STATE	1870–1880	1880–1890	1890–1900	1900–1910	1910–1920	1920–1930	1930–1940	1940–1950
Virginia	−8.3%	−10.1%	−11.5%	−8.9%	−4.8%	−20.6%	−6.6%	−5.2%
West Virginia	10.4	13.5	18.5	33.8	26.1	15.9	−3.7	−16.5
North Carolina	−2.4	−8.5	−8.2	−5.4	−5.0	−2.6	−7.6	−14.8
South Carolina	3.8	−3.6	−9.1	−10.7	−10.6	−29.5	−14.3	−23.6
Georgia	−3.9	1.8	−1.8	−1.8	−7.3	−26.2	−9.6	−20.8
Florida	2.1	13.1	16.0	18.9	2.0	17.3	12.4	1.6
Kentucky	−6.5	−9.8	−3.4	−9.2	−7.3	−8.1	−4.4	−12.2
Tennessee	−8.7	−5.4	−3.4	−8.1	−7.1	−3.5	−2.0	−8.4
Alabama	−8.0	−1.1	1.3	−2.9	−9.0	−10.2	−7.6	−20.0
Mississippi	4.0	−2.4	−0.2	−3.9	−15.3	−8.6	−6.6	−30.0
Arkansas	19.3	21.5	−1.1	6.7	−0.4	−11.2	−8.0	−30.0
Louisiana	.2	1.4	−2.4	−2.6	−8.1	−4.0	−1.3	−15.5
Oklahoma	a	a	a	70.5	0.8	1.1	−8.8	−28.5
Texas	8.4	3.5	3.2	−1.9	0.7	1.3	0.5	−8.3

SOURCE: Eldridge and Thomas, *Demographic Analyses and Interrelations*, Table A1.22, p. 262.

Note: Net out-migration is indicated by negative numbers. Net in-migration is indicated by positive numbers. The rate of net migration is expressed as a percentage of the average Negro population of each state for each decade.

aFigures were not given in the source because census data were nonexistent or because using the data given for the nonwhite category would have yielded a misleading picture of the size of the black population.

the form of net migration rates, or percentages of the black population of each state. In the decade 1910–1920, Mississippi lost over 15 percent of its black population. In the next decade, South Carolina lost almost 30 percent of its. Then, in the Depression decade, it lost another 14 percent. In the 1940s, the numbers became even more dramatic. South Carolina, Georgia, Alabama, Mississippi, Arkansas, and Oklahoma each lost at least 20 percent of their black population in those years. Numbers of that magnitude are simply inconsistent with a picture of the South as a vast jail. There was oppression aplenty in the South, and one side of it was the effort to immobilize the black population. Yet the number of migrants suggests that from the decade of World War I onward, blacks were relatively free to move as they chose.

How, then, is it possible to make sense of the crosscurrents manifest in the last three chapters—of blacks denied the vote and segregated, of the black codes resurrected in a host of laws aimed at limiting black mobility, of a white South in which planters had a fearsome arsenal with which to hold their black laborers in thrall, of a federal legal system that said no to laws institutionalizing debt slavery yet remained willfully blind to most violations of black rights, of peonage on the ascendance early in the twentieth century but then starting to decline shortly after its emergence, and of the apparent ease with which black migration conformed and reconformed itself to labor demand in both the South and the North?

Perhaps it is illuminating to conceive of the South from the end of Reconstruction to 1915 as an incipient South Africa.[59] From 1877 to 1915, it developed the legal apparatus of racial oppression, which paralleled an intensification of already-existing white antipathies toward blacks. Like South Africa, the American South was on the path toward a legal structure whose central rationale was the holding of an "inferior" race in subordination.[60]

59. In fact, the development of segregation came a little earlier in the American South than it did in South Africa. See Cell, *The Highest Stage of White Supremacy*, 192.

60. As George M. Frederickson has noted, there were large differences as well as similarities between the American South and South Africa. One of the most important was that in South Africa the whites were in the minority, whereas they were in the majority in the American South (*White Supremacy*, xxi).

But the South was a South Africa with a difference, for even as white southerners were rushing to codify segregationist practices and to enact laws further limiting black movement, the region was making the barest beginning at turning away from state-sponsored racial oppression and authoritarianism. Its movement in that regard came in consequence of three central facts of southern life. First, unlike South Africa, the American South was a minority section within a larger nation. It could not isolate itself from unwelcome trends in the country of which it was a part. Second, regardless of the laws, blacks were unwilling to give up their right to move. Like William Pickens' father, they would run away in order to escape an exploitative employer. Third, within the South itself there were many whites who had not the slightest interest in limiting black movement.

Although the great majority of whites were united in allegiance to the doctrine of white supremacy, they divided sharply on the question of black mobility. For the most racist of reasons, those without a stake in using black labor were often strong supporters of black migration. The counterpoise of their outlook served to limit the effectiveness of planters' efforts to prevent black movement and gave blacks room in which to fight the system.

The link between the nation and the South is seen especially clearly in the three federal judges Thomas Jones, Emory Speer, and William Brawley. Each was a native southerner committed to his region, yet each represented an extension of the power of the nation at large and each represented the ideas of the larger culture when it came to matters of peonage and involuntary servitude. If it is true that as late as 1939 the power of the federal courts did not quite reach into the backwaters of William Cunningham's Oglethorpe County, Georgia, it is also true that the power of the courts was too great to be ignored in most of the South. Ultimately it penetrated even to Oglethorpe County.

APPENDIX A

ABOUT MIGRATION STATISTICS

Statistical studies of migration in the United States rely largely on two types of data: census state-of-birth figures and census state-population figures broken down by race, age, and sex. Census information in the latter form can be used to produce *net* migration estimates. The net migration figures are estimates of the number of people a state gained or lost owing to migration after correcting for the effect of births and deaths. Net migration figures are not estimates of the total number of migrants entering or leaving a state but are instead the result of subtracting gains from losses or vice versa at the end of each census decade.[1] State-of-birth figures provide a more direct measure of migration, but unfortunately this set of data gives information about movement that has taken place over many decades. State-of-birth numbers can tell us how many people living in New York in 1870 were born in Virginia, but they say nothing about when the Virginians arrived in New York. Even comparing state-of-birth figures from one census year with those from the previous census does not tell the whole story, because the mortality of those who came in earlier waves of migration frequently acts to mask later gains.[2] The census office began recording state-of-birth data for whites in 1850, but did not

1. Lee *et al., Methodological Considerations and Reference Tables*, 15–25, 32.
2. *Ibid.*, 57–60.

give comparable information about blacks until 1870. As a result, about the best that can be done for the earlier period is to present information on the number of free blacks in 1850 who lived in the state in which they were born and the number who lived outside the state in which they were born.

Migration data for the decade from 1860 to 1870 are particularly unsatisfactory. Because of the unsettled conditions during Reconstruction, the census of 1870 was marred by a substantial undercount in many southern states. The extent of the undercount varied widely. Moreover, it is not possible to calculate the black population of particular southern states by extrapolating from information in later and earlier census, since that would not reckon with all the migrations of the time. All that it is possible to estimate by extrapolating is the size of the black population of the United States as a whole. Roger Ransom and Richard Sutch have concluded that the black population of the United in 1870 was undercounted by 6.6 percent. By their arithmetic, the black population in that year was really about 5,202,090 rather than the 4,880,009 recorded in the census.[3]

The undercount of 1870 affects both net migration estimates and state-of-birth figures for the decade 1860–1870. Although net migration estimates for the black population have been made for the decades both before and after the 1860s, none has been done for the Civil War era. Such estimates would pose particularly formidable problems because, among other things, war-related deaths could be expected to interact with the undercount to distort the results. Although the undercount makes it virtually impossible to use the 1870 state-of-birth figures for blacks living in the southern states, it does not affect at all the utility of the state-of-birth figures for blacks living in the North. This is notably true of the data for blacks residing in Kansas at this time.

3. Ransom and Sutch, *One Kind of Freedom*, 54, 329n.

APPENDIX B

THE EXTENT OF THE EXODUS TO

KANSAS, 1870 – 1880

Modern scholars are generally agreed that the Exodus of 1879 involved the movement of about twenty-five thousand southern blacks and that the greater number of the migrants came from the border states rather than from the states of the Deep South like Mississippi and Louisiana. Still, the impression persists that the exodus was a large-scale departure from the Deep South.[1]

What follows is designed to put that idea to rest by exploring statistical avenues that might lead one to infer that the exodus was larger than the data of the censuses of 1870 and 1880 suggest. Someone might argue, for example, that many migrants quickly became disillusioned and returned to their home states, thereby escaping enumeration as residents of Kansas in 1880. Similarly, it could be argued that many migrants left Kansas to move on to other northern states. It is also possible that significant numbers of blacks who migrated to Kan-

---

1. Painter, *Exodusters,* 146–47, 184; Athearn, *In Search of Canaan,* 167. For the purposes of this discussion, the Deep South includes the states of Alabama, Mississippi, Louisiana, Texas, and Arkansas. The purpose of defining yet another South is to distinguish this area from the western border South that sent so many migrants to Kansas, and from the South Atlantic area, which really played little part in the story of the exodus to Kansas.

sas from, say, Louisiana did not appear as Louisiana residents who had moved to Kansas, because Louisiana was not their state of birth.

The undercount of 1870 is not an issue for purposes of the present question. Although the census of 1870 undercounted the black population of the South by about 6.6 percent, there is nothing to impugn the quality of the enumeration in Kansas and the rest of the North.[2] Still, census data have their limitations. Censuses are taken at ten-year intervals, and therefore census information can be used to arrive at generalizations about population changes only between 1870 and 1880 and not within shorter periods. Fortunately, the census of 1880 occurred on June 1, 1880, a date that coincides conveniently with most estimates of when the Exodus of 1879 came to a halt.[3] If the census period 1870–1880 includes a considerably larger time span than is ideal, at least the period completely embraces the Exodus of 1879.

The census figures on state of birth are especially useful because they permit us to see the geographic origins of a state's population. Still, such figures do not discriminate between those who migrated to the state shortly before the census and those who came fifty years earlier or between those who came to the state directly from their place of birth and those who made intermediate stops. Had Henry Adams migrated to Kansas in 1879, the census of 1880 would have listed him as a Georgia-born black living in Kansas. It would have given no indication of his long residence in Louisiana. Furthermore, migrants of forty or fifty years earlier who die off blur the impact of more recent arrivals with the same state of birth. In the case of Kansas, however, the imponderables arising from earlier black settlement in the state are negligible since the black population there was minuscule in 1860 and small even as late as 1870.[4] State-of-birth figures are, hence, particularly revealing with respect to Kansas blacks. Although they give no information about intermediate stops the migrants made,

2. Ransom and Sutch, *One Kind of Freedom*, 54, 329n; U.S. Bureau of the Census, *Negro Population*, 26–27.

3. Painter, *Exodusters*, 200; Athearn, *In Search of Canaan*, 260, 262.

4. The figures for 1860 and 1870 are 627 and 17,108 respectively. See U.S. Bureau of the Census, *Negro Population*, 44. For a discussion of state-of-birth data as a source of migration estimates, see Lee *et al.*, *Methodological Considerations and Reference Tables*, 57, 60.

TABLE 15

Place of Prior Residence of U.S.-Born Blacks Living in Kansas, 1870 and 1880

STATE OR REGION	WITHOUT ALLOCATION		WITH ALLOCATION	
	1870	1880	1870	1880
Kentucky	2,360	6,985	2,778	7,984
Tennessee	696	5,418	819	6,193
Missouri	5,924	6,488	6,974	7,416
Alabama	168	854	198	976
Mississippi	132	2,776	155	3,173
Louisiana	98	1,300	115	1,486
Texas	178	2,464	210	2,816
Arkansas	893	768	1,051	878
Indian Territory	352	355	414	406
Unknown	10	0	12	0
Subtotal	10,811	27,408	12,727	31,328
South Atlantic	1,916	3,920	0	0
North and West	532	1,550	532	1,550
Kansas	3,797	10,921	3,797	10,921
U.S. total	17,056	43,799	17,056	43,799

SOURCES: U.S. Census Office, *The Statistics of the Population of the United States* (1872), 328–35; U.S. Census Office, *The Statistics of the Population of the United States at the Tenth Census* (1883), 488–91.

Note: The great majority of those born in the South Atlantic states but living in Kansas migrated there after first living in states nearer to Kansas, like Kentucky. Therefore, blacks born in the South Atlantic states have been allocated among the remaining southern states in proportion to each state's contribution to the black population of Kansas.

the raw data are relatively uncontaminated by the impact of previous waves of migration to Kansas. Table 15 presents the basic state-of-birth data on which any appraisal of the extent of the Exodus of 1879 must rest.

The table gives information for the Indian Territory and for each of the southern states except those in the South Atlantic region. Because it is known that very few blacks migrated directly from the South Atlantic region to Kansas, the states in that area have been aggregated. As purely an educated guess, I suggest that it would be surprising indeed if direct black migration from the South Atlantic region to Kansas exceeded one or two hundred in the 1870s. The experience of the North Carolina blacks who tried to go to Kansas under the leadership of Sam Perry is instructive in this regard.

The great majority of blacks who lived in Kansas and were listed as having been born in the South Atlantic states must have been persons who had made one or more stops along the way. Most of those who were over the age of fifteen or twenty in 1880 had almost certainly been imported to the border states or the Lower South as slaves before emancipation.[5] For understanding the Exodus of 1879, those blacks are best understood as coming from the states to which they had been imported.

To represent this situation statistically, it is necessary to allocate the persons listed as being born in the South Atlantic region among the various southern states to which they must have gone. The procedure that has been used to achieve this end is imperfect, since it ignores the fact that some southern states imported slaves in greater numbers than others and that after the war other states may have attracted a greater number of black migrants than their neighbors. Still, this procedure brings us closer to historical reality than does the uninterpreted information that in 1880 there were 1,876 blacks in Kansas who had been born in Virginia or West Virginia.[6] A further complication is that the number of northern-born blacks living in Kansas was not insubstantial. Of the 43,799 blacks living in Kansas in 1880, 1,505 had been born in northern and western states other than Kansas. In 1870, 532 had been. From where did the increase of over a thousand come? Were they northern blacks migrating from the South? Or were they discontented nonsouthern blacks who had moved west in the 1870s? Or were they some of each? Since there is simply no evidence

5. On the extent of the domestic slave trade, see Fogel and Engerman, *Time on the Cross*, I, 46–47, II, 43–48; Richard Sutch, "The Breeding of Slaves for Sale and the Westward Expansion of Slavery," in *Race and Slavery in the Western Hemisphere: Quantitative Studies*, ed. Stanley L. Engerman and Eugene D. Genovese (Princeton, 1975), 199–210; Tadman, "Slave Trading in the Ante-Bellum South," 195–220; and Bancroft, *Slave Trading in the Old South*.

6. *Tenth Census, Population, 1880*, 491. The procedure used for allocating South Atlantic blacks among the various other southern states is given in the note to Table 15.

to answer these questions, no attempt will be made to deal with the northern-born blacks in assessing the extent of the Exodus of 1879.

State-of-birth figures, by their nature, cannot provide a precise estimate of the number of migrants. What they can do, however, is provide a range within which the number must lie. If, for example, at the beginning of the 1870s there were 2,360 Kentucky-born blacks living in Kansas, and if there were 6,985 in 1880, then the number of black migrants must lie somewhere between 4,625 and 6,985. In the unlikely event that all the Kentucky-born blacks residing in Kansas in 1870 lived through the decade and remained in Kansas, the figure would be 4,625. In the equally unlikely event that they all either died or moved from Kansas, the number would be 6,985. Clearly, the actual figure falls between those extremes, its precise value being a function of such things as mortality rates, economic conditions, and opportunities elsewhere.

From Table 15 it is evident that in the 1870s it was the border South rather than the Deep South that funneled the greater number of blacks to Kansas. For example, the number of Tennessee-born blacks living in Kansas rose from 969 to 5,418, while the number of Mississippi-born blacks increased from 132 to 2,776. Tennessee supplied a greater number than Mississippi did even though the black population of Tennessee in 1880 was considerably smaller than that of Mississippi (403,151 as against 650,291).[7] Roughly the same comparison is possible between Kentucky and the Deep South states.

Moreover, no matter how one manipulates the figures, the picture does not change materially. As Table 15 makes clear, allocating South Atlantic blacks to the various sending states does nothing to change the impression that the migration of the 1870s was rather small and that it derived especially from the border states of Kentucky and Tennessee.

For some blacks, Missouri may have been the final destination of a migration that was originally meant for Kansas. Certainly there were some who made their way to St. Louis and then found that poverty prevented them from going farther.[8] The question of what to do about Missouri is a difficult one. For blacks, Missouri was far more a south-

7. U.S. Bureau of the Census, *Negro Population*, 44.
8. Athearn, *In Search of Canaan*, 9–23.

TABLE 16

State of Birth of Southern-Born Blacks
Living in Missouri, 1870 and 1880

STATE OF BIRTH	1880	1870
Kentucky	9,368	10,254
Virginia or West Virginia	7,895	9,098
Tennessee	4,713	3,858
Mississippi	2,004	1,375
Louisiana	1,591	933
North Carolina	962	1,111
Arkansas	931	1,117
Alabama	833	4,421
Maryland	665	674
Texas	601	497
Georgia	562	464
South Carolina	439	407
District of Columbia	67	8
Florida	59	47
Delaware	12	26
Total	30,702	34,290

SOURCES: U.S. Census Office, *The Statistics of the Population of the United States* (1872), 328–35; U.S. Census Office, *The Statistics of the Population of the United States at the Tenth Census* (1883), 488–91.

ern than a northern state. It was, after all, a former slave state. At the same time, because it did serve as a final destination for some in the Exodus of 1879, it deserves consideration here.

As Table 16 shows, the evidence of the state-of-birth figures is ambiguous, suggesting that although black migration to Missouri was hardly massive, some blacks were indeed coming to Missouri from Tennessee, Louisiana, Mississippi, and Texas. What makes the figures difficult to interpret is that in 1870 Missouri already had a sizable population of blacks. Many had probably been brought to the state by the slave trade. The figures for Alabama give a dramatic instance of that, since clearly there were few migrants coming to Missouri from Alabama. But can the same be said for Kentucky? Is it not possible that as an older generation of black Kentuckians began to fade from the scene, others from the same state came to take their place? Without further evidence, there is no good answer to this question.

What is evident, however, is that the migration of the 1870s to Missouri from the Deep South was not dramatically large. Even if one makes the counterfactual assumption that all the natives of Mississippi, Louisiana, and Texas who lived in Missouri in 1870 were out of the state by 1880, the resulting estimates from the 1880 figures would hardly betoken a massive migration. Surely, then, omitting Missouri from consideration as a receiving state will introduce only minimal distortion into the overall picture.

It remains possible, of course that some of those in the exodus made their way to Illinois and other more distant northern states, but the number of such migrants was certainly quite small. Black migration to Illinois, for example, amounted to only about 8,700 in the 1870s. During the decade, the number of Mississippi-born blacks living in the state increased from 929 to 1,401, a rise that could easily have taken place had there never been a migration to Kansas. On the other hand, the number of Kansas-born blacks living in Illinois did rise from 22 in 1870 to 52 in 1880, suggesting that a few of the migrants to Kansas may have moved on to Illinois bringing newborn children with them.[9] If discontented migrants to Kansas did not choose Illinois as a new destination, they certainly did not choose places farther east. All over the North and West the evidence of black migration is minimal, and what evidence there is suggests that any migrants came from nearby southern states.[10]

Thus far, there have been no attempts to make concrete estimates of the extent of black migration to Kansas in the 1870s. Normally the problems associated with interpreting state-of-birth figures render futile any effort to convert the figures into concrete migration estimates. In the case of Kansas, however, many of the problems usually encountered in such efforts are obviated by the fact that the state was new and that, prior to 1860, its black population was of negli-

9. Lee et al., Methodological Considerations and Reference Tables, 136, 310; Ninth Census, Population, 1870, 330; Tenth Census, Population, 1880, 489. In assessing the extent of black movement from Kansas to Illinois, it needs to be remembered that migrants are generally young adults of prime childbearing age.

10. See the data for all the northern states given by Lee et al. in Methodological Considerations and Reference Tables, Table P-1.

gible size.[11] Because there is not much need to worry about pre-1860 cohorts of black migrants to Kansas dying off or moving out, it is possible to use state-of-birth figures for the derivation of migration estimates which, if hardly exact, can be expected to have a reasonable relationship to historical reality. We have fairly exact counts of the number of blacks who lived in Kansas in 1870 and 1880, and we know where they were born. What we lack is any idea of the number who died or left the state in the intervening ten years. There is no perfect remedy for that defect, but if we make the assumption that 50 percent of the black population that was present in 1870 was gone by 1880, we will probably not go far wrong. Other studies of mobility in nineteenth-century America make that a reasonable assumption.[12] Given the magnitude of the figures we are dealing with and given the method of statistical analysis that is to be used, the supposition can hardly lead us very far astray.

Table 17 is premised on the assumption that only 50 percent of the blacks who were present in 1870 persisted through the decade. Even if that is not precisely correct, the basic directions indicated by the table will remain the same. The contribution of the border states was large in relation to the contribution of the states of the Deep South, and the overall size of the Exodus of 1879 was rather modest.

There remains the crucial question of how many blacks came to Kansas in 1879 and how many came earlier in the decade. On that point the census figures are completely silent. It is known that by the beginning of 1879 the population of the black colonies established by Benjamin Singleton and others was somewhere around two thousand, and it seems reasonable to guess that group migration was paralleled by individual migrations of perhaps equal magnitude. If that is so, the total number of migrants for the period 1870–1878 would be about four thousand and the number that came in 1879 and early 1880 would be about twenty-two thousand.

Such figures are in line with estimates of the size of the exodus by some knowledgeable contemporary observers. In January, 1880,

11. See n4 above.

12. Stephen Thernstrom, *The Other Bostonians: Poverty and Progress in the American Metropolis, 1880–1970* (Cambridge, Mass., 1973), 221–24.

TABLE 17

Estimate of the Place of Prior Residence of Black Migrants to Kansas,
1870–1880

STATE OR REGION	WITHOUT ALLOCATION	WITH ALLOCATION
South Atlantic	2,962	0
Deep South[a]	7,427	8,474
Missouri	3,526	3,923
Kentucky and Tennessee	10,875	12,392
Southern total	24,790	24,790
North and West	1,458	1,458
U.S. total	26,248	26,248
Selected States		
Kentucky	5,805	6,601
Tennessee	5,070	5,791
Mississippi	2,710	3,100
Louisiana	1,251	1,430

SOURCE: Table 15.

Note: The estimates are based on the assumption that 50 percent of those who came to Kansas from any given area and were present at the census of 1870 died or left the state before the census of 1880. Let P1 be the black population of Kansas from any given state or aggregation of states in 1870; let P2 be the comparable figure for 1880; then the estimated number of migrants for that area will be $P2 - \frac{P1}{2}$. Allocation and its rationale are described in the note to Table 15.

[a]The Deep South is here defined to include Alabama, Mississippi, Louisiana, Texas, and Arkansas.

Governor John P. St. John, of Kansas, who was closely involved with efforts to relieve and aid the migrants, estimated that after April, 1879, "from 15,00 to 20,000 refugees have arrived in Kansas." Others close to the situation gave similar figures.[13] It is this concentrated influx that captured the attention of the public and raised the possibility of a general exodus from the South. Even when the exodus was at its height,

13. Athearn, *In Search of Canaan*, 261–62. Some contemporary observers gave larger estimates, but the one cited here is more consistent with the census evidence.

TABLE 18

State or Region of Residence of Blacks Born in Kansas
but Living in the South, 1870, 1880, and 1890

STATE OR REGION OF RESIDENCE	1870	1880	1890
Missouri	150	491	1,329
Texas	37	65	136
Arkansas	16	46	72
South Atlantic	3	13	42
Mississippi	3	12	36
Louisiana	1	27	32
Tennessee	12	57	24
Kentucky	1	6	23
Alabama	0	5	2

SOURCES: U.S. Census Office, *The Statistics of the Population of the United States* (1872), 330; U.S. Census Office, *The Statistics of the Population of the United States at the Tenth Census* (1883), 489; U.S. Census Office, *Compendium of the Eleventh Census* (1897), III, 35.

however, the movement was more a migration from the border South than a flight from the Deep South.[14]

When the migrants came to Kansas in 1879, many were disappointed with what they found and some turned around and went home. The extent of the return migration is unknown, but if it was very large, census figures on states of birth would be a misleadingly low indicator of the size of the exodus to Kansas. Lawrence Rice estimates that at least 10 percent of the blacks who migrated to Kansas from Texas in 1879 returned home.[15] Rice may be correct, but clearly the return movement cannot have been greater than he estimates. If the blacks who went to Kansas returned to their southern homes in massive numbers, the state-of-birth figures for their home

14. On this point, apply the figures of 4,000 and 22,000 to the figures given in Table 17. As can be seen, even if one subtracts out the estimated 4,000 border-state blacks who came early, the exodus was still largely a border-state phenomenon.

15. Lawrence D. Rice, *The Negro in Texas, 1874–1900* (Baton Rouge, 1971), 204. Athearn, *In Search of Canaan*, 83–86, 276.

states should manifest a sharp increase in the number of persons born in Kansas, since the migrants were generally young adults of child-bearing age. If large numbers of blacks went to Kansas and returned home, some would certainly have come back with children who had been born on Kansas soil. Table 18 gives figures for the number of Kansas-born persons living in the southern states between 1880 and 1890. The table provides no support for the view that return migration was extensive. The figures in the table are generally small and are about what could be expected even if there had been no exodus in 1879. Undoubtedly, some who show up as statistics in this table were the children of return migrants, but clearly the number of such returnees cannot have been large. Certainly the number was not greater than 10 percent; probably it was much smaller.

No matter how one analyzes the statistical data pertaining to the Exodus of 1879, there is no escaping that it was preponderantly a movement of border-state blacks to Kansas. Given that most blacks lived in places like Mississippi and Alabama rather than Tennessee and Kentucky, the migration to Kansas from the Deep South must be considered quite small when compared with the black population of that region.

BIBLIOGRAPHY

This includes all sources cited in the footnotes with the exception of court cases, case digests, the session laws of the states, the legal codes of the state and federal governments, and city directories.

MANUSCRIPT COLLECTIONS

Affleck, Thomas. Collection, 1842–1868. Troy H. Middleton Library, Louisiana State University, Baton Rouge.

American Colonization Society. Records of the American Colonization Society, 1817–1964. Library of Congress, Washington, D.C.

Batchelor, Albert A. Papers, 1852–1930. Troy H. Middleton Library, Louisiana State University, Baton Rouge.

Boinsett, Thaddeus S. Letters, 1855–1871. William R. Perkins Library, Duke University, Durham, N.C.

Gay, Edward J. Family Papers, 1805–1925. Troy H. Middleton Library, Louisiana State University, Baton Rouge.

Gillespie, James A. Family Papers, 1840–1890. Troy H. Middleton Library, Louisiana State University, Baton Rouge.

Liddell, Moses St. John R. Family Papers, 1838–1870. Troy H. Middleton Library, Louisiana State University, Baton Rouge.

Moore, Thomas O. Papers, 1856–1876. Troy H. Middleton Library, Louisiana State University, Baton Rouge.

Tucker, James. Papers, 1863–1893. University of Texas Library, Austin.

U.S. Bureau of Refugees, Freedmen, and Abandoned Lands. Records, 1865–1872. National Archives, Washington, D.C. Record Group 105.

U.S. Department of Agriculture, Bureau of Plant Entomology and Quarantine. Boll Weevil Clipping Files, *ca.* 1898–1920. National Archives, Washington, D.C., Record Group 7-60.

U.S. Department of Justice. Classified Subject Files Relating to Peonage, 1914–1941. National Archives, Washington, D.C., Record Group 60.

———. Source-Chronological Files, 1871–1884. National Archives, Washington, D.C., Record Group 60.

U.S. House of Representatives. Records of the Committee on Education and Labor, 45th Cong., 2nd Sess. (H. R. 45-H8.5, Colonization of Liberia by American Negroes). National Archives, Washington, D.C., Record Group 233.

GOVERNMENT DOCUMENTS

FEDERAL DOCUMENTS

Congressional Record, 43rd Cong., 2nd Sess., 45th Cong., 2nd Sess., 45th Cong., 3rd Sess.

Failure of the Scheme for the Colonization of Negroes in Mexico. 54th Cong., 1st Sess., House Document No. 169.

On the Relations and Conditions of Capital and Labor Employed in Manufactures and General Business (Second Volume on This Subject). Vol. XIV of *Report of the Industrial Commission.* 57th Cong., 1st Sess., House Document No. 183.

Report and Testimony of the Select Committee of the United States Senate to Investigate the Causes of the Removal of the Negroes from the Southern States to the Northern States. 3 parts. 46th Cong., 2nd Sess., Senate Report No. 693.

Report by the Commissioner of the Freedmen's Bureau of All Orders Issued by Him or Any Assistant Commissioner, March 19, 1866. 39th Cong., 1st Sess., House Executive Document No. 70.

"Report of Hon. Charles W. Russell, Assistant Attorney-General, Relative to Peonage Matters, October 10, 1907." In *Annual Report of the Attorney-General of the United States for 1907.* 2 vols. Washington, D.C., 1907.

Report of the Commissioner of the Bureau of Refugees, Freedmen, and Abandoned Lands, December 19, 1865. 39th Cong., 1st Sess., House Executive Document No. 11.

"Report of the Commissioner of the Bureau of Refugees, Freedmen, and Abandoned Lands, November 1, 1866." In *Annual Report of the Secretary of War: Appendix.* 39th Cong., 2nd Sess., House Executive Document No. 1.

"Report of the Commissioner of the Bureau of Refugees, Freedmen, and Abandoned Lands, November 1, 1867." In *Annual Report of the Secretary of War,* 40th Cong., 2nd Sess., House Executive Document No. 1.

"Report of the Commissioner of the Bureau of Refugees, Freedmen, and Abandoned Lands, October 20, 1869." In *Annual Report of the Secretary of War [1868–1869]: Accompanying Reports*. 41st Cong., 2nd Sess., House Executive Document No. 1.

Report of the Joint Committee on Reconstruction. 39th Cong., 1st Sess., 1866.

Reports of the Assistant Commissioners of Freedmen and a Synopsis of Laws Respecting Persons of Color in the Late Slave States. 39th Cong., 2nd Sess., Senate Executive Document No. 6.

Reports of the Assistant Commissioners of the Freedmen's Bureau Made Since December 1, 1865. 39th Cong., 1st Sess., Senate Executive Document No. 27.

Schurz, Carl. *Report on Condition of the South*. 39th Cong., 1st Sess., Senate Executive Document No. 2.

South Carolina in 1876: Testimony as to the Denial of the Elective Franchise in South Carolina at the Elections of 1875 and 1876. 3 vols. 44th Cong., 2nd Sess., Senate Miscellaneous Document No. 48.

Statutes at Large of the United States . . . from December, 1863, to December, 1865. 38 vols. Boston, 1866.

U.S. Bureau of the Census. *Historical Statistics of the United States, Colonial Times to 1970*. 2 vols. Washington, D.C., 1975.

———. *Negro Population, 1790–1915*. Washington, D.C., 1918.

U.S. Census Office. *Compendium of the Eleventh Census, 1890*. 3 vols. Washington, D.C., 1897.

———. *Population of the United States in 1860*. Washington, D.C., 1864. Vol. I of *Eighth Census*.

———. *The Seventh Census of the United States, 1850*. Washington, D.C., 1853.

———. *The Statistics of the Population of the United States*. Washington, D.C., 1872. Vol. I of *Ninth Census [1870]*.

———. *Statistics of the Population of the United States at the Tenth Census, June 1, 1880*. Washington, D.C., 1883. Vol. I of *Tenth Census, 1880*.

U.S. Commissioner of Labor. *Tenth Annual Report . . . 1894*. Washington, D.C., 1896.

U.S. Congress. *Report of the Joint Select Committee to Inquire into the Condition of Affairs in the Late Insurrectionary States . . . and Testimony Taken*. 13 vols. Washington, D.C., 1872.

U.S. Senate, Committee on Education and Labor. *Report on the Relations Between Capital and Labor*. Washington, D.C., 1885.

Use of the Army in Certain of the Southern States. 44th Cong., 2nd Sess., House Executive Document No. 30.

The War of the Rebellion: A Compilation of the Official Records of the Union and Confederate Armies. 130 vols. Washington, D.C., 1880–1901.

STATE DOCUMENTS

Alabama House Journal. 1876–77, 1878–79.

Georgia House Journal. 1873.

South Carolina Board of Agriculture. *South Carolina: Resources and Population, Institutions and Industries.* Charleston, S.C., 1883.

Virginia House Journal. 1869–70.

NEWSPAPERS AND PERIODICALS

Aberdeen (Miss.) *Examiner,* February 15, March 8, March 15, 1883.

African Repository, 1865–80.

Atlanta *Constitution,* 1890–1900.

Birmingham (Ala.) *News,* February 20, 1899.

Charleston (S.C.) *News and Courier,* 1878, 1908.

DeBow's Review, 1866–69.

Elberton (Ga.) *Gazette,* April 5, August 4, 1875.

Greensboro *Alabama Beacon,* September 15, 1865.

Hinds County Gazette (Miss.), January 26, 1876.

Huntsville (Ala.) *Advocate,* 1865, 1868.

Huntsville (Ala.) *Gazette,* January 7, 1882.

Jackson (Miss.) *Daily Clarion,* December 6, 1865.

Jackson (Miss.) *Weekly Clarion,* 1869, 1879.

Jacksonville *Daily Florida Union,* March 4, 1882.

Liberia Bulletin, February, 1900.

Memphis *Daily Appeal,* 1865–77.

Meridian (Miss.) *Mercury,* December 20, 1879.

Milledgeville (Ga.) *Federal Union,* July 17, 1866.

Mobile *Daily Register,* December 7, 1872, February 3, 1876.

Montgomery *Daily Advertiser,* 1865–86.

Natchez (Miss.) *Democrat,* November 20, 1865.

National Republican, 1879.

New National Era, 1876

New Orleans *Picayune,* December 25, 1865.

New Orleans *Times,* 1866–75.

New York *Age,* November 21, 1912, February 6, 1913.

New York *Herald,* September 19, 1874.

New York *Times,* 1865–68, 1871–79, 1889–91, 1903–1909.

Richmond *Daily Enquirer,* March 3, 1866, February 16, 1867.

Richmond *Dispatch,* 1867–77.

Richmond *Planet,* February 17, 1900.

Savannah *Morning News,* 1882–92.

Selma (Ala.) *Southern Argus,* January 3, 1870, December 15, 1876.
Southern Cultivator, 1866–76.
Southern Recorder (Ga.), November 17, 1868.
Teche Pilot (La.), June 29, 1889.
Vicksburg (Miss.) *Daily Commercial,* 1877.

BOOKS

Anderson, Eric. *Race and Politics in North Carolina, 1872–1901: The Black Second.* Baton Rouge, 1981.

Andreas, Alfred Theodore. *History of the State of Kansas . . .* Chicago, 1883.

Andrews, Sidney. *The South Since the War, As Shown by Fourteen Weeks of Travels and Observation in Georgia and the Carolinas.* Boston, 1866.

Athearn, Robert G. *In Search of Canaan: Black Migration to Kansas, 1879–80.* Lawrence, Kans., 1978.

Ayers, Edward L. *Vengeance and Justice: Crime and Punishment in the Nineteenth-Century American South.* New York, 1984.

Baker, Ray Stannard. *Following the Color Line: American Negro Citizenship in the Progressive Era.* 1908; rpr. New York, 1964.

Bancroft, Frederic. *Slave Trading in the Old South.* 1931; rpr. New York, 1959.

Bardolph, Richard. *The Negro Vanguard.* New York, 1959.

Bentley, George R. *A History of the Freedmen's Bureau.* Philadelphia, 1955.

Berlin, Ira. *Slaves Without Masters: The Free Negro in the Antebellum South.* New York, 1974.

Billings, Dwight B. *Planters and the Making of the "New South": Class, Politics, and Development in North Carolina, 1865–1900.* Chapel Hill, N.C., 1979.

Billington, Ray Allen. *Westward Expansion: A History of the American Frontier.* 4th ed. New York, 1974.

Bittle, William E., and Gilbert Geis. *The Longest Way Home: Chief Alfred C. Sam's Back-to-Africa Movement.* Detroit, 1964.

Bond, Horace Mann. *The Negro in Alabama: A Study in Cotton and Steel.* 1939; rpr. New York, 1969.

Bowen, Louise DeKoven. *The Colored People of Chicago.* Chicago, 1913.

Brandfon, Robert L. *Cotton Kingdom of the New South: A History of the Yazoo Mississippi Delta from Reconstruction to the Twentieth Century.* Cambridge, Mass., 1967.

Burton, Charles Wesley. *Living Conditions Among Negroes in the Ninth Ward, New Haven, Connecticut.* New Haven, 1913.

Campbell, Sir George. *White and Black: The Outcome of a Visit to the United States.* London, 1879.

Carleton, Mark T. *Politics and Punishment: The Story of the Louisiana Penal System.* Baton Rouge, 1971.

Carpenter, John A. *Sword and Olive Branch: Oliver Otis Howard.* Pittsburgh, 1964.

Cartwright, Joseph H. *The Triumph of Jim Crow: Tennessee Race Relations in the 1880's.* Knoxville, Tenn., 1976.

Cell, John W. *The Highest Stage of White Supremacy: The Origins of Segregation in South Africa and the American South.* Cambridge, Eng., 1982.

Clark, Thomas D. *The Southern Country Editor.* Indianapolis, 1948.

Clowes, W. Laird. *Black America: A Study of the Ex-Slave and His Late Master.* London, 1891.

Coffin, Addison. *Life and Travels of Addison Coffin.* Cleveland, 1897.

Commager, Henry Steele, ed. *Documents of American History.* 7th ed. Vol. I of 2 vols. New York, 1963.

Conway, Alan. *The Reconstruction of Georgia.* Minneapolis, 1966.

Cooper, William J., Jr. *The Conservative Regime: South Carolina, 1877–1890.* Baltimore, 1968.

Cornish, Dudley Taylor. *The Sable Arm: Negro Troops in the Union Army, 1861–1865.* New York, 1966.

Coulter, E. Merton. *James Monroe Smith: Georgia Planter, Before Death and After.* Athens, Ga., 1961.

Cox, LaWanda. *Lincoln and Black Freedom: A Study in Presidential Leadership.* Columbia, S.C., 1981.

Crockett, Norman L. *The Black Towns.* Lawrence, Kans., 1979.

Daniel, Pete. *The Shadow of Slavery: Peonage in the South, 1901–1969.* Urbana, Ill., 1972.

Dawson, Joseph G., III. *Army Generals and Reconstruction: Louisiana, 1862–1877.* Baton Rouge, 1982.

DeCanio, Stephen J. *Agriculture in the Postbellum South: The Economics of Production and Supply.* Cambridge, Mass., 1974.

Draper, Theodore. *The Rediscovery of Black Nationalism.* New York, 1969.

Du Bois, W. E. Burghardt. *The Philadelphia Negro: A Social Study.* 1899; rpr. New York, 1967.

Du Bois, W. E. Burghardt, and Augustus Granville Dill, eds. *The Negro American Artisan.* Atlanta University Publications, XVII. 1912; rpr. New York, 1968.

DuBose, John W. *Alabama's Tragic Decade: Ten Years of Alabama, 1865–1874.* Birmingham, Ala., 1940.

Eaton, John. *Grant, Lincoln, and the Freedmen: Reminiscences of the Civil War.* 1907; rpr. New York, 1969.

Eldridge, Hope T., and Dorothy Swaine Thomas. *Demographic Analyses and Interrelations.* Philadelphia, 1964. Vol. III of *Population Redistribution and*

Economic Growth, United States, 1870–1950, edited by Simon Kuznets and Dorothy Swaine Thomas. 3 vols.

Engs, Robert F. *Freedom's First Generation: Black Hampton, Virginia, 1861–1890.* Philadelphia, 1980.

Evans, W. McKee. *Ballots and Fence Rails: Reconstruction on the Lower Cape Fear.* 1966; rpr. New York, 1974.

Fee, John G. *Autobiography of John G. Fee, Berea, Kentucky.* Chicago, 1891.

Ficklin, John Rose. *History of Reconstruction in Louisiana, Through 1868.* Baltimore, 1910.

Flynn, Charles. *White Land, Black Labor: Caste and Class in Late Nineteenth-Century Georgia.* Baton Rouge, 1983.

Fogel, Robert William, and Stanley Engerman. *Time on the Cross.* 2 vols. Boston, 1974.

Foner, Eric. *Politics and Ideology in the Age of the Civil War.* New York, 1980.

Franklin, Jimmie Lewis. *Journey Toward Hope: A History of Blacks in Oklahoma.* Norman, Okla., 1982.

Franklin, John Hope. *The Free Negro in North Carolina, 1790–1860.* Chapel Hill, N.C., 1943.

Frederickson, George M. *White Supremacy: A Comparative Study in American and South African History.* New York, 1981.

Garrison, William Lloyd. *Thoughts on African Colonization.* 1832; rpr. New York, 1968.

Gerber, David A. *Black Ohio and the Color Line, 1860–1915.* Urbana, Ill., 1976.

Gerteis, Louis S. *From Contraband to Freedman: Federal Policy Toward Southern Blacks, 1861–1865.* Westport, Conn., 1973.

Going, Allen. *Bourbon Democracy in Alabama, 1874–1890.* University, Ala., 1951.

Goodwyn, Lawrence. *Democratic Promise: The Populist Movement in America.* New York, 1976.

Gosnell, Harold F. *Negro Politicians: The Rise of Negro Politics in Chicago.* 1935; rpr. Chicago, 1967.

Greene, Lorenzo J., and Carter G. Woodson. *The Negro Wage Earner.* 1930; rpr. New York, 1970.

Gutman, Herbert G. *The Black Family in Slavery and Freedom, 1750–1925.* New York, 1976.

Harlan, Louis R. *Booker T. Washington.* 2 vols. New York, 1972–83.

———, ed. *The Booker T. Washington Papers.* 13 vols. Urbana, Ill., 1972–84.

Harrington, Fred H. *Fighting Politician: Major General N. P. Banks.* Philadelphia, 1948.

Harris, Sheldon H. *Paul Cuffe: Black America and the African Return.* New York, 1972.

Harris, William C. *Presidential Reconstruction in Mississippi.* Baton Rouge, 1967.

Haynes, George Edmund. *The Negro at Work in New York City: A Study in Economic Progress.* New York, 1912.

Helper, Hinton Rowan. *Nojoque: A Question for a Continent.* New York, 1867.

————, ed. *The Negros in Negroland; the Negroes in America; and Negroes Generally.* New York, 1868.

Higgs, Robert. *Competition and Coercion: Blacks in the American Economy, 1865–1914.* Cambridge, Eng., 1977.

Holt, Thomas. *Black over White: Negro Political Leadership in South Carolina During Reconstruction.* Urbana, Ill., 1979.

Johnson, Franklin. *The Development of State Legislation Concerning the Free Negro.* 1918; rpr. Westport, Conn., 1979.

Jordan, Winthrop D. *White over Black: American Attitudes Toward the Negro, 1550–1812.* Chapel Hill, N.C., 1968.

Katzman, David M. *Before the Ghetto: Black Detroit in the Nineteenth Century.* Urbana, Ill., 1973.

Key, V. O., Jr. *Southern Politics in State and Nation.* New York, 1949.

Kirwan, Albert D. *Revolt of the Rednecks: Mississippi Politics, 1876–1925.* 1951; rpr. Gloucester, Mass., 1964.

Kolchin, Peter. *First Freedom: The Responses of Alabama's Blacks to Emancipation and Reconstruction.* Westport, Conn., 1972.

Kousser, J. Morgan. *The Shaping of Southern Politics: Suffrage Restriction and the Establishment of the One-Party South, 1880–1910.* New Haven, 1974.

Kusmer, Kenneth L. *A Ghetto Takes Shape: Black Cleveland, 1870–1930.* Urbana, Ill., 1976.

Lee, Everett S., Ann Ratner Miller, Carol Brainerd, and Richard A. Easterlin. *Methodological Considerations and Reference Tables.* Philadelphia, 1957. Vol. I of *Population Redistribution and Economic Growth, United States, 1870–1950,* edited by Simon Kuznets and Dorothy Swaine Thomas. 3 vols.

Litwack, Leon. *Been in the Storm So Long: The Aftermath of Slavery.* New York, 1981.

————. *North of Slavery: The Negro in the Free States, 1790–1860.* Chicago, 1961.

Logan, Frenise A. *The Negro in North Carolina, 1876–1894.* Chapel Hill, N.C., 1964.

Logan, Rayford W. *The Betrayal of the Negro: From Rutherford B. Hayes to Woodrow Wilson.* New York, 1965.

McFeely, William S. *Grant: A Biography.* New York, 1981.

————. *Yankee Stepfather: General O. O. Howard and the Freedmen.* New Haven, 1968.

McPherson, James M. *The Struggle for Equality: Abolitionists and the Negro in the Civil War and Reconstruction.* Princeton, 1964.

Mandle, Jay R. *The Roots of Black Poverty: The Southern Plantation Economy After the Civil War*. Durham, N.C., 1978.

Mangum, Charles S., Jr. *The Legal Status of the Negro*. Chapel Hill, N.C., 1940.

Marshall, Jessie A., ed. *Private and Official Correspondence of Gen. Benjamin F. Butler During the Period of the Civil War*. 5 vols. Norwood, Mass., 1917.

Morris, Richard B. *Government and Labor in Early America*. New York, 1946.

Myrdal, Gunnar. *An American Dilemma: The Negro Problem and Modern Democracy*. New York, 1962.

Nieman, Donald G. *To Set the Law in Motion: The Freedmen's Bureau and the Legal Rights of Blacks, 1865–1868*. Millwood, N.Y., 1979.

Nordhoff, Charles. *The Cotton States in the Spring and Summer of 1875*. New York, 1876.

Novak, Daniel A. *The Wheel of Servitude: Black Forced Labor After Slavery*. Lexington, Ky., 1978.

Oubre, Claude F. *Forty Acres and a Mule: The Freedmen's Bureau and Black Land Ownership*. Baton Rouge, 1978.

Painter, Nell. *Exodusters: Black Migration to Kansas After Reconstruction*. New York, 1977.

Percy, William Alexander. *Lanterns on the Levee: Recollections of a Planter's Son*. 1941; rpr. Baton Rouge, 1973.

Phillips, Ulrich B. *American Negro Slavery*. 1918; rpr. Baton Rouge, 1969.

Pickens, William. *Bursting Bonds: The Heir of Slaves*. Enl. ed. Boston, 1923.

Pleck, Elizabeth Hafkin. *Black Migration and Poverty: Boston, 1865–1900*. New York, 1979.

Powell, Lawrence N. *New Masters: Northern Planters During the Civil War and Reconstruction*. New Haven, 1980.

Rabinowitz, Howard N. *Race Relations in the Urban South, 1865–1890*. New York, 1978.

Ransom, Roger L., and Richard Sutch. *One Kind of Freedom: The Economic Consequences of Emancipation*. New York, 1977.

Rawick, George P., ed. *The American Slave: A Composite Autobiography*. 19 vols. Westport, Conn., 1972–78.

Redkey, Edwin S. *Black Exodus: Black Nationalist and Back-to-Africa Movements, 1890–1910*. New Haven, 1969.

Reid, Whitelaw. *After the War: A Tour of the Southern States, 1865–1866*. 1866; rpr. New York, 1965.

Rice, Lawrence D. *The Negro in Texas, 1874–1900*. Baton Rouge, 1971.

Richardson, Joe M. *The Negro in the Reconstruction of Florida, 1865–1877*. Tallahassee, Fla., 1965.

Ripley, C. Peter. *Slaves and Freedmen in Civil War Louisiana*. Baton Rouge, 1976.

Roark, James L. *Masters Without Slaves: Southern Planters in the Civil War and Reconstruction*. New York, 1977.

Rogers, William Warren. *The One-Gallused Rebellion: Agrarianism in Alabama, 1865–1896*. Baton Rouge, 1971.

Rose, Willie Lee. *Rehearsal for Reconstruction: The Port Royal Experiment*. Indianapolis, 1964.

Schweninger, Loren. *James T. Rapier and Reconstruction*. Chicago, 1978.

Seebold, William. *Old Louisiana Plantation Homes and Family Trees*. 2 vols. New Orleans, 1941.

Shaw, Barton C. *The Wool-Hat Boys: Georgia's Populist Party*. Baton Rouge, 1984.

Shick, Tom W. *Behold the Promised Land: A History of Afro-American Settler Society in Nineteenth-Century Liberia*. Baltimore, 1977.

Simkins, Francis Butler. *Pitchfork Ben Tillman: South Carolinian*. Baton Rouge, 1944.

Simkins, Francis B., and Robert H. Woody. *South Carolina During Reconstruction*. 1932; rpr. Gloucester, Mass., 1964.

Sitterson, J. Carlyle. *Sugar Country: The Cane Sugar Industry in the South, 1753–1950*. Lexington, Ky., 1953.

Somers, Robert. *The Southern States Since the War, 1870–1*. New York, 1871.

Spear, Alan. *Black Chicago: The Making of a Ghetto, 1890–1920*. Chicago, 1967.

Spero, Sterling D., and Abram L. Harris. *The Black Worker: The Negro and the Labor Movement*. 1931; rpr. New York, 1968.

Stampp, Kenneth. *The Peculiar Institution: Slavery in the Antebellum South*. New York, 1956.

Staples, Thomas S. *Reconstruction in Arkansas, 1862–1874*. 1923; rpr. Gloucester, Mass., 1964.

Starobin, Robert S. *Industrial Slavery in the Old South*. New York, 1970.

Staudenraus, Philip J. *The African Colonization Movement, 1816–1865*. New York, 1961.

Steiner, Jesse F., and Roy M. Brown. *The North Carolina Chain Gang: A Study of County Convict Road Work*. Chapel Hill, N.C., 1927.

Tadman, Michael. *Speculators and Slaves: Masters, Traders, and Slaves in the Old South*. Madison, Wis., 1989.

Taylor, Alrutheus A. *The Negro in South Carolina During the Reconstruction*. Washington, D.C., 1924.

———. *The Negro in Tennessee, 1865–1880*. Washington, D.C., 1941.

———. *The Negro in the Reconstruction of Virginia*. Washington, D.C., 1926.

Taylor, Joe Gray. *Louisiana Reconstructed, 1863–1877*. Baton Rouge, 1974.

———. *Negro Slavery in Louisiana*. Baton Rouge, 1963.

Thernstrom, Stephen. *The Other Bostonians: Poverty and Progress in the American Metropolis, 1880–1970.* Cambridge, Mass., 1973.

Thompson, C. Mildred. *Reconstruction in Georgia: Economic, Social, Political, 1865–1872.* 1915; rpr. Gloucester, Mass., 1964.

Thorpe, Francis, ed. *The Federal and State Constitutions . . . of the . . . United States.* 7 vols. Washington, D.C., 1909.

Tindall, George Brown. *South Carolina Negroes, 1877–1900.* 1952; rpr. Baton Rouge, 1966.

Trefousse, Hans L. *Ben Butler: The South Called Him Beast!* New York, 1957.

Trelease, Allen W. *White Terror: The Ku Klux Klan Conspiracy and Southern Reconstruction.* New York, 1971.

Trowbridge, John T. *The South: A Tour of Its Battlefields and Ruined Cities.* Hartford, Conn., 1866.

Turner, Arlin, ed. *The Negro Question: A Selection of Writings on Civil Rights in the South by George W. Cable.* Garden City, N.Y., 1958.

Voegeli, V. Jacque. *Free but Not Equal: The Midwest and the Negro During the Civil War.* Chicago, 1967.

Wesley, Charles H. *Negro Labor in the United States, 1850–1925: A Study in American Economic History.* 1927; rpr. New York, 1967.

Wharton, Vernon Lane. *The Negro in Mississippi, 1865–1890.* 1947; rpr. New York, 1965.

Wiener, Jonathan M. *Social Origins of the New South: Alabama, 1860–1885.* Baton Rouge, 1978.

Wiley, Bell Irvin. *Southern Negroes, 1861–1865.* 1938; rpr. Baton Rouge, 1974.

Williams, Alfred B. *Hampton and His Red Shirts: South Carolina's Deliverance in 1876.* 1935; rpr. Freeport, N.Y., 1970.

Williamson, Joel. *After Slavery: The Negro in South Carolina During Reconstruction, 1861–1877.* Chapel Hill, N.C., 1965.

——. *The Crucible of Race: Black-White Relations in the American South Since Emancipation.* New York, 1984.

——. *New People: Miscegenation and Mulattoes in the United States.* New York, 1980.

——, ed. *The Origins of Segregation.* Lexington, Mass., 1968.

Wilson, Theodore Brantner. *The Black Codes of the South.* University, Ala., 1965.

Wolfe, French Eugene. *Admission to American Trade Unions.* Baltimore, 1912.

Woodman, Harold D. *King Cotton and His Retainers: Financing and Marketing the Cotton Crop of the South, 1800–1925.* Lexington, Ky., 1968.

Woodward, C. Vann. *Origins of the New South, 1877–1913.* Baton Rouge, 1951.

——. *The Strange Career of Jim Crow.* 3rd ed. New York, 1974.

————. *Tom Watson: Agrarian Rebel*. New York, 1953.

Wright, Gavin. *Old South, New South: Revolutions in the Southern Economy Since the Civil War*. New York, 1986.

Wright, Richard Robert. *The Negro in Pennsylvania: A Study in Economic History*. Philadelphia, 1912.

Wynes, Charles E. *Race Relations in Virginia, 1870–1902*. Charlottesville, Va., 1961.

Zangrando, Robert L. *The NAACP Crusade Against Lynching, 1909–1950*. Philadelphia, 1980.

ARTICLES

Alilunas, Leo. "Statutory Means of Impeding Emigration of the Negro." *Journal of Negro History*, XXII (1937), 148–62.

Bartley, Numan V. "In Search of the New South: Southern Politics After Reconstruction." *Reviews in American History*, X (1982), 150–63.

Bauman, Mark. "Race and Mastery: The Debate of 1903." In *From the Old South to the New: Essays on the Transitional South*, edited by Walter J. Fraser, Jr., and Winfred B. Moore. Westport, Conn., 1981.

Bell, Howard H. "The Negro Emigration Movement, 1849–1854: A Phase of Negro Nationalism." *Phylon*, XX (1959), 132–42.

Berthoff, Rowland T. "Southern Attitudes Toward Immigration, 1865–1914." *Journal of Southern History*, XVII (1951), 328–60.

Bonner, James C. "The Georgia Penitentiary at Milledgeville, 1807–1874." *Georgia Historical Quarterly*, LV (1971), 303–28.

Boyd, Willis D. "Negro Colonization in the Reconstruction Era, 1865–1870." *Georgia Historical Quarterly*, XL (1956), 360–82.

Brier, Stephen. "The Career of Richard L. Davis Reconsidered: Unpublished Correspondence from the National Labor Tribune." *Labor History*, XXI (1980), 420–29.

Burton, Vernon. "Race and Reconstruction: Edgefield County, South Carolina." *Journal of Social History*, XII (1978), 31–56.

Cable, George W. "The Convict Lease System in the Southern States." *Century*, n.s., V (1884), 582–99.

Calderhead, William. "How Extensive Was the Border State Slave Trade? A New Look." *Civil War History*, XVIII (1972), 42–55.

Chafe, William H. "The Negro and Populism: A Kansas Case Study." *Journal of Southern History*, XXXIV (1968), 402–19.

Cohen, William. "Black Immobility and Free Labor: The Freedmen's Bureau and the Relocation of Black Labor, 1865–1868." *Civil War History*, XXX (1984), 221–34.

————. "Negro Involuntary Servitude in the South, 1865–1940: A Preliminary Analysis." *Journal of Southern History*, XLII (1976), 31–60.

Daniel, Pete. "The Metamorphosis of Slavery, 1865–1900." *Journal of American History*, LXVI (1979), 88–99.

Eaton, Clement. "Slave-Hiring in the Upper South: A Step Toward Freedom." *Mississippi Valley Historical Review*, XLVI (1960), 663–78.

Eckert, Edward K. "Contract Labor in Florida During Reconstruction." *Florida Historical Quarterly*, XLVII (1968), 34–50.

Fleming, Walter L. "'Pap' Singleton, the Moses of the Colored Exodus." *American Journal of Sociology*, XV (1909), 61–82.

Franklin, John Hope. "History of Racial Segregation in the United States." *Annals of the American Academy of Political and Social Science*, CCCIV (1956), 1–9.

Goldin, Claudia. "'N' Kinds of Freedom: An Introduction to the Issues." *Explorations in Economic History*, XVI (1979), 8–30.

Goodwyn, Lawrence C. "Populist Dreams and Negro Rights: East Texas as a Case Study." *American Historical Review*, LXXVI (1971), 1435–56.

Green, Fletcher M. "Some Aspects of the Convict Lease System in the Southern States." In *Essays in Southern History Presented to Joseph Gregoire de Roulhac Hamilton*, edited by Fletcher M. Green. Chapel Hill, N.C., 1949.

Gutman, Herbert G. "The Negro and the United Mine Workers of America." In *The Negro and the American Labor Movement*, edited by Julius Jacobson. Garden City, N.Y., 1968.

————. "Reconstruction in Ohio: Negroes in the Hocking Valley Coal Mines in 1873 and 1874." *Industrial and Labor Relations Review*, October, 1962, pp. 232–64.

Gutman, Herbert, and Richard Sutch. "The Slave Family." In *Reckoning with Slavery: A Critical Study in the Quantitative History of American Negro Slavery*, edited by Paul A. David *et al*. New York, 1975.

Holmes, William F. "Labor Agents and the Georgia Exodus, 1899–1900." *South Atlantic Quarterly*, LXXIX (1980), 436–48.

Kellor, Frances A. "Assisted Immigration from the South: The Women." *Charities*, XV (October 7, 1905), 11–15.

————. "The Evils of the Intelligence Office System." *Southern Workman*, XXXIII (1904), 377–80.

Kelsey, Carl. "Some Causes of Negro Emigration." *Charities*, XV (October 7, 1905), 15–17.

Koch, Charles R. "All the Land That's Next to Mine." *Farm Quarterly*, Autumn, 1958, pp. 62, 98–106.

Krebs, Sylvia. "Will the Freedmen Work? White Alabamians Adjust to Free Black Labor." *Alabama Historical Quarterly*, XXXVI (1974), 151–63.

Lee, Everett S. "A Theory of Migration." *Demography,* III (1966), 47–57.

Lowenberg, Bert J. "Efforts of the South to Encourage Immigration." *South Atlantic Quarterly,* XXXIII (1934), 363–85.

MacDonald, John S., and Leatrice MacDonald. "Chain Migration, Ethnic Neighborhood Formation, and Social Networks." *Milbank Memorial Fund Quarterly,* XLII (1964), 82–97.

Messner, William F. "Black Violence and White Response: Louisiana, 1862." *Journal of Southern History,* XLI (1975), 19–38.

Morris, Richard B. "The Measure of Bondage in the Slave States." *Mississippi Valley Historical Review,* XLI (1954), 219–40.

Myers, John B. "The Freedmen and the Law in Post-Bellum Alabama, 1865–1867." *Alabama Review,* XXIII (1970), 56–69.

Nordhoff, Charles. "West Virginia: A Horseback Ride Through the Wilderness." *American Missionary,* XVI (1872), 1–24.

Ravenstein, E. G. "The Laws of Migration." *Journal of the Royal Statistical Society,* XLVIII (1885), 167–227, LII (1889), 241–301.

Reid, Joseph D., Jr. "Sharecropping as an Understandable Market Response—the Postbellum South." *Journal of Economic History,* XXXIII (1973), 106–30.

———. "White Land, Black Labor, and Agricultural Stagnation: The Causes and Effects of Sharecropping in the Postbellum South." *Explorations in Economic History,* XVI (1979), 31–55.

Reynolds, Alfred W. "The Alabama Negro Colony in Mexico, 1894–1896." *Alabama Review,* V (1952), 243–68, VI (1953), 31–58.

Rubin, Morton. "Migration Patterns of Negroes from a Rural Northeastern Mississippi Community." *Social Forces,* XXXIX (1960), 59–66.

Schwendemann, Glen. "Nicodemus: Negro Haven on the Solomon." *Kansas Historical Quarterly,* XXIV (1968), 10–31.

Shlomowitz, Ralph. "'Bound' or 'Free'? Black Labor in Cotton and Sugarcane Farming, 1865–1880." *Journal of Southern History,* L (1984), 569–96.

———. "The Origins of Southern Sharecropping." *Agricultural History,* LIII (1979), 557–75.

Sjaastad, Larry A. "The Costs and Returns of Human Migration." *Journal of Political Economy,* LXX (1962), 80–93.

Sutch, Richard. "The Breeding of Slaves for Sale and the Westward Expansion of Slavery." In *Race and Slavery in the Western Hemisphere: Quantitative Studies,* edited by Stanley L. Engerman and Eugene D. Genovese. Princeton, 1975.

Sweig, Donald M. "Reassessing the Human Dimensions of the Interstate Slave Trade." *Prologue,* XII (1980), 5–21.

Tadman, Michael. "Slave Trading in the Ante-Bellum South: An Estimate of the Extent of the Inter-Regional Slave Trade." *Journal of American Studies,* XIIII (1979), 195–220.

Talmon, Yonina. "Millenarism." In *International Encyclopedia of the Social Sciences,* edited by David A. Sills. Vol. X of 18 vols. New York, 1968.

Tilly, Charles. "Race and Migration to the American City." In *The Metropolitan Enigma: Inquiries into the Nature and Dimensions of America's "Urban Crisis,"* edited by James Q. Wilson. Cambridge, Mass., 1968.

Turner, Charles W. "The Chesapeake and Ohio Railroad in 1865–1873." *North Carolina Historical Review,* XXXI (1954), 150–72.

Wiener, Jonathan M. "Class Structure and Economic Development in the American South, 1865–1955." *American Historical Review,* LXXXIV (1979), 970–92.

Woodman, Harold D. "Post–Civil War Southern Agriculture and the Law." *Agricultural History,* LIII (1979), 319–37.

Woodman, Harold. "AHR Forum: Class Structure and Economic Development in the American South, 1865–1955." *American Historical Review,* LXXXIV (1979), 997–1001.

Wright, Gavin. "Freedom and the Southern Economy." *Explorations in Economic History,* XVI (1979), 90–108.

Wright, Richard R., Jr. "The Economic Conditions of Negroes in the North: III, Negro Communities in New Jersey." *Southern Workman,* XXXVIII (1908), 385–93.

THESES AND DISSERTATIONS

Boyd, Willis D. "Negro Colonization in the National Crisis." Ph.D. dissertation, University of California at Los Angeles, 1953.

Carter, Dan T. "Prisons, Politics, and Business: The Convict Lease System in the Post–Civil War South." M.A. thesis, University of Wisconsin, 1964.

Everly, Elaine. "The Freedmen's Bureau in the National Capital." Ph.D. dissertation, George Washington University, 1972.

Fishel, Leslie H. "The North and the Negro, 1865–1900: A Study in Racial Discrimination." Ph.D. dissertation, Harvard University, 1954.

Hamilton, Howard Devon. "The Legislative and Judicial History of the Thirteenth Amendment." Ph.D. dissertation, University of Illinois, 1950.

Hill, Mozell C. "The All-Negro Society in Oklahoma." Ph.D. dissertation, University of Chicago, 1946.

Lathrop, Barnes Fletcher. "The Pugh Plantations, 1860–1865: A Study of Life in Lower Louisiana." Ph.D. dissertation, University of Texas, 1945.

Lindsey, Almont. "Freedmen's Rights in the South, 1865 to 1866." M.A. thesis, University of Illinois, 1930.

Moore, Ross H. "Social and Economic Conditions in Mississippi During Reconstruction." Ph.D. dissertation, Duke University, 1938.

Omari, Thompson P. K. "Urban Adjustment of Rural Southern Negro Migrants in Beloit, Wisconsin." Ph.D. dissertation, University of Wisconsin, 1955.

Robb, John M. "The Migration of Negro Coal Miners from Alabama to Southeast Kansas in 1899." M.A. thesis, Kansas State College of Pittsburg, 1965.

Sigler, Phil Samuel. "The Attitudes of Free Blacks Towards Emigration to Liberia." Ph.D. dissertation, Boston University, 1969.

Steelman, Joseph F. "The Immigration Movement in North Carolina, 1865–1890." M.A. thesis, University of North Carolina, 1947.

INDEX